MESOB ACROSS AMERICA

Ethiopian Food in the U.S.A.

Harry Kloman

iUniverse, Inc.

New York   Bloomington

Mesob Across America
Ethiopian Food in the U.S.A.

Copyright © 2010 Harry Kloman

iUniverse books may be ordered through booksellers or by contacting:

iUniverse
1663 Liberty Drive
Bloomington, IN 47403
www.iuniverse.com
1-800-Authors (1-800-288-4677)

ISBN: 978-1-4502-5866-1 (pbk)
ISBN: 978-1-4502-5867-8 (ebk)

Printed in the United States of America

iUniverse rev. date: 9/24/2010

Contents

Foreword		vii
A Prologue: The Ferenj at the Table		xi
1.	The Ethiopian Meal	1
2.	A Stroll Through Ethiopian History	33
3.	A History of Ethiopian Food	48
4.	Acquiring a Taste: Europe's First Encounters	66
5.	Where To Eat, What To Eat	74
6.	Injera & Teff	94
7.	Ethiopia & Coffee	115
8.	T'ej: The Ancient Honey Wine	126
9.	Ethiopians in America: Who Lives Where?	141
10.	The First Supper	147
11.	Communities of Cuisine: Addis Ababa in America	157
12.	Communities of Cuisine: Urban Life	184
13.	Communities of Cuisine: Village Life	213
14.	Preparing an Ethiopian Feast	257
	An Epilogue: Ferenj Tales	273
	Appendix A: Finding Ethiopian Restaurants & Markets	285
	Appendix B: Restaurant Names	289
	Appendix C: The Recipes for the Feast	293
	Sources Cited	303

Foreword

Throughout this book, you may notice that I introduce my Ethiopian sources by their full names, and then refer to them after that by their first names rather than by their last names. I do this in recognition of Ethiopian custom.

Every Ethiopian's last name is the first name of his or her father. If Tadesse Aklilu has a son he names Dinaw, the boy will be known as Dinaw Tadesse. He'll never be called Mr. Tadesse but rather Mr. Dinaw, for Ethiopians always address each other by first names, adding courtesy titles when talking with someone who's not a close friend. If he becomes a doctor, he would be Dr. Dinaw to his patients. If he marries Miss Azeb Bekele, his wife will become Mrs. Azeb Bekele, or Mrs. Azeb to a stranger. Ethiopian women never change their names upon marriage. They merely change their titles. Of course, Ethiopians use the words for Miss, Mrs. and Mr. in their own languages. In Amharic, the official state language, those words are Waizerat, Waizero and Ato, respectively.

This patrilineal custom has resulted in the naming of an international religion.

In the 1930s, a group of Jamaicans came to believe that Haile Selassie, the emperor of Ethiopia, was a messiah of Biblical teachings: a black leader of an independent African nation. Before he chose his imperial name, which means "the power of the trinity," the emperor's given name was Tafari Makonnen. He was serving as a regional governor, or "ras," when he ascended to the thrown.

So Ras Tafari became Emperor Haile Selassie in 1930, but not before lending his name to a religion: Rastafari (commonly called, incorrectly, Rastafarianism). The religion also believes that Jesus was black and that the emperor was his incarnation.

Next, a word about words. Ethiopians and their ancestors have used a unique alphabet to write Amharic and several other Ethiopian language for nearly 2,000 years, and in all of that time, nobody has bothered to create a standard for transliterating it into any other language. This makes it challenging to write the names of some Ethiopian foods and dishes in English.

Proto-Ethiopians began to use this alphabet in the early centuries of the first millennium A.D. to write Ge'ez, and today Ethiopians and Eritreans use it to write Amharic and Tigrinya. All three are Semitic languages that evolved from an ancient Ethio-Semitic mother tongue.

The Ethiopic alphabet is, linguistically speaking, an abugida, which is a type of alphasyllabary: Each of its letters represents a vowel-consonant combination, except for 14 stand-alone vowels, and about two dozen special letters that represent *two* consonant sounds plus a vowel. All together, the alphasyllabary has 276 letters. Each consonant has seven forms, or orders, corresponding to the seven Ethiopic vowel sounds. English, of course, has more than a dozen vowel sounds.

The particulars of these letters, or fidels, aren't important to the English-speaking reader. What gets tricky is writing certain Ethiopian words in English. Five of the orders are easy to transliterate because they correspond well enough to common English "a-e-i-o-u" vowel sounds. The other two vowels aren't so clear.

Some transliterations write the first-order vowel as a simple "a," while others render it as "ä" or as "e." This letter is best pronounced like the "u" in "but," although it's never written as a "u" in transliteration.

And then there's the knotty (and naughty) sixth-order vowel, which is muted and sometimes even silent, a very short, blunt "uh"-like sound at best. Most people throw up their hands and simply render it as an "e." But some linguists use the English schwa, represented by ə, while some use the phonetic symbol ï, and some use no vowel at all after the consonant.

I've tried to keep the transliterations simple in this book, in most cases forgoing phonetic symbols like "ä" and ə. These I'll write as "a" and "e." I trust linguists and Amharic-speaking readers will forgive my shorthand, and I hope that someone will someday fully standardize the transliteration of this challenging language so that, if nothing else, the menus of Ethiopian restaurants around the country will all spell their dishes the same way.

During the two years I've spent researching and writing this book, I've talked with myriad Ethiopians across the country and the world. I'm grateful for all they've taught me, and I hope I've rendered their lessons well.

Special thanks go to Araya Selassie Yibrehu of New York City, Iasu (G.E) Gorfu of Los Angeles and Seifu Haileyesus of Pittsburgh for their insights and friendship. To the many other Ethiopians and Eritreans, whom I quote in this book but will not mention here, I extend my appreciation once more.

In my travels to visit restaurants and Ethiopian communities in America, I've counted on the kindness of friends who have served as my hosts. I could not have done my reporting without the help of Phil Anderson, Anthony and Jill Breznican, Steven Abbott, Susan and Neil Sheehan, and Will and Catherine Bruno, all of whom are fortunate to live in cities with large Ethiopian populations and many fine restaurants and grocery stores.

I dream of some day visiting every Ethiopian restaurant in the country and telling its story. I visited the communities in many of the biggest cities for this book and talked with restaurateurs and grocers in other places by telephone and e-mail. The stories I tell throughout the book only touch upon a small portion of the many fine Ethiopian and Eritrean restaurants in the United States, and so I beg the forgiveness of the places I haven't visited and whose stories I haven't told.

Finally, you can look for information and updates about *Mesob Across America* at the website I've created: **www.pitt.edu/~kloman/ mesobacrossamerica.html**, which includes a complete guide to restaurants in the U.S. (see Appendix A for details), and you can read a lot more about *t'ej*, the Ethiopian honey wine, at **www.pitt.edu/~kloman/tej.html.** I welcome your thoughts on any of this at **kloman@pitt.edu**, especially if you decide to make *t'ej* at home. I'm happy to share some tips, and I'd enjoy hearing how yours turns out.

Harry Kloman
Pittsburgh, PA
12 August 2010

A Prologue:
The Ferenj at the Table

THERE'S NOTHING QUITE LIKE an Ethiopian meal. Literally, nothing: It's a cuisine unique in the world in a variety of ways, and history suggests that it has been for millennia.

Other cultures eat without utensils and use bread to scoop up the food. But none do it with a spongy fermented sourdough flatbread like Ethiopian *injera*, and none use it to grab onto food soaked in a rich sauce made with *berbere*, a brick-red powder of hot peppers and as many as a dozen other spices. Many cultures drink coffee, but the Ethiopians first cultivated it in their temperate highlands. And some say that honey wine, called *t'ej* in the dominant language of Ethiopia, emerged here, even before the rest of the world came to know it as mead.

That's a lot to chew on, and you should savor it: A good Ethiopian meal stays with you on your fingertips, even if you wash your hands well after dining, and it lingers in the air delectably when you cook it at home.

In this guide to Ethiopian cuisine, I want to show and tell as much as I can about Ethiopians and their food, mostly in America but also back home. I'll offer some history, some recipes, and some preparation tips, including a lesson in making *t'ej*. I'll introduce you to many Ethiopians who live in America. And I'll encourage you to experience Ethiopian food if you haven't already — or if you have but didn't quite know what you were experiencing.

At a traditional Ethiopian meal, there actually is no table: The server places your food in a large colorful woven basket called a *mesob*, the dishes themselves arranged on a round platter that rests in the center of the basket. Some restaurants even give you the option of sitting at a *mesob*.

Ethiopian restaurants across America range from the elegantly appointed to mom-'n'-pop-style diners and bars. And while you'll mostly find them in big cities, some have branched out into small towns.

Eastern Virginia is an epicenter, but in the western Virginia town of Blacksburg, Haregewin Bekele's Excellent Table Ethiopian Cuisine offers a variety of authentic dishes for takeout only. In the Amish-flavored community of Lancaster, in central Pennsylvania, a business called Expressly Local serves a variety of foods, including Ethiopian dishes made by Etayehu Zeneba, a city resident whose Gursha Organics sells her native Ethiopian cuisine and even offers cooking lessons. David's Place in Iowa City doesn't sound Ethiopian, but it's owner, Dawit Kidane, was born in Eritrea, and his restaurant is the only place in Iowa you'll fine the cuisine. The upscale resort mountain town of Asheville, N.C., even has a local Ethiopian couple who serve the food once month at venues around the area.

Urban legend has long claimed that Ethiopian food made its international debut in Washington, D.C., in 1978, with the opening of Mamma Desta, believed by many to be the first Ethiopian restaurant anywhere outside of Ethiopia. In truth, it began a dozen years earlier, in California, at a restaurant that was launched, its owner claimed, with help from the Emperor himself.

Even Alaska once had a restaurant, located in a structure that was almost Ethiopian, and owned by a member of the Ethiopian royal family, which claims descent from King Solomon.

I'll explore all of this history in *Mesob Across America* and look back at how some Ethiopian restaurant communities in America formed and grew.

And let's not forget Eritrea: This small country lies just to the north of Ethiopia, and their histories are inseparable. Two thousand years ago, the Aksumite kingdom of northern Ethiopia — Aksum was, more or less, the infant Ethiopia — extended into what's now Eritrea. In 1994, after centuries of conflict between the two nations, during which time Eritrea was for a while a federal state of greater Ethiopia, Eritrea finally became an independent nation.

It's no surprise, then, that these two contentious modern neighbors share a cuisine. Eritreans prepare the same dishes as Ethiopians and use the same ingredients, occasionally changing the name of a dish from Amharic, the Semitic language of Ethiopia, to Tigrinya, the Semitic language of Eritrea. Both languages use the same unique Ethiopic alphabet, and both evolved from the same Ethio-Semitic roots.

Thus the Ethiopian *gomen* is called *hamli* among Eritreans, *misir* is *birsin*, *tibs* becomes *kulwa*, *wot* become *tsebhi* or *zegeni*, *niter kibbee* becomes *tesmi*, *t'ej* is called *mes*, *gursha* is *mukilas*, *doro* changes slightly to *dohro*, and *mar* barely changes at all into *ma'ar*. *Injera* is also the carbohydrate staple of Eritrean dining, although Eritreans also call it *taita*.

As Amanuel Kiflu, the owner of the Eritrean restaurant Ambassador in Washington, D.C., told me: "The food is the same. Only the cook is different."

For the purpose of our culinary journey, then, "Ethiopian food" will mean "the food prepared by Ethiopians and Eritreans." The online restaurant guide that accompanies this book lists both Ethiopian and Eritrean restaurants, and if you're ever looking to enjoy the cuisine, a restaurant of either culture will give you what you crave.

Ethiopians — and until 1994, that also meant citizens of the federated state of Eritrea — make up the second largest African immigrant population in America. Nigerians are first, and their immigration pattern has followed that of Ethiopians: In times of political strife in each country, people who could afford to leave often did, and many came to the U.S. to work or attend college.

The population of Ethiopia is about 75 million, compared with a population of 148 million in Nigeria. And the official language of Nigeria is English, where in Ethiopia, it's Amharic (although educated Ethiopians all learn English).

These circumstances surely account for why Nigerians outnumber Ethiopians in the U.S. But how do we account for the fact that Ethiopian *restaurants* are copious here, while Nigerian restaurants are comparatively few? There's even an Ethiopian restaurant now in Beijing, quite a spectacle in a country whose culture eschews eating with your hands.

As exotic as Ethiopian cooking may seem when it appears before you on the table, its ingredients are all common to the American palate: lentils, potatoes, peas, green beans, carrots, onions, chicken, lamb, beef — you can get them all in any grocery store, along with most of the spices that give them their flavor on the Ethiopian table.

That's not always the case with the ingredients of Nigerian cuisine. Sure, Americans can readily find yams and black-eyed peas, two common ingredients. But what about groundnuts, melon seeds, locust beans, or plantains? And when was the last time you craved a drink made of millet and sorghum, or a paste made from cassava, or a steamed bean pudding, with onions, wrapped in a moimoi leaf?

Just look at the two cultures' menus. An Ethiopian menu might offer *atakilt alicha*. But then there's the explanation: a stew of potatoes, carrots and green beans, simmered in a mild sauce of onions, ginger, turmeric and garlic. That's veggie cuisine no matter what you call it or how you cook it. Or *siga tibs*: lean cubes of beef simmered in onions and *berbere*, the Ethiopian red pepper spice.

Nigerian menus, too, will list a dish's name and then explain it. Somehow, though, it just doesn't sound as — well, American. *Jollof* rice is simple enough: rice mixed with vegetables, tomatoes, onions and a meat. *Amala* is a porridge of yams. But what about *eba* (fried cassava flour dumplings), *sobo* (roselle juice), *fufu* (a soup of starchy vegetable root), or *ogbono* (a soup of ground *ogbono* seeds, with crayfish, prawns, goat and locust beans).

So when you boil it all down — which is what you do with most of the dishes — Ethiopian cuisine is just like ours. Only different.

I'LL ALWAYS REMEMBER my first time. It happened at The Blue Nile, a restaurant in Ann Arbor, Mich., where I was visiting a friend. We found the place in the phone book's restaurant listings. *Ethiopian food? What's that?* We gave it a try.

It was the perfect initiation because we didn't have to make decisions about dishes so utterly foreign to us. The Blue Nile offers two levels of dining: The vegetarian feast, all you can eat of seven dishes; or the Ethiopian feast, which adds four meat dishes to the ensemble. We ordered the full monty.

The meats looked like what they were: beef, lamb and chicken (two varieties). Some of the vegetable dishes looked like cabbage, potatoes, carrots, green beans and lentils. But some of the others looked like — what *is* that? It's…it's…it's …delicious!

We had two refills that night and left fatted and fêted. I had found a new gastronomic horizon.

The date: Friday, March 10, 2000, or on the Ethiopian calendar, *Arb, Magabit* 2, 1992.

The next week, on a business trip to New York City, I looked for more Ethiopian food. I found it at Meskerem, just a few blocks from my hotel, on 47th Street as it approaches 10th Avenue. This neighborhood still goes by the name Hell's Kitchen, but in its gradual gentrification of the past few decades, it's also come to be called Clinton (no relation to the former president).

Meskerem had a diverse menu from which I needed to choose my selections. I didn't exactly know what I'd eaten the week before, so I chose a *beyaynetu* — a vegetarian combo platter, common at Ethiopian restaurants — and a chicken dish. *Exquisite!*

And the *injera* was different: darker than the snow-white *injera* of Blue Nile, and with a lemony taste. I would later learn that Blue Nile uses white flour to make its *injera* and doesn't ferment the batter. In Ethiopia, and at other Ethiopian restaurants in America, *injera* is made in part with teff, a native Ethiopian grain, and the batter ferments for a few days to give it a gentle sourdough taste that complements the food and accentuates the flavors of the sauces.

After those two encounters, Ethiopian food became my obsession, then my passion, and now my avocation. I began to read about the culture and the country's history. I learned to make the food myself. I studied Amharic and learned its 276-letter alphabet. I even began to make *t'ej*, the Ethiopian honey wine, which adds a tang of sweetness and spice when sipped (or guzzled) with an Ethiopian meal. Now I've become the *ferenj* (foreigner) who always gets a smile when he exchanges a few words in Amharic with his restaurant server.

For every fortunate diner who has tried Ethiopian food and loved it, there are probably 10 times as many who don't even know it exists, or who have tried it and don't want to try it again. Of course, many people (like me) refuse to eat raw chunks of fish wrapped in little wads of rice. There's no accounting for taste.

But if Ethiopian food isn't as ubiquitous in the American diet as chow mien or hummus, that may be because too many people haven't had a chance to try it: 17 states don't have Ethiopian restaurants, and some have only one or two.

If you live anywhere in New York state outside of Manhattan, Brooklyn or little Mount Kisco, it had better be Rochester if you want Ethiopian food. The five boroughs have more than twice as many Chinese restaurants as the entire nation has Ethiopian ones. And every supermarket in America has frozen Chinese cuisine — along with frozen Indian, Thai, Japanese, Mexican, Italian and Middle Eastern meals. One long-time Ethiopian restaurateur in America hopes to change that in the next few years with a line of Ethiopian food.

What follows is a closer look at all of this, from a neo-Ethiopianist *ferenj* to, I hope, the curious quotidian gourmand.

Enjoy your meal.

The Ethiopian Meal

Eating Indian food can be a messy business if you eat it like Indians do. That's because, in traditional Indian culture, you eat with your fingers.

The Indian-born film producer Ismail Merchant, who worked with the American director James Ivory, kept down costs during the production of his films by preparing some meals himself. Yet despite his many years in America — before his death, in 2005, he lived for decades in upstate New York — Merchant continued to eat his Indian food in the traditional way.

Ethiopians, too, eat with their fingers, as do many other cultures, in one way or another. But more than a millennium ago, Ethiopians found a way to put something between flesh and food.

It's called *injera*, a spongy flatbread made in round pieces of about 12 to 20 inches in diameter. The *injera* covers a large round plate or tray, and the cook places the various juicy dishes on top of it. Revelers then tear small portions of *injera* from another large piece and use it to grab some food.

In the best of cases, there are some rules. First, you should only use your right hand when you tear off pieces of *injera* to use for picking up your morsels. It takes a bit of practice to learn how to manipulate your thumb and first two fingers for the task. Once you've torn off your piece of *injera*, you wrap it around a portion of food and form a sort of mini-dumpling between your thumb and fingers. The *injera* should be the only thing that your fingers touch.

Then — and here's where it gets tricky — you should never let your fingers touch your lips when you eat. Just place the food inside your mouth without contact.

The edifying menu at Rosalind's, the oldest Ethiopian restaurant in Los Angeles' Little Ethiopia neighborhood, teaches diners a bit about Ethiopian cuisine and challenges them to eat properly.

"The person with the most spotless hands after a meal," the menu explains, "can be classified a true Ethiopian gourmet, as this is a sign of having mastered *injera*. Moreover, it is considered very bad manners if someone licks their fingers — a habit you can often watch at typical snack bars."

All much more easily said than done. The messy truth is that in most Ethiopian restaurants across America, things get sticky. But no matter. Who, after all, eats American food with a pinky in the air? And rare is the knife and fork at a pizza party.

In his book "Amharic for Foreign Beginners," Alem Eshetu pauses between grammar lessons to discuss a few "cultural considerations."

"When you eat food from the same plate with somebody else," he writes, "it is advisable to eat what you have in front of you. Eating food from the other's side is impolite. When you eat with elders, you have to give them a chance to start first. In addition to this," he adds, "you have to take care not to sing, not to talk too much and not to touch your hair while you are eating with somebody else."

Of course, if the dish you want is on the other side of the tray, there are ways to go about getting it. Always wait until another guest has moved his hand away before you reach for your desired morsel, then apologize gently as you reach across. Or better yet, Alem says, spin the tray around until the dish you want to grab is closer.

In her homey Ethiopian recipe book — which includes many photos of her friends, family and Ethiopia, where she was born and raised — Hagossa Gebrehiwet-Buckner adds a few more tips to the art of *injera*. After tearing off a piece of *injera* about the size of your palm, "use your fingers to control it so pieces won't fall down as you put the scoop to your mouth. It's okay to grab/sample more than one sauce or dish on each scoop-trip. Finally, you can proceed to eat the bottom/tablecloth *injera* where the sauce was first served. By now it is soaked with the tasty juices and is full of flavor."

As for the Ethiopian custom of *gursha* — the act of placing a morsel of food directly into the mouth of someone at the table — Alem advises, "You have to understand that it is a sign of love and respect, hence you have to take care not to refuse when it is offered."

And *gursha* — the word literally means "mouthful" — should always come in threes from your generous hostess. If she only offers to feed you once, she's skimping on her hospitality, although you should politely refuse the second offering, not wanting to seem piggish — until, of course, you give in. But why the third time? "It could be a reference to the Trinity," author Daniel Mesfin speculates in *Exotic Ethiopian Cooking*, "which would be in total disharmony solo or duo."

Hagossa cautions that an offer of *gursha* "often grabs foreigners by surprise," so it's "OK to decline a *gursha* if you are uncomfortable. People won't take offense from this." She notes that "often *gurshas* are much larger than the regular scoop due to tradition, so you might find your mouth full from front to back." Many 19th Century European visitors to Ethiopia were at once fascinated and repelled by the act of *gursha* and the size of the proffered repast.

Deresse Lekyelebet, who owns Fassil Ethiopian restaurant in Vancouver, explains the Ethiopian custom of communal eating nicely. "The way you eat means you are sharing whatever you have," he says, "in good times or in bad times." And while some "northern families" may use individual plates, he adds, "90 percent of the Ethiopian population eats together. The family eats together."

By northern families, Deresse means the more upscale residents of Addis Ababa, and his anecdote concurs with the findings of Donald Levine, the noted University of Chicago Ethiopianist, whose 1965 book, *Wax & Gold,* explores old and new customs in Ethiopian culture.

One portion of his book surveyed 700 Ethiopians about their views on native customs compared to foreign ones. Levine found that college-educated Ethiopians, who make up less than one percent of the population even today, were more likely to prefer "European" or "foreign" ways of doing things, which he defined as *any* variation of the Ethiopian custom of eating with your hands from a shared plate in the middle of the table.

Although 80 percent of Levine's respondents preferred Ethiopian food to non-Ethiopian dishes, 58 percent preferred to have individual plates in front of them. These modernists also shied away from *gursha*.

"The slight majority who reject this old custom," Levine wrote, "do so because they find it 'noisy,' 'childish,' 'unsanitary,' or simply 'out of fashion'; while those who still enjoy it do so chiefly because it 'expresses affection.'" But *gursha*, he observed, remains a cherished customs that "plays up the erotic component of eating."

In fact, *injera* is so important to the culture, Levine noted, that the Amharic word for "companion," *balinjara*, has the same etymology as the English word: literally, someone with whom you share bread. Whether *balinjara* is an Ethiopian original, or a sign of foreign influence on Ethiopian language, he doesn't speculate.

Levine spends several pages discussing the eminence of food in Ethiopian culture. "The duration of any large celebration is said to depend on how long the food and drink last," he writes. "Successful ones go on for three days." Even the Amharic words used to talk about a celebration emphasize food. "One 'eats at,' rather than attends, a christening party," Levine explains. "One 'drinks in,' rather than belongs to, a *mahebar*," which is a fraternal religious organization.

"The mood at mealtime is supposed to be deeply serious," Levine says. "Food is to be masticated aloud, indicating total involvement in the task at hand." And he notes that much of Amharic verse and idiom talks about food. For example: "Hand and fly-whisk; mouth and *injera* [go together]." Or: "No matter how much one plows, nothing tastes so good as *gomen*." Or: "*T'ej* has no specks; a poor man has no friends." Clearly, words to live by.

But how can a culture that revolves so thoroughly around food emerge in a country that so often has too little of it? If Americans know only one thing about Ethiopia, it probably has something to do with poverty and starvation. News reports of Ethiopia's periodic droughts, which turn an already bad situation into a humanitarian emergency, occur every few years, and the world usually comes to the rescue, if only temporarily.

In the mid-1980s, when Ethiopian restaurants were new in America, some people had trouble reconciling their indulgence in Ethiopian food over here with the situation over there. So a United Press International reporter, Iris Krasnow, wrote a piece in which she talked with restaurateurs and their patrons in Washington, Chicago, Dallas, New York and the Bay Area about their trepidations. Her story appeared in the Los Angeles Times in 1985 — almost 20 years after the first Ethiopian restaurant opened in the United States — under the headline, "Ethiopian Eateries Off to a Mixed Start."

One restaurant owner pointed out that Ethiopians in America send money to their relatives in the homeland, so patronizing a restaurant owned by an Ethiopian offers a little help. Some aficionados of the cuisine even took part in famine relief efforts.

Abate Mulugeta, a Dallas restaurant owner at the time, speculated that Americans may be afraid to eat with their hands, and then reminded them, "They go and eat Kentucky Fried Chicken with their fingers — why not Ethiopian food?"

Krasnow reported an Ethiopian presence in Washington of about 10,000 people and nine restaurants. Chicago, she wrote, has an Ethiopian population of less than 1,000 and only one restaurant. She ended her piece with a question that remains to be answered: "Indeed, on New York's overly kitsch Columbus Avenue, a spanking new Blue Nile restaurant recently opened its doors. Could Ethiopian cuisine be a rising star among yuppies in America?"

One of her sources, a Dallas writer, called the food "hearty, spicy, exotic — it's everything yuppies want." But it's heavy, noted a San Franciscan who loved the stuff, and "it's not the prettiest food in the world. It's not presented with the visual impact of nouvelle cuisine. Basically, it's sort of stew lapped on the platter in front of you." Finally, a Washington, D.C., lawyer offered this: "After years of elegant sushi and perfect little pâtés, I love the lack of sophistication." Hard to tell from that remark whether she was a Democrat or a Republican.

The Essentials

What the world knows as "Ethiopian food" is the food of the dominant northern Amhara-Tigrayan culture. Most of Ethiopia's more than 80 cultures have their own special foods as well, and we'll look at some of those for the largest cultural groups, like the Oromos and the Gurage.

The 2007 Ethiopian census showed this makeup: Oromo, 34.5 percent; Amhara, 27 percent; Tigrayan, 6 percent; Somali, 6 percent; Gurage, 4 percent; and Sidama, 3.5 percent. Various other cultures fill out the remaining 19 percent, with some of the smallest tribal groups numbering in the decimals. The religious breakdown is 43.5 percent Ethiopian Orthodox, 34 percent Muslim, 18.5 percent Protestant, and the remaining 4 percent either Catholic or traditional religions.

These many cultures and religions all eat the northern "national cuisine," which has spread throughout Ethiopia, but some cultures are sensitive that so few people know or understand their regional culinary specialties. The Oromos especially feel oppressed in Ethiopia because they're the majority culture, yet they've never held power in the national government.

Simply put, food in Ethiopia — and Ethiopian food in American — can get political.

Before we get to the foods that Ethiopians eat, and how they combine them to make their unique dishes, let's look at some of the hardware and culinary staples that make up the Ethiopian table and its cuisine.

As you read these words and terms, keep in mind that there is no standardized way to transliterate Amharic, the state language of Ethiopia, into English, and nobody seems eager to come up with one. That's why some of the terms of Ethiopian cuisine have several spellings, which I'll note. Almost all of the restaurants in America use the Amharic names for dishes. If a restaurant is owned by an Ethiopian from the northern Tigray region, or by an Eritrean, the names may be in Tigrinya. A few restaurants owned by Oromos will use the Afaan Oromo names. All, of course, transliterate the names into English letters, and they usually describe the content of each dish.

With that in mind, here are the Amharic words for key terms and elements of an Ethiopian meal that are *not* main course dishes and the foods used to make them. We'll get to those main courses a little later.

♦ *Injera*. A spongy, pliable, unleavened sourdough bread used as plate and utensil. It's smooth on its underside and bubbly-looking on top. *Injera* freezes well and reheats easily in the microwave to restore its texture. (Let it defrost a while on the tabletop.) It's traditionally made on a large round hotplate-type devise called a *mitad* (in Amharic) or *mogogo* (in Tigrinya). Sometimes you'll see it spelled *enjera*, which is probably a better transliteration of the Amharic. But *injera* is the most common English spelling.

♦ **Teff.** A unique native Ethiopian species of grain used to make *injera*. It's now grown in America and some other places. The genus *Eragrostis* has about 300 species. The one called teff is *Eragrostis tef.* Once again, "tef" is a more accurate transliteration of the Amharic, although "teff" is the most commonly used spelling.

♦ *Gebeta*. This word refers to a large wood cup or bowl, or a table made of bamboo. But it's also used more generally to mean the platter on which the communal meal is served. At restaurants, the *gebeta* is often made of colorfully painted metal. Some restaurants simply use a large pizza pan, or a metal serving tray that you can buy at Asian grocery stores.

♦ *Mesob*. A large, round, woven basket, often very colorful, from which you eat your Ethiopian meal. The *injera*-covered *gebeta* is placed in the middle of the *mesob*, and the diners all eat from the same central array of dishes. Sometimes it's written *messob*. Most Ethiopian restaurants in America have a few *mesobs* for guests who choose to eat in the most traditional way. But *mesobs* sometimes come with stools rather than chairs, and you have to bend over to get closer to your food. So in most Ethiopian restaurants, people sit at Western-style tables.

♦ *Berbere*. A spicy red pepper powder that gives heat to Ethiopian dishes. Each cook will have his or her own variations on a recipe for *berbere*, but it always contains red chili pepper of the genus *Capsicum*, along with such things as garlic, ginger, basil, cinnamon, cloves, cardamom, salt and onion. A hotter version, made with the seeds of the chili pepper, is called **mitmita**. A milder version is called **awaze**.

♦ **Wot.** A spicy dish made with *berbere*. Just about anything can be a *wot*, from *yemisir wot* (lentils) to *doro tibs wot* (chicken breast pieces fried in onions and butter). It's sometimes written *wat* or *w'et*. *Doro wot*, a chicken leg in spicy sauce, served with a hard-boiled egg, is often call the "national dish of Ethiopia."

♦ *Alicha*. A mild dish made without *berbere*. An *alicha*, sometimes written *alich'a*, gets its flavor from onions, ginger, garlic, turmeric — anything but *berbere*. Dishes that have just a touch of *berbere* will sometimes be called a rather confusing *alicha wot*.

♦ *Tibs*. This term refers to fried meat. If a menu just offers *tibs*, it's most likely beef. If the *tibs* are chicken or lamb, the menu will specify. Be sure to ask about the preparation when you order to discern if the *tibs* are *derek* ("dry") or in a juicy *berbere* sauce. At most restaurants, a dish called *derek tibs* or just *tibs* will be meat (beef, chicken or lamb) fried with chunks of green or red pepper, slices of onion, and occasionally tomatoes, all lightly spiced with *berbere* powder. *Tibs wot* usually means the dish is spicier and comes in a *berbere* sauce.

♦ **Niter Kibbee.** Spiced, clarified butter, similar to Indian *ghee*. In the Indian preparation, you merely boil the butter to separate the milk solids from the liquid fat, then refrigerate the liquid to solidify it. But as the butter boils for *kibbee,* you add numerous spices, like ginger, garlic, fenugreek, cardamom, turmeric, cumin, basil, onion — it's chef's choice. There are various spellings, like *nitir qibe* or *kibe* or *kibè*.

♦ **T'ej.** Ethiopian honey wine, made by mixing honey and water, then adding the stick or leaf of the gesho, a species of buckthorn native to Ethiopia. Gesho adds a slightly spicy, pungent flavor to the mixture and causes it to ferment. This wine is thousands of years old and an Ethiopian legend. Sometimes written *tej, tejj, t'ejj* or other such variations. Its companion beverage is **tella** or **talla**, a beer made from barley. Non-fermented honey mixed with water is called **birz** or **berz**.

The Ingredients and Their Progeny

Most Ethiopian restaurants in America offer the same general lineup of dishes, with variations from place to place based on the predilection and imagination of the chef, who's often the restaurant's owner. The cuisine uses no ingredients unfamiliar to American palates, although some dishes will look like they've been puréed in a food processor. They're not: The process of thoroughly cooking them in the pot gives them this texture and appearance.

Here's a rundown of the most common ingredients used in Ethiopian cuisine and some of the dishes you can make from them, along with the name for each item in Amharic after the English name. The dishes are all common offerings on the menus of Ethiopian restaurants in America.

♦ **Onions (shinkurt).** There is no Ethiopian dish made exclusively of onions, and there needn't be: This vegetable is the foundation of virtually every Ethiopian stew, so important to the culture and the cuisine that Ethiopians call it "king onion." You usually won't even know it's there because it will be so finely chopped and simmered into the sauce. But it's hard to imagine Ethiopian food without it. In fact, Dalo's Kitchen, an Ethiopian restaurant in Portland, Ore., says it offers a "variety of vegetables cooked in mild caramelized onion sauce." This is an excellent way to describe the foundation of Ethiopian dishes.

♦ **Lentils (*misir*).** This is a staple legume of Ethiopian cuisine and used to make numerous dishes, from a mild stew of whole brown lentils (*defin alicha*) to the fierier *misir wot,* a spicy red lentil stew. *Azifa* is a cold dish made with green lentils, onions, jalapeños and spices. Some restaurants will serve *misir shorba,* or lentil soup.

♦ **Peas (*atar*).** You often won't even know you're eating peas when you eat them at an Ethiopian restaurant. Yellow peas are used for a dish called *atar kik alicha* — literally, "peas split mild." It's a stew of yellow peas in a mild sauce seasoned with ginger and garlic. The cuisine's unique pea dish is *shiro,* a thick soupy delicacy made from pea powder mixed with numerous spices, then reconstituted in water and simmered until it thickens. It's the most liquefied dish on the Ethiopian table, and it's scrumptious when prepared by a chef who knows just the right mix of seasonings.

♦ **Potatoes (*dinich*).** Another staple vegetable, used in numerous dishes.

♦ **Green Beans (*fosolia*) and Carrots (*karot*).** You'll find these two common vegetables deep fried together in a dish called *fosolia,* which is also the word that Amharic (borrowing from Italian) uses for green beans, or stewed in *atakilt alicha* (*atakilt* is Amharic for vegetable). The latter dish includes potatoes, and sometimes cabbage, green peppers or even cauliflower, depending upon what *atakilt* the chef chooses to include.

♦ **Beets (*kay sir*, literally, "red root").** If you find a restaurant that serves a beet dish, give it a try. *Kay sir dinich,* usually an *alicha* but sometimes a *wot,* is a nicely textured mix of beets and potatoes, always deep red from the influence of the beets.

♦ **Mushrooms (*inguday*).** You don't find mushrooms as an ingredient in too many Ethiopian dishes. But some restaurants will serve the hearty *inguday wot,* a spicy dish made with diced pieces of mushroom in a thick purée.

♦ **Pumpkin (*duba*).** Lucky is the dinner guest who finds a restaurant that prepares *duba wot,* a spicy stew made with chunks of freshly cut pumpkin. The preparation is time-consuming — chopping up a whole uncooked pumpkin isn't easy — and naturally, you're only likely to find it in the late fall, when pumpkins are abundant in America. Look as well for *duba shorba,* or pumpkin soup, a creamy appetizer made from puréed pumpkin. *Duba* is also the Amharic word for squash, and some restaurants will serve *duba wot* made with squash.

♦ **Collard Greens (*gomen*).** Perhaps an acquired taste, *gomen* is another staple of Ethiopian vegetarian cuisine. The preparation makes the difference: If it's undercooked or inadequately seasoned, it can be a bit coarse or chewy.

♦ **Cabbage (*tikil gomen*).** A simple but tasty dish, *tikil gomen* is cabbage stewed until it's very tender, and usually mixed with carrots.

♦ **Chick Peas (*shimbra*).** This vegetable gets a lot of attention during religious fasting days and seasons, when Ethiopians can't eat meat and need additional vegetable dishes to fill the table. One treat is *butecha*, a dish of chick pea powder in water, cooked until it thickens, and then mixed with onions, jalapeños and lemon juice. The dish looks like scrambled eggs, and it's sometimes served cold. Every now and then, you'll find *butecha* prepared in a way that looks like hummus. Not too many restaurants offer *butecha*, and some only make it on fasting days. Chick peas are also used to make *shimbra asa*, literally, "chick pea fish." Another fasting dish, it's chick pea powder shaped to look like little fish pieces, then deep fried in a *very* rich *berbere* sauce. It usually seems to be more sauce than "chick pea fish" because the pieces tend to dissolve in the sauce.

♦ **Chicken (*doro*).** Often called the "national dish of Ethiopia," *doro wot* is a chicken leg in spicy sauce, served with a hard-boiled egg. The mild version is called *doro alicha*. You'll also find *doro tibs wot*, chunks of breast meat fried in *kibbee* with green peppers and onions. Ethiopians themselves eat *doro tibs wot* less frequently than *doro wot* or *doro alicha*. There's also *doro minchet abish*, shredded white meat chicken in a spicy *wot*.

♦ **Beef (*siga*).** These dishes tend to mirror their poultry counterparts: *siga wot* is spicy beef in juicy *berbere* sauce, a staple preparation, and *siga tibs*, which you'll sometimes see called *zilzil tibs* or *derek* ("dry") *tibs*, are fried chunks of beef with pepper and onions, mildly spiced. *Kay wot*, literally "red *wot*," is pretty much the same as *siga wot*. In fact, the names for the these several beef dishes are often interchangeable on menus, so be sure to read the description. *Minchet abish* is ground beef in a spicy sauce. *Kitfo* — often called Ethiopian steak tartar — is raw or lightly cooked ground beef, spiced with *mitmita* powder (hotter than *berbere*) and cardamom, and made rich with *kibbee*. *Gored gored* are chunks of seasoned raw beef. *Goden tibs* are short ribs of beef.

♦ **Lamb (*beg*).** Some Ethiopian lamb dishes, whether a *wot* or an *alicha*, will come with the meat still on the bone. Generally, *ye'beg tibs* are boneless chunks of lamb. As with beef and chicken, these dishes can come *derek* or as a *wot* in *berbere* sauce.

♦ **Fish (*asa*).** Not too many Ethiopian restaurants will serve fish, and when they do, it may look different on the plate than other Ethiopian food. Sometimes restaurants will offer just a piece of fried fish, or a piece of baked fish stewed for a short while in a *berbere* sauce. Because fish is such a flakey and delicate meat, the preparation is different than with chicken, beef and lamb.

So there you have the basic ingredients, along with some of the more common dishes made from them. On some restaurant menus, you'll see the prefix *ye* before the name of a dish. This is the Ethiopian word that indicates

9

possession or that simply means "of." So *ye'misir wot* is a "*wot* of lentils." Many restaurants don't bother using *ye* on their menus because it means nothing to an American patron.

By the way, if you're dining with a friend who can't stand the heat of a hearty Ethiopian *wot*, just give your companion a little superiority smile and say, "*Ye'wend alicha*," which Daniel Mesfin explains is a "derogatory phrase... coined for a man who displays cowardice."

Here again is *ye*, meaning "of." *Wend* is the Amharic word for "man." An *alicha*, of course, is a mild dish. So when you point to your friend with the bland palate and say "*ye'wend alicha*," you're calling him "an *alicha* of a man." An Ethiopian might translate this as "sissy." In English, you've more or less just called your friend a wimp.

Here are a few more important dining terms to know:

♦ ***Beyaynetu***. A vegetarian combination platter. If you want meat with it, ask for a *beyaynetu b'siga*.

♦ ***Ye'tsom wot***. Another name for a vegetarian combination, but it will be *only* vegetarian. "Tsom" or "som" — depending upon how you transliterate the Amharic letter that begins the word — means "fast." On fasting days, Ethiopians don't eat meat.

♦ ***Maheberawi***. On a menu, this refers to a platter of food intended to be shared, usually one with a variety of different dishes.

Finally, a word about spaghetti, lasagna, pizza and *cotoletta*, a breaded cutlet of veal, beef or chicken, often served over pasta (and spelled differently on almost every restaurant menu that offers it).

From 1890 until 1941, Italy colonized Eritrea, which is now independent, but which Ethiopia had claimed for years was its farthest-north province. During the colonial period, many elements of Italian cuisine became part of Eritrean culture, and now Eritrean restaurants in America almost always feature spaghetti dishes. This culinary custom migrated south into Ethiopia over time, especially into the northern provinces. It further took hold from 1936-1941, when Mussolini's army invaded Ethiopia and occupied it.

So don't be surprised to find Italian dishes on the menu of an Ethiopian or especially an Eritrean restaurant. Many Ethiopians even eat spaghetti at home, a remnant of the Italian occupation and Italy's subsequent influence in the country, where many Italians remained after the occupation. Some Ethiopians make their pasta sauce spicy with *berbere*, and they may even grab their spaghetti with *injera*.

Meal and Mealtimes: Who Eats What?

Despite all this talk of Ethiopian cuisine, there's a lot of poverty and hunger in Ethiopia. Much of the country is fertile, and in major cities, many Ethiopians eat well, or well enough. But eight out of 10 Ethiopians are agrarian in a country prone to drought, and this has a devastating effect on the well being of the population. The government has also often not been very good at getting food from places of abundance to places of need.

The World Bank reports that 52 percent of Ethiopians live in "chronic and transitory poverty in urban and rural areas in Ethiopia." In urban areas, the poverty rate is 58 percent, and "half of these people are desperately poor." The bank's study estimates that 30 percent of the country's farm households are "chronically poor." The mortality rate for children under the age of 5 is 20 percent.

And yet, the cuisine of Ethiopia has survived for millennia, often through the hardest of times. Ethiopia is such a diverse country, with so many cultures and customs, that one rule can't possibly fit all. Tribal and nomadic people eat differently than urbanites, and educated professional urbanites eat differently than the uneducated laborers who serve them. Coffee is a common denominator, as is some form of wine, often made from honey, or beer, made from grains or honey or both.

Ethiopia has two primary geographic features: the temperate highlands, largely in the center and north of the country, and sometimes called the Roof of Africa; and the arid lowlands, to the south and east, where drought and poverty often reign. The highlands are the most fertile, and what we know as "Ethiopian cuisine" comes largely from the culture and civilization that emerged there early in the first millennium A.D.

The most primitive Ethiopians, those in the southwest Omo Valley, wear little clothing, paint their faces, use plates to extend their lips, and eat a variety of basic foods: the farmers grow maize, sorghum, barley and other vegetables, while the nomadic hunters kill game that's often protected by the government — of which some have little, if any, awareness. They raise goats and buffalo, and a feast may consist of buffalo meat on a stick, roasted over a fire.

Jason McLure, an American journalist who spent a few years working in Ethiopia, traveled to the South Omo region and enjoyed a meal of "unseasoned goat shank on a stick cooked unevenly over a charcoal fire — and that was the celebration food," he says. "Normally the folks down there eat some awful concoction of millet and sorghum."

These cultures are not starving: They are, in fact, adequately fed according to their very modest needs. For liquid protein, they'll puncture an artery in the neck of a cow, drain the blood into a bowl, and drink it. During the driest

11

seasons, the young men and boys who tend the cattle subsist on diets of milk, beef and blood.

The closest thing to this in urban Ethiopian cuisine — and it's not very close at all — is *kitfo*, or seasoned raw ground beef, the Ethiopian equivalent of sushi or steak tartar. It's originally a delicacy of Ethiopia's Gurage people, but long ago it spread to the wider culture, and now it's a popular meal among Ethiopians, both at home and in the U.S.

The Gurage will sometimes eat their *kitfo* with *qocho*, a fermented bread-like *injera* substitute made from enset, or "false banana," one of the Gurage's most important plant foods. No one in Ethiopia would dare eat the cooked version of *kitfo* or its related dish, *gored gored*, chunks of raw meat stirred in a sauce of heated *berbere* and *kibbee*.

The most authentic Gurage-Ethio type of *kitfo* is called *birindo*, which refers to any dish prepared with raw meat, or simply *tere*, which means "raw." But you can ask for it *lebleb*, which means lightly cooked, or *yebesele*, which means fully cooked — a tourist's safest bet in the homeland, some Ethiopians have told me. McLure had some tasty *kitfo* in the southern city of Wolayta, and although the waitress swore it was cooked, "it looked pretty bloody to me," he says.

Eating raw meat goes back millennia in Ethiopia, and it's still a favorite of those who can afford it. In his bilingual cookbook, *A tavola con la Regina di Saba/Cooking with the Queen of Sheba*, the Ethiopian-born Italian restaurateur Teshome Behre explains: "Ethiopians enjoy the ritual of cutting off a portion of meat from a large piece brought and served by a waiter or from a section of meat hanging on the wall. Western guests may be slightly perturbed by such a scene as it may remind them of some of the gruesome tasks of a butcher."

Gruesome to foreigners perhaps, but celebratory to Ethiopians.

The late 19th Century Russian explorer Alexander Bulatovich noted that this predilection had one drawback. "All Abyssinians without exception have the inevitable consequences of that — tapeworm," he wrote. "Therefore, it is established practice among them to eat once every two months the cooked berries of the *kusso* tree to expel the parasitic worms."

Ethiopians still love their raw meat, and they eat it today in a variety of dishes, like *kitfo* (ground), *gored gored* (in chunks), or *tere siga* (literally "raw meat," sometimes also called *kurt* or *qurt*). Marcus Samuelsson — the Ethiopian-born, Swedish-raised York restaurateur and cookbook author — recalls a legend about Christian Gurages, engaged in wars with invading Moslems, and forced to hide from their attackers in the mountains, where they learned to enjoy raw meat because a fire for cooking would have given them away.

Tigrinya culture of northern Ethiopia and Eritrea contributed the *ambasha* or *hambasha*, a doughy leavened bread, to the Ethiopian table. An *ambasha* will have a design carved into the top of the dough before the baker places it in the oven. Sometimes the finished bread is smeared with vegetable oil spiced with *berbere*. Another Eritrean dish is *ga'at* or *akelet*, a very thick barley porridge, often served in the form of a round cake with a hole in the center, where the cook places a pool of thick hot *kibbee* spiced with *berbere* for dipping, and with some yogurt on the side.

Barley is an important grain among northern Ethiopians in Tigrinya-speaking regions, and another unique Tigrinya dish is *tihlo*, made from roasted barley flour that's rolled into balls and served with a rich spicy sauce. The dish is sometimes served alone and sometimes with *injera* — or *taita*, as it's also called in Tigrinya — and it's eaten by spearing it with a stick and dipping it into the sauce. *Tihlo* can be served at any meal, but it's especially important at celebrations, like weddings and christenings.

In a 2004 study of the more southern Oromo people, the largest ethnic group in Ethiopia, and one of the most diverse, Nobuko Nishikazi found that maize can comprise up to 80 percent of the diet, along with enset and sweet potatoes. Half of the ingredients in Oromo side dishes come from vegetables grown in home gardens, and dairy products from family-owned livestock account for about 25 percent.

Livestock (beef and mutton) is important to the livelihoods and diets of many Oromo people, and the Oromo diet of grains, vegetables and dairy products is typical of non-urban Ethiopians. Often they'll use any of their grains, and not just the more expensive teff, to make *injera*, or as it's called in the Afaan Oromo, *budeena*.

One favorite Oromo bread of the pastoralist southern Borana region — usually made with barley flour, and somewhat similar to an *ambasha* — is called *chumbo*, and the process of making it is somewhat elaborate. The cook begins by heating a concave *mitad*-like oven with hot coals. She places the dough or batter onto the hot surface, covers it with enset leaves, then places a second identical concave oven on top. The finished bread comes out moist and juicy.

Similar to this is the Borana *mugera*, another bread baked with hot ovens on top and bottom. But *mugera* has a special place in the Oromo diet. When a group of farmers from a community get together to help a neighbor with his harvest, they expect to be served *mugera* as a treat in the field at the end of the day's work. If a child helps his neighbors by tending their cows or horses, he anticipates *mugera* when he completes his chores.

The making of *chumbo* and *mugera* are older country traditions, not practiced as much, if at all, by Oromos who live in cities. Bulatovich described these breads in his book about his travels through Ethiopia. "The leavened bread is spread out on an earthenware pan," he wrote, "and from the top in the middle of a round loaf another smaller pan is squeezed. Fire is lighted under the large pan and on top of the small one. A somewhat heavy but tasty bread results." He never names this bread, but he does mention "unleavened flat cakes" called *kita*, a treat that Ethiopians still enjoy today.

For centuries now, the Oromo have felt marginalized by the dominant northern Amhara-Tigrayan culture, and some separatists consider Oromia to be an occupied country. Damee Ormaa, who came to America from Oromia in 2003, and who lives in Minneapolis, a center of the Oromo diaspora in the United States, operates a website about the concerns of the Oromo people, and he's passionate about his cause and his culture.

"Oromo traditional food is totally different from what most people refer to as Ethiopian food," he says. "In the sense that it is known to the rest of the world, everything Ethiopian is Amhara. If Ethiopia is represented in the Olympics, you see Amhara traditional clothing or some other element of Amhara culture. If Ethiopia is represented in a food-tasting event of some sort, *injera* with *wot* is what will be presented as the national dish."

In remote tribal parts of Oromia, traditions govern mealtime. "When an animal is slaughtered for sacrificial or other purposes," Damee writes in his blog, "there are parts of the animal body that are not edible. Religious leaders known as Qaalluus don't eat anything with feathers. Different Oromo tribes also have parts of the animal body that they can't eat. The story is long, but it is believed that a forefather for each particular tribe has died from eating the now forbidden part of the animal. Thus, the tribe leaders have so declared that no one in that tribe is allowed to eat that particular item in an animal's body."

How widespread is this custom? Certainly nobody knows for sure, although "today most Oromos have embraced Judeo-Christian beliefs," Damee says, "and most Oromos do not practice those sacrificial and other traditional rituals." But the custom still exists in rural and remote areas of Oromia.

In his blog, Damee notes that "Oromo urban dwellers consume the same or similar foods as what is categorically known as 'Ethiopian' food — the staple among them *injera* (*budeena* in Afaan Oromo). The taste, the cooking styles and ingredients may vary from one household to another." Oromo cultures have also "modified and perfected" some Ethiopian foods: In eastern Oromia, he writes, "*laftoo* is a freshly cooked rather smaller type of *budeena*, similar yet a totally different kind of *injera*."

"But again really, who gave the patent/ownership of the recipe for *injera* (*budeena*) to the Amhara?" he reflects. "*Injera* might have been started in Amhara areas of Ethiopia, but arguably, through long years of cultural interactions, it has been transformed and modified according to cultural preferences. For instance, my Somali acquaintances in the states prepare a different kind of *injera* than what you find at Oromo or other Ethiopian household."

So whereas urban dwellers in the Oromo region also eat what we know in our American restaurants as "Ethiopian food," Damee says that most Oromo also eat their traditional foods and dishes that originated in Oromo culture.

One such dish is a breakfast porridge called *marqa* made by mixing wheat with butter and boiling water. The Oromo also eat *qinche* (or *kinche*), another cereal dish, and popular in Amhara culture, made of shredded barley or wheat. It's often prepared at Oromo weddings and served to guests along with *chiko*, a thick bread-like barley meal mixed with spices and copious amounts of butter. At one point during the wedding, to anoint the father or the bride and the best man, guests will pour jugs of melted butter and *daadhi*, the Afaan Oromo word for honey wine, over their heads. This again is an older tradition, characteristic of village life, and not practiced too religiously today among more urban Oromo people.

Still common at a modern Oromo wedding is a ceremony where an older man will spoon feed the bride, the groom and the members of their wedding party. First comes *bunakala*, an appetizer of uncrushed coffee beans roasted in butter, salt or other spices, served from a decorated container. He goes down the line, giving each a spoonful. "Multiply like coffee beans," the man might say as he beckons them to remain humble in their love for one another. Next comes fresh milk from a vessel that he holds to their mouths, allowing them to drink. Finally, there's *daadhi*, rich and yellow, once again fed to them from a pitcher or jar. The table will be decorated with freshly cut grass, a symbol that signifies the newness of the union and encourages the couple to spread their roots and multiply. The vessels with liquid must always be full, lest the couple be cursed, so when the ceremony ends, someone quickly refills them.

The Oromo eat roasted meat (*food wadi*) and a snack called *korso* or *akaawii* which is made of roasted grains (barley, corn, sorghum, wheat). There are many others — *irra busaa, maroo, rimixoo, bordee* (a fermented cereal beverage) — all unknown in Ethiopian restaurants in the U.S. It's a diverse culture, and sometimes the foods of certain Oromos are unfamiliar to others. And because Afaan Oromo has many dialects, the names can differ from region to region.

Oromos enjoy a lot of dairy products: milk, butter, cheese and *anan ititu*, a milk that's almost as thick as cheese. In fact, says Damee, "Oromos add a lot of milk and milk products to their foods. The northern Ethiopians might not be so fortunate to do so." Coffee originated in Oromia, and it's still a favorite beverage of the culture, along with *daadhi* and *farso* (a beer made from barley).

"In Oromo country, where I grew up," Damee says, "almost every food item is served with some mix of dairy products, mainly milk or butter. Oromos offer milk to guests and strangers alike as tea or water is offered to visitors in the United States."

Oromo *budeena* (or *bideena*, depending upon the dialect) isn't always made from teff because people often can't afford it. Oromo cultures will instead use wheat, barley or xafi (a native grain) to make their *injera*. The ancootee (or anchote) is a climbing leafy plant whose potato-like fruit the Oromo enjoy, especially in the western Oromo region.

Oromos who can afford sugar will add it to their milk, but in general, Damee says, "I am not sure if there is a concept of desserts among the Oromos. After a meal, people normally drink coffee, milk or pass some time talking as they chew on *korso*." In fact, the absence of dessert is true across all Ethiopian cultures: Afaan Oromo dictionaries have no word for it and Amharic dictionaries struggle to find one.

As for Amhara-Tigrayan food in Oromia, "the names do vary," Damee says, "but for the most part the food is similar, and the differences are less noticeable — sort of the differences between pasta at an Italian restaurant or at an American-Mediterranean restaurant."

But he adds: "Oromos do not like using the Amharic word because of the historical contention that has endured for well over a century. If a name doesn't exist in Oromo, they turn to descriptive names."

Thus the Amhari *kay wot*, a red spicy stew, becomes *kochee diima*, which literally means "stew red" in Afaan Oromo, and the milder Amharic *alicha* become *kochee bora*, or "stew yellow," just as an Amharic *alicha* is often yellow. The Afaan Oromo *waaddii* refers to tibs — that is, meat fried in a pan with onions and peppers, but not in such a juicy, stew-like *berbere* sauce.

"The quantities of the ingredients and spices are different just because of the difference in taste and culture," Damee says. "But the differences are less obvious." Ingredients might even vary in some of the dishes: Some parts of Oromia use more butter than others, and some use oil instead of butter.

The Gurage beef dish *kitfo* is popular all over Ethiopia, but each culture and region might add its own special touches. "Oromo *kataffi* is similar," says Damee, "but it is as if Burger King is serving a Big Mac. Big Mac is identified with McDonald's, but that doesn't mean Burger King won't make it better. There will be a difference in taste unless Big Mac gives up its treasured recipe. And Burger King adheres strictly to its recipe."

Enset is especially vital to the Oromo and to many Ethiopian cultures in the southern parts of the country, although centuries ago it was cultivated and eaten in the north. That practice seems to have largely stopped, something observed by 19ᵗʰ Century European travelers in their accounts of the Ethiopian diet.

The enset tree itself is enormous and bears no edible fruit: The tree *is* the food — boiled, chopped up, ground into meal, then made into a sauce, or into a *qocho* bread. The large leaves and their stalks are also used for making mats.

Middle Eastern and European explorers of the 18ᵗʰ Century even observed the importance of enset. Ibn Fadl Allah, who visited Ethiopia in the 14th Century, mentioned it, and the Portuguese explorer Manoel de Almeida said the plant had a trunk so thick that two men struggled to carry it. When cut, several hundred new plants would grow in its place, he reported.

Jerome Lobo, an 18ᵗʰ Century Portuguese explorer, marveled at its usefulness: "Its leaves, which are so large as to cover a man, make hangings for rooms, and serve the inhabitants instead of linen for their tables. They grind the branches and the thick parts of the leaves, and when they are mingled with milk, find them a delicious food, and the trunk and the roots are even more nourishing than the leaves or the branches. The Abyssins report that this tree, when it is cut down, groans like a man."

Bulatovich offers a nice description of the way Oromos used enset to make bread. "Once a tree has attained four years in growth," he writes, "they dig it up and strip it of the leaves. Then, they bury the thick lower part of the trunk in the ground and leave it there for several months. After that time, it begins to rot and turn sour. Then they extract the buried tree from the ground, clean off the spoiled outer layer, and scrape and grind the part which has turned sour and soft. Then they bake it in large earthenware pans." He didn't much care for the finished product, which had "an unsavory and unpleasant sour smell," and which wasn't very nutritious. But "if you add flour to it," he concludes, "then the bread is somewhat improved."

Enset is so important to the Gurage that its cultivation and distribution can become ritualistic.

"Dispensing enset unsparingly, to kinsmen and strangers alike," writes the anthropologist William Shack, "is a social act in which all Gurage who can afford to do so engage. It is one of the few socially acceptable means by which Gurage men can openly display power and prestige. A wide range of Gurage social relationships, which cut across kinship groupings and status differences, stem also from economic transactions involved in dispensing or receiving enset."

A Gurage may have three meals of enset a day, each consisting of about the same amount of food, Shack found. Only at holiday festivals will people gorge themselves. They keep livestock primarily for milk, but also for protein. Their culture eschews the consumption of eating the flesh of animals caught by hunting. Shack found that Gurage cattle is often weak and of poor quality, so much of the milk is churned into *kibbee*, which households may have in large quantities.

Many Ethiopians survive by the meager fruits of their own labor. But many of country's poorest people suffer from horrible malnutrition and may have only one or two spare meals a day, even those people who live in proximity to more prosperous urban areas. These meals will consist of *injera* — often made of barley, millet or sorghum rather than teff — and a few ounces of spicy *wot*, perhaps with some beans or other vegetables, and rarely with meat.

"Meals of wealthy Ethiopian families," writes the scholar Abbebe Kifleyesus, "were distinguished not by the composition of the dishes, but by the quantity of the ingredients and the number of dishes served. Their food is more refined, harmonious in flavors, sweeter, and more elaborately decorated and served." The food of the poor contains more *berbere*, which adds heat and encourages the consumption of more *injera*, and it contains less butter and possibly even fewer onions, substituting instead vegetable oils and water to stew the meal.

Abbebe's 2004 study, "The Construction of Ethiopian National Cuisine," is filled with valuable tidbits about Ethiopian cuisine in the homes of the wealthy compared with the home of the poor, although it begins its history around the 18th Century, when European narratives began to document what Ethiopians eat. He notes that what the world knows as Ethiopian cuisine largely represents the cuisine of the northern-central highlands — that's where ancient Aksum existed — and not the many regional cuisines, apart from dishes that have been adopted by the wider culture.

Not surprisingly, he says, the four largest cultures in Ethiopia — the Amharas, the Oromos, the Gurages and the Tigrayans — have contributed the most to what we now identify as Ethiopian national cuisine. When Ethiopians go abroad, they tend to cook national cuisine rather than "the regional cooking they learned in the hearth of their mothers," Abbebe says. "Local cooking and feast foods in the diaspora now thus appear in contexts so different as to transform the original meaning." This separates the food from its history and culture, turning ethnic food into national food, and "once divorced in this way, national foods can easily be mixed and matched."

"While it is important to examine these other indigenous bases," Abbebe asserts, "the Ethiopians have always been extraordinarily loyal to the foods of the north-central highlands." And because "there are very few historical documents relating to Ethiopian foods," it's a difficult study to undertake and a difficult evolution to untangle.

In the mid-1930s, the African-American journalist George S. Schuyler wrote two mystery novels, one set in Ethiopia, and both with plots and themes that he hoped would stir support for Ethiopia's fight against the Italian occupation of their country. In *Revolt in Ethiopia*, the novel's hero, a wealthy African-American oilman, sneaks an Ethiopian princess back into her homeland, where they share a meal with a brave rebel leader in a small town on the border with Sudan.

"A servant entered with a great bowl of turtle soup," Schuyler writes, describing their first meal on Ethiopian soil. "Then came excellent river fish, followed by giant snails cooked in palm butter thickened with cassava flour. Gourds of cool palm wine were soon emptied and refilled. The pièce de resistance was a great haunch of rare beef, which the Dedjasmatch carved with a huge razor-sharp hunting knife. For dessert there was watermelon, followed by excellent Italian cognac."

This very authentic fictional repast samples three elements of Ethiopian cuisine: The raw beef is typically Ethiopian, the cognac shows the Italian influence, and the dishes (and beverages) made of palm and cassava are more Sudanese, a characteristic found in those far western parts of Ethiopia that border the Sudan.

In some of the poorest regions of Ethiopia, scholars have identified myriad "famine foods," wild fruits, vegetable and plants that people eat when their crops fail due to drought, or when food runs out between harvests. People forced to do this consider it to be an indignity, but they must survive, so they eat what they can, sometimes on the spot while foraging for it.

One such food — the leafy, spinach like *hamle kulitch* — has led to the saying: "If I survive until July and August, I will survive until the next year due to *hamle kulitch*." July and August bring the rainy season, after which people can harvest their crops. Another famine food is *digla*, a fast-growing wild seed whose grain provides a substitute for teff. Scholars have identified many famine foods particular to the regions in which they grow, and Ethiopians only eat these foods when circumstance offers no alternative.

The Daily Meals

The presence of famine and famine foods in Ethiopia presents a bleak and startling contrast to the way Americans sate themselves at Ethiopian restaurants. Those meals are more akin to middle-class family life in Addis Ababa and other Ethiopian cities, where it's three meals a day: in Amharic, *qurs, mesa* and *erat* — that is, breakfast, lunch and dinner.

For financially secure urban Ethiopians, *qurs* might be milk, cereal, bread and dishes made with eggs, familiar items any morning in America.

But the cereal is a little different. It will probably be *kinche*, a cracked wheat or barley porridge that looks and tastes a little like grits or cream of wheat. It's often served with hot *niter kibbee* to make it rich and fatty. Or you might eat *atmit,* a hot cream of oats cereal, with sugar or honey swirled in. Even beef *tibs* are not out of the question for breakfast in the way Americans would eat bacon, sausage or ham. And in northern Ethiopia's Tigrinya-speaking region, sardines and chopped tomatoes, spiced with a bit of *berbere,* might be on the table.

The bread at this meal may be *injera,* but often it's *ambasha,* served with Ethiopian honey rather than the more American jam. Or the breakfast starch could be *chechebsa* or *kita,* flat wheat or barley pan breads fried in *kibbee* and spiced with *berbere. Chechebsa* tends to be served in little pieces, while *kita* is often called an "Ethiopian pizza."

Breakfast protein can come from *enqulal* (egg) *tibs,* the Ethiopian omelet, with tomato, onion, jalapeño peppers, cardamom and a sprinkle of black pepper. For a more elaborate version of *enqulal tibs,* pan fry some beef and onions, then add the eggs to it, then scramble them all together. *Ful,* introduced to Ethiopia by Arabic cultures, is a hearty dish of mashed fava beans cooked with diced tomatoes, jalapeños, onion and cottage cheese or yogurt. *Quanta firfir* is spicy Ethiopian dried beef (like beef jerky) with chopped *injera* (a *firfir* dish always means something, often *injera,* chopped and added to the main dish). *Doro firfir* replaces the *quanta* with chicken.

Country people eat what they can get or afford. Their cereal might be *genfo,* a porridge made of oats. A grittier type of porridge is called *bula,* made from the powdered bark of the enset plant. Be sure to add lots of *berbere* and *kibbee* to give it some flavor. An *ambasha* bread and coffee is another common country breakfast. Or they could have *shiro,* the tasty ground pea powder that you can make in large quantities and keep for a long time, reconstituting it with water and serving it with *injera* or bread.

For *mesa,* middle-class Ethiopians will eat what we know as a typical Ethiopian meal: *injera* and the dishes of their choice — vegetarian or meat, *wot* or *alicha.* Like an American meal, this midday Ethiopian meal is lighter. Soup (*shorba*) or broth (*merek*) is a nice complement and can be prepared with lentils, beans, potatoes, collard greens, lamb, ox, chicken or any combination of these ingredients. Kids going to school may take a lunch box packed with *injera,* a *firfir* of tomatoes mixed with injera, and maybe a *wot* or an *alicha* to put on the *injera.*

Then, for *erat,* it's *injera* again with soups, meats and vegetables, usually more of them than the afternoon meal. For a break from Ethiopian cuisine, many families have spaghetti or lasagna, and more Westernized families may have a green salad before or after the meal. This is unusual, for as an Ethiopian friend points out, "we don't have courses in Ethiopia." And as Levine found, sometimes the members of such families eat from their own plates rather than from a communal plate in the centuries-old Ethiopian way.

The one thing you won't frequently find at an Ethiopian meal is dessert — at least, nothing unique to the culture, like tiramisu or parfait or baklava in the cultures from which they come. "By it's nature," an Ethiopian friend told me, "our culture doesn't have desserts." So sweets after a meal at an Ethiopian home might be cakes and pastries influenced by Italian cuisine, or even more likely, a trip to a bakery or café, where friends will gather for coffee and talk.

There's no exact word in Amharic that means "dessert," so the easiest word to use is *tafach,* which means "sweets." *Matatamiya* comes from a word that means "to make balanced" or "to make tasty," although in context, it could also indicate an appetizer; and the more literal *takatay megeb* means "meal follower," or actually, "follower meal" in Amharic word order — or for a more figurative meaning, "palate cleanser."

Amharic dictionaries variably use *matatamiya, tafach* or *takatay megeb* to translate "dessert." But some feel the need to explain: "*Kewana megeb behwula yemikerb tafach megeb,*" offers one loquacious dictionary as its first translation of "dessert." This phrase means, "After the main meal, [you are] served a sweet meal." This dictionary's second word for dessert is simply *takatay megeb.*

Iasu Gorfu, an Ethiopian writer and poet who has lived and worked in America for decades, calls *matatamiya* "a new addition to the language. The real issue is that 'dessert' is a European concept," he says, "and we do not have it in our tradition. Most Ethiopian foods are hot and spicy, and one does not finish with dessert after the meal. One just drinks *talla* or *t'ej,* and that is all. Honey or any sweet food is sometimes used at breakfast or eaten by itself whenever the occasion permits, but not in any regular fashion as dessert."

This lacuna on the Ethiopian table may be because sugar is largely a 20th Century addition to the culture, says Araya Selassie Yibrehu, a pioneering New York restaurateur and *t'ej* maker. Once sugar caught on, pastry shops of various nationalities — Italian, Greek, Arabic — began to speckle the landscape of cities and towns, especially in Addis Ababa. Sugar has even found its way into Ethiopia's honey wine, allowing some *t'ej* makers to sweeten their brew without using quite as much expensive Ethiopian honey. Purists like Araya would never taint their *t'ej* this way.

One sweet treat enjoyed by Ethiopians is *pasti,* a pastry made of fried dough that looks a bit like a contorted donut without a hole, sometimes sprinkled with powdered sugar. It's Italian in origin, but it's become a part of Ethiopia's dessert-less indigenous culture. It's often sold in *pasti* shops around Ethiopia, and you'll especially find such shops near schools (including colleges) because young people love the treat. There's also the *chornaki,* another deep-fried sweet pasty, crispy hard on the outside, chewy soft in the middle, and about the size of a baseball.

Ras Dashen, an Ethiopian restaurant in Chicago, serves an *injera* bread pudding created by its proprietress/chef, Zenash Beyene. You won't find it in Ethiopia, but it's certainly a dessert based on something uniquely Ethiopian. A few blocks up the street, Chicago's Ethiopian Diamond served a chocolate *injera* crepe cake for a special event in 2010. And Almaz Dama, the pastry chef at the family-owned Dama restaurant and bakery in Arlington, Va., makes a tall, moist, creamy, fruity teff cake that brightens any table lucky enough to host it.

Just as uncommon at an Ethiopian meal is the appetizer, although Ethiopian restaurants in America often have them to please their American customers and create a new revenue stream. A common appetizer — in fact, *the* common appetizer — is the *sambussa,* a fried pastry, usually triangular, stuffed with spicy lentils or meat. It's very much like the potato-filled Indian *samosa,* but smaller and crispier. Some restaurants offer *ayib*, or Ethiopian cheese, as an appetizer, and they'll mix in a little *mitmita* to give it some heat. A few will offer *butecha*, a chick pea dish more often served as a main veggie selection. Another especially good appetizer is *sinig*, a raw jalapeño pepper stuffed with onions, lentils or *ayib*. It's crunchy, spicy and very nourishing.

Ethiopian snacks, or *maksas,* which you could say substitute for dessert, are often crunchy or grainy, and they play a social role after a meal. There's the popular *kolo*, a treat of gently roasted barley, usually with roasted chick peas added, but sometimes with peanuts, then lightly dusted with *berbere* or other seasonings to taste. The best *kolo* comes from Ethiopia, where the barley grains are bigger than those found in the U.S. *Kolo* is also sometimes an appetizer, eaten with coffee before a meal, or when guests drop over to visit. Ethiopians also munch on "popcorn" made from pan-roasted sorghum kernels. It looks just like true popcorn, but it's a little fluffier, and nothing gets caught between your teeth.

Some Ethiopians will snack on *kita* or *chechebsa*, or perhaps even *quanta*, which can be an entrée stewed in *berbere* sauce. There's also *chiko*, prepared by roasting barley on a *mitad* (or in your oven), grinding into a flour, and then flavoring with a multitude of seasonings (cardamom, fenugreek, ginger, cloves), all mixed with *kibbee. Dabo kolo* is a doughy treat of sweetened, seasoned, kneaded dough, cut into little snack-sized pieces, and then lightly roasted or pan fried in oil until browned.

Coffee (*buna*) is the Ethiopian staple beverage, and drinking it can be ritualistic for those who choose to make it so. It can begin or end a meal, and sometimes it does both. Tea (*shay* in Amharic, although usually written as *chai*) is also popular — many Ethiopian companies package home-grown varieties — and of course, there's the legendary Ethiopian honey wine *t'ej* and its foamier kin, *talla*, a grain-based beer. Ambo mineral water is a popular drink and a profitable export. Fassil's Mineral Water is a new product, made in Argentina and exported to North America as a sort of Ambo substitute. There's also Coke, Pepsi, Sprite, Fanta and other soft drinks, manufactured now in Ethiopia. At weddings, the host might serve a popular aperitif of vodka and sweet vermouth.

Some Cultural Customs

The typical household in Addis Ababa doesn't dish up a lot of non-Ethiopian food. The one exception is spaghetti, a holdover from those decades of Italian influence. From time to time, a family will eat chicken and lamb in a more western style, baked or roasted, rather than stewed in a spicy *wot*. But Ethiopians say that's the exception rather than the rule.

At the most customary meal, the people surrounding the *mesob* or table will wash their hands in a bowl of warm water or have warm water poured over their hands from a vessel over a basin that catches the excess. This is very much like the order of business at a Jewish Passover seder, and many of the customs of Ethiopia's Christian church borrow from Old Testament customs (Ethiopian Christians don't eat pork, for example). It's also a good idea when everyone reaches for food from the same platter in the middle of the table. In fact, cleanliness is important in all aspects of Ethiopian food, from the way an animal is slaughtered to the way vegetables are washed before they're cooked.

You should never, *ever* lick your fingers at an Ethiopian meal. Because proper etiquette dictates that you only tear your *injera* and eat your food using your right hand, at some hand-washing ceremonies, that's sometimes the only one you'll wash. But just as often people will wash both. Using a hot towel is an alternative to washing with water, or sometimes you'll still get a hot towel after washing with water. Some Ethiopian restaurants in America will bring a towel to your table to give you a taste of this custom. After the meal, you wash your hands again with a towel or in a bowl of water brought to the table.

The most traditional Ethiopian parents are very strict about using only the right hand to eat, and if their children naturally gravitate toward using the left hand, the parent might scold them and retrain them.

Some families will burn incense, another centuries-old custom. And during fasting holidays, of which there are many in Ethiopian Christianity, animal products of any kind — including butter and milk — are banned. Fish is permitted, but many strict practitioners will shun that as well.

Religion accounts for some of what people eat or don't eat, and how they prepare their meals, and some Middle Eastern dishes have even made their way into Ethiopian's Moslem culture, a result of numerous historic encounters with — that is, conquests by — Moslem invaders.

Abbebe Kifleyesus has published numerous studies in which he describes the history and customs of food in Ethiopia. In "Muslims and Meals," a look at the Moslem Argobba culture of central Ethiopia, Abbebe names food after food common to all Ethiopians. At the Argobba table, the men eat first, and the women and children eat what's left after that.

"Argobba men not only eat before women," he writes, "but consider prized food items such as meat to be their exclusive prerogative. Women and children learn to refuse meat and, on formal occasions, to eat when the men leave. Women carry this modesty to extremes, and if they are guests they will often swear that they have already eaten, and if they have not, that they are not hungry."

Because Islam forbids alcohol, most Moslems in Ethiopia don't drink it, and some Moslem-owned grocery stores in the U.S. won't even sell gesho, the woody plant used to ferment *t'ej*. (They will, however, chew *chat*, a plant that delivers a mildly hallucinogenic effect, not unlike marijuana.) But Moslem Ethiopians do ferment their *injera* for two or three days because, in such a short period of time, no alcohol forms. They tend to make smaller, thicker pieces of injera — not unlike the size of pita bread.

Somali Moslems — there are many living in Ethiopia's vast eastern Ogaden region — bake a bread called *canjero* or *laxoox* ("laa-hoh"), also found in some Arab cultures. Made on a stove called a *daawo* (the Somali *mitad*), it's smaller and thicker than *injera*, yellowish in color, made with wheat rather than teff, fermented just overnight, and bubbly on top, but brown on the bottom. When you eat it, you can sprinkle sugar on top (very un-Ethiopian) or coat it with some melted butter. It's something of a cross between *injera*, a pancake, and the Indian lentil crepe *dosa*. Somali cuisine also includes the *sambussa*.

Moslem stews are sometimes more fluid, and in Harar, fenugreek seed is used to make stews with and without meat. In general, Moslem cooking will have more dishes that mix meats and vegetables together in the stew. This is done in some Christian Ethiopian cooking, but it's rather rare. Moslems also like to mash up pieces of bread and mix it into the dishes.

Ethiopian Moslems often eat rice, a custom that entered their culture through contact with Middle Eastern Moslems, and they tend to eat more lamb than Ethiopian Christians. The culture also has some unique dishes that further show an Arab influence. There's *kebsa*, a dish of rice and lamb ribs; and *hanid*, made by cooking spiced lamb ribs wrapped in foil, and then mixing the lamb with rice. *Ful,* a dish made from fava beans, comes from Arab culture, but it's now widely eaten by everyone in Ethiopia, especially for breakfast.

Apart from those differences, Moslem meals in Ethiopia are the same as they are in other religions: there's *injera* and *wots* and *alichas* — none of it accompanied, at least in observant households, by *t'ej.* Of course, many Moslems break the rules and drink *t'ej,* if perhaps on the sly from friends and neighbors.

The strictest Moslems and Christians adhere to Biblical principles when they eat, and even though those principles are largely the same, people of the two cultures may not agree to eat meat together, each group being unsure of the whether the other properly slaughtered, cleaned and blessed the meat. And while this may be more common among uneducated and tribal people, Ethiopians tend to live and socialize with others of their own class, culture and religion (not unlike so many of their American counterparts).

Most of the Jews of Ethiopia, who call themselves Beta Israel ("the house of Israel"), moved to Israel during Operation Moses and Operation Solomon, two daring airlifts in the '80s and '90s, and their new generations have become more Westernized in their practice.

In Ethiopia, the Beta Israel ate like all other Ethiopians. Most lived in towns surrounding the old Ethiopian capital of Gondar, and many were poor, just like their Christian compatriots. In addition to *injera,* Ethiopian Jews would sometimes eat a leavened bread with sesame seeds on it, as well as using sesame seeds in other ways. But this was a Gondar regional custom, not a uniquely Jewish one. Because of fear and cultural taboos, Christians and Jews would rarely break *injera* together, even though their food was largely the same.

Ethiopian Jews celebrate the Sabbath with a special large loaf of bread called *berekete,* which the woman of the household bakes all night under an open flame on a hearth. She also lets buttermilk cook for a long time until it turns to cheese. After synagogue on Saturday morning, the family eats the bread, sometimes adding spicy *berbere* to the cheese and soaking the bread in it. There's also *tebugna,* a small loaf of bread often served to guests with coffee, and *engotcha,* about the size of a biscuit, given to children.

Ras Dashen's Zenash Beyene grew up Beta Israel in Ethiopia, and she still cherishes her memories of *berekete.* As we talked about those days, a Tigrayan Christian friend joined our conversation and wrote the word in Amharic. Zenash says that the Beta Israel and Tigrayan people are very close. "If you test his blood and my blood," she says, pointing to her friend, "same thing."

When the Passover holiday ends, the Beta Israel enjoy a celebration called Gdeft, ending eight days of eating *matzos* with a feast that includes *engotcha* dipped in honey, whose stickiness represents the closeness of family, and whose sweetness is a holiday treat. (A salty variety of *engotcha* is called *dabeh*.) The meal features generous servings of *wots, alichas* and *t'ej,* along with singing, dancing and prayers.

Like their Christian and Moslem neighbors, the Jews of Ethiopia don't eat pork, as proscribed by biblical dietary laws. But kosher eating goes deeper than that, and only the Beta Israel follow all of the rules. Ethiopian Christians use *kibbee* in their beef dishes, even though the same rules that forbid the consumption of pork also forbid the mixing of meat and dairy. The Beta Israel don't mix the two elements because of kosher dietary laws, and some cooks won't even use *kibbee* in chicken dishes.

The Bible also forbids slaughtering and eating a wounded animal, and observant Ethiopian Jews obey. If their cow has a wound, they may give it to a Christian neighbor, who will gladly turn it into *siga wot*.

Orit Getanek — born in Ethiopia, raised from age 9 in Israel, and educated in clinical psychology in Chicago — observes Jewish dietary laws strictly, although her cousin believes it's kosher to use *kibbee* in chicken dishes. "With chicken," Orit says, "it's more rabbinic law, not Torah law." She followed the rules even in Chicago, which meant she rarely ate at restaurants, and she got her *injera* from Zenash. *Injera* among Beta Israel in Ethiopia was pretty much the same as it was in Christian homes, and Orit also remembers eating leavened bread covered with sesame seeds when she lived in Ethiopia.

In Israel, where most Ethiopian Jews now live, food customs have changed somewhat. Mothers still make *injera* to eat with traditional Ethiopian cuisine, as well as less traditional Ethiopian-style dishes, like a *wot* made of goat rather than lamb. But the Middle Eastern and European Jewish influence is strong in the kitchen, especially as new generations come along.

Couscous, falafel and schnitzel are common in the homes of Israel's Ethiopian Jews, many of whom remain strictly kosher. So is shawarma, which to an Ethiopian is a little like *tibs*. And because many of the children of Ethiopian Jews eat at school every day or even go away to boarding school, the emerging generation has become much more diverse at the *mesob*, often eating Israeli food during the week and Ethiopian food with the family at home on the weekends.

Fasting Holidays

As with any culture where people are free to choose their faith, religious practice among Ethiopians varies from person to person and family to family, and the more urban and educated the individual, the less he's likely to be a strict observer. But it's probably fair to say that on the whole, Ethiopians are an observant culture when it comes to their religions.

For Ethiopian Christians, and to some degree for Ethiopian Moslems, this involves a lot of fasting — that is, not eating until certain times on certain days, and not eating certain things during those fasting times. Ethiopian Jews have only a few fasting days.

Religious practice in Ethiopia is intriguingly syncretic, and none of these three religions eats pork, which is forbidden by the Old Testament. Ethiopian Catholics, however, eat pork, and some Italian restaurants in Ethiopia will serve it for Catholics and tourists.

In the tradition of the Ethiopian Orthodox Tewahedo Church — one of the oldest Christian churches on the African continent, with ancient ties to the Coptic Christianity of Egypt — there are about 250 fasting days each calendar year. Clergymen observe all of them, but the more devout laity reduce their obligation to about 165, and the casual observer only fasts during the 40 or so days of the Lenten season.

Observers eat no animal products (including eggs, milk, and butter) on fasting days and no food until about 3 p.m. in the afternoon on our Western clock. The Ethiopian clock would call this 9 in the daytime — that is, the ninth hour after sunrise.

The schedule of fasting is very complex. The simplest rule is that Ethiopian Christians fast every Wednesday and Friday in honor of the day Christ was condemned and the day he was crucified. But this changes somewhat during the approach to major holidays. For example, Ethiopians fast for the 43 days before Christmas, the day before Epiphany, three days beginning on the Monday before Lent, 40 days leading up to Palm Sunday, seven days between Palm Sunday and Easter, five days after Pentecost for *Tsom Hawaryat* (the Fast of the Apostles), and 15 days for *Tsom Filseta* (the Fast of the Holy Virgin Mary). In Amharic, *tsom* means "fast."

On these days, Ethiopians eat only fruits and vegetables, with no *kibbee* used in the preparation of any dishes. Ethiopian restaurants in American will sometimes add additional vegetable entrées to their menus during the long fasting seasons to offer more variety to the observant.

During "feasting days" — Easter, Christmas, Epiphany, and all non-fasting days — meat accompanies the vegetables on the *injera*, and beef is usually the meat of choice.

Ethiopian Moslems naturally fast for Ramadan, the ninth month of the Moslem calendar. They eat no food during daylight hours and then have a festive meal after sundown. Wealthier citizens may even close their businesses during the day. The Moslem observance tends to be more faithful than Christian fasting observances, and also more uniform among Moslems, whether they're wealthy or poor, rural or urban.

The simplest fasting tradition in Ethiopia comes from the Beta Israel, who fast for 24 hours — from sundown to sundown — on Yom Kippur, the holiest day in Judaism, and during a few other holiday periods throughout the year.

Ethiopian Jews have a unique holiday called Sigd, which means "to prostrate oneself." For centuries, this holiday has celebrated their kinship to Jerusalem and their desire to reunite with the Jews of the world outside of Ethiopia. This, too, is a fasting day, along with a few other special holidays, like *Tsom Dehnat* (the Fast of Salvation) or *Tsom Aster* (the Fast of Esther).

Unlike the Christian fast, which ends at midday, a Jewish fast is absolute: no food or water from sundown to sundown. The family will consume a large meal the night before the fast and then break the fast with another large meal.

Of course, the degree to which Ethiopians fast depends upon their kinship to their faith. This is especially true of a culture that's spread around the world, far from the traditions of home. Educated urban Ethiopians will tell you that they try to fast but don't always succeed. Doing it together with family makes it easier. The most likely time to fast is during the Lenten season. It's a long stretch, and in a way, it covers you for not fasting twice every week like orthodox believers do.

These customs will certainly change even further as new generations of Ethiopian-American children grow up and choose the customs that their own families will follow. It's a familiar story here: the fading away of the hyphen, and the cultural that precedes it, as the American side takes over.

The Enigma of Ethiopian Cooking

Can you keep a secret? Most Ethiopian cooks can. But it's not because they don't want to give away the special ingredients that make their *yemisir wot* or *siga tibs* better than anyone else's. It's simply because they can't quantify what they do.

Meskerem ("Meskie") Assefa, who owns two Ethiopian restaurants in the Detroit area, explains it well.

"When people ask me how did you cook it," she says, "I tell them I don't have measurements. It seems like I don't want to share my cooking secret, but that's not how it is." She notes, for example, that Gurage and Amhara *kitfo* are not the same. The way the Gurage people use *kibbee*, what they add to their *kitfo*, the types and amounts of spice — it all makes a difference, and it's hard to quantify.

"In the American and European way," Meskie says, "it's an ounce of this and a teaspoon of that. With Ethiopian food, you never use measurements. Your imagination, your eye is what measures it. Ethiopian cooking in general is something you don't rush. Boil the water, throw things in, and that's it — no, that's not how it is. Your timing is what makes it different. Your own judgment of the measurement, the sizes, the ingredients. Here in America, it's fast, fast, fast. That's not the Ethiopian way."

Roza Tesfaye concurs. She and her husband, Dereje Retta, own Red Sea restaurant in Ypsilanti, Mich., and for Roza, time is an essence of her cuisine. She likes a *lot* of onions and garlic in her *yemisir wot*, for example, and a lot of *berbere*. But you must cook the onions for a long time — perhaps an hour or two — and then you add the *berbere* and cook it a long time again.

"If you don't cook it well," Roza says, "it's going to be very hot and you can't even eat it. The degree of hotness changes by how much you cook it."

Some Ethiopian cooks claim it's the amount of butter or oil you use in a dish that makes it special, but Meskie disagrees.

"For me, it's not the *kibbee*," she says, "it's the timing, and the amount of the spices that I use."

James McCann spent time in Ethiopia for his book *Stirring the Pot: A History of African Cuisine*, and he talked with women about their cooking. Trying to get proportions for a recipe wasn't easy. How much of each ingredient do you use when making *shiro*? "The simplicity of the preparation of this dish," McCann writes, "belies the astonishing geography of its ingredients and the complexity of its constituent flavors." As one woman explained it to him: You might use a *weqiyt* of an ingredient (she cups one hand), or a *efign* (two cupped hands), or a *terign* (an open hand with extended fingers). "To tell you how to make this dish," McCann writes, "she has to show you using sounds and gestures. Written words convey little of the true sense of how to cook [*shiro wot*] sauce."

And then there's the big open secret of Ethiopian food. One cook might use more of a particular spice than another, one may cook it longer than her neighbor, and some will use more butter or less butter. But does it *really* make a noticeable difference?

"There is a degree of magic and secret factor about the Ethiopian restaurant menu," Hagossa Gebrehiwet-Buckner writes in her cookbook. "Diners are led to believe that dishes are lovingly prepared to some secret recipe, known only to that particular chef." But Hagossa admits that "most dishes in the typical Ethiopian restaurant don't vary much at all," and diners should "feel a bit of confidence when you go to a new Ethiopian restaurant across the street, town or in another city."

In other words, for the most part *yemisir wot* is *yemisir wot*, and *kibbee* is *kibbee*. From one good cook's version to the next, there may only be shades of difference, but they have more to do with an overall touch than a secret ingredient.

That's how Zenash Beyene sees it. When you ask her what makes one cook's food different from another's, she points to her head, rubs her fingers together, and just says, "It's this." Her husband, Kevin Swier, says good cooks have sensors.

For Araya Selassie Yibrehu, a pioneering restaurateur, the principle is simple: "In Ethiopian cooking, there are no measurements. You stir it, cook it and taste it."

Hirut Assefa doesn't have a restaurant, but she set one up for a week during the summer of 2009, in her hometown of Chicago, on the grounds of the stadium that hosted the annual gathering of the Ethiopian Sports Federation in North America. She, too, insisted that Ethiopian cooking is an art rather than a skill, with no secret ingredients and no measuring cups. "You cannot cook it, me and you, the same way," she said. "I know by my hand. I can see it."

At Ethiopia's embassy in Washington, D.C., Fikerte Kidanemariam has served as the ambassador's assistant since 1999. And while she isn't a cook by profession — Kebebush Demissie prepares meals for the ambassador and his family at their home two miles away — she's the embassy's unofficial chief consultant on cuisine.

Fikerte agrees that there are few, if any, secret ingredients in Ethiopian cooking. It's all about technique, and to some degree, predilection. For example, some cooks will chop up their garlic before putting into the mix, but Kebebush uses whole pieces. You can make *shiro* with chick peas, yellow peas or beans, and the choice slightly changes the outcome. (Tigrayan *shiro*, Ethiopians often say, is the best.) Naturally, the amount of spice and butter you use makes a difference, but Fikerte says that the order in which you add the spices, and when you add them during the process, affects the outcome as well.

Then there are the onions. You have to use just the right quantity, and you have to cook them for the proper length of time: until they brown, for a dark spicy *wot*, but not so long for a milder, lighter *alicha*.

"You have to take your time and cook it properly," Fikerte says. "Some people just use a few minutes to cook food." Still, she acknowledges that "even when people use the same ingredients," one woman's *wot* can taste different than her sister's version.

Johannes Aynalem, an expatriate artist and muralist, has a lot to say about his country's cuisine, and he loves saying it. He left Ethiopia and came to America in 1990 because, he says, "I am not a good follower of communism." He settled in New York, lived there for more than a decade, and now lives in Silver Spring, Md., closer to family.

Johannes "grew up in a family highly skilled in the art of cooking," and he learned to do it under the tutelage of his mother and grandmother. His family was especially known for its *talla*, which is "like Guinness, only better," and people would spend hours during holidays at their house.

There is a secret to Ethiopian cooking, Johannes says with a smile: "Preparation, preparation, preparation."

For example, the *kibbee*, which adds rich flavor to those meat dishes that use it. It begins with blending the spices, and then cooking the mixture for a long, long time — up to 12 hours, over a low flame, to let the solids separate from the fat, and then to let the fat absorb as much flavor as possible from the spices. Aging *kibbee* also influences its flavor, and the longer it sits, the richer it becomes.

Families don't always make their own *kibbee*. They often buy it at market from a trusted vendor, or sometimes from country people who come to the city to sell their goods.

It's the same for the essential spice *berbere* and the highly refined *shiro* powder: The cook must grind and mix a lot of spices in the right proportions, something she doesn't want to have to do very often. Some families stock up and only make *berbere* and *shiro* once a year.

Each family also has its own recipe, always just a little different from the family next door, although the more money a family has, the more spices the cook can include. The poorest families can't always afford to include all of the spices all of the time, so sometimes they'll make their *berbere* with fewer spices and then add touches of additional spice to the recipe when cooking an evening meal.

"That's where the cooking starts — in the preparation of the spices," Johannes says. "The process is very tiresome, and it takes a lot of time."

Even the cooking of the onions, an ingredient in every Ethiopian dish, makes a difference. You must cook them for a long time, with a steady hand, until they become mushy. This is hard to describe or measure in a cookbook.

Then there's the *shakla dest*, the clay pots used in Ethiopia to cook food. The difference between food made in a regular pot and one made in a clay pot is like the difference between pizza baked on a pan and in a clay oven, Johannes says.

Finally, consider the *injera*, which "is just like wine, very temperamental." Because *injera* is a fermented bread, it can be made with a sort of sourdough starter — that is, yeast left over from earlier batches. In some families, the yeast could be descended from a batch that's more than 100 years old. ("You never know," he says.) Each piece must be of even height and medium thickness.

Johannes is clearly a man with a passion for his native cuisine. Growing up in Ethiopia, he says, if dinnertime conversation grew slow, people could

always talk about food. He now enjoys food from a wide range of culture —
Chinese, Japanese, Thai, Mexican, Indian — but back in Addis Ababa, when
he went to a restaurant, it was almost always Ethiopian.

"This is what we like," he says of his compatriots. "Our food is very
addictive, even the *injera*."

This is all wonderful testimony for Ethiopian cuisine — far more
appetizing than what the government has to say.

Ethiopia: The Official Handbook, published in 1969, in the waning years
of the 700-year-old monarchy, spends about a page on "eating in Ethiopia,"
and some of it may discourage tourism.

The book explains *wot*, "the national dish of Ethiopia," as well as *injera*,
"a kind of spongy aerated pancake with something of the feel of foam rubber,"
and with a "bitter, slightly beery flavor." Meals often come with *t'ej*, the
national drink, which "tastes like a flat, rough cider, although it is not so
sweet." Everyone at the table eats from the same large plate, and while "it is
the custom for Ethiopian ladies to feed the men, visitors of either sex are likely
to find themselves being fed."

But to enjoy one of the greatest of delicacies, you'll have to find your way
from a restaurant to an Ethiopian home.

On public holidays and festivals, *The Official Handbook* explains, "a
carefully selected live beast [is] slaughtered just before the feast is due to begin.
The carcass is sometimes hung on steel frames, which are trundled to the table
so that each guest can cut off the piece of meat he fancies. He then dips each
mouthful in *berbere*, the favorite Ethiopian spice, which is also supposed to
be a precaution against tapeworm."

Supposed to be? For the sake of those bygone Ethiopians and tourists,
let's hope it was.

A Stroll Through Ethiopian History

How old is Ethiopian cuisine and the current fashion of eating it? That depends, in part, upon what you mean by "Ethiopia." But even if you could circumscribe the sprawling history of this complex country, very little documentation exists to confirm exactly when Ethiopians began to eat the way they do now.

For a few reasons — one ancient and historical, one modern and political —"Ethiopia" is as much an idea as a fact.

Today the term refers to a country with borders. But millennia ago, the civilized world of southern Europe and northern Africa used the term "Ethiopian" to refer to all of the dark-skinned people who inhabited the horn of Africa — that is, the lands immediately west of the Red Sea, in some cases stretching as far west and north as Egypt.

The name "Ethiopia" derives from two Greek words that together mean "burnt face," so it's easy to see how fairer-skinned culture would give this name to the Africans they encountered. The name appears in Homer's *Iliad*, referring to people who lived in the far east and far west, although Greeks regularly used the word "Aithiopia" to mean African people south of Egypt, and more generally, darker-skinned people they encountered anywhere in the world.

By the fourth century, the western world often used the word to refer solely to the kingdom of Aksum, the first great civilization in the territory that's now Ethiopia. A millennium later, the modern country formally took its name from that origin.

Then there's Abyssinia, another ancient name for Ethiopia, and one that persisted into the 20th Century. This name comes from an Arabic word, *habashat* or *habesha*, meaning mixture or half-breed, and it appears in ancient Yemeni inscriptions, which is significant: There's been a lot of exchange, both cultural and genetic, between Yemen on the east side of the Red Sea and Ethiopia on the west side.

The Ethiopian scholar Wosene Yefru speculates on another possible origin. "The term Abyssinia is foreign," he writes, "and Ethiopia has never, in its long history, called itself Abyssinia." He then notes the commonly accepted evolution of the name from "Habesha." But in Amharic, the Blue Nile is called the Abay, which is the ancient Ge'ez and modern Tigrinya word for "big," and "Abay Sina" is the name of a mountain around the Blue Nile, with "sina," derived from Mt. Sinai. This "Abay Sina," or "big Sinai," sounds suspiciously akin to "Abyssinia," and Wosene wonders if the name for this mountain produced the name by which Ethiopia was sometimes known well into the second millennium A.D.

An Overview

In the middle of the millennium before the Christian era, Yemeni tribes crossed the Red Sea, forming communities in what would become Ethiopia. They brought with them an ancient Saebean writing system that developed into the 276-letter syllabic alphabet used to write Ge'ez and later Amharic, the language of the Ethiopia government today. During this pre-Christian period, tribal kingdoms emerged throughout the region, and historians believe that one such kingdom, ruled by the Habasha people, eventually formed powerful Aksum.

These Semitic Habashas from Arabia naturally intermingled with the people who were already there, creating the Amhara-Tigrinya culture of northern Ethiopia and Eritrea that would become the ruling class in the millennia that followed, dominating the descendants of the Africans who lived there long before their arrival.

As certain as this seems now, it took a while for the ancient and the emerging modern world to stop calling everything east of Egypt "Ethiopia."

The third century romantic novel *The Aethiopica*, by the Greek writer Heliodorus, begins and ends in a place called "Ethiopia" and revolves around Chariclea, the daughter of King Hydaspes and Queen Persinna of Ethiopia. But this Ethiopia was more likely the ancient Nile Valley kingdoms of Nubia or Kush, which existed in what became Sudan. In his fifth century *Histories*, Herodotus later extended the borders of "Ethiopia" as far east as India, drawing again on the Greek meaning of the word. Greeks of this era regularly used the name Aithiopia to refer to Kush and its famous capital, Meroë.

The British writer George Ditson never actually visits the Ethiopia we know today for his 1858 book, *From Paris to Ethiopia*: After a trip through Egypt, he explored Nubia and Kush — once again, modern-day Sudan. These cultures may have extended slightly into the territory of modern Ethiopia, but they certainly aren't what historians now consider to be the Ethiopia of the ancient world.

Even the great King Ezana of Aksum, who brought Christianity to his empire, added to the confusion: "Ezana, King of Aksum, and of Himyar, and of Raidan, and of Aithiopia, and of Saba," says a fourth century A.D. stone inscription proclaiming his achievements, which soon included the conquest of the fading Kush and the destruction of Meroë.

When Ezana wrote "Aithiopia," he meant the African lands west of Aksum, even though the Aksumite kingdom itself is now considered to be the first true antecedent of Ethiopia. By the sixth century A.D., the Roman empire, acknowledging the importance of Aksum to the region, had begun to refer to Aksum as "Ethiopia."

Yet the liberal use of the name "Ethiopia" persisted into the 19th Century and found its way across the Atlantic. A Philadelphia company sold a product called "Ethiopian Black Enamel," with racist drawings of African children on its label. An 1888 newspaper ad for Ethiopian Pile Ointment features a caricature of an African-American and the promise to clear up "itching internal and external piles." In the 1840s, an American minstrel group called the Ethiopian Serenaders performed for President John Tyler. Sheet music from the 19th Century features such ditties as "the celebrated Ethiopian song" *Oh! Susanna*, written by Stephen Foster for a minstrel troupe. Such music in that era was commonly labeled "Ethiopian."

Daniel Flickinger's 1873 book, *Ethiopia, or, Twenty Years of Missionary Life in Western Africa*, is off by the width of the entire continent. Henry Llewellyn Williams' racist track, *Go And Get Tight!: An Ethiopian Farce in One Scene*, appeared in 1880: Its central character is "Edgar Percy Vere, a dandied young colored gentleman." Clayton Adams' 1917 book *Ethiopia: A Land of Promise* is a series of stories told to engender compassion for the human rights of African-Americans; George Washington Moore's 1918 *Ethiopian Anecdotes and Goaks*, written in slang and dialect, is a collection of racist "black utterances" about African-American life. In all of these instances, "Ethiopian" simply meant African or African-American.

Nor were museums immune. A 1945 bulletin from the Museum of Fine Arts in Boston discusses an exhibit of an "Ethiopian royal sarcophagus" of King Aspalta, who died from 568 B.C. Aspalta was actually a Kushite king who ruled long before there was an Ethiopia.

Even Verdi got it wrong. His Aida is an "Ethiopian princess" taken into slavery in ancient Egypt. She's the daughter of King Amonasro, whose vengeful armies advanced on Thebes. But there was no such Ethiopian king, and Egypt never fought a war with Ethiopia.

In the southern regions of Ethiopia today, there are isolated tribal people — pastoralists and nomads — who probably have some vague idea that they're citizens of "Ethiopia." But largely, they identify themselves by the names of their ancestral cultures. They're only a part of Ethiopia because, in the 18th and 19th centuries, a series of powerful emperors who ruled the burgeoning nation to the north conquered them and incorporated them, once and for all, into the borders of Ethiopia, having long claimed that these lands and these cultures were historically theirs.

In some cases, other nations still claim sovereignty over what has become, at least geopolitically, Ethiopian territories. The vast arid eastern Ethiopian region known as the Ogaden is ethnically and culturally Somali, and because of this, Somalia claims a right to it. The border between Somalia and the Ethiopian Ogaden has never been at peace. Eritrea, once a part of Aksum, and later a disputed part of Ethiopia, became an independent country in 1994 after years of armed rebellion (with ongoing borders wars and skirmishes since independence).

Ethiopia's largest culture, the Oromos, were long ago dominated by the northern Amhara-Tigrayan culture. Afaan Oromo is a Cushitic language that existed in eastern Africa longer than the Semitic languages Amharic and Tigrinya. Addis Ababa, the capital of Ethiopia, is in the vast Oromo region, not the more northern region known as Amhara, and the city is called Shegar or Finfinne in Afaan Oromo. Conflict and resentment exists to this day, and some Oromo people call themselves an occupied nation that was annexed by imperialist Ethiopian leaders in the 19th Century.

Of course, the Oromos themselves were conquerors, an ancient culture whose territory was the borderlands between Ethiopia and its southern neighbors. In the 16th Century, a series of powerful Oromo leaders began to move north, engulfing lands that the Ethiopian emperor considered to be his, and absorbing them into Oromo culture. The incursions would sometimes move northward into the Ethiopian territories of Shoa and Amhara — until the matter was settled in the late 19th Century by Emperor Menelik II, who conquered and absorbed the southern Oromo territories.

Yet this diverse idea called "Ethiopia" has largely held together, partly because of a national myth that ancient emperors circulated very effectively, and partly because of the early influence of Christianity.

The Bible tells the story of Makeda, the great queen from the land of Saba — or Sheba as it's more commonly known — who journeyed across the horn of Africa to meet Solomon, the mighty Hebrew king. The Biblical tale, which would have taken place around 1000 B.C., tells us little more, and historians today can't even locate Saba with certainty. Some believe it was across the Red Sea on the Arabian peninsula. Others say it was somewhere in the region north of modern-day Ethiopia. There may even have been civilizations by that name in both places.

Adding to the confusion, English translations of the Old Testament and Greek translations of the New Testament use the words "Ethiopia" and "Aithiopis," respectively, for the Hebrew name "Kush," once again labeling all ancient sub-Saharan Africans as "Ethiopians," whether or not they lived in what we now call Ethiopia.

But 2,000 years after the queen of Sheba met the king of the Hebrews, an astute Ethiopian emperor named Yekuno Amlak came to power in 1270 and spun a mythology out of their story that began the 700-year process of forging modern Ethiopia.

When Makeda visited Solomon, the newly fabricated story went, she gave him many gifts, the greatest one being a son, whom she named Menelik. When Menelik became a man, Makeda sent him to meet his father. He later returned to rule Saba, which the story claimed was ancient Ethiopia.

Two thousand years later, Yekuno Amlak claimed to be a descendant of Menelik, and when he seized the Ethiopian throne, he "restored" the ancient Solomonic Dynasty of Ethiopian emperors. A book, called the *Kebra Negast* ("the glory of the kings"), was written somewhere between 1314 and 1322 to document and embellish this ersatz history.

The lengthy saga asserts Ethiopia's place in history as the ordained successor to Israel and the ancient Hebrews, and it claims that Menelik, with God's permission, took the Ark of the Covenant from Jerusalem to Aksum, where it has since resided at St. Mary of Zion, an ancient church, protected by clerics and seen only rarely when they bring it out for worship service.

Some scholars claim that the *Kebra Negast* dates as far back as the sixth to 10th centuries A.D. But there's little evidence for that claim, and the fact that the book begins to appear so prominently in Ethiopian history right after the rise of Yekuno Amlak suggests a provenance contemporary to his reign. It also seems unlikely that so monumental a book could have been written during the decline of Aksum and right after its fall, a period from which no other written records exist.

The Solomonic dynasty ruled for more than 700 years, until the deposition and murder of Ethiopia's last emperor, Haile Selassie, in 1974. Along the way, there were a few fleeting invaders and interlopers: In the early 16th Century, for about 15 years, a Somali-born Moslem, Ahmad Gragn, conquered portions of Ethiopia (the Portuguese later helped defeat him), and from 1936 to 1941, Italy occupied the country. The whole world took notice of this 20th Century "Abyssinian Crisis," and governments around the world scolded Italy for its aggression — without intervening.

In between the decline of Aksum, around 800 A.D. or so, and the ascent of Yekuno Amlak in 1270, power centers in the nascent Ethiopia waxed and waned. Aksum occupied northern Ethiopia's Tigray region and Eritrea north of that. When Aksum fell, various tribes and cultures struggled for power for three or four centuries. Even after Yekuno Amlak established the Solomonic dynasty, its subsequent emperors often had trouble holding the center. Their territory would expand and contract from century to century.

But these events never finally broke the chain of Solomonic emperors, and today Ethiopia rightfully claims to be the only African nation that was never colonized.

In *Ethiopia,* a beautiful 1956 history of the country, French author Jean Doresse says that the Western world first heard rumors of the country's "Prester John" as early as 1165. That was the name Europeans gave for centuries to reports of a Christian emperor who ruled an ancient African land. In the centuries that followed, the presence of Christianity in sub-Saharan Africa gave Europeans some hope of gaining a foothold against the spread of Islam. The Portuguese especially sent missions to Ethiopia in the 16th and early 17th century, one of which produced the first important book about Ethiopian history and culture: Published in 1540 by Francisco Alvarez, a priest on a Portuguese mission that landed in 1520, it confirmed much of what Europeans had heard about Africa's Christian Prester John — in Alvarez's case, Emperor Lebna Dengel (also known as Dawit II), who ruled from 1508-1540.

Just how far back can we go in tracing the history of Ethiopia? How about 4.4 million years? In 1974, at an archaeological dig in the Danakil region of Ethiopia, Donald Johansson and his team discovered the remains of an upright-walking ape that the world now calls Lucy (and that Ethiopians call Dinkenesh, meaning "you are beautiful," or Birkenesh, meaning "rare"). At 3.2 million years old, she's the most complete fossil of an *Australopithecus afarensis,* a hominin (i.e., pre-human) species that laid the foundation for *Homo sapiens* — that is, us. Thirty-five years later, a team led by Tim White — part of the group that studied and analyzed Lucy, just after Johansson found her — told the world about Lucy's ancestor Ardi, a 4.4-million-year-old specimen of *Ardipithecus ramidus,* found near Ethiopia's Awash River.

Were Lucy, Ardi and their kin the progenitors of our "mitochondrial Eve," a theoretical female ancestor who created a gene pool roughly 150,000 years ago that evolved into modern human beings? The geneticist Sarah Tishkoff studies the DNA of tribes in east Africa, and among some Tanzanians, she has found the most diverse gene pool anywhere on earth. Tishkoff posits that these cultures formed through the migration of people from the north, once again making Ethiopia a likely place for the origins of the human species.

If all of this is true — and it seems fairly certain that it is — then Ethiopia is the cradle of civilization on earth. Still, it's a stretch to call these very ancient fossils "Ethiopian," for it would be myriad millennia before anyone would name this (or any other) emerging world.

The Rise of Aksum

The certifiable destiny of Ethiopia began to transpire in the century before the Christian era with the emergence of Aksum — sometimes written Axum — the first great independent African nation along the Red Sea in the region that's now northern Ethiopia.

Aksum reigned the region until about 800 A.D., and every culture in the ancient world knew about it. The Aksumites left behind a wealth of artifacts to account for themselves, none more significant than their coinage. These were the only unique African coins — other African cultures used Greek and Roman coinage, if they used coins at all — and because each coin depicted the emperor who minted it, we have a thorough account of the lineage.

We also know that Aksum became a Christian nation in the third century by fiat of King Ezana. It was the first sub-Saharan African nation to embrace Christianity, which remains Ethiopia's dominant religion today.

So where did Aksum come from? That's where the picture gets sketchy.

The earliest known distant ancestor of the Aksumite kingdom was probably Punt, a culture of at least the third millennium B.C., when Egyptians first wrote about it. The name of this ancient nation appears as "P-w-n-t" in Egyptian hieroglyphics, and it may have been pronounced "Pewanet" or "Epwonat." Nobody knows for sure.

Punt's location has never been precisely identified, but it seems to have stretched from what's now northern Ethiopia around Aksum into Eritrea, and also into neighboring Sudan. This range accounts in part for why Ethiopia and Eritrea are so manifestly linked by history, culture and cuisine.

After Punt came D'MT (spoken "Da'amat"), another mysterious ancient land located in the northern regions of Ethiopia, once again spilling over into Sudan on the west and Eritrea on the north. The small Ethiopian city of Yeha, perhaps a millennium old than the city of Aksum, was the capital city of D'MT, and because of this, some consider it to be Ethiopia's first ancient capital. The people of this loosely formed civilization were almost certainly the descendants of colonizers from the fertile southern Arabian peninsula (modern-day Yemen), and their entry into the horn of African brought a lineage that became fully African over the centuries. Although some historians, especially Ethiopian ones, dispute this, more and more it's becoming an accepted theory about the origins of the dominant Amhara culture of modern Ethiopia.

But of course, these Arabian settlers must trace their roots back millions of years to pre-historic Ethiopia, the cradle of all civilization, whose southern and central regions have given us Lucy, Ardi and their kin.

From these Arabian sojourners, the civilization of D'MT arose around 800 B.C. and faded just 300 or 400 years later, making way for the rumblings of Aksum in the century before the Christian era. D'MT left little evidence of its culture, and scholars have only recently begun to unearth what's there. The archaeologist David W. Phillipson says that the mid-first millennium B.C. is "generally assumed to mark the beginning of the historical period in northern Ethiopia." Those were the days of D'MT, whose citizens may fairly be called the first "Ethiopians."

From this *ur*-culture grew Aksum, and the artifacts left by the Aksumites tells us much of what little we know for sure about the origins of Ethiopian cuisine.

In fact, the American archaeologist Karl Butzer conjectures that Aksum declined and fell *because* of its mastery of agriculture: By 650 to 800 A.D., deforestation had brought about soil erosion, and this destroyed the Aksumite food chain. Add to that the growth of Islam across the Red Sea, which soon spread into the African territories surrounding the Christian Aksum, and you precipitate the end of an empire.

The first mention of Aksum in historic documents comes in the *Periplus of the Erythraean* [Red] *Sea*, written by an anonymous Greek merchant in the first century A.D. The manuscript refers to "the city of the people called Aksumites," located eight days from the Red Sea port of Adulis. Aksum's proximity to Egypt in the west and to Red Sea ports in the east fostered its success. The rulers of Aksum called themselves the "King of Kings" because they conquered and ruled so many of the weaker civilizations in the areas. Aksum's reign sometimes stretched through most of what is now modern-day Ethiopia, and the kings of Aksum ruled in a sort of federal system, granting autonomy to its provinces in exchange for the payment of taxes as tribute. This is how Ethiopia's emperors ruled from the time of Yekuno Amlak, and also why they had always claimed a right to call these southern territories Ethiopian.

Aksum fell around 800 A.D., and when Yekuno Amlak came to power in 1270, he took cues from the way Aksumite kings conquered and ruled the many cultures and kingdoms surrounding them. In between Aksum and Amlak, four centuries of turf wars among rival cultures produced a series of rulers and eventually the more durable Zagwe dynasty, whose emperors reigned from about 1125 until their conquest by Amlak, about a century and a half later.

The most notable Zagwe ruler, King Lalibela, carved superlative rock-hewn churches out of the stony hillsides of northern Ethiopia, where the emerging nation was still centered. Many of these have survived, drawing tourists to the region. The city of Roha was later renamed Lalibela in the king's honor, and you'll find Ethiopian restaurants today named for both incarnations of the city. Lalibela's reign ended around 1229, and 40 years later, in 1270, Yekuno Amlak came to power by killing Lalibela's son, Yetbarak, the last Zagwe king.

Ethiopia Emerges

The mythology-as-history crafted by Yekuno Amlak, who also claimed descent from the last Aksumite king, allowed Ethiopia to emerge as a modern nation. The persistence of Christianity, imposed by the emperors, helped keep the nation together. In the 18th and 19th centuries, a series of conquests by some strong Ethiopian emperors finally incorporated the many cultures, each with its own emperors and kings, who had always paid tribute — in money and goods — to the *negus negast*, or "king of kings," as the Ethiopian emperor referred to himself.

Slowly, from the time of the Aksumite empire into the 19th Century, "Ethiopia" expanded irrevocably southward. The city of Aksum could well be considered the first capital city of what would become modern Ethiopia, but after the Aksumite empire collapsed, the nebulous nation had no fixed capital until the 16th Century. The emperors of these eras would travel the country, keeping an eye on their many integrated kingdoms. Emperor Fasilides finally established a permanent capital at Gondar in the 1635. Southwest of the city of Aksum, Gondar is 25 miles north of the mighty Lake Tana, a source of the Blue Nile.

Gondar remained the capital until 1889, when the celebrated Emperor Menelik II, who would bring Ethiopia into the modern era, consolidated his power by establishing a new capital, south of Gondar in the center of the country. He named it Addis Ababa, which means "new flower" in Amharic. Ironically, the city is located in restless Oromia, and if the Oromo people every break away to create (or recreate) their own country, Ethiopia will lose its modern capital.

Menelik's successor, Emperor Haile Selassie, is the man most closely associated with Ethiopia in the memories of people today. He ruled for almost half a century, and his reign had a sanguinary end: In 1974, a Communist dictatorship called the Derg overthrew the 700-year-old Solomonic dynasty and executed its final emperor. By the end of his reign, Selassie had become ineffective and dangerously autocratic. But in his prime, his commitment to education, economic development and social progress made Ethiopia an international power in an emerging Africa.

The Derg ruled until 1991, when the many resistance movements that had needled its leaders since its inception finally came together and deposed dictator Mengistu Haile Mariam, who fled to exile in Zimbabwe, where he still lives today, despite having been found guilty in absentia of crimes against the nation. The leader of the resistance, Meles Zenawi — who is Tigrayan, not Amhara — emerged as Ethiopia's new prime minister, a job he retains in an economically troubled country that still doesn't give its citizens the freedom promised by its claim of constitutional democracy.

Cultural conflicts persist in the 21st Century, and the loss of Eritrea — as well as border wars with Somalia, an Oromo resistance movement, and growing discontent among the Moslem population — have continued to splinter Ethiopian identity.

The Oromo situation is especially acute. For centuries, the Ethiopian emperor moved the northern nation's capital around the country's northern regions of Tigray, Amhara and Shoa to manage the relatively defenseless kingdoms over which he reigned as their "king of kings." The emperor exacted "tributes" (i.e. taxes) of money and goods from these cultures, and he controlled them through a loose federation.

Then the powerful Emperor Menelik II, who ascended to power in 1889, finally used his military superiority to incorporate the southern Oromo tribes and many other cultures, once and for all, as part of a greater Ethiopia, uniting a country with many languages and many cultural conflicts. He also established Addis Ababa, in the Oromo region, as the nation's new permanent capital, replacing Gondar, in the Amhara region. This is why the Oromos feel that they were forced into alliance with the nation of Ethiopia, and some historic accounts back them up.

"Divided into endless houses," the British historian Cornwallis Harris wrote in 1844 in his *Highlands of Ethiopia*, "the majority of the southern Oromo tribes, who boast independence from Shoa, are governed by hereditary chieftains." (The Oromo region is just south of the Shoa region.) Harris notes that in Ethiopia's past, the Oromos, "united under one head, overran the fairest provinces of Ethiopia, and had they remained united, they might have completed the conquest of the greater portion of the African continent."

Documents like this give Oromos a strong argument to claim the right to independence after their conquest and incorporation by Menelik.

The Somalis, in the eastern horn of Ethiopia, are so poor, hungry and nomadic that they can't mount any reasonable opposition, and neighboring Somalia has been in turmoil for decades. But the Oromos, whose language and culture predate the Amharas and Tigrayans, believe they have been oppressed, and numerous international human rights groups agree with them.

There are separatist groups in Ethiopia today that want Oromia to secede and form a separation nation, which it was at times in the last millennium. Others simply want Oromos to be allowed to participate fully in government.

Gheleta "Gil" Kitila, who co-owns Soretti's Ethiopian Cuisine in Burtonsville, Md., is especially passionate on the subject: He's Oromo, from Nakamte, west of Addis, yet he doesn't believe Oromia should form a separate nation. He sees a simpler and more obvious solution.

Pointing to people who say that Ethiopians aren't mature enough for "American-style democracy," he says: "There are not 10 kinds of democracy. There is only one type of democracy, and that would suit every human being." He wants fair and free elections, which would allow Oromos a bigger share in government, and he notes the troubles Eritrea has faced since its independence. "I am not emotional about it like many others," he says. "I don't know if [the separatists] have really studied the situation, or if it's like revenge. They haven't pictured a free Oromia state and how it functions."

His countryman Aklilu Senbeth, who owns Era restaurant in Philadelphia, concurs. "Believing in it and working practically is a different situation," he says. "Eritrea is not doing well since its separation. It's better for Ethiopians to work together than to separate." And he adds, "If Oromia secedes, there is no more Ethiopia. Only Amhara and Tigray will remain. So much of the land is Oromo."

Ethiopia & Eritrea: Politics at the Dinner Table

The cultures that formed the pre-history of Eritrea are in some ways as mysterious as the cultures from which Ethiopia grew, and the fact that ancient Aksum stretched well into Eritrea has linked the two countries for more than 2,000 years. In modern times, the kinship has rarely been an amicable one.

The agrarian people of very ancient Gash, nearly 5,000 years ago, once occupied part of Eritrea. So did (perhaps) the fabled Punt, and the better-documented D'MT and Nubia, both of which tilled a part of the soil that's now modern Eritrea.

But the most compelling history of this small, poor, struggling nation on the Red Sea begins with the Aksumite empire of the early and middle first millennium A.D.

There's no question that the empire's eponymous capital was in territory that's always been what we now know as Ethiopia. But the kingdom of Aksum extended north into modern Eritrea, and after the fall of Aksum, Ethiopia's emperors always maintained that Eritrea was their nation's northernmost province. No matter that neighboring Sudan often controlled some of Eritrea, nor that the Arabic influence from across the Red Sea took root there. As Ethiopian power grew, so did its interest in "reuniting" with Eritrea.

The European scramble for Africa waylaid those plans for a while when, in 1890, Italy colonized Eritrea. The Italians tried to add Ethiopia to their empire, but the stalwart Emperor Menelik held them off in 1896 at the Battle of Awda, fought in a border town whose name is now legendary in Ethiopian history. Italy finally succeeded in occupying Ethiopia in 1936, but Mussolini's folly ended in 1941. When the Italians left Ethiopia, Eritrea also gained its independence.

The British oversaw Eritrea for several years, but in 1952, the United Nations declared that Eritrea should be federated with Ethiopia as the larger country's northern province. This pleased no one but the landlocked Ethiopians, who gained a valuable coastline and the ancient port of Massawa.

Soon a host of rebel groups formed, some in conflict with others. Border wars and all-out wars took place for years, escalating in 1991, when Ethiopia's military dictatorship was deposed and replaced with a nascent democratic government. Finally, in 1993, Eritreans voted for independence in a United Nations referendum. But armed conflicts still continue to flare up between the two rival nations — each blames the other for the excursions — and some border towns remain in dispute.

Where Ethiopia counts as many as 90 indigenous languages, Eritreans speak fewer than a dozen, with foreign languages like Arabic, Italian and English among them. The state claims no official language, and English appears on Eritrean currency. The most widely spoken native language is Tigrinya, which grew from the same Ethio-Semitic root language as Ethiopia's Amharic, and which is also spoken in the northern regions of Ethiopia that border Eritrea. Both modern languages use the Ethiopic alphabet, and they share many words.

But the kinship between the languages sometimes does more to exacerbate than attenuate the tensions between the two countries and their émigrés.

Lucia Ann McSpadden, who studied Ethiopian refugees in America, sometimes alienated the people she interviewed if she addressed them incorrectly. "By referring to a refugee from Eritrea as 'an Eritrean,'" she wrote, "I was seen [by Ethiopians] as supporting the Eritreans in their struggle for a separate state." But when she addressed an Eritrean as an Ethiopian, her subject would tell her: "I am an Eritrean."

"The subject of this issue was brought forcibly home to me when I was trying to get [a questionnaire] translated into Amharic and Tigrinya," she recalled. "An Eritrean woman, highly educated, a public health instructor at an Ethiopian college, totally fluent and literate in Amharic, refused to do the

Amharic translation, saying, 'I don't write the language of the oppressor.' She would only do the Tigrinya version."

This was before Eritrean independence, and during a time of open warfare, when tensions between people of the two nations were especially high.

Since independence, Eritrea has struggled with economic problems and a strong-armed government, and now "even some Eritreans are beginning to realize what a big mistake it was," said Iasu Gorfu, an Ethiopian who's lived in America for decades, and who, as G.E. Gorfu, has published books of poetry and philosophy.

When Ethiopia lost Eritrea, it lost its access to the seas. But as Iasu points out, "What's the point of a port if you can't export. Eritrea doesn't produce enough to feed itself. It's the politicians that caused this," he says of the split. "They exploit the situation for their own ends."

Prideful Eritreans disagree, of course, saying that the powerful Ethiopian government exploited their resources and relegated their culture. Despite hard times in Eritrea today, and despite a government that can't seem to improve the quality of life for its people, few of its citizens would agree to a reunification with Ethiopia.

Henok Tsehaye was born in Eritrea but raised for a while in Ethiopia when his parents moved there. He came to the U.S. in 1981 and has lived in Washington, D.C., his entire American life. He's fine with eating at a good Ethiopian restaurant, although as a board member of the city's Eritrean Cultural and Community Center, he usually eats at the center's restaurant. And he's happy with Eritrea's independence.

"When you are starting a new country from scratch," he says to the detractors, "there are a lot of challenges you face. Eritrea is on the right path, investing a lot in resources and creating the necessary infrastructure. I don't think there's anybody who would look back and think we should be a part of Ethiopia."

And then there are the dreamers. Tesfaye Tereke of San Francisco, who's lived in America for two decades, doesn't believe that Ethiopia and Eritrea can every reunite as one country. Too much has happened between them. But he imagines a time when the people of both countries can move across the border as freely and comfortably as Americans and Canadians do.

"I hate to hear we are a lot alike," he says. "We are the same. You can slice it and dice it however you like. It's a drama, and sooner or later it has to end."

Through all of these political and linguistic difference, one thing remains the same between the warring nations and their dominant Amhara and Tigrayan cultures: their cuisine. The manner of cooking and eating that developed in Aksumite times took hold in both nations, and today only the names for some of the dishes differ. No other nations in Africa make this food, a testament to the ancient ties between the two countries.

The Idea of Ethiopia

This complex cultural history is why many historians today say that "Ethiopia" is more of an idea than a reality, more of a political boundary than a unified culture.

Although the Amhara people finally dominated, and their language became official, Ethiopians speak as many as 90 other languages. Many have begun to wither away, replaced by Amharic as state-sponsored education spreads, or simply as elders die and the new generation begins to Ethiopianize.

Almost everyone in Ethiopia who can read and write can also speak English, for the Ethiopian elite has for centuries sought contact with the wider world. Fewer than one percent of Ethiopians are college educated, although an aggressive education program in the last few decades has raised adult literacy to about 43 percent. The literacy rate is even higher among the newest generation of school-aged children.

Educated Ethiopians today understand their country's cultural complexity and, on the whole, honor it. In the introduction to his thoughtful cookbook, *Exotic Ethiopian Cooking*, Daniel J. Mesfin puts it this way: "Ethiopia is not a monolithic culture. Hence, 'Ethiopian culture' remains a misnomer — a result of the country's political and social history over the last hundred years. Cultural integration has been attempted at various times, but its failure is thankfully due to the resilience of the cultures of its constituent nationalities, each no less sophisticated than the dominant Amhara culture."

This is nicely put. And yet, just four pages earlier, Mesfin writes: "Coffee did not become an intrinsic part of Ethiopian *culture* [emphasis added] until the 1880s, when [Emperor] Menelik himself drank it. It is true, however, that coffee was widespread in Muslim-Oromo inhabited areas from Harar through Yifat to Wello."

Those areas cut a wide swath through Ethiopia, and the Oromo, many of whom are Moslem today, are especially proud of having first cultivated coffee a millennium before the rest of the world knew about it.

So why does Mesfin say that coffee only became an intrinsic part of "Ethiopian *culture*" in the 19th Century, when an emperor of the dominant Amhara culture (but not the majority Oromo culture) gave it his imperial sanction? It seems the word "culture" slipped in where Mesfin meant "economy," for as he continues, "By the early 20th Century, coffee had become an export commodity." You can guess which "culture" profited from this boon, and which ones didn't.

So what *was* Ethiopia? What *is* it?

Niall Finneran, in his comprehensive book *The Archaeology of Ethiopia*, eschews the notion of a "monolithic cultural identity that is Ethiopia," choosing instead to reconstruct its history by emphasizing "the many and varied strands of archaeology of the region." Much of his work focuses on the Ethio-Eritrean highlands, the most fertile region of the country, from which agriculture and cuisine transpired.

It's an intriguing project, appropriate to the country's complex, multi-faceted history, and it offers some insight about what foods ancient Ethiopians ate.

But it doesn't really help us understand the history of how Ethiopian *cuisine* — that is, the Ethiopian way of *preparing* food — originated and then spread to the many other cultures that now live in modern Ethiopia and Eritrea.

Thus, for our purpose, it's clear what "Ethiopia" means today: It's the place where African people eat what we in the West know as "Ethiopian food" in Ethiopian ways. Exactly how it got that way is — and probably always will be — a riddle wrapped in an *injera*.

A History of Ethiopian Food

The ancient people of pre-Aksumite, pre-Christian cultures like Punt and D'MT left no records of what they ate, and what we know of these cultures comes mostly from the writings of the more advanced cultures that encountered them.

The scribes of ancient Egypt portray Punt as a land of myrrh, incense, perfume, spices and cattle-herding pastoralists, although drawings depict their cattle as being short-horned. This is significant, for the later Aksumite kingdom used sturdier humped cattle to plow fields and harvest teff. Egyptian pharaohs sent trade missions to Punt, the most famous ordered by Hatshepsut around 1500 B.C. Punt, too, sent caravans to trade with its neighbors.

The people of D'MT made iron tools and weapons, and they built a large stone temple whose remains stand near the Ethiopian village of Yeha. They also used irrigation and plows, just as the Aksumites did in the centuries that followed.

The area around Aksum, about 60 kilometers east of Yeha, has revealed deposits of what scholar believe may be traces of D'MT. When Aksum rose to power in the first centuries B.C. and A.D., it replaced the fading D'MT as the regional power. So what we know about D'MT may well be what we know about pre-Aksumite culture in northern Ethiopia.

The archaeology of D'MT and Aksum is much more revealing than that of Punt, and in the past two decade especially, scholars have made many critical discoveries. Reconstructing this culinary past is an intriguing puzzle with numerous pieces still missing. It's a picture that has emerged grain by grain, bone by bone, and shard by shard.

In the fourth millennium B.C., agriculture began to emerge in the fertile highlands of what is now western Eritrea and the Sudan. It then spread to the lowlands and eventually the plateau. These proto-Ethiopians grew sorghum, and by the end of the millennium, they had begun to herd cattle. By the first or second millennium B.C., they ate sorghum, wheat, barley and possibly teff, along with many other grains, vegetables and pulses (lentils, peas, fava beans, chick peas and more).

But the scholars disagree on when Ethiopians began to cultivate each of these crops and, in some cases, how they got to Ethiopia.

Some argue that ancient Ethiopians discovered agriculture on their own; others say they learned it through contact with Egypt and the Arabian peninsula. All we know for sure is that Ethiopians have long cultivated certain things — teff, enset, gesho — that no other culture has cultivated, which strongly points to Ethiopian origins. Whether they did it without help, or learned to farm from others, may never finally be known.

It may help to distinguish between the domestication of food plants and the enterprise of agriculture: The former sustains an individual, and the latter supports a thriving society. Once domesticated plants became subject to full-scale agriculture, identified by the presence of such advances as plows and irrigation, then a civilization and a culture could emerge.

The people of ancient Ethiopia certainly grew things collectively and ate them. The question is what they grew, when they started growing it, and the form in which they ate what they grew.

In the late 1960s, the archaeologist Jean Dombrowski explored two caves near the eastern shores of Lake Tana, the source of the Abay, or Blue Nile. Her discoveries date from around pre-Aksumite 500 B.C., and she found evidence of barley, chick peas and legumes. These caves are among the earliest evidence of agriculture in Ethiopia.

In the centuries after the fall of D'MT, small kingdoms jockeyed for dominance until Aksum finally began to emerge in the two centuries before the birth of Christ. The Aksumites rested their civilization in the fertile Ethiopian highlands, which make up only four percent of the country today, but which account for roughly 20 percent of its population and livestock.

What, then, did the Aksumites and their pre-historic ancestors eat? And beyond *what* they ate, how much do we know about how they *prepared* their food?

The answers to those questions have emerged largely through the findings of archaeologists working in Aksum, with some help and speculation from linguists. And while some mysteries remain, the evidence strongly suggests that the Aksumite people made some of history's first "Ethiopian food."

There's no question about whether the Aksumites and the cultures that preceded them had domesticated cattle. Copious cave drawing and archaeological evidence trace domestication back to the third millennium

B.C. These cultures apparently raised a wide variety of long- and short-horned cattle, as well as some camels, sheep, goats and humped zebu.

Unfortunately, the cattle of Ethiopia today provide little genetic link to their ancestors of the past. Drought and epidemic over the centuries wiped out virtually all of the native gene pools of Ethiopian cattle.

One of the earliest written records of what Aksumites ate comes from inscriptions on stones translated in 1962 by the Dutch scholar A.J. Drewes in his book, *Inscriptions de l'Ethiopie Antique.* His revelatory work requires no reading between the lines: The ancient Ge'ez inscriptions that he deciphers tells us explicitly what some Aksumites ate.

"Memorandum concerning the food of the royal court according to the law of the country," begins one text, written in the middle of the third century A.D., less than a century before the height of Aksum's power under King Ezana (321-360). The inscription goes on to describe the victuals: There's virgin mutton, virgin beef, honey, wheat, beer, bread, a bucket of butter and — best of all — honey wine.

In the Ge'ez inscription, it's called *mes*, the word still used in Tigrinya today. But we know it as *t'ej*, and here we have proof that the Aksumites fermented it. The inscription says the *mes* came served in a *gabata*, which Drewes translates as *sargato* (a frying pan). Ethiopians today serve their *wot*-covered *injera* atop a large round plate called a *gebeta*.

To this we can add — very gently — a finding of the archaeologist A.J. Arkell, who in 1942 studied four sites in the Eritrean city of Agordat, an ancient town proximate to Aksum. Arkell describes what he calls "large beer-pots with narrowed necks and out-turned rims." This shape perfectly describes a *berele*, the modern Ethiopian vessel for drinking *t'ej*, although Arkell's vessels were clearly much larger.

Arkell doesn't explicitly date them, but he says they're "probably contemporary with the New Kingdom in Egypt," which places them around 1550-1050 B.C. If these were beer pots, this makes them more than a millennium older than Drewes' discovery of a reference to *t'ej* in the second century A.D. And the beer pot is "possibly" even older yet: Akell further says that they could date back as far as the Second Intermediate Period in Egypt, adding another 100 years to their age.

A reference to bread in Drewes' inscription is too general to say for sure what kind of bread these Aksumites baked. The writing gives no hint as to the shape and texture of the bread, although it does mention wheat, presumably the flour used to make it.

But the Ge'ez word for "bread" in the inscription is *hbst*, which could be a clue. Centuries later, when Portuguese explorers described what was clearly *injera*, they called it *apas*, could be a clumsy transliteration of *hbst* (ancient

Ge'ez writing didn't indicate vowels). This is hardly evidence that the early Aksumite *hbst* is the later Ethiopian *injera*, but it's another reason to imagine. In Amharic today, the word *hibist* means manna.

Stuart Munro-Hay, a leading authority on Aksum, has little to say about Aksumite food in his book *Aksum: A Civilization of Late Antiquity*, and what he says draws more upon speculation than fact. The Aksumites left behind coins and artifacts, but very few written accounts of how they lived. And so Munro-Hay is forced to make some well-educated leaps.

In her handsome Ethiopian cookbook, *The Recipe of Love*, Aster Ketsela Belayneh, who owns an Ethiopian restaurant in Toronto, says that the traditional dish called *doro wot* — a chicken leg in spicy red pepper sauce — "goes back to the days of the Aksumite kingdom."

Munro-Hay says only this on the subject: "One or two pottery figures of birds exist from Aksumite times, and (with a little imagination) we can perhaps identify chickens and pigeons or doves." Other scholars have noted the absence of the chicken in rock art of the culture, although some archaeo-zoologists have found what they believe to be chicken bones.

Munro-Hay's book includes a page about Aksumite food, which consisted of locally available beef, mutton, bread, beer, honey, vegetables and fruits. Coastal Aksumites might have added turtle to their diets, and wealthier folks could afford imported wines and olive oil from Italy or Greece.

But Munro-Hay does offer a tidbit that furthers the emerging story of modern Ethiopian cuisine.

"Almost certainly," he writes, "some foodstuffs would have been eaten from wooden or basketwork vessels (the typical Ethiopian 'table' today, the *mesob*, is of basketwork) ... Basketwork storage bins can also be presumed with some likelihood."

The *mesob*, then, is our next documented element of Ethiopian cuisine among the Aksumites.

Manfred Kropp, a German scholar of Ethiopian history and culture, reported in 2006 that Maryam Anza, a stele discovered in the 1940s in northwest Ethiopia, speaks of the rations given to the workers who built it. Kropp translates the writing on the stele like this: "Read what is written here: This stele of the King of Agabo has been transported and erected in Agabo by his people in 15 days of statute-labour while they have been supplied by 520 jars of beer and 20,620 pieces of bread." Drewes, too, works with this stele in his 1962 book.

The brief text of the stele offers nothing more specific about the texture of the bread, but Kropp is willing to take the leap of faith. "There is a good chance and probability," Kropp ventured in 2008, "that along with teff, which is attested in archeological sites, the preparation of bread has not changed essentially for the last 3,000 years." So maybe the earliest pre-Christian Aksumites, and even the people of D'MT, ate *injera* after all.

Then what did they bake it on? Ethiopians today make their *injera* on a large round skillet called a *mitad*. In cities today, these are often electric; in the country, the *injera* bakes on a clay *mitad* placed over an open flame. But regardless of the technology, the principle is the same: Making a piece of *injera* requires a big round skillet.

Enter Neville Chittick, whose 1972-74 excavations at Aksum yielded myriad treasures — and a handsome 1989 book, written by Munro-Hay and others, describing and discussing Chittick's discoveries.

In a close look at the pottery from the Chittick site, Richard Wilding reveals the discovery of some Aksumite *mitads*, placing them in the late fifth or sixth centuries, thus some time before 600 A.D. "The presence or absence of so basic a piece of specialized equipment," Wilding writes, "might tell much of the diet and the principal cereal crop of Aksum."

In all of Chittick's collection, Wilding found only three pieces of *mitad*. They're 30 to 40 centimeters in diameter — that's 12 to 16 inches, the size of a piece of *injera* — and they're shaped like the *mitad* that Ethiopians use today, with a flat surface and raised edges.

Finally, Wilding makes it clear: "Unless a metal tray was used in the early period, only to be replaced later by pottery, the cereal teff was not used for the manufacture of *injera* until the late fifth or sixth century, and not extensively until after that date." He further notes that "none of the items so far recovered in metal from Aksumite sites has been at all appropriate to the service performed by a *mitad*," and he admits that it's "tempting to associate the appearance of the *mitad* with the initial extensive use of teff as a staple cereal."

It's more than tempting: It's the strongest piece of evidence we have about the origins of *injera* and the Ethiopian way of making it. No other archaeologist claims to have found a *mitad*, although some rare fragments of *mitad*-like ovens and griddles were found at Lalibela and dated to the middle of the first millennium B.C., even more reason to speculate on the genesis of *injera*.

If the Aksumites did make *injera*, we can only say with some certainty that they did so late in their development, and they certainly ate other breads. Inscriptions mention that a man would sometimes eat five loaves of bread a day, so the loaves must have been small, and not 12- to 20-inch pieces of *injera*.

The fact that stalks of emmer wheat appear on Aksumite coins probably means that the culture's small loaves of staple bread were made of wheat, and that teff *injera* was either a later innovation or a lesser source of sustenance.

For if Aksumite coinage, unique among African cultures, was a source of such great prestige, why do their coins have wheat on them and not teff?

In his 1995 book *People of the Plow,* a study of Ethiopian agriculture mostly since 1800, James McCann says that teff, "the highest prestige food" in the agricultural life of Aksumites, "requires intensive seedbed preparation possible only with the ox plow." The first solid evidence of an ox-plow device in Ethiopia comes from cave art "tentatively attributed to the first millennium B.C." This means that pre-Aksumite culture could only have began cultivating teff no more than 3,000 years ago.

McCann further asserts that "the evidence of both language and plant biology indicates that the Ethiopian highlands were a center of secondary dispersal for a wide variety of crops," including barley, wheat, sorghum, chick peas, lentils, and of course, teff.

The ancient highland gene pools for some of these plants are among the most significant in world agriculture, McCann says, and ox-plow farming was so important that it "seems to have been almost a *sine qua non* of imperial hegemony," a system that allowed emperors to levy taxes that supported government functions.

McCann's book is comprehensive, pulling together centuries of research and combining it with his own. Yet his index has no listing for *injera* — or *enjera*, as he spells it — and he mentions the bread only in passing here and there. Once again, the scholarship focuses on what ancient Ethiopians grew, and not on what they did with the harvest.

The story of the growth of teff in Ethiopia is now reasonably well documented, and the very latest archaeology at Aksum has even found physical evidence of the grain.

The book *Lost Crops of Africa,* a study by several international science agencies, has only this to say about the provenance of Ethiopia's staple bread: "Teff was grown in Ethiopia before recorded history and its domestication and early use is lost in antiquity." A 2003 genetic study of teff by Amanda Ingram and Jeff Doyle speculated on the ancient species from which it evolved, but the research doesn't guess at how long ago that might have happened. The study does note that "for most of its history as a domesticate, it has grown almost exclusively in Ethiopia, a country that is isolated from neighboring countries by its high mountains and surrounding deserts."

Since the mid-1990s, a number of leading scholars have done extensive work on pre-Aksumite and Aksumite agriculture. Some, like McCann, are cultural historians; others, like David W. Phillipson and Sheila Boardman, are archaeologists. Their work has allowed a portrait to emerge of what Aksumites and their predecessors ate.

Even the linguists have something to say. Christopher Ehret, a long-time scholar of Ethiopian languages, asserts that Ethiopians developed agriculture on their own without being taught how to do it by Southern Arabians. He has compared ancient Cushitic and Semitic languages of Ethiopia, and he speculates that teff "began to be cultivated at least several millennia before Christ, and possibly as early as the Near Eastern shift" — that is, about 5,000 B.C.

Teff was a "local independent invention," Ehret says, originating in the "northern and eastern fringes of the highlands." The word teff comes to Ethiopia's Semitic languages as a loan from its older Cushitic languages, but that was all in the family. "The idea that agriculture in Ethiopia and the Horn is relatively recent and owes much to Arabian influence can no longer be entertained in any form," he wrote in 1979. "By the beginning of the Southern Arabian impact on the Horn, the agricultural heritage of the different parts of Ethiopia was already largely established."

The latest scholarship seems to position teff as the first Ethiopian grain, with grains like wheat, barley, sorghum and oats following soon after, or perhaps coming into use simultaneously with the ascent of agriculture, Tertia Barnett reports in *The Emergency of Food Production in Ethiopia* (1999). Corn (maize) took longer to join the buffet.

The first millennium B.C. also saw the introduction of lentils, peas, chick peas and beans. Soon came the oil seeds, like linseed, or the native Ethiopian *noog* (niger seed), with others (safflower, sesame, sunflower, flax) following them. Potatoes, onions, garlic and tomatoes came during the first millennium A.D. The important plant enset also emerged in pre-Christian times, in the remote southern Omotic regions of Ethiopia, possibly at the same time that teff was emerging in the north, Ehret speculates.

Finally, there are the elemental spices, like turmeric, ginger, fenugreek, black pepper and red pepper — the latter being a key ingredient today in *berbere*.

Ethiopia and India were trading partners before the Christian era, although there's little documentation for exactly what got traded between the two cultures in those early times. There's more evidence of it in the first century A.D., and many Aksumite coins have turned up over the years in India, just as archaeologists have found Indian money in ancient Ethiopia.

The *Periplus of the Erythraean* [Red] *Sea*, a Greek trade manual written some time during the first century A.D., discusses trade between India and Aksum from the Indian point of view, noting items — iron, steel, belts, cloth, garments — that India exported through Adulis, a key Aksumite Red Sea port. The unknown author doesn't mention spices. Two ancient geographers also noted this proto-Ethiopian civilization: Ptolemy (90 — 168 A.D.) mentions Aksum as the capital of a kingdom west of Red Sea ports, and Strabo (63 B.C. — 24 A.D.) wrote about the honey wine made by early Aksumites.

The preeminent Ethiopian scholar Richard Pankhurst has written that contacts between Ethiopia and India "date back to the dawn of history," with India giving "cotton and silk, pepper and other spices" to the Ethiopians, who gave gold, ivory and slaves in return. Pepper is important here, for Ethiopians used it to add fire to their dishes before the arrival of cayenne by the 18th Century.

Barnett notes that whereas coriander and fenugreek apparently had Ethiopian origins, other key spices arrived much later, when Ethiopia began to have contact with Europe. This includes the New World spice *Capsicum*, or cayenne, essential to *berbere* today.

But Boardman also notes that the Aksumites grew cress, a milder peppery native spice, which they probably used to flavor their *wots* along with rarer non-native black pepper.

"Cress is widely grown in Ethiopia as a medicinal and culinary plant," Boardman wrote in *Archaeology at Aksum, Ethiopia*, Phillipson's account of a mid-1990s excavation there. "Before the introduction of New World spices, its seeds were widely used as the main flavouring in *wot* sauces, although the wealthy preferred to use black pepper, imported from Arabia and further afield."

Boardman cites Sue Edwards, co-founder and director of the Institute for Sustainable Development in Ethiopia, as her source of information about cress. Edwards says that Ethiopians have long used such spices as black cumin, sweet basil and rue, as well as *noog*, which today gives Ethiopians an important cooking oil.

But even Edwards admits that it's risky to extrapolate from these accounts of other cultures' spice trade. "There are many unresolved questions about the development of Ethiopia's unique crops, particularly teff and enset," she says. "It seems probable that teff was not used in the kitchens of the Aksumite nobility because it needs its own cooking technology."

Catherine D'Andrea, of Simon Fraser University, has studied food in the Ethiopian highlands, and she concurs that scholars "know very little of the early history of spices and flavorings." She, too, notes that *berbere*, a blend of spices, takes most of its taste from *Capsicum*, which the Aksumites certainly didn't have.

So even if Aksumites made teff *injera*, they probably couldn't have made the same kind of fiery *wots* or milder *alichas* of the Ethiopian cuisine we know today, all of which depend upon red pepper, ginger, turmeric and other spices for their heat and zest. Aksumite *wots*, if they existed at all, were no doubt milder, flavored first with cress and then with black pepper when cooks could get it.

Finally, Phillipson's groundbreaking excavation at Aksum from 1993 to 1997 — the first since the Chittick expedition of the 1970s, when the Derg took over — and his two-volume report, *Archaeology at Aksum, Ethiopia*, confirms some of what other archaeologists could only surmise.

The team collected seeds and fruit samples during its excavations, and an analysis suggested the possible presence of teff in pre-Aksumite culture, with teff definitely present in the kingdom of Aksum. This is the proof that scholars had been seeking for decades.

Phillipson's team also found traces of chicken, the animal that now lends itself to Ethiopia's national dish: Although 90 percent of the bones at their sites came from cattle, a portion of the other 10 percent contained chicken bones. The scholars don't speculate on what the Aksumites and pre-Aksumites did with their chickens — nor with the dogs and donkeys whose bones also turned up.

Despite the many remarkable finds of Phillipson's team, Boardman — a member of that team — had this to say when the dust settled on the four-year excavation: "There is currently little agreement over the date(s) for the introduction of crops of Near Eastern origin (wheat, barley, pulses, flax) and their route of entry, or for the domestication of Ethiopian crops such as teff, *noog* and enset."

By "little agreement," she means exact dates and the evidence to prove it. But all of the scholars agree that the Aksumites and probably pre-Aksumites grew teff, the grain most essential to modern Ethiopia's unique cuisine.

Thus the evidence of *what* these cultures ate has become increasingly bountiful:

♦ The most ancient civilizations of the land now called Ethiopia grew millets and sorghum as early as five millennia B.C.

♦ Linguistic analysis suggests that these cultures may have had teff more than 5,000 years ago. A variety of archaeological evidence confirms teff in Aksum early in the first millennium A.D., and probably in pre-Aksumite cultures of the first millennium B.C., when they had the proper cattle and plows to harvest it.

♦ The proto-Ethiopian cultures before D'MT kept domesticated cattle three millennia B.C. and farmed fields in the first millennium B.C.

♦ Pre-Aksumite people ate barley, wheat, oats, emmer, lentils, *noog*, flax, linseed and chick peas by the first millennium B.C.

♦ The kings of Aksum drank *t'ej* and beer as early as the third century A.D., made *injera* by about sixth century A.D., and during the time of the empire, throughout the first millennium A.D., feasted on a wide range of grains, legumes, mutton, beef and chicken. They served their meals on a *gebeta* placed atop a *mesob*, and seasoned their *wots* with cress and black pepper before *Capsicum*, the hotter European red pepper, arrived in the 17th or 18th Century and allowed them to create *berbere* as we know it today.

All we need now is an Aksumite recipe book, a lacuna that may forever remain the central mystery of the earliest Ethiopian cuisine.

After Aksum: Modern Ethiopian Food

Between the artifacts of Aksum and the dawn of the Solomonic dynasty in 1270, little was written of what and how people ate in the land we now call Ethiopia.

From the ninth through 13th centuries — that is, between the end of the Aksumite empire and the birth of the Solomonic dynasty — Ethiopians didn't leave behind much writing about their politics and daily life. Only the superlative rock-hewn churches of King Lalibela (1189-1229), the greatest monarch of the century-long Zagwe dynasty, provide some architectural clues about how these medieval Ethiopians lived and prayed.

The eminent Ethiopian historian Edward Ullendorff wrote that this period was "enveloped in such impenetrable darkness owing to the political upheavals which occurred at that time and which greatly disturbed the continuity of Ethiopian history." The written history of Ethiopian cuisine suffered along with everything else. Only foreign manuscripts, mostly from Arab cultures, tell this part of the Ethiopian story, and what people did write had little to do with food.

But these early Ethiopians occupied the same region as the Aksumites did, and they grew out of Aksumite culture. There's no reason to believe that Aksumite cuisine didn't become a more engrained part of an emerging Ethiopia.

We do have one clue — if we can call it that — about Lalibela's dinner table.

In his 1892 book *Vie de Lalibala* ("Life of Lalibela"), Jules Perruchon reprints and translates an Amharic manuscript about the king's 12th Century life. The manuscript resides in the British Museum and dates to the 15th or 16th Century, so it's more oral than documented history. It's also a glorious hagiography, filled with stories of the king's humility, kindness and reverence for God.

Lalibela's diet gets little mention. At one holiday meal, he eats bread dipped in "a bouillon of herbs." He dips two pieces — then generously gives the third morsel to his servant. Could this bouillon be some sort of *wot*, and could the bread be *injera*? The Amharic manuscript doesn't contain either word, and so we can only imagine.

But it does use the word *hbst* for bread, and that's intriguing: Again, this is the word poorly transliterated by early Portuguese narratives as *apas*, which was clearly *injera*, and it's further reason to speculate that the *hbst* of Lalibela is the *injera* of the Ethiopia that followed.

We also learn that Lalibela set a table "well garnished" with wine and, not surprisingly, *mes*, or honey wine. This continues the potable tradition begun by the Aksumites in the third century A.D.

In 1270, Yekuno Amlak seized power from the Zagwe rulers, and the Solomonic dynasty took hold of Ethiopia's destiny. Emperors lived like kings, and they had bountiful banquets to trumpet their power and status.

From this opulence, an important document emerged in several editions throughout the centuries, and it's a feast of information on Ethiopian cuisine as we know it today.

Called the *serata gebr*, which means "the proceedings of the royal banquet," it describes the royal banquet, or *gebr*, of Ethiopia's middle ages, as early as the reign of Amda Seyon I, who ruled from 1314-1344. The document is written partly in an earlier form of Amharic and partly in Ge'ez. This all makes translating it a challenge.

In a seminal 1988 essay, Kropp published a manuscript of the *serata gebr* and, in an essay preceding the text, discussed its contents and revelations. But his essay doesn't translate the document word for word, and since then, no one has published a full translation, although Kropp continues to work with the text.

Kropp can't say exactly when his text of the *serata gebr* was written, but it seems to have come from the era or Zara Yakob (1434-1468). Its mention of Amda Seyon, who ruled a century earlier, documents how royal traditions survived from emperor to emperor.

Kropp's *serata gebr* presents detailed instructions for preparing a royal banquet and includes many anecdotes about daily life in the emperor's court. The text "gives all sorts of details about the complicated procedures in the royal kitchen and household," and Kropp speculates that the information might have come from the two top officers charged with supervising the procedures. "In general," Kropp says, "regulations of this kind were transmitted orally," so a text like the *serata gebr* is a rare and valuable resource.

The document provides "a detailed list of the daily royal table, which is astounding for its variety of bread, vegetables, and drink." It describes "yä-Afreng-enjera, 'foreign, European bread,' in regulations dating from the time of Baeda Maryam (1468-1478 A.D.). The preparation of any of this food is the task of a special cook or brewer bearing the respective title."

The presence of European-style bread in the *serata gebr* shows that the earliest Western explorers had already begun to influence the country, but not so much that it co-opted the traditional Ethiopian way of eating.

Full menus appear in the *serata gebr*, and they include *mogarya*, a hard bread used as a dish; a vessel filled with *wot*; *injera*, a bread made of teff; and rations of beer and *t'ej* (called *sägg* in the ancient language), sometimes served in vessels of silver or gold.

No part of a slaughtered animal went to waste: The tendons became part of umbrellas, and the hides became stirrups and other elements of the transportation system.

There were even special rules governing the use of the latrine, called *gemga meftah*, or "the place where one opens the fine robe." Violate the rules and "the culprit is stripped of his clothing, be he a man or a woman, and as a punishment smeared with his own excrement."

But did these medieval Ethiopians eat with their hands the way their ancestors do today?

According to Kropp, these banquets took place over two days, and "only the highest-ranking officials and royals were permitted to eat with knifes." This implies that others ate without cutlery. Meals were served on *gebeta*, just as they are today, another indication that the revelers scooped up their food with *injera*. Lower-level people ate from plain *gebeta*, but royalty had theirs adorned with silver and gold.

Thanks to the *serata gebr*, we know that Ethiopians ate *wot* with *injera* and accompanied it with honey wine as early as the beginning of the 14th Century. It seems highly likely that the cuisine and its customs predate this documentation. We can at least say with relative confidence that by 1270, when Yekuno Amlak rose to the throne and declared the Solomonic Dynasty, the Ethiopian way of eating was already in place. This is just 44 years before the ascension of Amda Seyon I, who's mentioned in the *serata gebr*.

Kropp's findings are seminal, and as he continued to plumb his manuscript for additional morsels, he learned of the discovery, in 2008, of a new *serata gebr* dating back to the 16th Century. Deresse Ayenachew is working with the text, but Kropp believes it probably won't yield any new insights because its based on older known documents.

"We were interviewing some priests in churches and monasteries," Kropp said in early 2010, "but the result was the same one we always had: the text and its technical terms in old Amharic are definitely very far away from nowadays, even from the oral tradition. Only the careful study of contemporary documents will ever give more positive results."

An Ethiopian embassy visited Europe in 1306 during the reign of King Wedem Arad (1299-1314), but the members of this earliest-known Ethiopian excursion to Europe didn't leave behind much insight into their manner of eating. Then, beginning in the early 16ᵗʰ Century, European exploration of Ethiopia began with earnest, and the Portuguese led the way.

The Venetian Alessandro Zorzi never visited Ethiopia, but in the early 16ᵗʰ Century, he published a series of detailed itineraries of travel to and from Ethiopia based upon his research among monks who had been there. Most of these volumes discuss travel routes, but here and there they speak of food.

"There grow corn, vines, beans, cropped twice a year," Zorzi writes of Aksum. "There grow all fruits except chestnuts, and there grow peas, beans, chick-peas, and in the best and richest ground there grow many trees and date-palms. There grow lemons, citrons, oranges to full perfection. There grow not melons but gourds and other things and herbs, honey, much sugar, countless domestic animals such as buffaloes, oxen, cows, sheep, goats, dromedaries, great store of fair horses, mules, asses, and very great dogs." Merchant ships from other countries "bring all the spices except ginger, which is found in this land."

In 1520, just as Zorzi was publishing his work, the Portuguese sent a mission to Ethiopia to forge relations with Prester John, the European moniker for Ethiopia's Christian emperor. The Europeans used this name to refer to the Ethiopian monarch for many generations, and at the time of the mission, "Prester John" was Lebna Dengel (née Dawit, the Ethiopian form of "David"), who ruled from 1508 to 1540.

The missionaries spent six years in the country, and when they returned, Father Francisco Alvares wrote an invaluable account of their explorations. He spoke mostly about the religion and culture of the country, as well as his own tribulations. But sprinkled throughout his narrative are many morsels about food.

Alvares found that Ethiopians cultivated a wide variety of grains and vegetables. He reports frequently of seeing gardens and fields of wheat, barley, oats, beans, pulse, peas, garlic ("very big"), onions, rue, cabbage, lemons, limes, peaches, "very fine" grapes, figs, nuts, parsnips, watercress and "much mustard." He saw "many other species of vegetables which we do not have and which they eat, [and] they are very good as the country goes."

Alvares also noted that Ethiopians would trade almost anything for pepper, and described *wots* made spicy with cress, linseed, and in the case of the emperor, black pepper. In fact, Alvares says that black pepper was the gift most prized by the emperor when the Portuguese presented it to him. This surely means that Ethiopians didn't have the red hot *Capsicum* in the mid-1500s. The fact that Alvares never mentions it further leads scholars to believe that it had not yet entered the Ethiopian diet.

Tewolde Berhan Gebre Egziabher, an Ethiopian botanist and scholar, says that *Capsicum* "requires such extensive care that it dominates the farmer's life, especially at the seedling production phrase. If it were present when Alvares visited Ethiopia, it would be expected that he would have noted it." Tewolde's well-documented 1984 essay about New World foods in Ethiopia notes that the Scottish explorer James Bruce, in his 18th Century account, specifically mentions *Capsicum*. Tewolde then reasonably concludes that "chili pepper was introduced into Ethiopia in the two and a half centuries from 1520 to 1770."

So what did Ethiopians do with this bounty? On that account, Alvares offers only limited help in understanding the emergence of the modern Ethiopian way of eating.

He's very helpful on bread, which he describes in ways that sound familiar today. In pots, they mix the dough, then place it in a furnace on a plate of iron or copper. "The plate is round and of a good size," he writes. "They place fire underneath it, and when it is hot, they clean it with waxed cloth, pour on it a good portion of dough, and spread it out with a wooden spoon of such size as they intend to make the bread, and they make it very round."

Clearly, this in *injera*: big, round, and made from a batter that you pour (rather than knead) onto a surface that sounds like a modern-day *mitad*. They made this bread with maize or barley, but also with "taffo, a small, black grain." This is how Alvares recorded teff, the primary grain of today's *injera*, and his description is accurate enough. Alvares calls taffo "a very good and delicate crop. It is highly esteemed because maggots that eat wheat and other vegetables do not eat it, and it keeps a fairly long time." Agronomists today also note the resiliency of teff.

With this large round flatbread, Ethiopians ate a lot of beef. Alvares reports the slaughtering of myriad cows for the feasts in which he participated, many of them thrown by monks who didn't eat meat. At least, they didn't eat it when anyone is looking.

"But when they are outside with us Portuguese," he says, "they drink wine and eat meat, so long as there is only one, but if there are two they do not do it, being afraid of each other." Ethiopians also bought fowl at marketplaces and served it at meals.

Alvares often dined with clerics, who served only modest meals. The monks of Ethiopia ate a lot of fruits and vegetables. But they also made a very hot sauce ("it burns the mouth") that Alvares calls *tebba*, and they soaked their bread in it.

According to Tewolde, *tebba* is Alvares' recording of *tsebhi*, the Tigrinya word for *wot*. Poorer Ethiopians today will eat meals of *injera* soaked in *berbere*, perhaps with a bit of meat or vegetables if they can find or afford it.

It's hardly a stretch to think that the ascetic monks of 16th Century Ethiopia did the same thing.

As for the act of eating, Alvares once again provides tantalizing tidbits that echo the Ethiopian meal of today. For breakfast, "two hours before midday" in the town or Barua, his hosts invited him to sit on mats placed on the ground (some Ethiopians still do this today), and there they served "a large wooden trencher of barley meal, but little kneaded, and a horn of mead." This describes *kinche*, a common Ethiopian morning food today. Later in the day, he received a similar meal, "toasted barley, made into flour, and they mix it up with a little water."

An evening meal in the town of Angote is more substantial. The revelers again sat on mats, this time covered with black sheep skins. They ate from "flat trenchers, like trays of great width, without napkins or tablecloths." Alvares calls them "ganetes," certainly a poor rendering of *gebeta*. "These were handsome and large," he says, "and very broad."

The participants washed their hands with water, "but no towel came to clean our hands, neither for putting bread upon, except it was put upon the same *ganetas*. There came bread of many kinds, namely, of wheat, barley, millet, chick-peas and taffo."

Before everyone partook, their host "ordered to be placed before him rolls of that inferior bread" — this is probably rolled *injera*, a common way of serving it today — "and upon each roll a piece of raw beef, and so he ordered it to be given to the poor who were outside the gate waiting for alms."

Then came the appetizers, "three sauces or relishes in small sauce dishes, of a black clay, and well made. They put into them the most inferior bread, broken small, and butter with it." Today, this is called *firfir* or *fitfit*: *injera* mixed with sauces, meats or vegetables. Alvares and his delicate companions didn't eat this native cuisine, and their very generous host provided them with well-cooked food more to their liking.

Finally, the main course: a raw breast of beef, which Alvares did not eat, choosing instead to stay with his specially prepared, "very well cooked" victuals — which he doesn't describe — and with plenty of mead.

At a later banquet with the Prester John himself, Alvares describes an occasion that could well have taken place in a European palace.

"The dishes were different kinds of meat," he writes, "cooked in various ways, almost in our style. Among them were fowls, whole, big and fat, some boiled, and some roasted. Then they came with fat meat of the larger animals, so skillfully cooked that we did not know whether it had been boiled or roasted. We were amazed to think how they could possibly do such delicate cooking here."

One revealing observation comes when a dinner host rolls pieces of meat in the *injera*-like bread and gives it to peasants before beginning his own meal. At this point in Ethiopian history, it seems like this way of eating was mostly practiced by people in the social hierarchy below emperors and their elite guests.

Another Portuguese explorer, Baltazar Telles, confirms this culinary evolution. He spent time in Ethiopia in the early 17ᵗʰ Century, about 100 years after Alvares, and recorded his finding in *The Travels of the Jesuits in Ethiopia*, which wasn't published until 1710. His account of mealtime might describe an Ethiopian restaurant today.

"The women bring two or three *macobs,*" he writes, meaning *mesobs,* "which are like large table baskets, and very lofty, because [they are] covered with high lids, like caps, the whole made of straw. In these *macobs,* or baskets, were 20 or 30 *apas,* that is thin cakes, like our frying oat cakes, made of wheat and their grain called *tef.* Their *apas* are very large, and thin, at least half a yard diameter." Telles is describing teff *injera.*

"This is all the state of the Ethiopian table," he continues, "for they have neither knife, fork, nor spoon, salt, pepper casters nor any other utensil. These very *apas,* which serve instead of napkins and dishes, are also part of the food. The table is covered with the *apas,* and on them, without any plates or dishes, the meat is laid, whether it be roast or raw, as they eat it."

Thus, by the 1630s, Ethiopians ate their meals like they eat them today. They also enjoyed honey wine, which Telles says "is not so well tasted as our wine, [but] more wholesome." Ethiopians only drink it after the meal, and Telles marvels at their capacity. "It is wonderful to think how they can hold so much," he says. "This wine is very weak, yet the quantity makes it have the same effect as the best in Europe for turning the brain, making the tongue run, and weakening the legs."

In all of their talk of food and drink, Alvares and Telles never use the word *injera* and never call the abundant Ethiopian mead *t'ej,* even though they clearly describe both items. Later accounts by European explorers are more detailed, as is their affection — or lack of it — for certain elements of Ethiopian cuisine. Their many journals document the history of the Ethiopian cuisine we enjoy today.

Manuel de Almeida, a Portuguese Jesuit, visited Ethiopia in the 17ᵗʰ Century and published a very detailed and helpful account shortly before his death in 1646.

"As they ordinarily sit on the ground," he wrote, "the great nobles on carpets and the rest on mats, their tables are all low and round. They have neither tablecloth nor napkin on them. They wipe their hands on the *apas* they eat, and the table is full of them in houses where there are plenty."

This echoes Alvares' observations about the presence and use of *injera* and the *mesob*, those low round tables that Almeida describes. But he adds more to the story of *apas*.

"They put their food on them," Almeida explains, "without using plates, if it is raw or roast meat. If it is a stew of chicken or mutton or their staple fare, which is a kind of thin pap in which they moisten their *apas*, made from the meal of different pulses, such as lentils, chickpeas, linseed and others peculiar to this country, all this comes in bowls of black clay. This is the dinner service of poor and rich so that down to our own times nothing better was seen even on the table of the Emperor himself."

This revealing passage does more than simply describe a way of eating. The dishes he describes are typical of Ethiopian restaurants and meals today, and his "thin pap" is certainly the *berbere* sauce of a contemporary Ethiopian *wot*.

By the 18th Century, Ethiopian food had become fully what we know today. Bruce's five-volume account of his trip to Ethiopia, from 1769 to 1771, describes fiery Ethiopian foods seasoned with cayenne, which he says the Ethiopians mixed with black pepper. This is *berbere*, at last. Tewolde even speculates that the name *berbere* derives from *papare*, the ancient Ge'ez word for pepper.

Yet Bruce doesn't call it *berbere*, and in his account, Ethiopians use cayenne *and* black pepper to season their foods. Did he just not encounter the word, or had Ethiopians, as late at the 1770s, still not discovered that mixing cayenne with other spices could make a fiery seasoning unique to their culture?

Finally, we should note that history is always told by the victors, and in the case of Ethiopia, the victors were the people of the Amhara tribe. In Ethiopia today, according to a 2007 census in the country, Amharas are about 27% of the population, and people of the Oromo tribe are about 35%. But long ago, the Amharas dominated, imposing their language and their rule.

Before they became part of Ethiopia, the Oromo and other southern cultures simply ate the foods available to them where they lived. For some, in the arid lands, this often meant starvation, or bare subsistence. They grew vegetables and legumes where the land was arable, and they raised cattle where there was water. We know little of the ancient customs of theses cultures, and even today, many are illiterate, so no written records exist. What we now call Ethiopian cuisine slowly spread to the entire nation.

This merger was not without reverse influence, and some of these cultures' foods joined the Ethiopian table. The popular dish *kitfo*, or raw ground beef, comes from Gurage culture. Enset, too, is a staple of the Gurage and other groups of the southern highlands.

In *Stirring the Pot*, McCann digs into the historic records and recounts a grand feast thrown in September 1887 by Menelik, the king of the southern Shoa region of Ethiopia, and his epicurean wife, Queen Taytu, who set the menu and did a lot of the cooking.

McCann draws his account from historic records, and he positions the feast, which lasted for five days, as a defining moment in the development and expansion of Ethiopia's national cuisine. Eighteen months after the feast, King Menelik of Shoa became Emperor Menelik II of Ethiopia, and suddenly, all of the neighboring kingdoms he had conquered and incorporated as the Shoan leader became part of the expanding Ethiopia.

The food at this banquet included *t'ej*, rich spicy *wots*, cooked and raw meat, and a mountain of *injera*. McCann argues that Menelik and Taytu created this event not just as a unifying culinary act but as a political one as well, drawing on "many regional and cultural traditions" that ultimately served to "establish a shared culinary heritage."

This feast, McCann says, laid the groundwork for a historical process and created the Ethiopian national cuisine that has since spread around the world. By 1921, the French physician Étienne Mérab published his *Impressions d'Ethiopie*, which included a long list of the Ethiopian dishes we know today: *tibs, wot, alicha, gomen, shiro, doro, dulet,* and even *butecha*, a chick pea dish rarely found in restaurants (in fact, I once found a restaurant owner who had never heard of it). Many of these dishes and preparations go back centuries at the Ethiopian table, but as McCann points out, Mérab's list demonstrates just how codified and ubiquitous they all had become as essential elements of classic Ethiopian cuisine.

In these more modern politicized times, many of the cultures incorporated by Menelik into a greater Ethiopia have come to see themselves as conquered and now occupied nations. This remains a central political issue (and struggle) in Ethiopia today. Each of these groups has its own language and customs, and each has foods unique to its culture. But we know little about the history of their cuisines, for as Phillipson notes, "the archaeological evidence for early food production… in the south and southwest is almost non-existent."

To account for them we can only turn to the ancient Greeks and Romans, whose writings distinguished primitive "Ethiopians" by what they consumed, not by how they spoke. There we have accounts of fish eaters (ichthoyophages), ostrich eaters (trouthophages), locust eaters (acridophages) and elephant eaters (elephantophages).

This certainly isn't all they ate, but it's all we'll ever know.

Acquiring a Taste:
Europe's First Encounters

I once gave lodging to an English lad who had arrived in my hometown to attend graduate school.

He needed a place to stay for a week before finding a flat of his own. To thank me for my hospitality, he invited me to dinner when he settled into his new place. He provided me with a typical English repast — a blandly seasoned "meat and two veg," as he described it.

This fellow would never have survived in Ethiopia.

About a sesqui-century earlier, when European exploration of Ethiopia began in earnest, the high-minded men taking those first footsteps in Africa didn't always appreciate Ethiopian cuisine and the customary method of eating it. They wrote with a mixture of amazement, humor, disdain and disgust at the sight and taste of spongy *injera*, spicy *wots*, and the piquant inebriant, *t'ej*.

In his mid-16th Century book, Alvares reported what he saw on the Ethiopian table. But he also commented on it, and none if it really appealed to him.

"Their food is raw meat," he wrote "and we could not bear to look at it, let alone eat; nor of the bread unless it was of wheat, or at least chick-peas." The travelers instead had their servants prepare their meals — thoroughly cooked — although at times, to be polite, they were obliged to eat something of what their hosts provided.

Job Ludolphus, a German scholar, wrote about every aspect of Ethiopian life in his classic 1682, although he never visited the country, instead basing his comprehensive work on the published journals of Alvares, Telles and other explorers and missionaries, among them an aged Ethiopian monk named Gregory, who lived in Rome. Some of Gregory's source material has long been out of print, so Ludolphus' amalgam is a valuable document. He talks about food here and there throughout his vivid book, and his notes will resonate with 21ˢᵗ Century diners.

"Their diet is not only very homely," Ludolphus wrote, "but also far different from ours, for they feed either upon raw flesh, or half boiled. They covet as a daintie the half-concocted grass and green herbs they find in the maws of the beasts which they kill, and greedily devour those morsels, having first seasoned them with pepper and salt, as if the beasts better understood what herbs were most wholesome than themselves, a sort of diet which none of our Europeans will envy."

Urban Ethiopians no longer practice such customs. But what Ludolphus writes next, they do: "Their bread they bake upon the embers, made in the fashion of thin pancakes. Their tablecloths served them for bread, which there was no need for the servants to take away, fold up or wash."

As for the manner of eating, it's hard to tell whether Ludolphus approves. Observing the habits of a nobleman, he wrote, "The children belonging to court take the meat and put it in their mouths, and if the gobbets be too big, they thrust them in, as they do that cram capons." To a European reader of the time, it surely sounded barbaric.

Manuel de Almeida, the Portuguese Jesuit, picks up the story.

"Although there is so much food and in such plenty," he wrote, in words that are still true today, "hunger is common and food is often not to be had." He cites numerous reasons. Locusts often kill crops, especially grains, and much food is lost to "the lawlessness with which many troops of soldiers are always going about the whole country, eating, plundering and looting everything. Another explanation is that they do not carry food from one district to another, from a place where there is some to a place where there is none, because the roads are difficult and porterage is very costly."

And then there's the problem of too much drink.

"They not only eat their food," Almeida writes, "but, in a beverage like beer which they make (they call it *cala*), they drink more than they eat in [*injera*]." Later, he observes: "There is no conversation without the [honey] wine circulating and being drunk in turns until either they are laid out on the spot or else withdrawn, so much warmed up that they cannot easily find the door. They achieve this by drinking to such excess that no one knows how they can hold so much. The wine is really very mild and if it were drunk in moderation no harm could be done."

His mention of "cala" refers to what we now know as *talla*, or Ethiopian beer, although it's doubtful that Ethiopians of his era went hungry because they drank too much. In fact, his passage on honey wine notes that Ethiopians only imbibe so heavily *after* they complete their meal.

Almeida also observed teff, "a food peculiar to this country and highly esteemed because it grows well and gives adequate nourishment. It is a seed so fine that a grain of mustard might be equal to ten of teff."

As for more substantial fare, "beef they eat raw, calling it *berindo,* and it is the food they esteem most highly. They put a great deal of salt and pepper on it, if they have the pepper, and the most important people who can have the gall of the animal that is killed squeeze it by hitting it often on the piece in front of them so the meat should soak it up well; they claim that it gives it a great relish. This is their mustard, though mustard itself is found in the country. They make another more peculiar dish from the soft matter inside certain entrails with their salt and pepper. It is a dish for princes and they would not abandon it for any other."

Another Portuguese explorer, Jerome Lobo, published an account in 1789 of his mission to Ethiopia in which he describes *kibbee* and *gursha.*

"Everything they eat smells strong, and swims with butter," he wrote. "They make no use of either linen or plates. The persons of rank never touch what they eat. Their meat is cut by pages, and put into their mouths. When they feast a friend, they kill an ox, and set immediately a quarter of him raw upon the table, for their most elegant treat is raw beef, newly killed, with pepper and salt; the gall of the ox served them for oil and vinegar. Some, to heighten the delicacy of the entertainment, add a kind of sauce made of what they take out of the guts of the beast. This they set on the fire, with butter, salt, pepper, and onion."

He didn't really care for this cuisine, especially *manta,* the sauce made from the guts of the slaughtered ox. "They have often done the favor of helping me to some of this sauce," Lobo wrote, "and I had no way to decline eating it, besides telling them that it was too good for a missionary." He also observed that they eat raw beef "with the same appetite and pleasure as we eat the best partridges."

The most comprehensive early look at Ethiopia by a European came from James Bruce, a Scottish explorer who, in 1790, published his vivid five-volume book, *Travels to Discover the Source of the Nile.* He describes not only the content of an Ethiopian meal but the ritual of eating it, again witnessing *gursha.*

"No man in Abyssinia, of any fashion whatever, feeds himself, or touches his own meat," Bruce wrote. "The women take the steak and cut it length-ways like strings, about the thickness of your little finger, then crossways into square pieces, something smaller than a dice. This they lay upon a piece of the teff bread, strongly powdered with black pepper, or cayenne pepper. They then wrap it up in the teff bread like a cartridge."

When the morsel is ready, the man places each hand upon his neighbor's knee, "his body stooping, his head low and forward, and mouth open, very like an idiot." The woman places the food in his mouth, "which is so full that he is in constant danger of being choked. This is a mark of grandeur. Having dispatched this morsel, his next female neighbor holds forth another cartridge, which goes the same way, and so on till he is satisfied. He never drinks till he has finished eating; and, before he begins, in gratitude to the fair ones that fed him, he makes up two small rolls of the same kind and form; each of his neighbors opens their mouths at the same time, while with each hand he puts their portion into their mouths."

By the 19th Century, with the scramble for Africa underway, European empires began to grapple for the largely independent horn of Africa, which the prized and legendary Ethiopia occupied. As governments bargained with each other for territory and influence, explorers brought home tales of an exotic land.

Henry Salt, a British visitor, seems to have had only contempt for what he witnessed at the Ethiopian table.

"The food of the Abyssinians," he wrote, "in no way resembles normal, proper food, and the natives are not familiar with intelligent methods of preparing meals. In fact, many Abyssinians do not really know how to cook and eat or even how to sit correctly at a table."

In the Ethiopian highlands, Henry Dufton had his first encounter with teff. It looked at first like "long grass run to seed," he wrote in his 1867 account. "It stands about a foot high, and yields a small round grain no larger than a pin's head. It makes a good sweet bread, however, which is much preferred by the natives to that made of maize, or even to wheaten bread."

He marveled at the Ethiopians' tolerance for spicy foods: "Not only do they use pepper on meats, but it is mixed in their bread, in milk, and even in the water they drink. It is here called *berbere*, probably from the Berber country to the north, where much is grown. On one occasion I was able to eat the hot dishes pretty well, but before my mouth had grown accustomed to it they were intolerable."

Dufton attended an Ethiopian meal that began with a "large pile of teff-cakes, about a foot and a half in diameter and half an inch thick. The surface of each was covered with large holes, like a sponge, which in their soft spongy nature they did not a little resemble."

Soon, there appeared "a seething pot of minced mutton, almost lost in a thick red-pepper butter-gravy. The servant, having washed his hands, now takes half of a teff-cake, and using it as a cockney often does a cabbage-leaf, scoops up an allotment of the mutton and thick gravy and places it on the summit of the bread pile. We tuck up our sleeves and fall to, breaking off pieces of bread and rolling up a mutton-pill inside, which we swallow as well as we can, using tedge [honey wine] to wash it down. If there is not enough pepper, you can dip it into a pile of cayenne, which is placed on some convenient part of the bread-plate."

The cayenne mentioned here is certainly *berbere*, possibly mixed with a little water and used as a dipping sauce to make a morsel especially flaming. You can ask for this garnish at Ethiopian restaurants today if the food isn't spicy enough on its own.

In 1848, the British explorer Walter Plowden toured Ethiopia and visited the more southern Oromo region, where he found some variations in the northern way of eating. His hosts served him supper "in a large wooden bowl with a circular stand, all carved out of a single piece of wood." He ate inch-thick "teph bread," as he called it — he meant *injera*, made of teff — which came accompanied with a *wot* spiced with *berbere*, "a small hot pepper resembling cayenne, ground fine." The servants ate "beans, boiled or roasted, and nook (from which oil is extracted in Abyssinia), also roasted." This is the important Ethiopian oilseed we call *noog* today.

Plowden topped off his meal with "a jar of beer, thick, and resembling paste, with which water is mixed in as often required: the taste is somewhat like that of cider. We drank from horns, which are filled up by the domestic, or by your host, while in your hand, until you signify satiety by returning it nearly full." This beverage is *talla*, the Ethiopian beer, or *farso* as it's called in Afaan Oromo.

James Barker's 1868 memoir presents Ethiopia as "a nation who generally live on raw meat, [and] it cannot be supposed that they have made great advancement in their cuisine." He had little affection for the bread made of "flour and water mixed together in a frying pan, then beaten out between the hands to somewhat the shape of a pancake but much thicker, and baked dry in the pan." Dissatisfied with his culinary choices altogether, he concludes of the bread: "This was a luxury!"

Emilius Cosson's 1871 account is less judgmental. He attests to the variety of breads eaten by Ethiopians, "some white, some brown, according to the corn they were made of."

To begin the meal, "a servant now came round and poured water over our hands out of a brazen vessel, after which he spread some kind of sauce on the bread in the basket before us, and we were invited to begin the repast. Everybody ate with their fingers, dipping bits of the bread, which was soft and spongy, into the sauce which pleased them best. The bread was in large wafers, about as thick as a pancake, and a foot and a half in diameter. There were more than a dozen of these wafers in each basket."

The basket was surely a small *mesob*, and the sauces were spicy *wots*. In fact, among tribal Ethiopians today, meals often consist of little more than saucy *wots* spread on spongy *injera*, with the rare treat of meat when the people can afford it.

Cosson's meal also included *gursha*, for "if the Ras [governor] saw any of the native guests he wished especially to honor, he broke off a piece of bread, rubbed it in *all* the sauces, and rammed it into their mouths with his own hand. They however managed to handle their food with such skill that very little mess was made in eating it, and though the bread was rather bitter, some of the sauces were good, and the meal was not so unpalatable as might be supposed."

The bitterness of the bread reveals that 19th Century Ethiopians fermented their *injera* batter just as modern Ethiopians do today. The hand-washing at the table is also a custom retained by some modern Ethiopians.

The *fin-de-siecle* Russian explorer Alexander Bulatovich also witnessed the ritual hand washing when one of his servers "brought a copper wash-stand of intricate form, and we, in accordance with the Abyssinian custom, washed our hands before the meal." His young servant girl then dished out slices of *injera* and placed on them an array of foods: "hard boiled eggs cooked in some unusually sharp sauce, a ragout of mutton with red pepper and chicken gravy with ginger, and tongue, and ground or scraped meat, all abundantly seasoned with butter and powdered with pepper."

"We ate with our hands," Bulatovich wrote in 1897, "tearing off little petals of *injera* and collecting with them large amounts of all sorts of food. My mouth burned from the quantity of pepper. Tears came to my eyes. My sense of taste was dulled. And we devoured everything indiscriminately, cooling our mouths, from time to time, with sour cream or by drinking a wonderful mead — *t'ej* — from little decanters wrapped in little silk handkerchiefs." His book includes many more descriptions of foods and eating rituals, most of which he seemed to enjoy — or at least respect.

Europeans tended to appreciate *t'ej* more than they did the repast that accompanied it, and even some of the missionaries who visited Ethiopia enjoyed the sweet potable.

"Their drink is somewhat more dainty," Ludolphus observed, "and is the glory and consummation of their feasts, for so far they still retain the custom of many of the ancients, that as soon as the table is clear'd, they fall to drinking, having always this proverb in their mouths, *That it is the useful way to plant first, and then to water.*"

In 1856, the legendary explorer Sir Richard Burton said *t'ej* "exhilarates, excites and acts as an aphrodisiac." Two decades later, the Englishman Robert Bourke found *t'ej* to be "excellent, and very refreshing after our ride" on a visit to the home of some Ethiopian friends.

Some, like Cosson, enjoyed it but also couldn't handle it. "A good *t'ej* is rather heady," he wrote, "so we always took care, when out visiting, to keep a native servant, with a steady head, standing behind us, for the special purpose of emptying our bottles, a duty which it seemed to give the greatest satisfaction to perform."

Finally, there are the vivid accounts of food and drink written in 1898 by the Englishman Edward Gleichen, whose book describes the way in which the "lower classes" took their meals.

He begins by describing *injera*, "very thin, flat cakes, about the size of a handkerchief, which look and taste like sour, uncooked crumpets. They are also generally damp, flabby, and full of grit."

At the meal, while sitting "cross-legged or squatting on the floor," the Ethiopian uses the *injera* first as a sort of napkin, "wiping his hands on the top of one. The next one he folds in four and dips into a bowl full of red pepper mixed with clarified butter. Soaking it well in the mixture, he kneads it up in his hands, and crams it into his mouth. If you happen to be a particular friend of his, he may insist on your eating a bit that he has torn off. The red grease looks rather nasty, but tastes — for I have tried it in minute quantities — a good deal better than it looks."

His host then uses his sword to slice huge chunks of meat off the hind leg of a sheep or some ribs of beef.

"This he crams into his mouth as far as it will go," Gleichen reports, "and slices off the mouthful — with his sword — close to his lips. The upper classes, of course, take their food more tidily." He finds that Ethiopians eat very little fruits and vegetables, that they will "rarely touch, or even cook," the variety of game birds available to them, and that "the honey they eat is good, but it is always full of comb, dirt, and dead bees."

In fact, even today, Ethiopians will say that unprocessed honey, still in the comb, makes the best honey wine.

Gleichen didn't say whether he enjoyed *t'ej*, although his description seems to suggests that he didn't.

"It is the drink of the upper classes of the country," he wrote. "It is made by fermenting honey and hops and water together, and this process produces a strange-tasting drink rather like a bitter cider, and intoxicating, distinctly. The brands of *t'ej* differ according to the locality: Ras Makonnen's [father of Haile Selassie] best tastes like sweet, strong old Madeira, and [Emperor] Menelik's like still hock, whilst the inferior kinds vary between bad sherry and sourish water with dead bees and lumps of wax and bark and earth floating in it."

Later in his book, Gleichen attends an "excellent European luncheon" with the Emperor, although the meal is "interspersed here and there with Abyssinian dainties, of which red pepper formed the principle ingredient."

He clearly prefers this Western-influenced experience to the more authentic Ethiopian one.

So it seems that little has changed in the Ethiopian manner of eating for at least four centuries and probably much longer. Fortunately, the rest of the world's taste for the cuisine has changed appreciably.

Where To Eat, What To Eat

Addis Ababa has plenty of restaurants, and all of the tourist towns in Ethiopia have a hotel, usually with a restaurant, and at least a few other places to find decent food. But restaurants in Addis are frequented more by tourists and the Ethiopian upper classes. The average Ethiopian enjoys the evening meal at home, although naturally that varies from family to family and culture to culture.

Hiwot Woldu's life growing up in Ethiopia and attending college in America is a good microcosm.

The daughter of an Ethiopian Airlines pilot father and a flight attendant mother, she came to America in 1999 to go to college and then to get a medical degree. She was raised in a typical Ethiopian household, with a cook who prepared meals. This is common in middle-class homes, or "even a little less than middle class," Hiwot says. "There's always someone poorer than you."

Lunch growing up meant eating in school, and for Hiwot, it was always home cooking — that is, if she got to finish her meal.

"We — or rather, our cook — packed our lunch every day," she recalls. "It was the usual stuff that we'd have at home. We almost never packed utensils, so we'd eat even spaghetti with our hands. For some reason, I swear it tastes better that way. The one thing that we don't usually pack for school is *shiro*. I guess it was seen as too modest a dish to pack and share with people."

And she adds: "Most of the time, all the people in your group of friends were free to eat your food and vice versa, so usually, I'd eat maybe a couple of bites out of my lunch before everybody finished it."

Packing a lunch like this means that Hiwot's food isn't heated when she eats it, and sometimes at Ethiopian restaurants in America, you'll find

74

vegetarian dishes served at room temperature. Now and then a menu will even tell you this and give you the option of asking them to re-heat your food.

For dinner with Hiwot's family, it was almost always Ethiopian food, or else Italian dishes like spaghetti or lasagna. For parties, they might have a roast, but never just for family meals. Whole chickens were unheard of as well: When chicken was the evening meal, it would come as an Ethiopian *wot* or *alicha*. "For the most part," she recalls of her childhood, "the things we got excited about were things with a lot of meat in them — meat with no fat." She was especially fond of *kitfo*, but always cooked and never raw. Even now she cautions against eating raw meat in Ethiopia.

All of this food was made from scratch, and the *injera* was made of pure teff. No cook in Ethiopia bought her *injera* at market.

But because Hiwot's parents were world travelers, she and her siblings often traveled with them, and they grew up liking more than Ethiopian food. "Hamburgers were like the greatest thing," she says. "Take us to McDonald's every day!"

Even back home in Ethiopia, when she went to a restaurant, it would be a hamburger or pizza joint, or perhaps an Italian restaurant, not the more exotic places. She never visited the one Chinese restaurant in Addis that she knew about, and only the more "sophisticated" Ethiopians would dine out on foreign cuisine.

For breakfast in Ethiopia, Hiwot learned to enjoy American-style cereal, which her parents would bring home from trips abroad. Other kids her age didn't eat this type of cereal, but now she says it's more common in Ethiopian grocery stores.

When Hiwot came to America for college, she landed at a small school in a small town in Iowa, and she had no place to get Ethiopian food. "I missed it," she recalls, but because of her upbringing, "it wasn't culture shock. I just had to make do." Hiwot admits that she's a hopeless cook, but fortunately, she had relatives in the U.S., and on breaks from school she visited them in D.C. and California. It's "Ethiopian all the time" on these visits, either at restaurants or in someone's home. And when her mother came to visit her, she would bring Ethiopian food from Addis.

A decade ago, Hiwot says, even restaurants in American cities with big Ethiopians populations didn't always have the kind of *injera* she enjoyed back home. Sometimes it was "too white and sticky." Now it's "almost like the real thing" — not pure teff, but at least with some teff, and with a better texture.

For medical school she moved to Pittsburgh, a city with two Ethiopian restaurants, neither of them near campus, and because she had no community to connect with, she never ate at either of them. Instead, she found a substitute, common among Ethiopians in university communities.

"I did crave Ethiopian food a lot," she says, "but the more convenient way was to get Indian food on my way home. We share a lot of spices."

It's fair to say that Hiwot became a typical American college student once she moved to America: sandwiches, salads, Chinese, French, Thai, Japanese, Mexican — those cuisines and more sustained her, with Ethiopian binges during family visits on one coast or another.

When Hiwot lived with her family in Ethiopia, she fasted for holidays, sometimes "just to keep Mom and our cook company." She's not as observant now, a conversion common among younger Ethiopians who live abroad. In America, Hiwot says, the older folks tend to be more observant. But even they look for loopholes, like drinking skim milk instead of whole milk (all animal products are forbidden during fasting).

Hiwot hopes a career in psychiatry will give her an opportunity to live in a city with a larger Ethiopian community and a steady supply of Ethiopian food. But that's not a priority — in fact, just the opposite.

"The only part I'd like to be close to is my family," she says. "My whole point to leaving my country is to experience new cultures and meet people who are different from me, so just sticking to my community kind of defeats that purpose. Also, because our culture is so community oriented, you kind of would have a lot of obligations and a lot less time and autonomy to branch out and grow as an individual."

Restaurants in Ethiopia

Even Ethiopian families get tired of eating at home every day. In most Ethiopian cities and towns, you're likely to find a restaurant that serves spaghetti or other Italian dishes, although the farther you travel from a population center, the more limited your choices become — if you have any choices at all. But then, who goes to Ethiopia to eat Chinese food?

Only 3.3 percent of the people in Ethiopia cook with modern energy supplied by electricity, kerosene or gas, according to the government's 2004 Welfare Monitoring Survey, which didn't even include statistics for the Ogaden, the country's poorest and most isolated region. The concentration is highest in Addis Ababa, where more than half of the residents cook in modern ways. So it's no wonder that the phenomenon of the public restaurant is relatively recent in Ethiopia.

The Eritrean scholar Abbebe Kifleyesus, in his essay "The Construction of Ethiopian National Cuisine," observes that since at least the 1920s, Ethiopian towns have seen "the rise of small restaurants, food vendors at various corners of towns, push-cart food hawkers, sandwich and boiled egg sellers nearby entertainment pubs, and stalls selling spices and a variety of breads during market days."

J.I. Eadie's *An Amharic Reader*, an anthology of articles, stories and documents, has a page of "eating house signboards" from around 1913, when Eadie, a British officer, served in Ethiopia.

"In Ato Kabbad's house," proclaimed one of the restaurant signs, "there is highly recommended food for Christians, both for fast and non-fast days." ("Ato" is the Amharic word for "Mr.") Said another: "In Ato Alamu's house there is highly recommended pure food and teas." Each of these places seems to go only by the name of its presumably well-known owner. One unnamed eatery boasts: "The most excellent bread shop in the whole of Addis Ababa, celebrated in the kingdom. There are also excellent drinks of every kind." And for a place to rest after your meal: "In Ato Ayala's hotel there is excellent food for Christians. Enter! Buy! There are dishes for fast and non-fast days."

The book presents all of its entries in their original Amharic, with English translations following each one, and includes recipes for *t'ej, talla, shamet* (a barley and honey beverage), two different cultures' preparations for *dillih* (a *berbere* sauce), and a promotion for Kola, an imported French wine-cola aperitif that only the elite would have enjoyed at finer Addis Ababa establishments.

A true restaurant culture only began to emerge in Ethiopia in the 1960s. Before that, Abbebe writes, "the choice of restaurants in, for example, Addis Ababa included a few family-owned restaurants serving national dishes. But by the early 1970s, Addis Ababa was sporting the sale of roasted beef (*tibs*) in and around the circle of the Soccer Stadium restaurants," as well as boiled gastro-intestinal parts, *kitfo*, and *quanta* (beef jerky) in various restaurants.

"These restaurants and their flavoured dishes," Abbebe says, "are not also unknown to low-rank customers. In other words, *haute cuisine* in Ethiopia is not only the prerogative of the rich."

It's fair to say that *haute cuisine* in Ethiopia no longer includes boiled gastro-intestinal parts. At the time, though, these restaurants flourished thanks to middle-class patrons, who also invited the opening of European-style restaurants at luxury hotels and soon as stand-alone businesses.

"Amidst the burgeoning industry of national food restaurants," Abbebe observes, "interest in foreign foods thus seemed by the 1970s to have taken roots in the capital." These places were especially important to single, middle-class men who had no maids or servants, or no time or talent for cooking.

In 1979, the Los Angeles Times reported the results of a study of 130 Ethiopian college students, construction workers and bank employees. Heart attacks were rare then in Ethiopia because of the country's traditional low-fat, high starch diet. Construction workers, who ate mostly "whole grain bread, vegetables, peas and tea," had an average cholesterol level of 110. College students, adding fat from things like margarine and sausage to the traditional foods, came in at 160. The bankers ate more meat, butter and eggs, and their cholesterol was 180. No doubt the numbers for urban Ethiopians are higher now, a combination of more prosperity and more ways to eat badly.

Solomon Addis Getahun, an Ethiopian-born American scholar, has written about the rise of a newer phenomenon in Ethiopian eating: the fast-food restaurant. At places like Spot Bar, King Burger, Burger Queen, Rand Fast Food and LA Burger in Addis Ababa, patrons can buy burgers and fries, with pizza joints just around the corner. In & Out, near the Ras Mekonnen Bridge, offers takeout service, and Big Burger provides fast-food catering.

These joints represent more than just a change in diet.

"In a country and society where the passage of time seems inconsequential," Solomon writes, "and in a culture where socialization is the hallmark of a good individual, the introduction of 'to go' is an indication of a shift in attitude towards socialization and the concept of time: while time becomes no more constant, socialization also seems to have ceased serving as a standard for good character."

And of course, meals "to go" can't be shared from a common plate in the middle of a table surrounded by friends and family.

In 2008, a group of Ethiopian businessmen announced plans to build a series of fast food restaurants in Ethiopia that served the national cuisine. Mulu Mesob Foods sought to "prioritize hygiene and sanitation in our delivery," founding partner Tekie Gebremedhin told Nazret, an online Ethiopian publication. Price, too, is important. "Civil servants are suffering due to the spike in food prices," Tekie said. "For instance, a plate of *kay wot* used to cost five birr, but now it has tripled. Our prices range from eight to 17 birr for a plate, depending on the type of food, but also includes a soft drink or bottled water." The company is apparently the first of its kind in Ethiopia.

If there's an upside to this Westernization of Ethiopian eating, Solomon suggests, it's the advent of an urban gym culture. In traditional Ethiopia, being plump meant you could afford the food — usually beef — to get that way. (Weregenu Restaurant in Addis promotes itself, in English, as "the meat place.") It was a status symbol, something to which poor Ethiopians aspired. But now a waistline is increasingly a sign of gluttony, and as a result, "fitness centers and health clubs are also mushrooming in Addis Ababa," Solomon says, and some of them even air their exercise programs on national TV.

The patrons of these fast-food restaurants are largely (as expected) students and foreigners. The middle-class urban Ethiopian family is more likely to visit a restaurant with table service, just as their American counterparts do, and they have nearly as many choices.

And as Abbebe points out, Western chains like Pizza Hut, McDonald's and KFC "have not yet taken root in Addis Ababa." Teen-agers mostly patronize the home-grown fast-food restaurants, and "for many Ethiopian traditionalists," he writes, "these are treated more like exotic oddities than as substitutes for indigenous meals and snacks."

Alem Eshetu, in "Amharic for Foreign Beginners," notes that bigger restaurants in Ethiopia have menus, but at the smaller ones, your server will "enumerate the list of dishes" available that day. If service is a problem, which is just may be, then "to get the waiter's attention, you can clap your hands softly. But don't click your fingers which is considered impolite."

This probably won't be a problem at the restaurant in the Addis Ababa Hilton, where the *haute cuisine* is almost entirely foreign, albeit sometimes with an Ethiopian spin. The hotel has several dining rooms, from the Jacaranda Restaurant that serves its "signature lobster dish," to the Kaffa House and its traditional Ethiopian entrées, like *kitfo*, *shiro* and the house specialty, *zilzil tibs*, a spicy, juicy beef dish. The hotel also has a brick-fired pizzeria, a poolside bar that serves club sandwiches, and a lobby bar that serves both Ethiopian dishes and international cuisine.

So what's on the menu at the Addis Hilton?

As an appetizer, you can get an "Ethiopian fresh fruit cocktail," "Red Sea shrimp cocktail" or lightly smoked salmon. Soups include Bavarian lentil, French onion, or "Ethiopian pepper pot."

You can follow that up with some delicious Wiener *backhaendl* (deep fried, breaded spring chicken), *osso bucco cremolata*, Swiss *oberland* pork chop (Ethiopian Christians and Moslems both shuns pork, so this is strictly for the tourists), Nile perch, prawns brochette Dahlak (named for an archipelago of Eritrean islands), or tournedos of *sanga* beef. "Sanga" is the Amharic word for steer, as well as an internationally known breed of cattle.

Not exactly "Ethiopian" food, although sometimes food with an Ethiopian take.

The Sheraton Addis provides similar options — and then some. In its Breezes restaurant you can order barbeque, and at Les Arcades the cuisine is French. Stagioni is typically Italian, Summerfields is international, and Shaheen is Indian. A few other eateries at the hotel offer snacks and lighter options. On weekends, the Sheraton's Gaslight night club is open until 4 a.m., and it has a dress code.

Then there are the city's fine Ethiopian restaurants. If you want true local cuisine, restaurants in Addis Ababa run the gamut. You can get good fresh spicy beef (*kay wot*) and *t'ej* at any number of homey little places — essentially, butcher shops that prepare beef dishes and serve them with *t'ej*. Men in white butcher smocks carve the meat from hanging sides of beef, prepare them to your specifications, and serve them with *injera*. This is the Ethiopian version of short-order cooking — fresh, filling, and made right before your eyes.

There are plenty of restaurants as well that serve full menus of the native cuisine, some renowned for their quality.

Agelgil is "one of Addis's swankiest restaurants, where the businessmen, diplomats and the Italian-suit-wearing crowd come to feast," The New York Times wrote. Part of it is American-style ersatz swank, with palm fronds in the bar and lounge. The restaurant itself is adorned with more traditional art, and the cuisine is all Ethiopian, including *asa kitfo*, a dish of chopped fried tilapia that the restaurant claims is unique among the city's menus.

There are many *kitfo betoch* ("*kitfo* houses") dotting the landscape, although Ethiopians in America caution against eating raw beef in Ethiopia. These restaurants will serve the dish *lebleb* — that is, lightly cooked — if you request it. "If you are too sensitive about hygienic measures with food," wrote Joaquin Gonzalez Dorao, a Spanish blogger, "don't get close to a butcher shop in Ethiopia. After visiting one of these shops you will undoubtedly become a vegetarian!!"

If you have room for dessert (Western-style, of course), stop into any of the city's numerous pastry shops. If you just want to drink, then select one of the myriad *t'ej betoch* ("*t'ej* houses") that pock city and town alike. Wikimapia.org lets you search for them online and see their locations from the sky.

And if you're really lucky, you may get an invitation to a *zegubin*, an informal gathering place that serves food and drink, without a license, and usually operates out of someone's home. The term is an Amharic word that means "close the door," and it can also refer to an exclusive bar or an after-hours bar.

For non-Ethiopian cuisine in Addis, you can choose from restaurants that serve Chinese, Indian, Thai, Turkish, Middle Eastern, Mediterranean, European, French, Mexican, Russian, Armenian, "Continental" and plenty of Italian. Well-off and educated Ethiopians will eat at these restaurants, and so will tourists. "In fact," says Selamta, a website promoting travel in Ethiopia, "it is possible to eat your way round the world without ever leaving Addis Ababa."

Prices at the restaurants vary, but they're always higher than their counterparts serving Ethiopian cuisine. You can get a meal served on *injera* at a traditional restaurant for a few dollars. At the higher-end non-Ethiopian restaurants, prices can begin at $25 for a dinner and go as high as $300. But if you order Italian cuisine in Addis, be forewarned: The sauce, like all the best Ethiopian food, may be spicy, so ask for it plain if you can't stand the heat.

This is all what you might expect in a city of more than 2.1 million people. Outside of Addis, in smaller but still major tourist towns, be prepared to eat mostly — although not exclusively — Ethiopian food. These tourist destinations have pastry shops and juice bars as well as traditional restaurants that serve only Ethiopian cuisine. Most have pizza shops, and there's always Italian. Many have regional specialties unique to the cultures of the area.

In Aksum, the place where Ethiopian cuisine began, you can choose from a variety of restaurants: the Abinet Hotel, the Yeha Hotel (named for the ancient D'MT capital) and Café Abyssinia serve native cuisine with some non-Ethiopian dishes, while Axumawit Pastery [*sic*], near the Abinet, is the place to go for dessert. For Ethiopian cuisine and a Western-style breakfast, try Tsega Café, and for European food, there's the Remhai Hotel. Most of these places are located in the center of the city, which has about 48,000 residents.

You'll find largely the same sort of options in Dire Dawa (population 398,000) Gondar (195,000), Dessie (169,000), Jimma (159,000) Harar (122,000), and Lalibela (15,000), where the better hotels serve a mixture of Ethiopian and Western meals — three-course dinners of steak or roasted lamb when it's not fasting season, and in some cases even when it is (for the tourists, not the locals).

From Dire Dawa's upscale Ras Hotel to its quaint Harar Road Restaurant, or in Lalibela, from pricier hotels like the Lal or the Lasta, to smaller restaurants like Blue Nile, you'll find good food in cities where tourists visit.

And by the way, if you're desperate for pork while you're in Ethiopia, you can find it, although not easily. In Ethiopia's second-largest city, the multi-cultural (and ancient) Dire Dawa in the eastern Harar province of Ethiopia, Italian restaurants may serve pork. Ethiopian Catholics enjoy it, as do tourists.

Finally, in the most isolated areas of Ethiopia, like the southern Omo region, you'll pretty much find only Ethiopian food and maybe some spaghetti. These are destinations for the bravest tourists, often for campers, and some guide books recommend that you plan to prepare your own food, if you can find a decent market.

Ethiopian Menus in America

Like Chinese restaurants in America, Ethiopian-American *megeb betoch* ("food houses") tend to serve a dozen or so dishes whose ingredients are familiar enough to American palates.

Rare is the restaurant that serves *milas* (beef tongue), *hod* (stomach), *dulet* (a stew of spiced beef, liver and tripe), or *milasna sember* (tripe and tongue), dishes you'll find in Ethiopia, and in the more diverse Ethiopian cookbooks, but only now and then in Ethiopian restaurants in the U.S.

Not so exotic, but still rarely seen, is *kategna*, toasted pieces of *injera* coated with *berbere* and *kibbee,* often offered as an appetizer. Just as rare is *bederjan* (eggplant) and *duba* (pumpkin, or sometimes squash). Each usually comes as a *wot.* These dishes emerged in Ethiopia in the last several hundred years, as more European vegetables found their way into the Ethiopian diet.

Then there's the delicious *butecha,* seen more and more on restaurant menus. It's sort of the Ethiopian hummus, although when done well, it looks like scrambled eggs. It's a blend of chick pea powder, onion, jalapeño, turmeric, lemon juice and olive oil, chilled and chopped to give it the appearance of eggs. Meskerem in New York City makes *butecha,* but it's not on the menu: You get a little side portion with the vegetarian platter. Other restaurants offer it mostly as an entrée choice but sometimes as an appetizer, and every now and then it *will* look like hummus — although it shouldn't.

Ethiopian restaurants may not be as ubiquitous in America as their Chinese competition, but they've certainly come a long way in the past 30 years.

America's first Ethiopian restaurant was opened in Long Beach, Calif., in 1966 by Beyene Guililat, who was born and raised in Ethiopia (see Chapter 10). The Ethiopian population in America at the time was off the economic radar: The census bureau only reported statistics for "African immigrants," with no breakdown for Ethiopians, and between 1930 and 1969, the country granted residency to only 1,144 people born in Ethiopia. So Beyene counted on adventuresome non-Ethiopians to stay in business.

Other restaurants eventually followed in California, and Beyene is now an almost forgotten piece of Ethiopian-American history: Most Ethiopians will tell you their cuisine spread from a seed planted more than a decade later.

That seed was Mamma Desta, which opened in Washington, D.C., in 1978 (see Chapter 11). Its Eritrea-born chef, Desta Bairu, is now a legend among her cultural descendants: She had lived here for almost 20 years, cooking for the Ethiopian ambassador to the United Nations, before she went to work at the restaurant bearing her name among the growing Ethiopian community of the nation's capital. Hers is the name Ethiopians speak when they remember their culture's "first" restaurant here.

The next year, a group of Ethiopians opened Sheba in New York City (see Chapter 12). Araya Selassie Yibrehu was a partner in that enterprise, and so was Yeworkwoha "Workye" Ephrem, the owner of Ghenet restaurant in New York City since 1998.

Ethiopian cuisine was so little known back then that these pioneer restaurateurs couldn't get teff to make their *injera.* They had to use pancake flour or a blend of other grain flours as a substitute until teff became more available a decade later, when restaurants had begun to sprout up in other major American cities of the Ethiopian diaspora.

"The mid-1980s saw an influx of Ethiopian restaurants," Washingtonian magazine reported in December 1992. "At first supported by the Washington area's sizeable Ethiopian community, this cuisine's spicy stews have found increasing favor with non-Ethiopian clientele."

This all happened in the shadow of Desta, whose restaurant closed after several years. She lived a few other places before lending her name and cooking talents in 1984 to Mama Desta's Red Sea, Chicago's first Ethiopian restaurant (see Chapter 11).

The blossoming of Ethiopian restaurants in America largely corresponds with the Ethiopian diaspora caused by Mengistu Haile Mariam, the dictator who, in 1974, overthrew the emperor, had him executed, and then imposed a bloody communist government that fell in 1991. Many of the people who left were those who could afford passage, and in America, no longer professionals and elites, they opened businesses. Restaurants and grocery stores, designed to serve their own burgeoning American community, were among them.

American Visions magazine estimated that America had about 70 Ethiopian restaurants in 1992. Today there are more than 350 (including Eritrean). The awareness of the cuisine has grown so much in the past decade that Beijing now has an Ethiopian restaurant, opened in 2008 by an Ethiopian-American and his wife. That's quite an innovation: In a country accustomed to eating with two long wooden sticks, the idea of eating with five short fingers doesn't come naturally.

Owners Daniel and Marlo Dagnachew — he's Ethiopian, she's American — moved to Beijing with their three children in 2007 from the Washington, D.C., area, where they owned some restaurants, and opened Ras Ethiopian Cuisine in March 2008, seating their guests at a mix of tables and *mesobs*. Originally in the city's far-out Lido neighborhood, the restaurant moved to Sanlitun a year later and how has a window that looks out onto the city's embassy area, a location that should be good for business.

Their menu features all the familiar items: *sambussa, doro wot, kitfo, awaze tibs*, combination platters, and *asa*. The restaurant names the dishes in transliterated Amharic and explains them in Chinese: *Dulet* is "spices with tripe, beef and innards," an accurate — if perhaps not terribly appetizing — description. The restaurant serves strictly Ethiopian food for dinner but mixes up the offerings at lunch, with some Vietnamese, Thai, Japanese and Italian dishes available, along with fried rice, Chinese style. The lunch buffet cost 48 yuan (about $7), and for 400 yuan (about $60), you can get a sample meal with 12 different dishes.

Ras' name in Chinese, 家埃赛俄比亚餐厅, translates as "Family Ethiopian

Meal House" (or "dining room," depending upon the translator). These last two words are similar to the Amharic phrase for restaurant, *megeb bet*, or "food house." The clientele is a mix of tourists, locals, and the Ethiopian community of Beijing, mostly people (like Daniel and Marlo) who moved there for business opportunities. The restaurant imports its spices from Ethiopia.

Jessica Wang, a reporter for the English-language magazine The Beijinger, says that "Chinese diners are quite open to the idea of eating with one's hands. In fact, the Chinese may even tell you Ethiopian food is similar to Chinese food." That may be more civility than fact, a result of the Chinese people's increasing fascination with that part of the world. The Chinese government now even encourages research, travel and cultural exchange with Africa. Certainly the presence of an Ethiopian restaurant in Beijing will encourage such an exchange.

When Prague got its first Ethiopian restaurant in July 2009, the Czech Republic got its first African restaurant. Ethiopia Café, in the city's Vinohrady district, was created by Jiři Škvor, who lived in Ethiopia in the 1990s, where he started a charitable mission. His Prague restaurant also has a heart: More than half of the café's employees are people with psychological conditions that make it hard for them to find work elsewhere.

Russia has had an Ethiopian restaurant since 1999: Adis Ababa, located along the Garden Ring in central Moscow, and for many years called Bungalo Bar. It serves traditional dishes, like *tibs* and *t'ej*, and some *very* untraditional (and expensive) ones, like alligator, ostrich, kangaroo — and "Mexican pork."

And these aren't the only place you'll find Ethiopian food around the world. Frankfurt has long had a large Ethiopian community: In terms of the diaspora, you could say it's the Washington, D.C., of Europe. You can get Ethiopian food in Australia, Belgium, Canada, Denmark, France, England, Greece, Israel, Jamaica (near the Bob Marley Museum), Japan, the Netherlands, New Zealand, Norway, Italy, Switzerland, Spain, Sweden, Thailand, and of course, numerous African countries. Just call it the new Chinese.

Most Ethiopian restaurants in America and around the world serve dishes that are readily familiar to people raised in big Ethiopian cities — spicy *wots* with beef and chicken, milder *alichas* made with vegetables, and all of it on top on *injera* made with teff.

But every now and then, a restaurant will innovate, serving American-style foods in Ethiopian ways, or simply adding American items to the menu to please families with fussy eaters.

Fasika in St. Paul, Minn., is a good example. The restaurant's large menu includes all of the Ethiopian standards, along with American items like the

Fasika Cheese Burger (charbroiled hamburger, American cheese, lettuce, onion, tomato and fries), or a spicy chicken sandwich.

But you can also get the unusual *yebalager tibs*, a dish of "home style smoke flavored lamb." The Amharic word *balager* means "countryside," so the name associates this dish and its smoky flavor with American country cookin'.

Fasika's *moja asa*, a pan-fried spiced catfish served with rice, is both unusual and ironic. The name literally means "wealthy fish" because catfish is rare in Ethiopia, so only the wealthy would eat it. Fried fish is a common Ethiopian food, and it's sometimes served at restaurants in America. But Ethiopians follow Old Testament dietary codes, which forbid the consumption of any fish that doesn't have scales — like catfish. Of course, the code also forbids mixing meat and dairy products, a rule followed by Jews who keep kosher but not by Ethiopian Christians: *kibbee* is a key ingredient in meat dishes, and some of the best *wots* will come swimming in the Ethiopian spiced butter.

Muzita Bistro in San Diego wants to "bring Ethiopian and Eritrean food into the cuisine level," says the restaurant's general manager, Michael Lunsford. It's sort of Ethiopian fusion cuisine, with many of the basic ingredients presented in imaginative ways. They use teff as a light breading for fried calamari or okra and serve a spicy lentil spread inside a toasted round of *injera*. There's tofu in *awaze* sauce, a leg of lamb seasoned with Ethio-Eritrean spices, and good old *kitfo*, cooked in *tesmi* (*kibbee*) and served with *ajibo* (*ayib*, or cheese). The menu names its dishes in Tigrinya rather than Amharic, and meals come with your choice of *injera* or rice.

Madget in Washington, D.C., doesn't have any especially unusual dishes, but it does have confidence: "The best Ethiopian food in the nation," boasts a large replica of its menu in the window. "Most Ethiopian restaurant *owners* dine at Madget ☺." The owner, who once cooked for the Ethiopian army, is the restaurant's cook.

Its menu also has a sense of humor in serving up some standard dishes. There's a dish called "Vayyagra," with the name also written in Amharic letters. It's the Ethiopian traditional beef *tibs*, "our house special," the menu explains. "Yes, we hear it does the trick."

Then there's "Taytanik," a larger portion of *tibs*. Says the menu: "You got it, it's big." Or try some "meltingly tender and juicy pan-fried chunks of beef." Just ask for the "Jelati" — a dish whose name is yet another pun, albeit a very subtle one, with a nod to the Italian influence on Ethiopian cuisine.

And speaking of Italian: Just a few blocks down the street from Madget in Washington is La Carbonara, offering "fine Italian cuisine" on a street lined with Ethiopian and Eritrean businesses and restaurants (nearly a dozen).

It's not out of place: The owners are Ethiopian, and their lunchtime clientele especially tends to be more Ethiopian than not.

At Nyala in Los Angeles, you can order a spicy "mixed seafood" meal of surimi, octopus, shrimp and mussels, all sautéed with onion, garlic, tomato, *berbere* and olive oil. At Meskerem in Las Vegas, there's an all-American club sandwich — that is, if you want to be a member of that club at an Ethiopian restaurant.

Queen of Sheba in Addison, Texas, offers a traditional dish with a local moniker: The "Houston Style" special is standard *kitfo* (steak tartar, the menu says), accompanied by another beef dish and collard greens (*gomen*). You could say it's what's for supper. Adey Abeba in Seattle offers "stir fried ribs" on its menu. But don't worry, it's Ethiopian: This is just the English explanation of *goden tibs*, a dish of short ribs (lamb or beef) cooked with onions and peppers.

Sacramento's Addis Ababa restaurant serves the traditional Ethiopian omelet with jalapeños and onions, but it also serves an omelet that adds beef to the mix. Seattle's Kokeb has a children's menu that simply offers smaller portions, but includes the caveat, "We recommend the milder dishes." Nearby, the city's Blue Nile offers a *yedoro* (that is, chicken) sandwich, and "green *doro tibs*," a dish of chicken mixed with a side of vegetables, *gomen* or cabbage, and a salad. Another Blue Nile — this one in Kansas City, Mo. — features nothing more out-of-the-ordinary on its menu than shrimp *alicha*. But the owner, Daniel Fikru, offers cooking lessons as the University of Missouri in Kansas City: For $9 tuition, plus $18 in materials, you can attended a two-hour class and learn to make *injera, misir wot* and *atakilt alicha*.

The fish offerings at Memphis' Abyssinia are quite unusual. There's "salmon gulash" (with a mix of vegetables), "amberjak gulash" and "white tuna fish" salad. The restaurant also serves a dish with goat along with the more traditional lamb. Meskerem in Charlotte, N.C., offers American-style tuna salad as an appetizer, but the rest of its menu is strictly Ethiopian, and they even have their own brand of winery-bottled *t'ej*.

Makeda in New Brunswick, N.J., offers an all-Ethiopian menu, except for its appetizers, which are all-Middle Eastern — *loubia* (sautéed string beans), *zaalouk* (eggplant), *kefta* (Moroccan meatballs) and *zitoune* (marinated chicken). The restaurant's website presents itself as the state's only Ethiopian restaurant, which may have been true when it opened. Now there are several more, like West Orange's Harrar Café and its very unusual "soy *tibs*" and Maryland crab cakes (under the "Chef's Alternatives" portion of the menu); or Montclair's Mesob, whose straight-up Ethiopian menu offers nothing more unusual than shrimp *tibs*.

At Queen of Sheba in Washington, D.C., you can enjoy any of a variety of smoothies, including the quasi-Ethiopian "Sheba Smoothie," which includes honey and flax seeds, two items common to Ethiopian cuisine. The restaurant also serves spaghetti, chicken cutlets and grilled chicken salad, and it has a breakfast menu with Ethiopian items along with "eggs the way you like them," and pancakes with syrup and butter.

And what to make of the restaurant's "*timatim* and peanut butter *fitfit*," a dish of tomatoes, onions, jalapeños and peanut butter, blended with mixed injera? Add some jelly and you've got an American favorite — Ethiopian style. The restaurant offers this unusual fare because it's a favorite of Washington cab drivers, who sometimes want a quick American-style meal.

Some Ethiopian restaurants in America serve dishes made with seafood not commonly found in Ethiopia. Asmara Restaurant in Cambridge, Mass., offers salmon or scallops in *berbere* sauce (as well as the very un-Ethiopian "spicy chicken wings").

One special item to look for is *sinig*, offered by only a few Ethiopian restaurants in America. It's a jalapeño pepper, stuffed with tomatoes and onions (or whatever the cook decides to stuff it with). Merkato in Los Angeles offers it, as does Omo in Silver Spring, Md., on its *beyaynetu*.

This is just a sampling of how Ethiopian restaurants in America tweak their menus for patrons. Fortunately, almost all of these restaurants explain each dish. You'll usually see the authentic Amharic name for the dish transliterated into English, sometimes with the dish written in Amharic letters after it. Then, the menu tells you what it is. But every now and then, you're on your own, and if you don't know what *yekeyser selata*, *inguday tibs* and *ye bere tibs* are, you'll miss out on cold beet salad, spicy mushroom stew, and beef roasted or stewed with onions, peppers and tomatoes.

Then there are the restaurants that take common dishes and fancy them up a bit. At Cottage Restaurant in Atlanta, the familiar *kitfo* dish of raw or lightly cooked chopped beef becomes *banatu*: *kitfo* and cottage cheese atop pieces of *injera*, with cubes of lean beef sautéed in red onions, garlic, jalapeno peppers, fresh tomato, herbs and spices. In Los Angeles, at Rahel Ethiopian vegetarian cuisine, a "veggie *banatu*" has tomatoes and green peppers, seasoned with garlic and onions, all mixed with *injera*. And at Café Colucci in San Francisco, *banatu* is either beef seasoned with *berbere* and cardamom, then mixed with *injera*, or for a vegetarian version, it's the same seasonings, but with tomatoes and onions, plus the *injera*. Each version comes with sour cream.

In fact, *banatu* refers to something added after a dish is cooked. In these menu items, it's cottage cheese (*ayib*), *injera* or sour cream, and possibly some of the spices. At an Ethiopian restaurant, you needn't worry about what things are called, as long as the menu describes them.

Another example: *yefisik beyaynetu*, a hearty mix of meats and vegetables.

Fasika is the Ethiopian Easter, and for the 40 days of the Lenten season, no meal may contain animal products. A *beyaynetu*, of course, is a vegetarian platter, and a *beyaynetu b'siga* is a vegetarian platter with meat. Calling the latter combo *yefisik* means that the Easter fast is over and you can eat meat again. Most restaurants simply call this a *beyaynetu*. The ones that add *"yefisik"* want to acknowledge its celebratory nature.

If you're lucky, you may find a restaurant that presents its dishes in Tigrinya or Afaan Oromo, two other widely spoken languages in Ethiopia.

Tigrinya is spoken in the north of the country and in Eritrea, and it's a Semitic language like Amharic, so the names of the dishes aren't too different in most case. You may see *kelwa* rather than *tibs*, *tegamino* for *shiro*, *hamli* and *birsin* for the staple vegetables *gomen* and *misir*, and possibly even *taita* for *injera*. *Doro* changes simply to *dohro*, and *azifa* is still just plain old *azifa*.

At Minneapolis' Blue Nile, owned by an Oromo man, you'll find, for example, *kataffi* instead of *kitfo* and *kurumba* for *tikil gomen*. Salt Lake City's African Restaurant, also Oromo-owned, serves *walmaka* (a combination plate), *waaddii* (*wot*), *raafuu* (*gomen*), *dabaqula* (squash, or *duba* in Amharic), *qimamii* (*kibbee*), *budeena* (*injera*), and *ashaakiltii* (*atakilt*, or veggie stew). But apart from the language difference, and a few dishes special to the culture, Oromo-owned restaurants serve the national cuisine, and explanations always accompany the unfamiliar Oromo names.

Your best bet at any Ethiopian restaurant is to order a *beyaynetu* and sample as many dishes as you can. If you go to the restaurant with a group of people, you can practically order everything on the menu.

But how many choices is too many choices? At The Ethiopian Restaurant in Berkeley, Calif., the menu boasts 792 of them when you order its *beyaynetu*.

The restaurant prepares 12 vegetarian dishes, and the *beyaynetu* lets you choose five. Do the math and you can concoct 792 five-dish combinations out of those 12 choices where no two combinations have the same five dishes.

It's a mathematical equation called a combination factorial, and you can apply it to the menu of any Ethiopian restaurant that offers a *beyaynetu*.

Here's how it figures.

In the equation, N is the number of dishes from which you can choose, and K is the number that you may choose. So at the Berkeley restaurant, N = 12 and K = 5.

First, multiply 12 x 11 x 10 x 9 x 8: That's N (12) multiplied down by K (five) ascending numbers. That comes to 95,040. Next, multiply K down to one: 5 x 4 x 3 x 2 x 1. That's 120. Finally, divide 95,040 by 120, and you get 792.

Let's try another one. Say your menu offers 10 veggie dishes, and the *beyaynetu* allows you to select four of them. N = 10 and K = 4. Here's what you get:

$$\frac{10 \times 9 \times 8 \times 7}{4 \times 3 \times 2 \times 1} = 210$$

Not quite as many, but still enough to have your server tapping her foot impatiently while you decide.

Finally, a word about service. If you're lucky, you'll be treated like *betegna* — that is, a welcomed guest, almost a member of the family — when you visit an Ethiopian restaurant, especially if you become a regular there. But Ethiopian restaurants seem to have developed a reputation for being less than snappy about tending to their customers' needs. And that's not me talking: It's Seleda, an online 'zine for hip young Ethiopians that published from about 1999 to 2004 (with a farewell issue in 2009).

Each issue of Seleda had a Top 10 list in the style of David Letterman, and sometimes the lists poked fun at culinary things.

In April 1999, the "Top 10 Signs You Have Become a Ferengie" — that is, foreigner — included: "No. 6., You still get bewildered by the slow service at Ethiopian restaurants." Other signs include asking for a beer list instead of just ordering a Heineken (Ethiopians in America tend to eschew their country's beer for more continental selections), describing *injera* as "those spongy burritos," and reflecting on the dangers of carcinogens at a coffee ceremony.

In June 1999, Seleda proposed the top 10 things never to do in Ethiopia, including "when ordering *kitfo*, demand it be prepared 'medium medium rare, but a little to the medium side…I don't want to die of Ebola before seeing Sodere again.'" The No. 8 sign, not about food, says something about the endless cultural conflicts in Ethiopia: "In the middle of a heated political discussion, shake your head and whisper, 'Can't we all just get along?'"

And in May 1999, Seleda proposed 10 businesses sure to go belly up in Ethiopia, including: "Pork Products 'R Us: All Pork All the Time," and of course, the doomed "*Injera* and *Wot* In-a-Can: just open, microwave, and m'….m'….good!"

The Buzz on Wine and Beer

While you're eating all of this spicy Ethiopian food, you'll need something to drink.

Water is always good, and some restaurants sell Ambo, bottled in Ethiopia from the natural springs of the Ambo Mountains. Coffee is both common and cultural, with many restaurants selling Ethiopian coffee and even conducting the traditional coffee ceremony. Or you could have some tea, probably American-made in restaurants, although there are numerous Ethiopian brand name teas, some of them for sale in grocery stores here.

You might also consider a potent potable to wash down you meal. Most of the offerings are wines, beers and liquors from the United States and around the world. But more and more, Ethiopian restaurants in America offer beers and wines from back home.

Numerous Ethiopian beers have become increasingly available in restaurants around the country: Harar, Meta, Bedele, St. George, Castel, Bati and Hakim Stout. Occasionally you'll find Addis, an American-made brew that presents itself as "genuine Ethiopian-style lager beer." That's a good trick, because these Ethiopian beers taste pretty much like their American counterparts — which, of course, tend to taste like one another. Hakim Stout is like a dark sweet ale — a "peculiar," as the British call it — and the others are solid lagers. You'll also sometimes find Asmara, the leading Eritrean beer: At New Eritrea Restaurant in San Francisco, a promotional card under the glass tabletops boasts, "We proudly serve the Eritrean King of Beers."

As for wines, you can often find the Ethiopian-made dry reds, Axumite and Gouder, the semi-dry red Dukem, and the semi-dry (actually, more semi-sweet) whites, Kemila and Awash Crystal. Most of them are pretty routine, but if you want a full Ethiopian experience, then give one a try.

If you ever have a chance to drink bootleg Ethiopian *t'ej*, do it. The winery *t'ej* you buy in bottles is often very good, but it's different than homebrew, which is usually fermented in a jug in someone's kitchen.

Unfortunately, you won't get that chance too often: It's hit and miss finding an Ethiopian restaurant that serves homemade *t'ej* or an Ethiopian grocery story that sells it. *T'ej* is relatively easy to make (see Chapter 8), and homebrew is always popular with Americans who try it. But it's against the law in many states to sell homemade alcohol, and the places that sell it do so at their own risk — and under the radar of local law enforcers.

A few markets and restaurants in the D.C. area sell their homemade *t'ej*, and they risk getting busted for it. But at least one probably never will: The market sells no other alcohol and doesn't put its *t'ej* in the display cooler. You'll only know the place offers it if you can read the Amharic sign in the window saying, "*T'ej* for sale."

So you'll probably need to settle for some winery *t'ej*. There are more than a dozen different brands, most of them from small wineries (see Chapter 8). They're almost impossible to find in wine shops, except in big cities with large Ethiopian populations.

You won't find *areque* (or *araki*) in too many Ethiopian restaurant in

America. This is an anise-flavored liquor — the Ethiopian ouzo — and it's potent stuff. New Eritrea in San Francisco offers an Eritrean-made brand of *areque* called Zibib, and it packs a wallop when downed in shots.

Andrew Heavens, a journalist living in the Sudan, has posted a recipe on his blog for "electric tea," made by first preparing a cup of Addis Tea — that's an Ethiopian brand — and then adding "a good slug of *araki*." It's clearly not a recipe for tea-totalers. In response to Heavens' blog, an Ethiopian who signed his name Safiya recalled a song from childhood:

Wake up in the morning and drink coffee
After lunch, *katikala* [another distilled liquor]
After dinner, *t'ej*
This is the remedy for human being's ailments

After the song, Safiya adds, "Now that I am old, I don't subscribe to the song's logic. I don't drink alcohol and feel great about it. It is the healthiest thing you can do."

NTS Enterprises of Oakland, Calif., began importing Ethiopian foods, spices and alcohol in the 1980s. There weren't many restaurants then, and with liquor laws written by the states, the company couldn't sell its alcohol around the country as easily as it sold its spices and grains. NTS has grown with the Ethiopian-American restaurant community, and it's still a major player in the field. But now it has competitors, like Kebede "Teddy" Tadesse's company, Global Air and Transport in Maryland, and two separate companies named Blue Nile Enterprises, one in Oakland and one in Chicago.

Their markets tend to criss-cross: You can find beer from California's NTS in Washington, even though Global sells it from nearby Maryland, and you can find Global's product in Milwaukee, even though the much closer Blue Nile of Chicago distributes as well. Sometimes the reach of a company has to do with it sales potential: To sell out of state, distributors must buy licenses one state at a time, and if a company can't sell a lot in, say, Massachusetts, it probably won't want to pay for the right to sell just a little.

The Ethiopian beer business doesn't get much more mom and pop than Chicago's Blue Nile Enterprises. It's owned by Denekew "Danny" Getahun, an engineer, and his wife, Abeba "Abby" Heroda, who raises their children and operates the business from a home office, with a warehouse nearby. Both are from the northwest city of Bahir Dar, a popular tourist destination on the south shores of Lake Tana, although they met in the U.S.: Danny arrived in 1987, living first in D.C. and then in Chicago, and Abby arrived in 1996.

Their company opened in 2007, and now it's trying to grow. But there are challenges.

First, getting the beer from Ethiopia to the U.S. takes 45 to 60 days because it comes by sea from a landlocked country, traveling by truck from Ethiopia to a port in Djibouti, and beginning its ocean voyage in the Red Sea, where ships can't dock in any Moslem country that forbids alcohol. This, Danny says, adds time to the length of the journey.

Then there's the issue of volume. Ethiopian law requires Danny to buy beer from any particular company in quantities of more than a thousand cases, and he's not allowed to mix brands from different companies to meet that threshold. Some companies make more than one brand, so he's allowed to mix brands within a company. But by not being able to mix from company to company, he can only order — and thus only offer his customers — a limited number of brands. If he has too much beer in stock before his still-small company can sell it, the beer will reach its expiration date. His window is about six months.

This limits his growth potential for now, although lower demand in the U.S. means no supply problems from Ethiopia. Danny says he's had no trouble so far getting beer from the Ethiopian companies that make it. He worries just a bit that increased demand will affect the supply side of the equation.

Blue Nile has licenses to sell its beer in Illinois, Florida and Seattle, and he's working on Denver, which has a sizeable Ethiopian community. His out-of-state product goes strictly to wholesalers, but in Chicago he sells directly to restaurants and markets as well. Visitors to Disney World in Orlando can now buy Ethiopian beer thanks to Blue Nile's expanding enterprise.

As for who drinks the beer, Danny knows it's mostly non-Ethiopians, for a few reasons. When non-Ethiopians go to an Ethiopian restaurant, they often want the full authentic experience, so they'll order a beer from back home. Ethiopian-Americans who drink beer at home buy it at distributors, and very few distributors stock Ethiopian beer. But even if they could get it at a distributor, they can be snobbish about drinking it because they feel they know it too well. "When you have gold," Danny observes, "you tend to think it's silver or brass."

Nega Selassie, the co-owner of NTS Enterprises, guesses that Americans down nine out of 10 bottles of Ethiopian brew sold in U.S restaurants. Ethiopians are more likely to choose Heineken or Guinness, and Nega thinks he knows why. "They feel proud to drink foreign beer," he says. "It's the mentality."

Only two wineries in Ethiopia make *t'ej* for commercial distribution. Tizeta Tej isn't available in America. Nigest Honey Wine is, and Teddy stocks it. But Americans find its taste to be too sharp, so he can't get too many Ethiopian restaurants to carry it.

Zerihun Bekele of Alem Ethiopian Village, a restaurant in Milwaukee,

Wisc., confirms this: He once sold Nigest but doesn't any more because his customers favor the American-made brands that he also sells. He gets his Ethiopian beers from Teddy in Washington.

Of course, when a restaurant's policy permits it, the best and most economical scenario is always to BYOT, especially if it's homebrew. Just be sure to bring enough to share with your Ethiopian hosts.

Injera & Teff

The world seems to have found teff.

Not bad for the smallest food grain on earth — one piece is the size of a grain of sand — and better yet when you consider that its name derives from the Amharic word *yätäfä*, which means "lost," because each grain is so easy to lose if you drop it.

Some scholars have even speculated that because teff is so small, Ethiopians cultivated it before other grains: Why would a culture harvest such a tiny grain if it had alternatives? Others doubt this, saying that the hardiness and nutritional qualities of teff account for its ancient cultivation.

No longer just the unique grain needed to make Ethiopian *injera*, it's now used as a gluten-free substitute for wheat, suitable for baking everything from cookies and muffins and cobblers to pancakes and pasta. Once available as a food product only from Ethiopia, entrepreneurs in the United States, Australia and Canada now grow and sell it, both for its grain and for its grassy stalk, which makes an excellent livestock forage.

About 300 species of teff grow on several continents, but Ethiopia hosts its greatest diversity. *Eragrostis tef,* the *injera* species, almost certainly originated there, although scholars can only speculate about how long ago that happened.

In the binomial nomenclature of science, the full name of the *injera* teff is ***Eragrostis tef* (Zucc.) Trotter**. This refers to Attilio Zuccagni, an 18th Century director of the botanical gardens in Florence who first grew teff in Europe, after the Scottish explore James Bruce brought some seeds back with him in 1773; and to Alessandro Trotter, who rediscovered Zuccagni's 1775 thesis, *Dissertazione Concernante Tef,* in 1918, and who published articles about teff in 1918 and 1938.

During the centuries after Zuccagni's work, teff came to be called by some other scientific names: There was **Poa abyssinica (Jacq.)**, which refers to N.J. Jacquin, the 18th Century botanist who named it (*Poaceae* is the grass family); or **Eragrostis abyssinica (Jacq.) Link**, a variation of the current name, adding a reference to the German botanist Johann Heinrich Friedrich Link, who refined Jacquin's classification. Trotter finally named it *Eragrostis tef*, and today its full name pays tribute to him and Zuccagni.

Eragrostis tef is the species of *Eragrostis* native to Ethiopia and grown now in America, although purists will say (and they're probably right) that the version grown in North American soil doesn't yield the same taste as native teff. It certainly doesn't produce the same finished product: In Ethiopia, pieces of pure teff *injera* are thinner, larger and more sour than the mixed-grain versions found around the world. The diaspora has learned to make do, and New World connoisseurs don't realize the difference.

In 1978, J.A. Ponti wrote that the ancient people who lived in today's Ethiopia first cultivated teff from between 1000 and 4000 B.C., even before they cultivated barley. In 1866, the scholar Franz Unger claimed to have found teff seeds in an Egyptian pyramid c. 3359 B.C. and in a Jewish town c. 1300 B.C., but later scholars have said Unger was almost certainly mistaken.

The science of the late 20th Century has documented its history with more certainty, but no scholar will swear that teff existed in pre-Ethiopian, pre-Aksumite cultures much before the late first century A.D., about 2,000 years ago.

And this is one very nutritious grain. A 1997 study by the Biodiversity Institute of Ethiopia, conducted by Seyfu Ketema, found that white, or *magna* (pronounced "manya") teff, the kind most popular for making *injera*, has 56 percent more calcium and 68 percent more iron than wheat. There are also red, black and mixed-seed varieties.

Teff is higher than wheat in a dozen amino acids, especially the essential lysine, and slightly higher in such nutrients as potassium, zinc and aluminum. It contains 11 percent protein, 80 percent complex carbohydrates, and almost four grams of fiber per ounce. Ethiopian athletes believe that teff makes them stronger in competition, so they'll eat it as *injera* or as a porridge made from the whole grain.

Lost Crops of Africa asserts that one large piece of *injera* a day supplies an Ethiopian with enough amino acids to sustain life without another protein source, and two pieces are "sufficient to ensure good health."

Teff has as much food value, or even more, as grains like wheat, barley and maize "probably because it is always eaten in the whole-grain form: the germ and bran are consumed along with the endosperm," the institute study says.

The largest grain crop in Ethiopia, its production exceeds the second most common crop, maize, by nearly 16 percent. No other African country grows teff as a significant crop. Some Ethiopians, especially in the country's poorer western provinces, will eat it several times a day, according to *Lost Crops of Africa*. "Teff is so overwhelmingly important in Ethiopia," the book asserts, "that its absence elsewhere is a mystery."

But now, thanks in part to the rising awareness and popularity of Ethiopian food, teff is catching on, with commercial production taking place in several countries.

Teff grows on stalks of tall reedy grass, and after harvesting the tiny grain, Ethiopians use the leftover stalks as livestock forage. Farmers in the United States have now begun to adopt the plant for this purpose as well.

The name *Eragrostis tef* comes from Greek and means "grass of love" (*eros*/love, *grostis*/grass). Of the nearly 300 genera of *Eragrostis,* about 43 percent of them seem to have originated in Africa, the Biodiversity Institute reports, with others coming from Asia, Australia, Europe and the Americas.

And by the way, *magna* isn't the Amharic word meaning white. The name of this teff comes from an Amharic phrase, *minigna nech new*, meaning (roughly translated) "how white it is." Although *nech* means white, the phrase's first word, *minigna*, is a pronoun that's been shortened and corrupted into *magna* to give this teff its name.

There are other kinds of teff — *sergegna* (a mix of white and brown), *kay* (red*)* and *tiqur* (black), for example — and Ethiopians harvest these for *injera* as well. There's also *abolse* teff, an improved variety being tested and studied in Ethiopia, with good results in early studies based upon its yield and baking quality. Some fields have mixed varieties, and in fact, such mixing often gives the grain its color.

But *magna* teff is most prized, and it's the kind Ethiopians export — when there isn't a shortage and a government ban on exports. Unfortunately, that's the current state of things, with teff demand in Ethiopia exceeding the supply, and with Ethiopian importers now looking for sources of teff even among growers in America.

Teff thrives from sea level to as high as 2,800 meters (about 1.7 miles), and in various temperatures, soils, terrains and rainfall conditions, although not in places with excessive rainfall. It's so hearty and easy to grow under the right conditions that in Yemen, it's called the "lazy man's crop." Farmers simply toss some seed into the ground after a flood, then return six weeks later to harvest the grain. Teff grows almost everywhere in Ethiopia, except for the eastern parts of the country, and especially in the vast eastern Hararge province, also known as the Ogaden, an arid, sparsely populated land made up largely of ethnic Somalis.

In English, the word almost always appears as teff rather than tef, although it needn't: The word in Amharic consists of two letters, the first one a "t'e" (an explosive "t"), and the second one a simple "f." In fact, just as we sometimes write *t'ej* to capture the sound of the explosive "t" at the beginning of the word, we might just as correctly write *t'ef.* But nobody does.

As for "*injera*," the pioneering Ethiopian language scholar Wolf Leslau claims that the word derives from the ancient Ethio-Semitic verb *gagära*, which means "to bake." The more contemporary linguist Chris Ehret says that can't be so, basing his analysis on the way words and sounds have evolved in Ethio-Semitic languages, and he offers *cangara* as the older word from which *injera* sprung.

Homegrown American Teff

Although many Ethiopian restaurants will import their teff from back home if they can, they haven't needed to do so for quite a while. Teff is now as American as *injera*, and you can buy the U.S.-grown product from specialty stores and on the internet. This is largely thanks to one American entrepreneur, who began growing teff in America two decades ago and selling the milled grain to Ethiopian restaurants.

Since then, teff grass has also become increasingly abundant as a forage for livestock, with more than a dozen states now growing it

Suddenly, teff seems to be sprouting up literally from coast to coast — in Oregon, Kansas, Idaho, Montana, Washington, Minnesota, Oklahoma, Pennsylvania, South Dakota, Nebraska, Nevada, New York, Virginia, Illinois, Delaware — and soon, maybe in your neighbor's backyard.

One such place is the 3,000-acre SS Farms, a company in Hydro, Okla., owned by the progressive commercial farmer Dean Smith, who has said, "We'll try a test plot of almost anything," but not before researching the market. He did that for teff in 1996, and he found that Workinesh Spice Blends, a Michigan-based company at the time (now in Minnesota), was eager to get as much teff as he could provide. The pioneering spice company, launched in 1978 by its eponymous owner (see Chapter 10), makes *berbere*, *shiro* and many other spices for sale to Ethiopian people and restaurants in the U.S. It also sells teff and *injera*.

So Smith looked into teff when he heard about it, learned that Ethiopians in the U.S. sometimes had a hard time finding it, and found his way to Workinesh. He planted 700 acres that first year and sold it to the company, thus launching a beautiful friendship. He also harvests the hay for fodder.

In a unique enterprise, the U.S. Agriculture Department provided a grant for a Kansas collective of black farmers, some descendants of African slaves, to grow teff. The effort led to a Civil Rights Achievement Award for a group that fostered the program.

Josh Coltrain, the project coordinator, said he had a hard time at first getting farmers to agree to plant teff with other grain prices so profitably high. In 2008, they planted 80 acres, mainly for the grain, although they looked for a market for the forage grass as well. They sold the grain to Workinesh, which was eager to get as much as they could. Coltrain says he learned about the company's needs from Smith.

Some ill-timed rains damaged productivity a bit, but even so, things went well, and in 2009, Coltrain says they doubled their acreage, and "there is a positive vibe with the project. Teff is growing in popularity in our region as a forage crop, so that has helped with publicity." As for the rain, which threatens every growing season, Coltrain is gently philosophical. "I learned long ago," he says, "that one shouldn't complain about the rain. It may go away. The producers need all the moisture they can get."

But most of the teff grown nationwide still turns into forage, and researchers at both the University of South Dakota and Cornell University have published brochures inviting farmers to consider growing teff in their states.

"Teff can rival New York grass hay dry matter yields and produce relatively high quality forage with proper management," wrote a team of researchers at Cornell. The South Dakota report draws the same conclusion but cautions that because teff is "susceptible to infestation from stem-boring insects, the potentially devastating effects of this insect severely limit predictability of teff forage yields at this time."

The Cornell project, which has no such fears, began in 2002 with funding from the McKnight Foundation and in association with the Ethiopian Agricultural Research Organization. The scientists sought to increase their yield through genetic manipulation, and in 2006, Ethiopia's National Variety Release Committee approved a new variety, *quncho*, for use in Ethiopia. This means more teff and better teff to feed Ethiopians.

In Oregon, university researchers in the southern part of the state have planted teff for several years and harvested it as forage. They sell the forage to local horse owners, who say their horses gobbled it up. Ken Rykbost, the project supervisor, noted the plant's heartiness, as long as it's planted after the risk of frost.

A program supervised by agronomists at the University of Nebraska produced a good first yield of forage teff in 2007 on several thousands acres of land, and now it's expanding. Bruce Anderson, an extension forage specialist with the project, said growers were happy with the look and quality of the hay. Agronomists in the region are now studying the plant and its results in Nebraska. Jerry Volesky, a hay and forage specialist with the University of

Nebraska, is conducting trials on three teff varieties, and he says horse owners particularly like teff as forage for their animals.

A 2007 trial in Pennsylvania produced a good crop that pleased and surprised Marvin Hall, a forage specialist at Pennsylvania State University. The state's farmers often deal with pesky mite problems that damage their spring timothy crops. Teff, which can't be planted until May or June, could help to overcome this problem, and it produces yields that are one-half to two-third larger than other summer forage grasses, Hall found.

Likewise, a 2004 Nevada test of the viability of teff led to a harvest that produced $200 more in revenue per acre than alfalfa and required less than two-thirds as much water, saving about 50 percent in operating costs, the University of Nevada reported in 2006. This means market competition for other forage grasses.

All of these projects harvest the teff while it's still green — that is, before it begins to produce the grain used in making *injera*. The grain heads may just be emerging when it's cut, but there's no profit in waiting: In Nebraska, for example, they get three yields from a field by planting the first in late May, the second in early August, and a third in mid-September. All are harvested just as grain heads emerge and well before the grain matures. Waiting any longer would produce a crop of forage teff with less protein and digestible energy, Anderson says.

Homestead Sport Horses of Waynesboro, Va., has a small website promoting teff as "a new kind of hay that is hitting the horse, alpaca and cattle community. It's palatable like a nice alfalfa, and it gives horses their bulk and nutritional needs without high amounts of sugar." In consultation with scientists from Virginia Tech, the company joined a local farm in nearby Middlebrook, Va., a few years ago in planting some fields of teff, and they're pleased with the results. "Loves it," writes one satisfied customers on the website, speaking of his horse. "Licks it clean in his stall." Says another: "Won't touch anything else."

Even the website Horse Talk has something to say about teff: It's "Hay for Sale" page directs teff aficionados to companies in Illinois and Virginia that sell it as a "high-protein, fine-stem alternative for alfalfa and timothy." The sale pitch gets pretty vivid: "Great hay for all horses. Especially IR and Cushing horses since it is GLUTEN FREE! Very palatable and tender like alfalfa but won't make horses hot like alfalfa sometimes can."

And so the horses' gain is the Ethiopian community's loss.

One way to grow more teff is to sell more seeds. That's what at least two companies now do.

CalWest Seeds of West Salem, Wis., has tested all of the available U.S. strains of teff — some 100 of them — and has now begun to breed proprietary strains of teff seed that it says will produce higher yields and quality. Their seeds produce a "leafy, fine-stemmed hay" of which "animal acceptance and palatability has been reported to be excellent by horse owners," the company's promotional material says.

Target Seed of Parma, Idaho, markets seed for "Tiffany Teff Grass," promising "high forage quality and yield" for this "great interim hay crop between alfalfa stands." The company has published a bold and colorful 54-page brochure promoting teff as forage grass, and a U.S. map in the brochure shows 17 different teff-planting sites in 14 states. Some of this is being done through private enterprise, and some through university-sponsored trials and experiments.

But long before the emergence of these forage teff enterprises, there was The Teff Co. of Caldwell, Idaho. America's largest teff producer, the company has grown the grain for more 25 years, marketing it to the Ethiopian and Eritrean communities in the U.S. as a product called Maskal Teff. The name means "cross," and in Ethiopian Christianity, Maskal is a holiday that celebrates the finding of the true cross on which Jesus was crucified.

The thriving enterprise is the work of Wayne Carlson, who became acquainted with Ethiopian food and culture in the early 1970s, when he lived and worked in Ethiopia as a biologist. That's where he learned about teff, which Ethiopians preferred to use to make their *injera* when they could get it. Back home in Idaho, near the Oregon border, he found the climate and geology of the Snake River Valley area similar to Ethiopia's fertile Rift Valley, a place where Ethiopians grow teff.

"Both are the result of major dynamics in the earth's crust, resulting in massive basaltic lava flows and tectonic movements," Carlson's website explains. "And both are subjected to hot summers with intense sunlight." So Carlson thought: "Why not change the direction of cultural influence? Rather than exporting 'development' practices to Ethiopia, why not take some wisdom from an ancient culture? From there," his website says, "it was a small step to contact Ethiopians living in the American metropolitan areas and re-establish the relation between the Ethiopians and their favorite grain."

He experimented at first with three varieties, and when the Ethiopian population of American began to grow significantly, he saw an investment opportunity. Now, he grows his teff in two varieties, brown and ivory. Teff Co. is privately owned, and Carlson doesn't discuss its finances or his operation. But The Boston Globe reported in 2004 that he grows about two million pounds of teff grain annually, almost four times what the company grew about a decade earlier, and Dun & Bradstreet estimates its annual sales at $1.2 million.

And that's still not enough to meet the demand. In 2002, the University of

Nevada at Reno launched an impressive and expanding cooperative extension project to grow teff.

The project started with just four acres and now plants 1,100 acres, according to Jay Davison, a university agronomist who works with the growers. Eleven farms produced 800,000 pounds of teff in 2008 and a little more than a million pounds in 2009. They sell it to producers, who clean it and then sell it to distributors, who grind it into flour for retail sale. Davison has a target yield of 1,700 pounds per acre, but sometimes the farmers get almost 2,500 pounds per acre.

For several years, Davison says, they sold it all to Carlson, and now they're selling it to distributors who prepare it for retail sale. Some importers from Ethiopia have even approached the Nevadans with an offer to buy as much as four million pounds of grain, which they want to sell to Ethiopians in countries experiencing teff shortages, but Davison says the price they offered wasn't high enough to justify doing it. The Nevada farmers also sell their leftover teff grass to farmers as forage for their horses.

Davison now makes a point of eating at every Ethiopian restaurant he can find when he travels, and in his conversations with restaurateurs, he's discovered a high demand for the increasingly more expensive and hard-to-get grain. He recently planted small fields of 13 different teff varieties supplied to him by a center in Washington state, and he'll soon acquire 15 varieties of teff from an Ethiopian university. These are both pilot projects to produce more seeds, which will enable him to expand his commercial output.

The farmers see teff as a way to diversify, and they hope to install equipment that will allow them to mill the grain into flour, which would cut out a middleman and increase profits. For now, they only have a new seed cleaner, installed in 2009, and they're trying to get more farmers in the area to grow some teff. They sell their product to an Ethiopian-American wholesaler who mills it into flour and sells it to the community. Some Ethiopians in America have told Davison that "teff grain imported from their country tastes and smells different than the variety grown in the U.S." He'd like to test their recollections some day by having them compare *injera* made with American and Ethiopian strains of teff.

Nevada uses about 92 percent of its crop land to produce hay, and Davison says the Nevada farmers wanted to "produce higher income using crops that require less irrigation water than alfalfa. Teff seems to fill that niche nicely." So the success of the Nevada project, and the long-time success of Carlson and a few others, should send a message to entrepreneurs in America and around the world: With the growth in popularity of Ethiopian food, and with Ethiopian immigrants now having become so accustomed to using teff like they did back home, the farmer who grows the grain and mills in into flour has a chance to capture a piece of a growing niche market.

Carlson began his enterprise as a business opportunity, but his love of Ethiopian culture and people infuses his work. "All anybody here has heard of Ethiopia is starving children," Carlson told the Associated Press in 1991. "We assume they ate dirt for thousands of years." In 1988, Carlson and his wife, Elizabeth, his partner in the business, gave 25,000 pounds of teff to a relief agency for distribution in Ethiopia, where the Derg couldn't adequately feed its people.

In the early 1990s, Elizabeth Carlson told the Associated Press, some Ethiopian women in America had not seen teff or cooked with it for 15 years, and "tears came to their eyes" when they smelled it cooking, she said. "Maybe it was a memory from when they were children. It must have struck a deep chord in them."

Although Carlson began his company to sell teff for making *injera*, he has since embraced the emerging possibilities of teff as forage grass. His newer company, Dessie Summer Lovegrass, received a U.S. government Plant Variety Protection certificate in 1996 for "Dessie," a variety of teff whose seeds he sells for people who want to grow teff as forage. It was the first such government certification for a variety of teff, and Carlson will own it exclusively until 2016. Dessie, which means "my joy" in Amharic, is a town in north central Ethiopia, and "lovegrass" is a translation of *Eragrostis,* the scientific name for the teff. His company calls it the "new-old forage crop."

Thanks to Carlson, Smith, and some other innovative farmers, along with the university projects like the ones in Kansas and Nevada, teff has become more available in America from numerous internet companies that buy it in bulk and then package it under their own company brands: Bob's Red Mill and Berry Farms are two such brand names. Most health food stories and neighborhood food co-ops sell these products, and some even offer teff grain in bulk, with a mill in the store that turns your grain into flour suitable for making *injera*.

Ethiopia's Bread of Life

A few years back, I had a student who was raised in Washington, D.C., a city rich with Ethiopian culture. She grew up eating Ethiopian food at the home of a close family friend. One day, she asked her Ethiopian "godmother" if *injera* was difficult to make.

"Not at all," said the older woman. "I get in my car, go to the grocery store, and buy it."

"*What?!*" said the girl, shocked at her godmother's indolence. "You don't make it *yourself?*

"Does your mother bake *her* own bread?" her mentor replied.

Times have certainly changed for Ethiopian women who make the daily meal. In Ethiopia today, most families still make their *injera* at home. But the government has begun to encourage the construction of condominiums, which means that some families now have smaller homes with less cooking space. This has driven more Ethiopians to buy their *injera* at market.

The traditional way of making *injera* in Ethiopia comes with certain requirements. You should never wash the container, called a *bohaka*, in which you mix the batter, for doing so washes away the *irsho* — that is, the remnants of fermentation from the previous batch. This thin yellow liquid is the Ethiopian version of sourdough starter — *irsho* is actually the Amharic word for yeast — and the most serious bakers will collect it to begin new batches and stoke the ones that come from a well-used *bohaka*. The batter must sit for anywhere from one to three days, depending on the temperature, the altitude, the strength of the *irsho* and the age of the *bohaka*.

If the cook hastens the process and the batter doesn't ferment enough, the *injera* is called *aflegna*, which means unleavened. This kind of *injera* is popular in rural areas. If it's made from highly fermented *irsho* and has a very sour flavor, it's called *komtata*, a term derived from the Amharic word for vinegar. Some people prefer their *injera* this way, but just as often it's a mistake, the work of a novice cook, like a newlywed, or just not a very good one.

Centuries ago, the Portuguese explorer Almeida observed the labor-intensive process of making *injera* (or *apas* as he called it).

"Simple as this food seems," he wrote, "it is no small labor to prepare it in Ethiopia, primarily because they have no mills to grind the meal. It is all ground by hand and it is women's work; men, even slaves, would not grind at any price. A woman grinds every day enough for forty or fifty *apas*. These have to be made daily because on the second day they are unfit to eat. Grinding meal for making *apas* calls for many slave women, and plenty of firewood, and is very great drudgery."

Plus ça change: In Ethiopia today, and at Ethiopian restaurants across the country, cooking is still largely women's work, although they're at least respected and honored for their contribution and have modern technology to help them.

The Scottish explorer James Bruce observed the making of *injera* a century or so later, and he described how Ethiopian women mix the flour and water in earthenware jugs to allow it to ferment. The women then pour the batter onto a piece of flat earthenware over an open flame and create an *injera* about two feet in diameter (larger than today's). The "soft spongy" finished product was "of a not disagreeable sourish taste," he wrote.

With mechanical mills to grind the teff, making *injera* today isn't quite as physically challenging. But if you want to make *injera* at home: good luck! It's not easy, and it still requires a large round cooking surface. In Ethiopia, this device is called a *mitad*, and every Ethiopian home has one. For maximum efficiency when making *injera*, you also need a *sefed*, a large, round, flat piece of wicker that slips under the *injera* when it's done baking and makes it easier to remove from the *mitad*.

The households of educated city Ethiopians have modern kitchens and durable *mitads,* or sometimes even electric ones. But the majority of Ethiopians live in rural villages, where they use clay *mitads* that they place over an open flame atop a primitive stove. These *mitads* break easily, and families usually have to replace them four or five times a year at a sometimes prohibitive cost of 40 Ethiopian birr (about $4). A family that can't afford a new *mitad* will borrow a neighbor's until they can.

But an Ethiopian company called Dama Enterprises, dedicated to making home life easier for the country's poor, recently began to market the Mighty Mitad, a simple steel band that wraps around a clay *mitad* and compresses it to prevent it from breaking (see Epilogue). If the government and the company can get it to people everywhere, the company says, it will save Ethiopians $200 million a year and one billion pounds of clay.

Many Ethiopians in America make their *injera* on the electric Silverstone Heritage Grill, sold by Target on its website for about $90. Ethiopian grocery stores around the country also sell them, and the people who use them say they work well as a substitute for the real thing from back home. They're red and very contemporary-looking, and in the hands of a skilled cook, they produce *injera* of the proper texture.

But if you want a more authentic American-made *mitad*, you need to turn to Niat Products Inc. of Seattle, Wash., which sells one that looks very much like the electric ones you find in Ethiopia. The company calls its product a *mogogo*, the Tigrinya word for *mitad*.

It's the brainstorm of Zekarias Tesfagaber, an Eritrean-born inventor who received the patent on his "Electric Cooker" design in 2006 after two years of work to perfect it. He sells his *mogogo* for abut $100 (plus $35 shipping) on a website (see Appendix A). He formed Niat (pronounced "nee-at") in 2000 after receiving a patent on his first invention, the Fernello Single Burner, a device for heating coffee (see Chapter 7). He now markets two coffee-related items and he's working on a third. The company name is a Tigrinya word that refers to something you're proud of, and it can also be a girl's first name.

To create his *mogogo*, Zekarias had to pay close attention to the nature of *injera* and the challenges of getting it just right.

"*Injera* is very sensitive," he says. "It needs very equal heat." So the winding coils under his *mogogo* are evenly spaced around the bottom of the device to insure this. *Injera* also requires just the right amount of steam when you cover the *mogogo* during the short cooking time, and the cover of his invention has a tiny hole on top to release excess steam when the cooker fills up with it.

Because the bottom coils are so well insulated, you can put Zekarias' *mogogo* right on top of the flames on a gas range and heat it that way rather than plugging it in. Some Ethiopians have done this, so Zekarias invented a variation with no coils and no legs, but of the same size and with the same cooking surface. For reasons he can't explain, this version has become popular with Ethiopians in Australia. He speculates that Australians use more gas heat than electric to cook.

Zekarias uses parts from the United States, Mexico and China to manufacture his *mogogo*. But don't picture an assembly line or a factory: He builds each device himself in his workshop, and if he's swamped with orders, he'll hire some assistants, supervising their work and inspecting each *mogogo* before he ships it. His children also help by folding the instruction brochure and inserting it into the box.

Born in Asmara, Zekarias lived in Ethiopia for 12 years before leaving for America just after the fall of the Derg. He lived briefly in Connecticut and South Dakota before settling among Seattle's large Ethiopian-Eritrean community. He has four children, none of them teen-agers yet, and selling his inventions doesn't feed the family: Zekarias works as an aircraft technician for B.F. Goodrich, and he's turning his associate's degree into a bachelor's in aeronautic engineering.

Since put his device on the market, Zekarias has sold around 10,000 units, all by word of mouth among the Ethio-Eritrean community. "The marketing is traditional," he says. "They have to see how it works. If they can see their friend using it, they will have confidence to buy one." But he's had a hard time getting his *mogogo* in stores because market owners are accustomed to selling products on consignment, and he's not willing to do that. "When they deal with me," he says, "they deal like they are back home. But we are in America, and we have to deal like we are here." He hopes to remedy this with some help from professional marketers because, he says, "I cannot reach everybody, I need someone to lead me there."

In 2003, the Energy Research and Training Center of Eritrea perfected a more modern oven for making household staples. The three-part clay structure includes a *mogogo* on the left to make *injera* more efficiently, a stove in the center on which to make sauces, and on the right, a *moqolo*, which offers

Eritreans a more efficient way to make *kicha*, the "Ethiopian pizza" that's called *kita* in Amharic. Traditional *injera* is made on a simple flat clay *mitad* over a flaming hearth. The modern unit still has an open flame at the bottom, but it's all encased in a clay structure that's sturdier than a thin, breakable *mitad*.

By the way, if you ever get the idea of bringing an electric *mitad* back from Ethiopia — don't! Ethiopians in America say its incompatible with U.S. outlets, so your genuine (if modern) Ethiopian *mitad* will be a conversation piece and little else. The dome-shaped straw cover of a traditional *mitad* used in Ethiopia is called, in Amharic, an *akimbalo*, and its insides are smeared with a mixture of teff straw and — cow dung!

Even with an American-made *mitad,* making *injera* isn't easy, and some Ethiopian women in America tell me they've given up trying. But Heather Moore, a North Carolina woman with Ethiopian friends, has mastered the craft of making *injera* in her kitchen. She uses the Heritage Grill, and her website includes step-by-step instructions and even video so you can watch her do it. You'll find it all at http://burakaeyae.blogspot.com/2007/02/step-by-step-injera-instructions-real.html.

Most *injera* sold in America contains a mix of grains: some teff — perhaps 25 to 50 percent — and then some flour of wheat, barley or sorghum. Teff grain has its own natural yeast, so *injera* made with pure teff ferments in the presence of that yeast. Make *injera* with different grains and you get a fermentation process stoked by different yeasts, which any winemaker knows will influence the flavor of the finished product.

At Ethiopian grocery stories in Washington, D.C., you can occasionally buy pure teff *injera*, which is a darker brown than the *injera* made with a mix of flours. It tastes a bit richer, but not too much so. The sourdough flavor of the fermentation tends to even things out. In Ethiopia, teff isn't the only grain used to make *injera*. When teff is too expensive, as it often is, pastoral people will use corn or sorghum. In fact, the largely Moslem Harari culture of eastern Ethiopia sometimes makes *injera* with various millet grains. They call it *bidena*, a variation of *budeena*, the Afaan Oromo name for the bread.

Injera Bakeries: Ancient & Modern

The Washington, D.C., area has lots of companies that make *injera* for the Ethiopian community and its many restaurants. It's a big little business, although some of these "companies" have kitchens no larger than the one in a family home (and in some cases even smaller). They're often literally mom-and-pop or brother-and-sister operations, with sons and daughters helping to cook and deliver the bread to restaurants and markets in the area.

Yagere, Ergoye, Zenebech, Tena, Alew Bilcha, Sergena, Taam Yalew, Woderyelew, Abyssinia, Melkam, Enat: These are the names of the hand-made brands of *injera* you can buy in Washington, Maryland and Virginia, baked in stores or kitchens sprinkled around the city and the region, and trucked daily to the many restaurants, grocery stores, and now even 7-Elevens in Ethiopian neighborhoods, serving a community's hunger for the taste of home.

There are dozens of them, and now they thrive, but back in the late 1980s, when the pioneering Ethiopian inventor and businessman Tedla Desta began to make *injera* in D.C. and distribute it to 7-Elevens, before there were Ethiopian markets, he couldn't sell enough of it for his business to survive. Kassa Maru, who would later become a D.C. *injera* maker, says he remembers hearing about Tedla's innovative American enterprise during his youth in Ethiopia in the 1960s.

These small businesses all create their *injera* the old-fashioned way, one piece at a time. The cook, often the business owner, will mix various flours and water in large bowls or buckets, allow it to ferment two or three days, then swirl ladles of the finished batter onto one *mitad* after another — as many as a dozen working at one time. A few minutes later, each piece is gently lifted from the *mitad* and stacked into piles of eight or 10, then wrapped in plastic bags for retail sale. The kitchens will sometimes have an employee or two, maybe Ethiopians and family members, but often Hispanic immigrants.

Some restaurants sell their *injera* to their city's Ethiopian markets and citizens. Some markets make fresh *injera* in back-room kitchens on rows of American-made *mitads* or a reasonable facsimile and sell it to area restaurants. In cities that can't support any such places, Ethiopians simply have to make due with *injera* baked in their own home kitchens, sometimes smaller in size if they don't have room for a proper *mitad*. Emanu Mogos, who owns the only Ethio-Eritrean restaurant in Cincinnati, will make takeout *injera* for customers with a few days' notice, but she can't make enough to supply markets, including places owned by her son and her nephew.

This scenario repeats itself in Los Angeles, San Francisco, New York, Seattle, Houston, Dallas, Atlanta and any city big enough to make the marketing of *injera* profitable, if just barely. The Boston company Family Injera does business from a small shop with its name typed on a piece of paper and taped to the front door. But it sells its *injera* in such places as South End Food Emporium, an upscale convenience store in Boston that also sells some Ethiopian spices.

If *injera* is difficult to make at home, then at least its easier to send thorough the mail. Around half a dozen Ethiopian entrepreneurs have online companies that allow you to order *injera*, which usually arrives in two days.

The shipping can cost more than the *injera* itself, but even with shipping, it's rarely more than $1 per *injera*, and sometimes less if you buy in quantities.

In you live in the D.C. area, you can even get *injera* made in Ethiopia and imported by EthioGreen, the enterprise of Rahel Beyene and Winny Yirga-Keefe. They call their product Yagerbet Injera — the name means "from the homeland" — and they import it by air from Ethiopia and delivery it to individuals throughout the city and suburbs. These *injera* are bigger than the kind made here — they're about 20 inches in diameter, compared with the common 12-inch pieces made domestically — and because they come from so far away, customers need to refrigerate them to keep them fresh.

EthioGreen gets a shipment of frozen *injera* every Friday. The boxes take 28 to 30 hours to travel by air from Addis Ababa to Rome and then to Dulles Airport, and along the way, they pass through an array of health and customs inspectors, both in Ethiopia and in the U.S. The *injera* is packaged in Ethiopia immediately after it cools, and it comes in sealed packages of three. It's made of pure teff, unlike American *injera*, and it comes in different natural shades of white or gray, depending upon the variety of teff used to make it.

The company imports about 30 to 45 boxes a week, and each box contains nine three-packs. Sales are by pre-order only, and a three-packs sells for $6.25, so a box with 27 *injera* costs about $56.

Rahel and Winny launched their company in early 2008, but by the end of the year, they were almost scuttled by politics. Rumors began to circulate that EthioGreen bought its *injera* from a company owned in part by the wife of Ethiopian President Meles Zenawi, who's reviled by many people of the diaspora. Protesters began a campaign on radio to discredit the company, and they organized a boycott of markets that sold Yagerbet. Soon no market would carry the product, and despite doing some radio interviews to counter the bad publicity, "some people had already made up their minds and didn't want to believe you," Rahel says. "They are few, but the sad part is that this opposition has access to the media, and people don't bother to check their facts. They just listen and react."

So now they sell directly to individuals, building a customer base by word of mouth. "Business is about finding solutions," Rahel says. "If one thing stops you, you are not in business. We had to work with people who knew us. These are people who oppose the opposers."

Rahel and Winny both work full time in information technology: Rahel, the daughter of a police officer in Ethiopia, came here in 1995 and has a master's degree from George Washington University; Winny, the daughter of a merchant, has been here a bit longer and has a degree from the University of Maryland. They have siblings here as well, and they still feel strongly about their homeland, where they realize they were lucky to have grown up comfortably. That's part of the reason they began EthioGreen.

"What Ethiopia is known for in the rest of the world is hunger," says Rahel, who certainly saw poverty during her childhood. "But that's not what Ethiopia is about." It was important to them that they work with an *injera* producer in Ethiopia with good business practices, and their first exporter wasn't too forthcoming about its production. So Rahel says they soon teamed up with Mama Fresh Injera, an Ethiopian company, with some Dutch investors, that treats workers well. The company had to hire a few people to work with EthioGreen, and "that really matters to us because we know we are making an impact," Rahel says.

Ethiopia has experienced teff shortages recently, so the government no longer allows it to be exported. Oddly, though, manufacturers can export *injera* made from Ethiopian teff, presumably because the factory that makes the *injera* puts people to work.

But that's a small industry now, and Rahel says that "people in Ethiopia are hungry not because of the lack of teff but because they lack the money to buy teff. The only way Ethiopians will grow out of poverty is by developing agriculture." She urges the government to do more to get away from ox-and-plow farming and the dependence on nature. "If you always depend on nature," she says, "it won't give you what you want."

Rahel hopes EthioGreen can expand beyond the "ethnic market" and sell *injera* to non-Ethiopians in America as well. She also wants to begin importing more Ethiopian products. "As long as there is anyone to promote Ethiopia, I will work with them," she says. "The government comes and goes, but Ethiopia will go on forever."

The two young entrepreneurs now have competition from the very company that supplies them. Mama Fresh uses a technology developed by a Dutch company to make pancakes, and its Ethiopian factory will eventually have as many as 400 efficient *mitad*-like stoves to do the job. It's a joint project with an Ethiopian businessman, Hailu Tessema Negede, and his Dutch counterpart, Jan Vink, and they make their *injera* at a factory in Sebeta, southwest of Addis Ababa.

The company says it produces 6,000 pieces of *injera* daily for sale in Ethiopia and 3,000 daily for export, and it hopes to increase capacity to 48,000 pieces daily in Ethiopia and 12,000 to sell to the rest of the world. The company operates 24 hours a day and employs people in three shifts, making its *injera* from white teff, red teff, or a mixture of the two.

The Dutch-Ethio company's output is impressive, but its technology is nothing like what you find in Washington's northeast quadrant, where the city's big dog has modernized the process: Zelalem Injera makes its daily bread with the Zelalem Injera Machine, the creation of Dr. Wudneh ("Woody") Admassu, an Ethiopian-born professor of chemical engineering at the University of Idaho.

The machine can turn out 1,000 pieces of *injera* an hour with only two employees stationed at the end of the process to package them, and then a few more to load them onto a truck and ship them out daily, seven days a week. It's an invention built to last: "Zelalem" is the Amharic word for "forever," a name Wudneh chose because *injera* and the food you eat with it sustain you for a lifetime. It's also the name of his first-born son.

Wudneh applied for a patent for his invention in 2002 and officially received it on June 20, 2006. There are now two Zelalem Injera machines at work in the world, and both are operated by members of the same family: the original machine, launched in Dallas in 1998, and run by Elfenesh Maru and her husband, Habte Retta, who also own the neighboring Maru Grocery; and the Washington machine, launched in 2004, and run by Elfenesh's brother, Kassahun ("Kassa") Maru, with the help of their two other siblings, brother Agegeneh ("Aggie") and sister Lemlem, who only more recently came to America.

This family connection goes even deeper: Wudneh and the Marus are "cousin-ish," as Wudneh puts it, another example of how kinship ties came to America with the diaspora. Like Wudneh, Kassa grew up far from the city, in traditional southern Ethiopia, and moved to Addis for high school. When he graduated, he got a job as an accountant with Wudneh's uncle. That's where the two men became friends, and as the communist revolution began to take hold, Kassa urged the younger Wudneh to go to America, which he did. Soon Wudneh invited his friend to join him, and the rest of the Maru family followed in the years and decades after that.

Wudneh got his bachelor's degree in chemical engineering at the University of Oregon and his doctorate at the University of Idaho. He worked for Dow Chemical in California for six years — he holds several patents from his work there — then returned to Idaho to join the faculty of his alma mater. Kassa says that he had "always pushed Woody to build something for Ethiopia." As Wudneh remembers it, his friend often talked about creating a better griddle to make *injera* and gently badgered him with comments about "good-for-nothing engineers." Finally, in 1995, at a soccer match in San Diego, Kassa introduced Wudneh to a man who wanted to talk about financing a machine to make *injera*.

"That's when I knew Kassa was serious about this thing," Wudneh says. "But nobody knew what the machine would look like. We had no idea."

So he set out to invent one, which turned out to be harder than he'd imagined.

"What I didn't know is how delicate *injera* is," he recalls. "You have the bubbly eye, the circular geometry, it's a little bit elastic, it's smooth on the back side, the fluffy texture — you have all of these things. And I said, 'Oh, man, what did I get myself into?'"

He began playing around with ideas for a belt system with a smooth surface, and then with a good heat transfer system. A prototype didn't work, and he consulted a mechanical engineering friend, whose advice solved some problems. He also watched Elfenesh and his wife, Elizabeth, make *injera*, jotting down the proportions of flour and water, something an Ethiopian woman never does when she cooks.

Three years later, after more trial and error, the Zelalem Injera Machine went from the drawing board to the assembly line. They formed a company, Zelfiwu Inc., which owns the patent. Wudneh is its president and chief executive officer. Kassa, Elfenesh, Habte and Elizabeth are the other shareholders.

At Zelalem in Washington, the making of *injera* begins with the mixing of the batter. Kassa uses a blend of many flours: buckwheat, whole wheat, barley, self-rising and, of course, teff. The ingredients are placed in heavy plastic containers the size of industrial garbage cans, where they're blended with a mechanical paddle.

It looks simple, but the paddle was one of Wudneh's first challenges: *Injera* must have "eyes" on top, and these eyes come from balancing carbonation and fermentation. If you agitate the batter, you won't get the balance right. A regular paddle would cause too much of the carbon dioxide to escape, so he developed a paddle that stirred these huge containers of thick batter at just the right angle and with just the right amount of sheer.

"When our mothers and sisters put batters side by side," Wudneh says, "I cannot tell, but they can tell you if it's ready or not. If you don't have the viscosity right, you will not make *injera*. You will make a pancake."

Next, the containers go into a pre-fermentation room for 24 hours and sit at room temperature (which, during the summer in Washington, is often in the 90s). Then they go into a refrigerated fermentation area for six to eight days. This keeps mold away and allows the fermentation to continue more slowly. Kassa has dozens of containers going at once, and the chamber is redolent with the tart aroma of fresh *injera*, the flavor of fermentation already in the air.

During this stretch of the process, Kassa skims the top of each barrel two or three times. The commercial flours he uses have salt and preservatives, and these elements float to the top, along with excess water. He uses two kinds of barrels: the gray, 32-gallon Rubbermaid Brute, and a brick-red oval-shaped container of nearly equal capacity, imported from Greece and used there to ship olives.

Ethiopians don't chill their fermenting batter at home. But in the long run, this part of the Zelalem process is one of several elements that give the company's *injera* a longer shelf life after it's baked.

When a batch of batter is ready, it gets stirred very gently to distribute the carbon dioxide without releasing too much of it. Now it's time to make the *injera*. Each barrel is fitted with a suction hose, which draws the batter up into the first station of the 35-foot-long Zelalem machine. Two side-by-side, computer-operated spouts drip batter onto the heat-resistant wire mesh conveyor belt. The computerized program measures just the right amount of batter for a piece of *injera*.

The next station spreads each dollop of batter out to a circumference of about 12 inches, the size of most American-made *injera*. This was another especially tricky part for Wudneh. It's done with an arm that swiftly swirls above each dollop, blowing a gentle stream of air onto it. A computer program and the speed of the conveyor belt time the process to perfection.

Now that each dollop of batter is the proper size, it goes into the oven. Four silver metal hoods encase the batter, with the temperature inside averaging 500 degrees (the material of the belt can withstand temperatures of up to 800 degrees). Women who make *injera* by hand on a *mitad* must cover each piece during the baking process, but they need to be careful to let moisture escape or else the eyes won't form. Inside the Zelalem machine, a process of flash vaporization cooks the bread, and at the end of the oven, a ventilation hose removes 80 percent of the water from the enclosure.

What exactly goes on inside the oven, apart from the application of heat, is something Wudneh won't reveal about his invention: "It we couldn't come up with that," he says, "it wouldn't work. The technique is to make it fluffy on the top, with eyes on the top. If you have eyes on both sides, it's not *injera*."

After a few minutes in the oven, the baked *injera* emerges from the other end, stuck to the surface on which it was baked. That's where Wudneh's final innovation steps in. In Ethiopia, women often remove the *injera* from a *mitad* first by gently blowing around the edges to loosen it, and then by slipping a large flat piece of wicker between the *injera* and the *mitad*. For health reasons alone, that wouldn't work in an industrial setting. So the Zelalem machine has two swirling mini-spatulas that slip under the edges of each piece of *injera* and gently lift it from the surface.

Finally, a worker at the end of the line picks up each piece of *injera*, piles them all on one another in stacks of seven or 10, then slips them into plastic bags with the Zelalem label. A twist tie seals the deal.

It's all pretty slick, but of course, it didn't come about easily. "It took

Woody a year just to get the eye part right," Kassa says. The D.C. operation turns out about 5,000 pieces of *injera* a day, stoking up the process each night around 9, and wrapping the last 10-pack about 12 hours later. Aggie and Lemlem run the operation all night, and Kassa takes care of business during the day.

The Zelalem machines are so efficient that just three of them could produce up to 72,000 *injera* a day — compared with 60,000 *injera* made by 400 ovens in the Dutch-Ethiopian project.

The company sells two varieties: "yellow label," with 10 pieces to a pack; and "green label," with seven pieces to a pack and more whole grain flour in the recipe. Each product's label includes nutritional information, the only commercially sold *injera* made in the D.C. area that does so (one 12-inch piece has 340 calories). Kassa's first draft of the labels had the name "Zelalem Injera" written in both English and Amharic. But the Food and Drugs Administration told him that if he did that, he had to translate all of the ingredients into Amharic. Some of the words were technical and hard to translate, so rather than bother, he removed the Amharic product name.

Ethiopians in Dallas and then in Washington were reluctant at first to accept *injera* made by machine, and Wudneh recalls the chatter among the community. People claimed the process added chemicals to the batter, which it does not, and that a machine would take jobs away from home *injera* makers. "But if that is the case," Wudneh says, "then technology has to stop, and that's not going to happen." Innovations like his, he notes, will provide jobs for people in the long run.

More than a decade into the enterprise, Zelalem Injera is now available at markets all around the Dallas and D.C. areas, and Kassa says it sells as well as the hand-made product. The company even offers its products nationwide through its website, shipping the *injera* from both Dallas and D.C. (see Appendix A).

The partners of Zelfiwu Inc. would like to build more Zelalem machines, but Wudneh says that will have to wait. He gets e-mails from Germany, Italy, England and Ethiopia, all from people who want him to build one. But he's still paying off the initial investment of the company's two machines, and he's seen too many people invest in Ethiopian enterprises, only to lose their investment because of the government's bureaucracy.

Still, he knows it will happen eventually. Making *injera* one piece at a time — or even in a factory with 400 individual wood-burning ovens — isn't very efficient. Ethiopia was once nearly 50 percent forest; now it's just 3 percent. And while technology in Ethiopia is improving, ovens still omit pollutants from burning wood and dung. He applauds the attempt to do *something*, but he says: "When you talk about trying to help 80 million people,

I don't think that's going to help." With a machine like his, mass producing *injera*, the price will come down, "and then you can supply everybody." And he notes: "There are lots of improvements to be made in our system. It's not the perfect system. That's what I want to do, but I've run out of money."

Kassa, the instigator who got it all started, would like the company to expand to Los Angeles, San Francisco and Seattle, all places with large Ethiopian populations. In fact, he dreams of returning some day to Seattle, where he lived for 11 years after his arrival in the U.S. in 1974. He escaped Ethiopia just weeks before the Derg seized control of the government and executed the emperor. Since then, he's lived in Dallas and now Washington. Aggie and Lemlem came here from Ethiopia six years ago to join the family business.

If he does return to the Pacific northwest, then maybe Seattle will get a Zelalem Injera factory. The city certainly has a community large enough to support one. But until the franchise spreads, most of America's Ethiopian community will continue to eat *injera* made the old-fashioned way, by pouring the batter onto a hot *mitad* and swirling it around to the proper size, one piece at a time.

Ethiopia & Coffee

On Nov. 11, 1974, the paleontologist Donald Johanson made a discovery that led to the re-imagination of human origins.

On a dig in the Danakil, a lowland region of Ethiopia formed millions of years ago by the Red Sea, which extended far into what's now the African continent, Johanson unearthed portions of a fossilized skeleton that appeared to be something between a human and an ape. A tape of the Beatles song "Lucy in the Sky with Diamonds" was playing, so the team named her Lucy.

The discovery of Lucy further affirmed Ethiopia's role in history, and today this remarkable specimen remains the most complete fossil of an early human ancestor. Scientists date Lucy at about 3.5 million years old. Other teams have found older fossilized bones. But no find from so long ago in our evolutionary past is more complete.

To call Lucy the ancestor of all humanity is an intriguing flight of fancy. But we do know one thing for certain about Ethiopia's seemingly infinite past: This is the land responsible for waking people up in the morning and keeping them up all night.

Ethiopia introduced the world to coffee.

Where It Began, How It Spread

Legend attributes the discovery of the palatable stimulant to Kaldi, a goat herder from Kaffa, circa 850 A.D., who noticed one day that his goats became frisky — dancing on their hind legs — when they ate the little red berries on a shrub in his field. Excited by his find, the goat herder took some of the beans to the local monks, who roasted them in a fire, crushed them into a powder,

115

and put them in water to create a new beverage, which gave them the energy to stay up all night in prayer.

The truth, alas, is far less fanciful. Some scholars believe that the coffee plant grows native only in Ethiopia, where the Oromo people may have been the first to use the bean. The Oromo ground the beans into a powder and then mixed it with animal fat to eat while traveling and to give them energy for the hunt or for battle. Other tribes also began to use the beans to make porridge or wine.

Historians speculate that coffee spread from Ethiopia to Yemen on the Arabian peninsula when slaves, taken across the Red Sea from Africa, were found to be eating the berries of the plant. These slaves entered through the Arabian port of Mocha, which may have given coffee one of its numerous sobriquets.

But nobody truly knows who discovered the coffee "bean" or who first turned it into something to drink. All we know is that it happened in the Ethiopian highlands — we don't know exactly when — and from there it spread to the world.

For millennia in Ethiopia, coffee grew wild in forests and was cultivated only for domestic use. The commercial coffee trade began in the 19th Century around the city of Jimma with the establishment of plantations, and as Addis Ababa, the country's new capital, grew in size and prestige, so did Ethiopia's place in the world coffee market.

The world has recognized the quality and value of Ethiopian coffee for centuries.

In 1902, as Ethiopia was expanding its trade with the modern world, the British Board of Trade's journal said coffee from Harar, Ethiopia's eastern province, was "greatly esteemed by connoisseurs for its aroma and strength." Grown in a temperate climate, on small plantations, the journal said, "the care with which the natives look over their plantations has a great influence on the quality of the coffee."

A 1918 report by the U.S. Commerce Department spends several pages discussing Ethiopian coffee, especially the coffee from Harar.

Those highly desired berries are "unusually long and well-shaped, and make such excellent coffee that the world market receives a great deal of Harari under the name of 'longberry Mocha.'" The report notes that coffee grows all over Ethiopia wherever the elevation is between 4,500 and 6,000 feet. This is true of Harar, as well as in the coffee-rich forests of the more western Jimma, Kaffa and Guma provinces.

But the world's discovery of the value of Ethiopian coffee has led to some injustices by Ethiopians against Ethiopians. When the international market for Ethiopian coffee began to grow in the 1950s, some small pastoral coffee-producing cultures had their land seized by the larger, more powerful cultures — with the approval of the Ethiopian government. This happened to the Majangir, who lost some of their land to more organized and powerful cultures like the Amharas and the Oromos.

The 1918 Commerce Department document reaffirms that the coffee bean is Ethiopia's gift to the world. But the quality of Ethiopian coffee, says the report, owes to outside influences.

When the Arabs exported coffee from Ethiopia and cultivated it on the Arabian peninsula, the soil and climate of the plant's new home produced seeds that improved the original stock. In the 15th Century, Arab Moslems briefly conquered and occupied portions of Ethiopia — especially the eastern portions, including Harar, which is still heavily Moslem today. The invaders brought some of this improved Ethiopian coffee back to its place of origin.

"Thus we have two kinds of [Ethiopian]-grown coffee," the report says, "the indigenous plant in southern and western [Ethiopia] and the cultivated Harar plant, which originated from the same indigenous stock, but which is very much superior, owing, presumably, to cultivation and to its having come into the eastern part of the country via Arabia."

In other words, Ethiopia didn't introduce this most excellent Ethiopian coffee to its eastern Harari region. Arabia did.

Antony Wild disputes this in his 2007 book *Coffee: A Dark History*.

Citing genetic findings, he writes, "As it is clear that the Harar type evolved from the Kaffa type, this would imply that there had been a migration of the plant to Harar before the plant went on to be cultivated in Yemen." He also claims that "until the mid-sixteenth century, the [world] demand for coffee was met by Ethiopia entirely," thus disputing assertions that coffee first came to be traded worldwide from the Arabian peninsula rather than from Ethiopia.

Some coffee drinkers today are almost cultist about their indulgence, and on the world financial market, specialty coffees are traded as commodities. This is bad news for Ethiopian coffee growers, who naturally get the short end of commodities market profiteering, which sometimes pays less for the coffee than it costs to grow and harvest.

But despite its history and reputation, Wild says, Ethiopia's legendary coffee is now considered to be mainstream by the specialty market, lacking flavor and pedigree, which means even lower prices for Ethiopian coffee producers.

Wild also posits an interesting theory of the relationship between Ethiopian coffee and — well, humanity as we know it.

Evoking the discovery of Lucy, he writes, "Genetic research suggests that all modern humans are directly descended from a group of about a hundred and fifty *Homo sapiens sapiens* who lived in the Ethiopian Highlands some 120,000 years ago." This is the common human ancestor that scientists call our "mitochondrial Eve." Wild then notes studies of "the so-called brain explosion that took place about 500,000 years ago," which led to an increase in man's brain size by 30 percent.

Putting this all together, mixing science with Western religious mythology, Wild reflects on whether these pre-historic wild coffee trees played a role in developing human intelligence: "Coffee has always been associated with speed of cognition and expression, and the sudden dawn of self-awareness in the Genesis story concerning the forbidden fruit of the 'Tree of Knowledge' is something that could have been prompted by a psychoactive substance such as caffeine. The previously docile brains of *Homo sapiens sapiens* would have been ill prepared for such an assault."

Even more intriguing is the "missing" Old Testament book of Enoch, which the 18th Century Scottish explorer James Bruce rediscovered in Ethiopia. The description of the Tree of Knowledge in that book, Wild writes, "could easily suggest a coffee tree, with its depiction of delicious fragrance and clusters of fruit."

So in Wild's fanciful and ironic re-imagining, you could say that coffee precipitated the Fall, which led to the pain of childbirth — and to modern medicine's admonition that a pregnant woman should not drink coffee. Both literally and figuratively, Ethiopia may well be the birthplace of everything, and Ethiopian coffee may be one of the seeds from which it all grew.

Black Gold

The name "coffee" may come from the Kaffa region of Ethiopia where it grows heartily. Or it may come from "qahweh," the word adopted by Arabic when Middle Eastern cultures exported Ethiopian coffee and introduced it to a wider community.

But that Arabic word might well derive from Kaffa, or perhaps from the Arabic phrase "*qahwat al-būnn*," meaning "wine of the bean." The Amharic word for coffee is *buna*, which sounds suspiciously like the Arabic word for "bean." Just as Arabia might have improved the stock of some Ethiopian coffee beans, so might the Arabs have given the Ethiopians their word for coffee.

Coffee today is Ethiopia's most valuable export, and the government sometimes keeps prices high in the country itself. Ethiopians consume about 45 percent of the coffee they grow, and the harvest accounts for 60 percent of the country's total export earnings, according to a study by American University. Only 2 percent of Ethiopia's coffee comes from state-owned farms, the study found. The rest comes from small parcels of land owned by peasant farmers, and they get very little for their effort, especially compared to the price of coffee worldwide.

Because of this, the Ethiopian Coffee Trademark and Licensing Initiative formed in 2004 to address the low prices paid to Ethiopians who harvest and sell coffee. In its mission statement, the group says it wants to "increase the prosperity and hope for all actors through the trading chain, from bean to cup, from the small scale coffee farmer through to the discerning coffee-lover."

The group has since negotiated trademark agreements to sell licensed coffee in nearly three dozen countries. It's a way of branding Ethiopian coffee in the hope that the brand name will increase the visibility and the value of the product, which will mean higher revenues for coffee growers. Countries that sign the agreement "acknowledge Ethiopia's ownership of the names Yirgacheffe, Harar, and Sidamo" — the three most prominent types of Ethiopian coffee — "and set the basis for joint marketing promotions and overall brand enhancement of the targeted Ethiopian coffees with the participating coffee companies."

The United States and the European Union are signatories, and it's a good thing: More Ethiopian coffee goes to Germany than to any other country, with Japan and Italy next on the import list. There are many types of Ethiopian coffee, each one slightly different in taste, at least to the connoisseur, and each one named for the region of Ethiopia in which it grows.

In 2007, after a public relations war, the Ethiopian government and the American coffee giant Starbucks reached an agreement that defines how the company can promote Ethiopian coffees. More than a dozen other American companies that sell coffee have also signed the accord, which is all about protecting the honor and name recognition of Ethiopia's Harar, Sidamo and Yirgacheffe coffees.

To further enhance their earnings, Ethiopian coffee growers have recently unified to create a network of fair trade coffee, which guarantees them a price that will allow growers to earn a living wage based upon their country's standard of living.

One such project is the Oromia Farmers Cooperative Union — Oromia is a region of Ethiopia where coffee grows in abundance — formed in 2004 by Tadesse Meskela, an agriculturalist who spent some time on a fellowship in Japan in 1994 and learned about unions. A decade later, after traveling around his country to educate people and organize them, he formed the coffee union, which was the subject of the 2007 film *Black Gold*, a documentary about his efforts to secure better prices for Ethiopian coffee and better wages for the people who grow and harvest it.

Dean Cycon's book *Javatrekkers: Dispatches from the World of Fair Trade Coffee* includes a lively chapter on Tadesse and on Ethiopian coffee in general.

His compassionate writing gives a vivid account of the struggles of Ethiopian coffee farmers to earn a subsistence living. Tadesse's efforts have helped, and so has the trademark agreement that grew from it.

Cycon also discusses the importance of potable water to the coffee trade. Connoisseurs pay less for beans that have been sun-dried after harvest rather than being wet-processed, which allows the beans to ferment. But in arid Ethiopian coffee regions like Jimma and Harar, water is scarce, and the growers often have no choice but to sun dry their beans when they can't get to a coffee washing station.

Black Gold, by the British siblings Marc and Nick Francis, shows what Cycon's book tells. Tadesse is central to the story, and the images of Ethiopia's lush isolated southwestern coffee-growing region are striking. So is the success of Tadesse's fledgling effort, which has already allowed some towns in coffee regions to build new elementary schools and medical clinics.

Tadesse even has something to say about exactly who gave coffee to the world, and his assertion opens an old Ethiopian wound.

Why was there no mention of coffee among the gifts that Makeda, the Queen of Sheba, gave to Solomon? Because Makeda was from the northern region of Ethiopia, and coffee was first discovered in the south by the Oromo people, who long ago lost their struggle to command the nation's political currents.

Tadesse, an Oromo, is adamant about this. "We fried the beans in butter and put them in our cheeks to stay alert for long treks with our cattle," he says. "Oromo people used coffee centuries before the Ethiopian or Abyssinian nation was created. We could go all day on these *bunakala* [coffee roasted in butter] without food and water. We used the leaves for tea and put the grounds on cuts."

He's talking about rituals that date back millennia, before the Oromo people — and the rest of the world — learned to brew coffee into a drink, and his cultural distinctions attest to ancient tribal conflicts. He makes a convincing argument.

But whoever discovered coffee, one way or another, you can be sure it came from somewhere in the land we now call "Ethiopia," where modern people are so proud of their contribution that they've built a part of their culture around it. Coffee is the last remaining undisputed Ethiopian emperor, especially in Tadesse's Oromia, where every day begins with a coffee ceremony, and where giant decorative Ethiopian-style coffee pots greet people who enter some of the towns in the nation's proud coffee-growing communities.

The Ethiopian Coffee Ceremony

In Ethiopia, you don't just drink a heaping mug of coffee that someone sloshes at you after a meal. There's a ceremony that surrounds its preparation and consumption, and if you do it by the book, it can take a while.

It may be a long, elaborate ceremony for special occasions, or it may be an abbreviated version among family and friends after dinner. But if they can help it, Ethiopians back home don't just grab their coffee on the run and drink it from a paper cup. For them, it's more than simply a custom: It's a matter of community.

The basic ceremony itself is pretty straightforward, and it includes all of the steps in the process of making coffee that you don't see when you simply order a cup at a restaurant. Of course, because it's ceremonial, it takes a bit more time: up to three hours, which includes the all-important socializing that enlivens the celebration. Restaurants that do it naturally compress the process and just give their patrons a taste of what it's all about.

The tools of the ceremony are commonplace: coffee beans, a flat pan (like a brazier) to roast the beans over a flame, a coffee pot, and cups from which to drink the finished product. Add a little incense and you have a ceremony. In Ethiopia, it's always a woman who performs it, and she often wears a *shamma,* a traditional long white dress with decorative colored edges. You'll sometimes see servers in Ethiopian restaurant working in one.

The ceremony begins with the washing of the beans. Then, they're roasted on a pan over an open flame. The woman conducting the ceremony stirs and shakes them frequently to keep them from burning and to make sure they roast evenly. As the beans get hot, they'll sometimes make a popping sound. Soon their outer husks fall away, and they begin to smoke. The woman waves her hands over the smoking beans to circulate the aroma, and the air becomes redolent with coffee and thick with white smoke. This is the step a server will often share with customers at a restaurant, bringing the pan to the table from the kitchen to add a touch of cultural authenticity.

When the beans are thoroughly roasted, they're ground to a powder with a *mukecha* (a heavy wooden bowl) and a *zenezena* (a stick used to crush the beans). This is the Ethiopian mortar and pestle. Some restaurants use the American version of the tools, but most will use a modern coffee grinder. Even Ethiopians in their homes today will make this concession. The result is the same, if slightly less ancient and authentic.

Finally, the woman places the roasted beans into a *jebena,* an Ethiopian clay coffee pot, usually black or rusty brown, with a wide round bottom that leads up to a spout and a handle. When using a *jebena,* you'll need a small wicker mat, called a *mattot,* on which to set it. Ethiopian grocery stores usually sell the two items together (there's no sense in buying one without the other).

Once filled with coffee and water, the *jebena* sits over an open flame until the coffee is hot. It's then served in a very small cup called a *sini* (or *finjal* in Tigrinya), and sometimes handed to the guest on a *makrebia*, a long wooden stick with a small round platform at the end where the *sini* rests.

While all of this happens, the people at the ceremony socialize and munch on snacks, like *injera*, *kolo* or "popcorn" made from sorghum, a lighter treat than the American variety (and the thin husk from the kernels doesn't get stuck between your teeth). When it's time to serve the beverage, the most theatrical of coffee makers will begin with the spout of the *jebena* a few inches above the cup and raise it high as the coffee continues to pour.

As with most rituals, it's considered polite to compliment the skill of the presenter and the taste of the finished product. In fact, truly passionate Ethiopian coffee drinkers will have three cups, each with a name: *abol*, *hulategna* (the Amharic word for "second"), and the very important third round, *bereka*, whose drinkers are "blessed" (the word's meaning in Amharic). The server brews each pot separately, with some of the freshly ground coffee reserved when making the *abol* round for use in making the *hulategna* and *bereka* pots. You can get away with drinking only one, but you never stop at two: If you take the *hulategna*, it's bad luck not to stay for the *bereka*.

And why three cups? Just as it's customary to offer *gursha* three times, the three cups of coffee could be a reference to the Trinity. Or they could just be a way to make the experience last.

In Ethiopia, the coffee ceremony quenches two thirsts: One for the stimulating beverage, and one for the even more important sense of community that accompanies each round. Ethiopians today tend to drink their coffee with sugar, a habit that became more culturally engrained during the Italian occupation of the late 1930s. But the traditional flavorings are spices, salt or even butter, a choice that the intrepid Andrew Zimmern found to be thoroughly unpalatable on an episode of his *Bizarre Foods* TV show.

In the more tribal communities of Ethiopia, coffee remains central to cultural and family life. In his 2006 study of coffee among the pastoral Daasanetch people of southwestern Ethiopia, Toru Sagawa found an adherence to ritual and a social structure related to coffee that stood out among the normally patriarchal culture of Ethiopian tribal people.

"The handling of coffee is under the wife's discretion," Sagawa writes, "and only she can brew and allocate it. This space has a political importance such as to entertain guests, to bless the society with peace and affluence, and to conduct many *rites de passage*." And the wife is more than just a laborer in this social space: She is "an active participant in the process of rituals and discussions."

The Daasanetch buy their coffee from northern merchants who bring it to their towns. They buy husks, not beans, and use some husks for multiple brews — sometimes as many as 11 servings per husk. They often even give used husks to friends and neighbors if the husks can still produce potent coffee. Only wives have the right to ask for a neighbor's husks or to give husks to a neighbor, Sagawa found. Whether or not she does it depends upon the situation: It would be inconsiderate *not* to give husks to a neighbor who has no husks to make coffee to entertain a guest.

Most Daasanetch drink their coffee without added flavoring. But when they do add something, it could be ginger, onions, salt, sugar or milk.

"When the Daasanetch feel sick," Sagawa writes, "they first attribute it to 'not having coffee' that day. In addition, if a person has a headache, others will spray coffee onto his/her head, and if a person has a chill, warm coffee is poured over him/herself to feel better. When a mother washes her baby's body, she spouts coffee from her mouth onto the baby's body wishing his/her health. Coffee is quite indispensable in the life of the Daasanetch."

This is the *ne plus ultra* of Ethiopian coffee "ritual," practiced among the cultures for whom ritual is life.

Few Ethiopians in America practice these old rituals, instead preparing their coffee on any available burner. But for a slightly more authentic modern experience, you might want to try the Fernello Single Burner and its related products.

Zekarias Tesfagaber, an Eritrean-American, now living in Seattle, began to market his sleek device in 2000 through his company Niat Products. A few years later, he added a *mogogo* for making *injera* (see Chapter 6). "Fernello" is the Italian word for "furnace," a nod to Eritrean's Italian colonial days, and Zekarias sells his product for $95 plus shipping through his website (see Appendix A).

He got the idea to design the Fernello one evening while attending a coffee ceremony at the home of some friends. They roasted their coffee the old-fashioned way, over charcoals, and Zekarias recalls, "I got a headache for three or four days." So he set out to create a way for Ethiopians and Eritreans to heat coffee evenly and effectively without burning down the house (traditional ceremonies inside a home tend to set off fire alarms, he says).

The Fernello has a wide silver base that's hard to knock over, a tapered middle section that's not as wide as the base, and a single coil burner that rests on top of the base and that you can remove simply by lifting it out. The base never heats, so you can leave it on forever, and the wires that heat the coil are grounded and thoroughly insulated.

The Fernello even has an alternative use. The coils are small, but they're still big enough to place a skillet on top to make a fiery *wot*. This comes in especially handy for cooks who want to spare their kitchens the heat and smoke of cooking: Just take the Fernello onto an outdoor patio or apartment balcony and you have Ethio-Eritrean *al fresco* cooking at its most contemporary.

And don't forget the *accoutrements*. Zekarias sells a *menkeshkesh*, the device for roasting raw coffee beans. It's a metal cup on a long handle, shiny and modern but still very much like the devices used in Ethiopia. (*Menkeshkesh* is the Tigrinya word for what Amharic call a *biret mitad*.) Now Zekarias is creating a *rokobet*, a rectangular table, with drawers and a cabinet, for serving coffee at a ceremony. He brought a prototype to Festival Eritrea in Washington, D.C., during the summer of 2009, but right now he's stymied by the delicate and bulky design of the item, which makes it almost as expensive to ship as it is to make.

Inventing is just a sideline right now for Zekarias, who works full time at B.F. Goodrich in Seattle. He hopes that will change some time. "I have quite a lot of ideas," he says, "and they're not only for Habesha people."

In urban homes and restaurants, across America and even in Ethiopia, the coffee ceremony is somewhat abbreviated — when people practice it at all.

Iasu Gorfu left Ethiopia in 1974 and has lived in Los Angeles since 1981, with some time spent in London in between. A widower, and the father of three grown children, when he has coffee at home, he says, "I just put it in the microwave."

But he fondly recalls the role that coffee played in the Ethiopian home life of his youth, even among people who lived busy professional city lives.

"More than likely," Iasu says, "they would never make coffee and drink it alone, rarely ever. People live in communities and neighborhoods, and you get together with your neighbors to sit down and chat. It's a whole ceremony."

This potable feast would take place every day in a different neighbor's home, where the hostess would roast the beans for all to see and wave them around to circulate the aroma. During the ceremony, Iasu says, everyone sits down together when it's time to pour, and "the children are supposed to be quiet."

This only happened in people's homes. At the office, professionals drank their coffee when they had time to fix a quick cup. That's true of Iasu's life today — he's an engineer for the Defense Department and works on Boeing projects — although he does look forward to visiting friends and family, where coffee becomes ceremonial once again and reminds him of home.

When Dawit Kidane came to Ethiopia in 1975, he was 15 years old, the adopted son of an American family who knew his parents in Ethiopia. His mother, father and four siblings live here now, but for a long, long time, he had no community — and no coffee ceremony.

He's not a big coffee drinker anyway, but the coffee itself isn't really the point. It's the community, and he missed it. Now it's back in his life: He owns an Ethiopian restaurant in Iowa City, Iowa, where he roasts three kinds of Ethiopian coffee and serves it to his customer. He also sometimes gets together for the whole day at the home of some Ethiopian friends in Cedar Rapids, and they do the full ceremony — three hours worth of coffee, conversation and snacks.

But in America, where life is busy and old customs tend to drift away, that sort of devotion is rare.

Almaz Dama, a partner in the family-owned Dama bakery, grocery and restaurant in Arlington, Va., enjoys coffee as much as any Ethiopian, and at home after dinner, she and her family usually serve it up in American fashion. If guests come over, they'll do a ceremony and munch some snacks. Only when "the grandmas" visit from Ethiopia will Almaz turn the evening cup of coffee into a full ceremony, a tradition that the elders expect and still cherish.

Araya Yibrehu has lived in America since the 1970s, owning Ethiopian restaurants and making *t'ej*. But he, too, remembers the role of coffee in his life back home.

The coffee ceremony brought families together, especially people retired from their jobs, or people who didn't have a job. These families would conduct a ceremony every day in a different home, and it bonded them in community. They would drink coffee and talk the day away, snacking on *shiro*, *kolo*, lentils and *injera*.

"They'd get together just for the coffee ceremony," Araya recalls. "This made families very close to each other. Of course," he adds, about Ethiopian life in America, "it's different here."

T'ej: The Ancient Honey Wine

Nobody can document for certain when Ethiopians, Aksumites or pre-Aksumites began to make *t'ej*. We know that gesho, the species of buckthorn that provokes the fermentation process, is native to Ethiopia, and that excavations at Aksum have found remnants of gesho and writing that mentions honey wine in the third millennium A.D. This confirms that *t'ej* is at least nearly 2,000 years old.

Accounts from as early as the 16th Century, when European exploration of Ethiopia began in earnest, copiously document the presence of this special honey wine. These historic chronicles offer many sweet tidbits about *t'ej*: its production and consumption, and its place in Ethiopian society. Once a drink of emperors and kings, it's now enjoyed by anyone who can afford the honey and gesho to make it. Some cultures in Ethiopia even use *t'ej* as a sort of sacramental wine in their religious practices, with the task of making it falling on a young man in the community.

Eva Crane, in her 1999 book *The World History of Beekeeping and Honey Hunting*, tells us that the Greek historian Strabo (63 B.C. — 24 A.D.) wrote about Troglodytes living in ancient Ethiopia. "Most of the people drink a brew of buckthorn," he reported, "but the tyrants drink a mixture of honey and water, the honey being pressed out of some kind of flower."

Strabo doesn't specifically say that these Ethiopians fermented this drink. But he mentions buckthorn, and that's gesho, so fermentation may have taken place. This appears to be the earliest reference to Ethiopians fermenting honey and water with gesho. To a Greek of Strabo's time, "Ethiopian" could have meant any of the black-skinned cultures of Africa. But remember: Only the *real* Ethiopians cultivated gesho.

"In many areas [of Africa], particularly in the east," Crane writes, "honey was fermented in water for a longer period, with the root of some other part of a specific plant which had been found to increase fermentation and thus give a higher alcohol content. One of the most famous of these drinks was *t'ej* or *t'edj* in Ethiopia; Christianity had arrived there in the 300s, and alcohol was not prohibited."

Some 16th Century European chroniclers write that Ethiopians added saddo wood, or *Rhamnus tsaddo*, to cause fermentation. Gesho is *Rhamnus prinoides*, clearly kin to the fermenting plant observed by the Europeans. It's full name, **Rhamnus prinoides (L'Herit)**, comes from Greek and means "tuft of branches resembling evergreen oak" (*prinos*). The name also honors Charles Louis L'Héritier de Brutelle (1746-1800), the French botanist who studied and named it.

Gesho is the ingredient that turns honey and water into *t'ej*. Without gesho, you have a beverage that Ethiopians call *birz*, a mixture of honey and water that's allowed to ferment on its own, very slightly, for a few days. *Birz* doesn't have the spicy pungency of *t'ej*, and it certainly doesn't have the alcohol content.

The gesho is a woody plant with leaves on its branches, and Ethiopians use both parts of the plant in making *t'ej*. The wood or stick of the gesho, when used for *t'ej*, is called gesho *inchet*, and the leaves are called gesho *kitel*. The leaves are also ground into a fine powder called gesho *duket* (or *duqet*).

Pieces of *inchet* can be as thin as a strand of linguini or as thick as your thumb. The dried crumbled leaves of *kitel* look like oregano, and *duket* looks like olive-green flour.

Each type of gesho produces a different color and flavor of *t'ej*. Most Ethiopians today prefer gesho *inchet*. *T'ej* made from *inchet* is pale yellow and tastes at once spicy and sweet, depending upon how long it ferments and how much gesho you use. *T'ej* made from *kitel* is amber and usually has more of a pungent flavor. You shouldn't use *duket* for *t'ej*: It's made for producing *talla*, the Ethiopian beer.

In their historic accounts of *t'ej*, many European chroniclers observed that Ethiopians used gesho leaf in making their *t'ej* and that royalty favored this sharper-tasting variety. The Europeans generally seemed to prefer the sweeter *t'ej* made with gesho *inchet*. Percy Powell-Cotton, a *fin-de-siècle* British big game hunter, dined with Emperor Menelik II, who treated him to some rare 12-year-old *t'ej*, "a sweet dark-colored liquid, looking and tasting like syrupy port." His dinner with the worldly *negus* featured a French claret. The mature *t'ej* came after dinner — along with Épernay champagne.

In 1924, Major J.I. Eadie, D.S.O. - that is, Distinguished Service Order, a British military designation - published *An Amharic Reader*, a book filled with essays, poems and documents that explored the life and culture of Ethiopia. His book is considered to be the first chrestomathy of the Amharic language and of Ethiopian culture, and he collected the material in 1913, when he was stationed in Ethiopia.

Everything in the book appears in both Amharic and English — it was translated in India, with a preface written by "the Ministry of Defence in Baghdad" — and on pages 88 and 89, Eadie presents a preparation for *t'ej* — or as the book writes it, Taj. It's a recipe for hard-core, old-fashioned *t'ej*, made by crushing up the whole honeycomb — sometimes with a few stray bees still in it — and mixing it with the water.

The English translation calls for six or seven parts of water to one part of honey. "The next day," says the recipe, "all the impurities and wax float on the top. The maker having taken out the impurities and having slightly heated some gesho, it goes into the *birz* whilst hot, and ferments all night. If it be in the highlands it is ready in eight or nine days, and if in the plains in four or five days." The different fermentation periods have to do with the diverse climate of Ethiopia: In the cool highlands, *t'ej* requires extra time to ferment, but in the torrid plains, it happens more quickly.

This passage, by an unidentified author, claims that the finished *t'ej* "will remain good for 20 years," although from time to time, you must stir some fresh honey into it. "This mixing again with honey is not just only once," the instruction say. "It must be done when needed, when the Taj is becoming sour."

Finally, the book offers one more helpful household hint. "The impurities being purified they give wax," it says. "What is left over from the wax also is called 'Fagulo' and is used for rubbing on *mitads*." This *fagulo* is dregs from the honeycomb, separated from the *t'ej* at the end of the fermentation process, then strained in a cloth and rubbed on the surface of your *mitad* to clean it. There are other types of *fagulo*: Some Ethiopians use the seeds from plants like flax (*telba*) or collard greens (*gomen*), roasted and ground into a fine powder, and then rubbed over the surface of the *mitad*.

T'ej isn't the only fermented beverage that Ethiopians drink. *Talla* is a beer-like drink made from grains, different ones for different cultures and regions, but barley is a common starter, along with maize, wheat or even teff. It also requires powdered gesho leaf. In Afaan Oromo, it's called *farsoo*. *Merisa* (made with gesho) or *keribo* (made without gesho) are Oromo variations of the brew. *Shamita* is the Gurage *talla*, seasoned with linseed, cardamom, coriander and bishop's weed, and *borde* is another fermented grain drink. Both *shamita* and *borde* — sometimes used as a meal replacement by the country's poorest people — are made without gesho and tend to have short fermentation periods.

But among them all, *t'ej* is the mainstay and the legend, and thankfully, it's easy to create in your kitchen.

Ask any two Ethiopians how to make *t'ej* and you'll get three or four different methods. Nini Gezachew, who formerly owned Nini's Market in Falls Church, Va., prefers to make her *t'ej* using gesho leaf. She doesn't stir the liquid during the several weeks of fermentation, and she places the lid on the jar loosely to allow the mixture to breathe. Nini taught me how to make *t'ej* one afternoon in her shop. She telephoned her mother at home in Falls Church, asked for instructions, and translated them for me as her mother spoke.

Martha Agedew Vasser, an Ethiopian-born woman living in Pittsburgh, prefers gesho stick and seals the lid tightly. Then, every two or three days, Martha opens the jar and gives it all a swirl. ("It likes to be stirred," she told me.) Martha gets her gesho from back home when she visits, or she has relatives bring her some when they come to America.

Azeb Girmay, a shopper at Sheger Market in Takoma Park, Md., rinses her gesho in cold water to remove the dust, then she boils it for a while in a cup or two or honey water before putting into back into the big jar to ferment for a month. Nini and Martha don't boil their gesho stick.

Bekele Bahiru, a professor on the science faculty at Addis Ababa University, has studied the microbial properties of *t'ej*, analyzing 200 batches of the elixir made at different times and in different places. His findings confirm what every home *t'ej*-maker knows from experience.

"As *t'ej* fermentation is a spontaneous process that depends on microflora naturally present on the substrates and equipment," Bekele wrote, "the different metabolic products of the randomized microflora at different stages, the physical and chemical environment, duration of fermentation and concoction practices would result in physico-chemical variations in the final product."

In other words: No two batches of *t'ej* are exactly alike.

Bekele also points out that the type and quality of honey used in making *t'ej* affects its taste, as do a host of secret ingredients unique to the maker.

"Some *t'ej* makers add different concoctions such as barks or roots of some plants or herbal ingredients to improve flavor or potency," he wrote. "Producers usually are not willing to tell about additives used and their compositions."

Truth is, sealing or not sealing a fermenting batch of *t'ej* doesn't make much of a difference. Stirring seems to help encourage fermentation after you've removed the gesho. Using gesho *inchet* or gesho *kitel* matters a lot, and so does the length of time you keep the gesho in the liquid and allow it to ferment. Which of these methods makes a better *t'ej*? Try it yourself a few different ways and see which one you like best.

What's In a Name?

The history and origin of the word "*t'ej*" — as with so many words in so many languages — is probably as clear as it will ever get.

It's the word, in Amharic, that Ethiopians have long called wine made from honey. Linguists have traced the word back a few thousand years to a hypothetical root word, *d'agay*, in the old Ethio-Semitic languages that later evolved into Amharic. In Tigrinya, a Semitic language dominant in northern Ethiopia and Eritrea, honey wine is called *mes*. This was also the word for honey wine in Ge'ez, the first language to evolve from ancient Ethio-Semitic, but now used today only in the liturgy of the Ethiopian Christian church.

In Oromo, honey wine is called *daad'ii*. Oromo culture reveres the drink, which comes in three strengths: the lightest, *hamtu*, means "bad" or "feminine"; *boru*, meaning "thick" or "heavy," is a medium variety; and *bekumu*, possibly a form of the word that means "intelligence" or "ingenuity," is the strongest and most prized.

Ethiopia is the home of as many as 90 languages, some of them now used by just a few hundred remaining speakers, and many of them have their own words for honey wine. In Hadiyya honey wine is *dik'aasa*, and in Majang it's *ogool*. Mursi speakers call it *gimma*, and the Shekkacho call it *bito*. Variations of *'ees* or *essa* appear throughout the large Omotic family of languages in southern Ethiopia. Perhaps the oddest incarnation is the Tsamai word *xoronko*. In Birale, a nearly extinct language, it's the similar *koronko*.

And many Ethiopian languages simply borrow *t'ej* and give it their own spin: *c'ajj, s'ajji, tajjita, t'ajay, t'ayye, dag'a*. The preparations and fermenting agents may different slightly from culture to culture, but it's all honey mixed with water and fermented into wine.

So important is *t'ej* to Ethiopian culture that as much as 80 percent of the country's honey — which could be a profitable export crop — goes to the making of the beverage.

The apostrophe often seen in the word *t'ej* represents what linguists call an explosive. This mean you spit or snap the consonant very slightly when you say it. Listen closely to an Ethiopian pronouncing "*t'ej*" and you may hear it — or you may not. Because of this, you'll usually see it written as *tej*, without the apostrophe. There's no standard, and the difference really only means that you need to enter both spellings into a search engine if you want to read about *t'ej* on the internet.

Making T'ej

It's virtually impossible to ruin a batch of *t'ej* once you have the basic ingredients. By "ruin," I mean that the *t'ej* doesn't ferment, and you're left with a soggy clump of *inchet* or *kitel* in a roué of honey and water. Nothing but gesho will do, and it's not a product that you'll find at your local Piggly Wiggly. But in this age of online shopping, good gesho is just a few clicks away.

Here are the basic instructions for making *t'ej* using gesho *inchet*:

♦ In a clear glass jar, mix three parts water to one part honey and stir rigorously until the honey goes into solution. Use liquid measures for the honey, even though it's sold in solid measures. I recommend making larger batches, if only because, after waiting for more than a month until it's ready, you don't want it to be gone all at one meal. A one-gallon jar works well.

♦ Add a quantity of gesho *inchet* and stir it into the liquid. How much gesho? Well, that depends on what sort of flavor you hope to achieve. Those devilish details follow.

♦ Put a lid on it, but don't tightly seal the lid, and let the gesho soak in the liquid for two weeks. At the end of the first week, stir the mixture for 20 seconds or so. At the end of the second week, stir it again, then remove the gesho, stir once more, and let the liquid ferment for three more weeks, stirring at the end of the third and fourth weeks.

♦ At the end of the fifth week, strain the liquid through cheesecloth, bottle it, chill it, and serve with Ethiopian food.

If you use gesho leaf, you'll need to strain the gesho out of the liquid after two weeks. Do this using cheesecloth, double thick, and change it as needed during the straining process. *T'ej* made with gesho leaf will be darker in color and more pungent in flavor. ("This one is an acquired taste," said a friend after I served him a glass made with stick and then a glass made with leaf.) It will also have more sediment in the bottle as it chills.

Because of all this, gesho stick is the novice's best choice. You don't have to strain it after two weeks: Just use a pair of tongs to pluck out the pieces of stick. At the end of five weeks, you finally strain it, but you won't get a lot of stuff in your cheese cloth: The stick doesn't crumble or dissolve in solution the way the leaf does.

Or at the end of six weeks. Or seven weeks. Or eight or nine weeks or three months or more. You can let it go as long as you like — the longer, the stronger. It tends to get clearer the longer it ferments, and the flavor slowly inches toward that of liquor as more of the sugar from the honey converts to alcohol.

To get your *t'ej* looking its best, you might consider investing a little extra effort in the straining process.

Because you can't get all of the yeast out of it, homebrew *t'ej* continues to ferment in the bottle, and you may hear the hiss of pressure being released when you open it. Once the *t'ej* begins to chill, most of the residual yeast will settle and form a brownish silt, which is harmless, if a bit unappetizing to the neophyte. With the yeast still in solution, your *t'ej* will look much more opaque; without it, the *t'ej* becomes a glistening transparent yellow.

So you may, if you like, add one step to the straining process. To get rid of the silt, put your strained and finished *t'ej* into the refrigerator for 24 to 48 hours, then gently pour this clearer golden chilled *t'ej* into another bottle, leaving the yeast sediment behind. Another way to do this: When you strain the still-warm *t'ej*, strain it into a pitcher, let the yeast settle, then pour the *t'ej* from the pitcher into your wine bottle. It's a little extra work, but it makes your *t'ej* look much more like a white wine.

The price of gesho stick in Ethiopian grocery stores varies from as low as $8 a pound to as high as $17 a pound. On the internet, you can get good gesho *inchet* for a reasonable $10 a pound plus postage. Gesho leaf is always more expensive per pound, but you use much less of it in each batch (see Appendix A).

Kafeynesh Tadesse, one of my *t'ej* teachers, had lived in America for just one year when we spoke, and she raised 10 children in Ethiopia before coming to America, where two were in college. She kept telling me that the gesho stick in Washington's Ethiopian markets is too small, so she preferred to have gesho sent to her directly from Ethiopia.

"Big," she told me, holding her outstretched hands almost as far apart as she could.

This baffled me. Gesho is gesho, I had found: At several Washington area markets, I bought some excellent gesho stick — thick and slightly pungent-sweet to the smell. It produced delicious *t'ej*. Some gesho stick it thinner, but those pieces are just the smaller branches of the plant. Even if Kafeynesh preferred the thicker pieces of gesho stick, you could still get them easily around the area.

Finally, after a few more tries, I understood. She was talking about value.

Even gesho at $8 a pound was *very* expensive compared to what she paid for it when she got some directly from Ethiopia. The "big" of her outstretched arms referred to quantity: For $10 in America, you get this much — she held her hands close together — but for the same amount of money, you get "big" from Ethiopia, she said with outstretched hands.

How much gesho to use is a matter of judgment and experience. In general, though, count on using about one-third of a pound of gesho stick for about 96 ounces of liquid — that is, three cups of liquid honey and nine cups of water, all mixed in a one-gallon jar. Some places sell thick pieces of stick, and some sell thinner ones. I recommend the thick stuff, but it's all good.

If you use gesho leaf, you'll need about four level tablespoons full for 96 ounces of the honey water mixture. Most gesho leaf will look like oregano with little chips of wood in it. For the finest and most concentrated gesho leaf, which looks like a green powder, two heaping tablespoons is sufficient.

Once it's mixed, you can use Nini's method or Martha's method — that is, put the lid on loosely and forget it until the appointed times, or seal it and stir it every two or three days. I split the difference: I place the lid on loosely and stir it once a week.

Two or three days after mixing the ingredients, microbes will begin to form. The microbes on gesho stick tends to grow like fine fuzzy white strands rising up from the top of the mixture. With gesho leaf, it's a bit more mold-like in appearance.

This won't look too appetizing, but don't worry: These are good microbes, a sign of the beginning of the fermentation process — that is, of the sugar in the honey being converted to alcohol in the presence of naturally occurring yeast. Bekele found that the primary yeast in *t'ej* is *Saccharomyces ellipsoideus*, although many different kinds of these little buggers will turn your honey and water into wine. Just remember that the mold of penicillin — which, like yeast, is a fungus — looks like this, too, so you can think of your fermenting *t'ej* as medicine.

Eventually, you'll begin to see tiny bubbles rising from the yeast that will collect at the bottom of the jar, and sometimes they look like they're forming little hot springs on the surface of your liquid. That's more fermentation. After you remove the gesho, these bubbles will confirm that the fermentation process is ongoing. And be sure to stir the gesho into the liquid just before removing it. You don't want to remove all of those good microbes when you pluck out the stick with your tongs or strain the leaf through cloth.

There's one thing that can go wrong, and it's called *Brettanomyces bruxellensis*. It's a naturally occurring yeast that threatens to give any wine a taste best described as resembling kerosene or lighter fluid. Some winemakers believe that a slight "Bretty" taste adds character to a wine. Others say it ruins the wine no matter how faint the effect.

In homemade *t'ej*, *Brettanomyces* can grow if your vessel isn't cleaned well from a previous batch, or if the yeast happens to be on your gesho. You can kill the *Brettanomyces*, a weak yeast, by adding a bit of commercial yeast, which is much heartier. Rinsing the gesho *inchet* before immersing it into the liquid might help to wash away the *Brett* if it's on your gesho.

You'll know your *t'ej* has gone Bretty if it smells like kerosene or lighter fluid after the first or second week, and if you see brown scum and large opaque bubbles forming on the top of the jar among the tiny white fermentation bubbles that you want to see. Drinking Bretty *t'ej* won't harm you, but the flavor of *Brettanomyces* will compete with — and possibly overpower — the sweetness of the honey and the pungency of the gesho. Your taste buds will have to decide how much you can handle.

All in all, it's best not to worry about your *t'ej* turning Bretty because there's really not too much you can do to stop it. Remember that this is science at its most ancient and raw. You may just have to accept the fact that *Brett* happens.

If you like your *t'ej* specially flavored, you can add a small quantity of any *one* of these ingredients for the last three or four days before bottling it: banana, coffee, ginger, orange peel, lemon peel or even jalapeño peppers. A server at Queen of Sheba restaurant in Washington, D.C., told me that jalapeño is her favorite add-in.

An eight-ounce glass of *t'ej*, mixed in these proportions and fermented for four or five weeks, will have about 250 calories, or perhaps a little less, depending upon the strength of the wine. The alcohol content should be around 8 to 12 percent. If you let your *t'ej* ferment longer, more of the sugar in the honey converts to alcohol, so the calorie count goes down and the alcohol content goes up.

This is the basic recipe, taught to me by several Ethiopians. But there are variations, and each Ethiopian attests to her or his way of doing it.

For example, you can boil some of the honey water with the gesho. Using this method, you mix the honey and water and let it begin to ferment on its own for three days. On the third day, remove a cup or two, put it into a pot, add the gesho, and boil it for about 10 minutes. Then, return all of this back to the rest of the honey water. Remove the gesho at the end of two weeks from the day you first mixed the honey and water, and let it ferment for two more weeks after that. Ethiopians who use this method say it cuts some of the bitterness of the final product.

To stoke the fermentation of your next batch, you might want to save a glass of unchilled *t'ej* from the batch you just completed. Then, mix your honey and water for the new batch, and blend in this "finished" *t'ej* before adding the gesho. The reserve glass will contain rich active yeast, and this helps the fermentation process begin more quickly in the new batch.

The ultimate fermentation starter is the lees left behind in the just-finished batch: Lees are the sediment in the bottom of the container, flush with active yeast. Mix your new batch of honey and water in the jar with the old lees, then add a cup of your freshly made *t'ej* (not yet chilled), and follow any of the methods above. This should get your fermentation started more quickly. You don't want to use the same lees over and over and over because yeast can get old. Start with a fresh batch of *t'ej* after using leftover lees three or four times in succession. And you certainly don't want to use lees from a batch that went Bretty.

So enjoy your *t'ej*-making adventure, and don't be intimidated by Seleda, an online Ethiopian 'zine. In its April 2004 issue's list of "The Top 10 Signs You Are Ready To Go Back to Ethiopia," No. 9 was, "Your 857th attempt to brew *t'ej* in your studio apartment just failed." If that ever happened to an Ethiopian, he probably wouldn't even be welcome back home.

Drinking T'ej

In ancient times, Ethiopians drank their *t'ej* from leather containers or from vessels made from the horns of animals. Ethiopians today usually drink *t'ej* from a glass, often in a *t'ej bet* — literally, "*t'ej* house," a bar that specializes in *t'ej*, always made by the proprietress of the place.

But beginning in the 18th Century, visitors to Ethiopia began to write about a special container used to drink *t'ej*.

This container, still used today, is called a *berele*. It resembles a Florence flask, with a wide round bottom, and a narrow neck with a small opening on top. It's easy to grip, rests nicely in the palm of an open hand, and holds more *t'ej* than a mere wine glass.

It also serves a practical purpose in Ethiopia.

"At first sight the use of the *brilla* [sic] seems rather strange," writes Edward Randolph Emerson in his 1908 book, *Beverages Past and Present*. "But when it is looked into more closely, it is seen these people have solved quite a difficult problem, and the practice shows a degree of niceness that one would hardly expect to find in a people of their character and environment.

"If there is any other country that has more flies in it than Abyssinia," he explains, "the traveler will do well to stay away from it. No matter in what part of the land you may visit, there will be flies so thick it is almost impossible to eat without getting them in the food, and *t'ej*, being made from honey, is sweet and of course more than usually attractive to these pests."

T'ej served in a wide-mouthed glass would soon be swimming with live insects. But with a *berele*, notes Emerson, "all this annoyance and trouble is obviated. The *brilla* is held in the hand with the thumb over its mouth, and conversation proceeds with only a momentary interruption now and then, caused by raising the bottle to the lips."

Many other European visitors of the 19th Century commented on the sanitary convenience of the *berele*, although some of them enjoyed *t'ej* more than others.

When modern towns and cities began to emerge in Ethiopia, so did the *t'ej bet*, a place where people drank — and gambled. From *qomar*, the Amharic word that means to gamble, came the *qomaret*, which refers to a person — almost always a woman — who makes *t'ej* or owns a *t'ej bet*. The word is now seen as being somewhat insulting or derogatory because of this origin.

Ethiopians will sit for hours in a *t'ej bet*, drinking and engaging in conversation, which of course grows more convivial as the day or night goes on. If there's music, someone will eventually dance with a *berele* full of *t'ej* on his head. Needless to say, he won't spill a drop. When *t'ej* is especially strong, Ethiopians will say it has "*betam teru moq'ta*," which means that it gives you a "very good buzz." (The word "*moq'ta*" literally means "heat.")

And the *t'ej bet* isn't the only places to drink: You can go to an *areki bet*, where you drink *areki,* the strong Ethiopian ouzo, or to a *talla bet* for Ethiopian beer, or to a more general *matat bet*, or "drinks house," where they serve all kinds of drinks.

You can guzzle your *t'ej* if you prefer, or you can sip it like a fine wine. Just remember to start out slowly: When your *t'ej* arrives at your table, it's customary to roll a bit of the first swallow around on your tongue for a few seconds to appreciate its full flavor.

And don't forget to make an Ethiopian toast: Raise a glass to your drinking companions and tell them *letenachin* — "to our health."

After that, it's *bereles* up.

Buying Bottled T'ej

If making *t'ej* sounds like too much trouble, you can always buy *t'ej* from one of the American wineries that bottles it for commercial sale. It won't have the sweet pungency of homebrew: It will taste more like a medium dry white wine with (in the best cases) a hint of spice from gesho. But it still makes a fine complement to your Ethiopian meal.

Winery *t'ej* is a relatively new phenomenon, an element of Ethiopian cuisine that came late in its development in the United States. It's no wonder: Starting a winery and marketing your wine is much more challenging than opening a market or a restaurant. Wines require a knowledge of the science of viticulture, and they take patience and experimentation to get right. An opaque homebrew may please the regulars at an Ethiopian *t'ej bet*, but in an American restaurant, patrons like to be able to see through their white wine.

A number of new brands of American-made *t'ej* have popped up in the last few years, the work of Ethiopian-American entrepreneurs looking to spread a little culture. Most use gesho stick to flavor their *t'ej*, along with yeast to stoke the fermentation. Some of these Americans brands of *t'ej* have won prizes in wine festivals, usually under the category of "mead." Araya Yibrehu, a long-time *t'ej* maker, objects to this, and he's urged the competitions to create a separate category for *t'ej*. So far, no competition has done it.

Their names are sometimes cultural and sometimes personal. Herb Houston got his recipe for Enat Tej from his Ethiopian mother-in-law, and *enat* is the Amharic word for "mother." Yamatt Tej blends the names Yared and Matias, the two sons of the wine's creator. The word also means "mother-in-law's," and as the company's owner explains it on his website, "I would say this is a win-win: The kids are happy, and the wife's side of the family is happy, too."

Then there are the names that simply tap Ethiopian cultural touchstones: Addis Tej, named for the nation's capital; Sheba Tej and Saba Tej, each named for the legendary queen; Meskerem Tej, named for the first month of the Ethiopian calendar, and also after the New York restaurant for which it was created; and Nibit Honey Wine, whose name is the Amharic word for a female bee ("nib" is a male bee).

Wineries in Ethiopia have made *t'ej* as far back as the 1940s, although such *t'ej* always was and still is rare: Most Ethiopians simply prefer to make their own at home or drink it at any of the local *t'ej bet* that liberally litter the landscape. This *t'ej* is usually unfiltered, which in Amharic is called *defres*, meaning muddy or unclear, or *lega*, meaning young. The "mud" is just the residual yeast — harmless and virtually tasteless. The Ethiopian wineries that make *t'ej* prepare it *tetara*, or filtered (literally, clear), so it looks like a white or amber table wine.

Wilhelmine Stordiau, who grew up in Ethiopia in the 1950s and '60s, heard stories of some traditional cultures fermenting their *t'ej* for months by burying it underground in clay pots, producing a very potent potable. She never got to taste this brew herself. Stordiau now makes and markets Begena Tedj and lives in Frankfurt, Germany, a center of Ethiopian life and culture in Europe.

One of the earliest brands of commercial *t'ej*, Agew Medir, appeared in Ethiopia in the 1940s. The word *medir* means "earth," and the term *agew medir* refers generally to the most exceptional *t'ej*, so calling your brand Agew Medir implies that it's the best you can buy. The Agew (or Agaw) are a tribe in Ethiopia's northern Tigrinya-speaking region, the birthplace of *t'ej*, and also the source of the finest honey in Ethiopia.

Then, in the 1960s, there was Saba Tej, a commercial brand produced by Mesfin Selashe and served for a while on Ethiopian Airlines. Mesfin, a famous

Ethiopian *ras* (regional leader or governor), was one of his country's richest men, very close to the emperor, and he was executed in 1974, soon after the Derg took over. His son Daniel Mesfin would later write *Exotic Ethiopian Cooking*, an excellent cookbook and guide to the cuisine.

At least two brands of commercial *t'ej* exist today in Ethiopia: Nigest ("Queen") Honey Wine, made by the state-owned Awash Winery; and Tizeta ("Memory") Tej, produced by an Ethiopian man who lived in Canada and returned home to begin his winemaking enterprise.

Finding Tizeta and Nigest in the U.S. is next to impossible, although in Washington, D.C., it's there if you know where to look. Kebede "Teddy" Tadesse, a Baltimore businessman who owns the import company Global Ocean and Air, distributes a variety of Ethiopian wines and beers to restaurants and grocery stores in the Washington metropolitan area. For a while he had dozens of cases of Nigest available for anyone who wanted to buy them. Unfortunately, that wasn't too many restaurants. Teddy says the taste of Nigest is too sharp for most American palates, and Ethiopians very often prefer to drink American beers like Becks and Guinness.

"The recipe should be the same for all *t'ej*," Araya explains. "Otherwise it is not *t'ej* at all. The basic formula in making *t'ej* is three parts of water and one of part of pure honey and less than a pound of clean gesho. Making it at home you can use the same formula. The only difference from one winery to another is essentially quality control, and using the right ingredients."

Years ago, Araya created Sheba Tej, one of the first in the U.S., and he now makes Axum Tej and Saba Tej. He also was a co-owner of Sheba, New York City's first Ethiopian restaurant, which opened in 1979.

He's not a big fan of adding flavorings, like ginger or banana, as some home vintners do. "A whole lot of other flavoring stuff is used to show one is better than the other," he says. "I do not like it, because you can not have consistency in the taste. I like to make it as simple as possible, water, honey, gesho, some good yeast, and heavy filtration." These last two details, of course, are for winemakers, not old-fashioned home brewers.

If you can't find a *t'ej* in a wine shop where you live, many of these wineries will ship their product to you, as long as your state liquor laws allow you to buy wine from out of state. They're all reasonably priced for a bottle of specialty wine, but shipping can double the price.

Here's where you can get your *t'ej* fix:

♦ **Axum Tej**, made by Heritage Winery of Rutherford, N.J. (888.835.2986). This *t'ej* adds a touch of Ethiopian honey to the mix along with its American firewood honey.

♦ **Agazen Tej,** made by Laddsburg Mountain Winery of New Albany, Pa. (570.363.2476). Along with its *t'ej*, this homespun winery makes other meads and sells them in 375 milliliter bottles as specialty wines. The name is the Amharic word for the animal we know as the mountain nyala, a native Ethiopian species that's kin to the kudu more than it is to the nyala.

♦ **Enat Tej,** made by Enat Winery of Oakland, Calif. (510.632.6629). *Enat* is the Ethiopian word for "mother," and this company bases its *t'ej* on a recipe provided by the Ethiopian mother-in-law of the company's owner. The winery makes two varieties: traditional and orange.

♦ **Addis Tej** and **Nibit Honey Wine,** both made by Elsa Winery, Orange, Calif. (714.639.6323). The company makes two varieties of Addis Tej: mild and sweet.

♦ **The Queen's Honey Wine,** made by Nigisti Abraha, an Ethiopian-born woman who lives in Denver. Her name, Nigisti, means "queen" in Amharic. She takes orders online at her website (303.929.7106).

♦ **Seifu's Tej,** made by Lakewood Vineyards, Watkins Glen, N.Y. (607.535.9252). Lakewood created this *t'ej* for Seifu Lessanework, the founder of Blue Nile Ethiopian Restaurant in Ann Arbor, Mich. The winery now sells it to other Ethiopian restaurants and wine shops.

♦ **Sheba Tej,** made by Brotherhood Winery, Washingtonville, N.Y. (845.496.3661). Brotherhood is considered to be the oldest operating winery in the U.S.

♦ **Meskerem Tej** and **Regal Tej,** made by Easley Winery, Indianapolis, Ind. (317.636.4516). The former is named for Meskerem Ethiopian Restaurant in New York City. Some relatives of the New York owners also have a branch of the restaurant in Charlotte, N.C., where one of the owners told me that a relative of hers makes this *t'ej* at Easley.

♦ **Yemar Tej,** made by Berrywine Plantations, Mt. Airy, Md. (301.831.5889). This winery makes two varieties: amber medium sweet and pale dry.

♦ **Yamatt Tej**, made by Rabbit's Foot Meadery of Sunnyvale, Calif. (408.747.0770). The name means "mother-in-law's tej."

♦ **Docho Tej,** made by a winery in Burtonsville, Md. It comes in two varieties: regular and coffee flavored (called *yebuna t'ej*). It's available at a few markets in the Washington, D.C., area, and the company can be contacted at: yebunateg@gmail.com. The name *docho* is an Oromo word that has come into use in Amharic. It means "short and husky," which describes the round-bottom *berele* from which *t'ej* is consumed in Ethiopia. The wine's label depicts a *berele*.

♦ **Begena Tedj.** This is one of at least two commercial brands of *t'ej* made in Europe. It's the creation of Wilhelmine Stordiau, who lives in Frankfurt and was born and raised in Ethiopia. She markets it all around the continent. A Swedish company also makes a honey wine that it calls, quite simply, Tej.

Each of these wineries makes a good sturdy *t'ej*, sparkling clear and thoroughly filtered.

But really, why go through all the trouble of tracking them down — only the most specialized wine shops in big cities sell *t'ej* — when you can easily order some gesho and make your own *t'ej* at home? It's an ancient treat worth taking the time to master.

Ethiopians in America:
Who Lives Where?

In the first few decades after World War II, Ethiopians came to America for the same reasons that so many other people did: to get an education, to take that education back to their homeland, and sometimes, in rare instances for Ethiopians, to live in America and seek opportunity here.

But then, in 1974, the Derg deposed the 700-year-old Ethiopian monarchy and began a policy of intolerance, censorship and persecution that became known as the Red Terror. Seventeen years later, in a 1991 survey conducted in Washington, D.C., fully 95 percent of Ethiopian living in America cited the Derg as their reason for leaving.

Before the Derg, Ethiopians studying in America — where their government had long sent some of the nation's highest-achieving young people — gladly returned home with their college educations and their knowledge of Western culture. By the mid-1970s, many of these students chose to stay here rather than return to troubled Ethiopia, settling in larger American cities, where other Ethiopians, few as they were at the time, already lived.

By the early '80s, a mass migration had begun as Ethiopians fled the increasingly merciless Derg. These emigrants — doctors, lawyers, teachers and laborers — sometimes lived first in refugee camps in the Sudan before finding nations that would accept them. From 1951 to 1960, government records show, the United States granted asylum to 61 Ethiopians. From 1981 to 1990, the number was 18,542.

The U.S. government settled its share of the refugees in Los Angeles, Atlanta, Chicago and Washington, D.C.. These cities today — along with Seattle and a few other big urban areas — host the largest Ethiopian populations in America. Some of them already had a growing Ethiopian population, especially the Los Angeles and bay areas, where Ethiopians had gone to college since the 1950s and occasionally stayed.

After the fall of the Derg, Ethiopians continued to emigrate to get a college education, to seek a better life, or to join family members. Ethiopia's current elected leaders aren't as oppressive as the Derg, but they don't permit all of the freedoms that we do here, and there's some press censorship, as well as ongoing conflicts with minority cultures and their resistance or liberation movements.

Some of the earlier waves of Ethiopian immigrants divided themselves into sub-communities by their level of education or their ancestral cultures. These distinctions have naturally begun to dissolve as the immigrants become Americans and their children are born and raised here. Ethiopians and Eritreans in America now own businesses side by side and even together, despite the ongoing border wars between their countries.

The U.S. State Department establishes the number of immigrants who may legally come to the country each year and distributes these slots among many countries. Ethiopia is granted immigration rights for about 5,000 families a year, and the slots are awarded in Ethiopia in accordance with the Unites States' Diversity Visa lottery.

Some of these immigrants are college-educated and seek to establish themselves here in their professions. But the many who don't have college degrees at least have family and friends here, and with those connections, they find jobs in community businesses. And of course, some Ethiopians in America are visitors who just never go home after coming to spend time with family members who have residency status.

Unfortunately for Ethiopia, the country has lost a third of its doctors to immigration, the majority of them now working in the U.S., where half of the Ethiopian professionals who come here to study remain here when they earn their degrees.

This all means that the stories Ethiopians in America tell about their lives here and back home represent only a portion of the wider Ethiopian experience.

In his 2007 book, *The History of Ethiopian Immigrants and Refugees in America: 1900-2000*, Solomon Addis Getahun presents the most important study yet of Ethiopian immigration to the United States, exploring where people settled and the communities they formed in their new homes. The San Francisco bay area has an especially large concentration of Eritreans. Seattle has an abundance of Ethiopians from the city of Gondar. Ethiopians in Minneapolis consider their city to be the "Oromo Capital in America." Columbus, Ohio, also has a concentration of Oromos and a good number of Eritreans.

Male immigrants have always outnumbered female immigrants by about two to one, but most early restaurant owners were women, simply because the men didn't know how to cook. Even today, many Ethiopian women own restaurants and grocery stores in disproportion to the male-female ratio within the community.

So how many people born in Ethiopia now live in the United States? That's hard to say, and trying to get precise data from government documents is a bit like herding Abyssinian cats.

The 2000 census reported 69,530 Ethiopian immigrants in the U.S., the nation's second largest African immigrant population, after Nigerians. Two years later, Ethiopia's ambassador to the United States at the time, Kasahun Ayele, told the BBC that more than half a million Ethiopians lived here. And in 2004, the California-based magazine Tadias, published in English for Ethiopians in America, claimed a population of 750,000, a number that may include the American-born children of Ethiopians, although even if it does, the number still sounds much too high.

Then there's Peter Hagos Gebre's *Making It in America,* a series of profiles of successful Ethio-American entrepreneurs. His book offers some population estimates: 100,000 Ethiopians in the D.C. area, 30,000 in Los Angeles, 25,000 each in the San Francisco bay area and Seattle, and 15,000 in Atlanta. He bases these estimates on embassy information and on his own discussions with people in the various communities. Meanwhile, the website of Los Angeles' Little Ethiopia asserts that "the Ethiopian population in LA county is unofficially estimated at over 60,000."

From 1930 to 1969, the United States granted permanent residency to 1,114 Ethiopians, according to the Office of Immigration Statistics. The numbers jump considerably in the next three decades: 2,588 in the 1970s, 12,927 in the 1980s, and 40,097 in the 1990s. From 2000-2008, 32,664 Ethiopians were granted citizenship, and 71,140 won permanent residency.

Meanwhile, from 1990 to 1998, 14,023 Ethiopian refugees arrived in America. That's one fifth of the entire population of 69,530 reported by the Census Bureau in 2000. And the Bureau of Immigration and Naturalization claims that from 1994 to 1998 alone, 47,528 Ethiopians immigrated to the Washington, D.C., metro area. That's more than half of the Census Bureau's 2000 figure for all Ethiopians in America.

The disparities between anecdotal estimates and census data arise from the number of people who return voluntary census forms and their fear of identifying themselves to the government. The disparities between government agencies is harder to explain. This troubles the census bureau, which sends its representatives, some of them Ethiopian-Americans who speak Amharic, to Ethiopian community events to explain the process and quell fears of returning census forms.

So while census numbers clearly aren't accurate, at least they allow a comparison from place to place and decade to decade based on a consistent data set.

The most helpful comparison arises when we combine the figures for the District of Columbia and its adjacent Maryland and Virginia suburbs. Here's what you find in the 2000 census, the latest for which complete hard data is available. These numbers count people born in Ethiopia, not their American-born children (a separate tally, as noted), and certainly not their relatives hiding under the bed when the Census taker came to call:

Area	Ethiopian Population
D.C. and suburbs	**19,353**
District of Columbia	2,158
Maryland	7,806
Virginia	9,389
California	15,867
Texas	6,433
Minnesota	5,413
Georgia	5,203
Washington (state)	4,414
New York (state)	3,309
Massachusetts	2,033
Ohio	1,988
Colorado	1,986
Illinois	1,798
Ohio	1,644
Pennsylvania	1,257
North Carolina	759
Michigan	722
Wisconsin	266
Iowa	170
Total Ethiopians in the U.S.	**69,530**
People with Ethiopian Ancestry	**86,918**
GRAND TOTAL	**156,449**

All of these numbers are ridiculously low, especially for the most populous states. But if we assume they're all proportionally wrong, they support long-standing colloquial wisdom: The District of Columbia and its Maryland

and Virginia suburbs — Takoma Park, Silver Spring, Arlington, Alexandria and several more — are the Ethiopian heartland of the diaspora in America, creating the largest community of Ethiopians outside of their homeland. Many of the Ethiopians who own restaurants and grocery stories in Maryland and Virginia say they moved there to live and work away from the crowded D.C. business cluster.

In California, the metro areas of Los Angeles and San Francisco each have substantial Ethiopian communities, as do Atlanta, Dallas, Houston and Seattle. These cities have plenty of Ethiopian restaurants and some grocery stores, although many of the Ethiopians who live there have college degrees, own businesses (often that serve their community) and work in a variety of professions.

Surprisingly, New York City's census found barely 2,500 Ethiopians. The numbers trickle down: This city of seven million people (plus tourists) doesn't have an Ethiopian grocery store. Chicago, with a city population of half that, has one grocery store and for a while had two, although the Census Bureau identifies fewer than 2,000 Ethiopians in the city (more reason to doubt the official figures). Seattle, with a fraction of New York City's population, has a whopping 18 restaurants (give or take a few in a volatile business).

Then there are all the others, who settled in smaller communities or less traditional cities, either for business opportunities or because they attended college there and stayed after graduating. They have little community in their new home towns, but if they're lucky, they have an Ethiopian restaurant where they can congregate.

Pittsburgh has a small, educated Ethiopian population and two restaurants (one owned by an Ethiopian businessman, one by an African-American attorney). The first one opened in 2004, the other four years later. Cleveland, a city larger than Pittsburgh, has just one restaurant, down from two a few years ago. Charlotte, N.C., has an Eritrean restaurant and a branch of Meskerem, a New York City restaurant that spread south when a family member moved to North Carolina.

Outside of the New York City boroughs of Manhattan and Brooklyn, you'll only find two other Ethiopian restaurant in the state, one in Rochester and one in Mount Kisco. Madison, Wis., once had two restaurants but now has just one. Nearby Milwaukee has two, as does Ann Arbor, Mich. Iowa City, a hip college town, has one restaurant, but it serves American dishes to complement its full "Eritrean and Ethiopian" menu. Its name, David's Place, hardly promotes its cuisine (the owner's name is Dawit, the Ethiopian form of David).

In big cities, Ethiopian restaurants tend to multiply as the Ethiopian population does. In smaller ones, they're an exotic respite for diners tired of the more typical "American" restaurant cuisine — like Italian, Mexican, Asian or Middle Eastern. And to those isolated Ethiopians who live in cities with little or no community, the restaurants provide comfort food on a night out, although that's becoming less essential with each generation.

Older Ethiopians in America tend to prefer Ethiopian food exclusively. Their sons and daughters enjoy Ethiopian food but don't insist upon it. They grew up minorities in their schools, and naturally, they wanted to blend in, eating pizza, fast food, and other ethnic cuisines with their friends. They may even request non-Ethiopian food at home, and their parents realize that these new Americans will probably have little, if any, Ethiopian food in their own homes some day.

This is a common immigrant pattern, with an exception: Russian and German and Polish and Chinese and Middle Eastern cuisine have all become a part of the American table, whereas Ethiopian cuisine has not. You can buy frozen pierogies and Hunan chicken, or kielbasa or toaster strudel or blintzes or baba ganoush or hummus at your local supermarket. Sure, they're all foreign inventions. But who really thinks of them as being exotic any more?

Not so with Ethiopian food. You don't find it in American kitchens, and in another few generations, you may not even find it in homes of Ethiopian ancestry.

The First Supper

Beyene Guililat was a wanderer.

His life began in Ethiopia, took him to both American coasts and a few points in between, and may have ended in Kenya, many decades and many enterprises later. The people who knew him speak of him with nostalgic chuckles, and they tell tales that seem more like urban legend than biography.

In 1966, it seems he even went missing, although nobody knows for how long. The only trace of this brief episode in his life is a classified ad that ran for five days in the Los Angeles Times from April 26-30, 1966: "Reward. $50 for positive information regarding Beyene Guililat. Last known address 1959 Locust Ave., Long Beach, Calif. Call 632-2572."

Eventually he turned up — and went on to make Ethiopian-American history.

For of the many things he did, nothing approaches the significance of one short-lived Long Beach enterprise: Ethiopian Restaurant was the first of its cuisine in the world outside of Ethiopia, and Beyene owned it.

Most Ethiopians on the east coast of the United States, and many on the west coast, believe that America's and the world's first Ethiopian restaurant was Mamma Desta, opened in 1978, in Washington, D.C., by an American entrepreneur, and named for its chef, Desta Bairu, who came to the U.S. in 1959 from Eritrea to cook for Ethiopia's United Nations ambassador.

In fact, Beyene opened Ethiopian Restaurant, in Long Beach, Calif., about 20 miles south of Los Angeles, in 1966, fewer than three months after someone ran the missing person ad in the Times. People who knew him back then say he began his restaurant career a year or two earlier with an old-fashioned American diner inside a recreational vehicle. Only a handful of older Ethiopian-Americans now remember the early enterprises of the peripatetic Beyene, who has become an almost forgotten restaurant pioneer.

The Long Beach Press-Telegram, the town's evening newspaper at the time, introduced Ethiopian Restaurant to the world on July 21, 1966, on page A-24, in its Table Talk column, a collection of squibs about interesting places to eat in the community. Here's what the newspaper reported:

> **FROM THE LAND OF THE QUEEN OF SHEBA —**
> Definitely the most unusual new café in town is the Ethiopian Restaurant, 732 E. 10th St. It's a former house converted into a modest dining place which seats 30 in two rooms. The owner is **Beyene Guililat**, a young Ethiopian man who is in this country studying to become a commercial air pilot. His dinners consist of authentic native dishes, including chicken. They're from $2 to $4, according to how many courses you wish.

Adjusting for inflation, that's about $13 to $26 for your meal. Presumably the higher price got you a feast of meat and vegetable dishes.

The next day, the Long Beach Independent, the town's morning newspaper, ran the Table Talk column on page C-12, exactly as it appeared in the Press-Telegram. The second squib of the column recommended The Barge, "Southern California's only floating beer bar."

What did people make of this "unusual new café" and its unheard-of cuisine? Did Americans give it a try? And if they didn't, were there enough Ethiopians in the Los Angeles area to help the restaurant thrive?

The Ethiopian community of Los Angeles at the time consisted mostly of students and a few college graduates who stayed in America after getting their degrees. An Ethiopian Student Association in Los Angeles staged cultural events in the city, and the week that Beyene's missing person ad appeared, the group performed at a festival honoring Israel. Ethiopian Airlines maintained offices in New York and Los Angeles and advertised in the LA Times for people seeking employment in a wide range of positions.

Perhaps inspired by Beyene's enterprise, the Los Angeles Times ran a piece on Oct. 20, 1966, with chicken recipes from around the world, included one for "Ethiopian Chicken" that replaced *berbere* — unknown to Americans, and impossible to get at the time anyway — with chili powder (cayenne would have been a better choice).

There seems to have been no followup in the Long Beach papers on Beyene's restaurant, and the Los Angeles Times didn't mention it at all. The restaurant was less than a mile and a half from Beyene's "last known address" in the missing person ad, and he clearly invested more in renovating the house on 10th Street than he did in naming the place, although his restaurant's minimalist moniker was perhaps a good choice at the time.

Many tales swirl around the enigmatic Beyene, and it's hard now to track down the truth of his busy life. One thing seems pretty certain: He never realized his dream of becoming an airline pilot, although he got around as if he had.

People who knew Beyene in the 1960s claim that on a visit home, he told the emperor of his desire to open an Ethiopian restaurant in America, and the emperor was so impressed that he gave Beyene some grant money.

Araya Yibrehu, a long-time Ethiopian-American restaurateur, lived in Ethiopia in the 1960s, and he remembers hearing that Beyene won the prestigious Haile Selassie Prize Trust Award, given to people who strengthen "the spiritual and cultural bonds between the Ethiopian people and the peoples of the African continent and the whole world," the Trust's preamble states.

Yigzaw Ambaye worked for Ethiopian Airlines back then and attended Ethiopian day school with Beyene when the two were children. A New Yorker now for many decades, Yigzaw remembers the adult Beyene flying back and forth in the 1960s, from Ethiopia to California, with teff given to him by the emperor, free of charge, to help promote Ethiopian food and culture in America. A tourist agency helped Beyene to promote Ethiopian food, arts, and crafts in America, Yigzaw recalls, and before Beyene opened a restaurant, he was a milkman, delivering door to door.

These anecdotes layer memory on memory and tale on tale, so who can say which are true, and which are more of Beyene's peculiar legend?

But Beyene certainly did renovate a two-story brick house in a residential Long Beach neighborhood to open his restaurant there. Ethiopian and American flags flew at the ribbon cutting, and the mayor of Long Beach attended.

So did Mohamed Ibrahim, a long-time Los Angelino who opened his own Ethiopian restaurant, Awash, in 1991, and who remembers eating at Beyene's place during its short lifetime. Mohamed came to America in the summer of 1963 after getting an art degree at Addis Ababa University. He studied for a while at Cornell before moving to Los Angeles, where he met Beyene. He knew him for decades, and over the years they kept in touch, which wasn't so easy to do.

"Beyene never stayed put in one place," Mohamed remembers. "He was good at starting things but he never finished. When he was done with Los Angeles, he moved to San Diego."

Beyene brought some Ethiopian friends and family members to America, and he employed some of them as servers at his restaurant, but he hired immigrants to work in the kitchen. "He was quite a cook himself," Mohamed says, "and I believe they learned really quickly. One thing at that time that impressed us was that he taught these Mexican girls to cook the *injera* for him. Nobody else knew how to do it." Mohamed recalls that Beyene couldn't always get teff, so he used pancake batter and self-rising flour to make his *injera*, just as his entrepreneurial descendants did more than a decade later in Washington and New York.

Mohamed is an excellent memory trace for social and cultural history like this. When Emperor Haile Selassie visited Los Angeles in 1969, Mohamed joined a group of Ethiopians to meet him at the Century Plaza Hotel. Among the group was Beyene's brother, Tesfaye. Mohamed recalls that a member of the welcoming party kept a hand in his pocket during their audience. One of the emperor's aides noticed this and scolded the fellow, telling him that it was "impolite and not Ethiopian," Mohamed recalls. He and the other guests only learned later that the man was missing a finger on that hand, which he kept in his pocket to avoid embarrassment.

As for whether Beyene ever took those flying lessons, Mohamed can't say. But he remembers the dream. "He was bragging to everyone that he went to buy a used plane," Mohamed says. "He was a real character. I had young children at the time, and my wife didn't like Beyene. But he was so creative, it was unbelievable."

Beyene's restaurant didn't survive long enough to make the record books. The 1965 Polk's Long Beach Directory lists Alladin's Lamp Antiques as the occupant of the house at 735 E. 10th St. The property was "vacant" in the 1966 directory, published too early in the year to include Beyene's restaurant. The 1967 Long Beach phone book lists no "Ethiopian Restaurant" in either its white or yellow pages. By 1968, the building housed the Headstart program of the Long Beach Community Improvement League. No doubt the kids ate well thanks to the kitchen that Beyene left behind.

Mohamed recalls that Ethiopian Restaurant only lasted for six or seven months before Beyene closed it — and then, a year or so later, he opened another Ethiopian restaurant in San Diego. That place, too, didn't last very long, although Emperor Haile Selassie himself may have visited it on his 1969 trip to California — or so some Ethiopians now reminisce, more than four decades removed. Beyene later lived in Arizona, New Mexico and New York, managing apartments and investing in a variety of other businesses, Mohamed says. The legend goes that he returned to East Africa later in his life and died in Kenya a few years ago. Nobody seems to know for sure, although many older Ethiopian-Americans have heard the stories.

Mohamed knew of only a few dozen Ethiopians living in the Los Angeles area in the 1960s, and the Census Bureau report for 1970 listed only Africans, with no breakdown for Ethiopians. So while Beyene's restaurant may not have survived because Americans weren't ready for such exotic cuisine, or because there were too few Ethiopians to keep it alive, "it was also probably just the way Beyene ran his business," Mohamed reflects. "That was Beyene."

In light of this legend, his name is a little bit ironic. The word *beyene* comes from an Amharic verb that means to decide as a judge does in issuing a ruling. *Guleh* means "evident, obvious, or conspicuous," and from that word comes a term for a highly visible decoration that an aristocrat puts atop his house to distinguish it from others. So you could say "Beyene Guililat" means "a conspicuous decision." He seems to have made many of them in his life, one after the other, as he sojourned from adventure to adventure.

Beyene's restaurants may not have lasted very long, but his dreams did lay a foundation for an Ethiopian restaurant culture in southern California. Addis Ababa opened in the late 1970s, on legendary Sunset Boulevard in Hollywood, and thrived for a number of years for its owner, Amare Teferi, who retired from Ethiopian Airlines to open his restaurant. Walia, Demera and Ghion opened elsewhere in the city in the years that followed.

Before their city's restaurant culture and Ethiopian population began to boom, Los Angelenos had to read their hometown paper very thoroughly to enjoy a few morsels about Ethiopian cuisine.

One of the earliest mentions of Ethiopian food in the Los Angeles Times came buried at the end of an Oct. 30, 1964, story by Evelyn de Wolfe, a reporter spending time in Ethiopia. She visited the cultural affairs office of an Ethiopian princess and reported that the Ethiopian Women's Welfare Association "runs a restaurant development not only as a money-making venture, but to afford tourists an opportunity to enjoy *injera* and *wot*, the authentic Ethiopian food." She offers no further explanation.

Three months later, in another piece from Addis Ababa, de Wolfe advised Los Angelenos, "Don't miss a real Ethiopian meal. The place to go is the Ethiopian restaurant, built in the manner of a tekul, the traditional Ethiopian circular house." Her recommended restaurant had no name, and by the way she referred to it, you'd think it was the only one in the country.

On June 16, 1966, P.F. Stare wrote a long piece in the Los Angeles Times about breakfast customs around the world. For breakfast in Ethiopia, the piece says, people "cook *kimchi* from wheat and eat it with *chike*, a kind of barley bread." Stare meant *kinche*, a porridge, and *chiko*, a bread-like barley paste with lots of spices and butter.

Jean McGrail visited Ethiopia in 1968 and wrote a piece for the Times in which she mentioned "the most unusual baskets, which are used as tables for serving *injera* and *wot* — the native dishes." She says nothing more about food.

Ken Reich's 1969 travel piece about Ethiopia in the Los Angeles Times describes "a spongy sourdough bread called *injera* and stew known as *wot*. The *injera* is used as a utensil instead of knives, forks or spoons, and the spicy stew is served in a large straw basket, one basket for everyone." This doesn't quite allow Los Angelenos to picture the *wot* atop the *injera*. Reich also tasted a "bland, delicious honey-based drink called *t'ej*," which was "served in large glass vials looking like they came out of a chemistry lab." He either didn't ask what they were called — it's a *berele*, of course — or didn't care to share the name.

Meanwhile, on the east coast, The New York Times had begun to discover the cuisine.

On Nov. 19, 1966, Thomas F. Brady's story about a conference of African leaders in Addis Ababa describes a state dinner: "Everyone carefully tasted the Ethiopian delicacies — a soft, flat, spongy gray bread that looked like tripe and had a pleasantly sour taste, and a meat stew so highly laced with pepper that the guests had to wash it down with a lot of *t'ej*, an Ethiopian mead or a fermented drink made of honey and water. The classic component of an Ethiopian banquet, raw meat, was left off the menu, apparently out of consideration for foreign palates."

Craig Claiborne published a lengthy piece in The New York Times in 1970 that described his encounters with Ethiopian food in Addis Ababa. He talks about *injera*, *wot*, *t'ej* and more, and he offers cooking lessons through the courtesy of Mrs. Assegedsh Walde, the "utterly charming" owner of Mara Denbeya restaurant, which offered both sit-down dining and takeout meals.

"There are, in general, two reactions to the native food of Ethiopia," Claiborne wrote. "It is consumed with considerable ardor or eschewed with comparable passion. In the American-European world, it resembles as much as anything the food of Mexico but only in its thoroughgoing use of hot red and green peppers. Most of the main dishes of the Ethiopian kitchen are based on *berbere*, which is nothing more than dried hot red chilies. The food is, to my mind and taste, among the world's most interesting, and it is taken in the most convivial manner."

His story is a good introduction to the cuisine for New Yorkers, who wouldn't get their own Ethiopian restaurant until 1979, although *berbere* is certainly more than just chili peppers, and *injera*, as he later says, is not made with millet.

The Los Angeles Times didn't notice the emerging trend of Ethiopian restaurants in Los Angeles until Aug. 14, 1979, when restaurant critic Lois Dwan had only this to say in a column of food-related squibs: "You have heard of an Ethiopian restaurant. Very good reports, too. It is Walia, 5881 W. Pico Blvd., Los Angeles." (This is just two blocks from Mohamed's Awash, which opened 12 years later). More than a decade after Beyene and his Ethiopian Restaurant, Dwan apparently hadn't yet deigned to try the cuisine at Walia herself, and she didn't mention the restaurant's signature dessert, an Ethiopian custard baklava. Her guides to Los Angeles restaurants published in the mid- to late-1970s don't list any Ethiopian cuisine.

So it seems that Ethiopian food had hit the Los Angeles radar by 1979. In a column on March 11 that year in the Times, Dick Roraback begins with this anecdote: "'What's the matter with American food?' writes P.F. of Fullerton. "Armenian, Ethiopian, Moroccan restaurants. Holy smokes! Don't you ever hanker for a good old *steak*?'" Roraback goes on to review a steakhouse. The newspaper's historical database turns up no earlier references to Ethiopian restaurants, although by this time D.C. had surpassed L.A.: The city had four restaurants, each of them thoroughly reviewed by The Washington Post.

Colman Andrews reviewed the Ethiopian restaurant Ghion for the Times in 1983, asking his readers, "Ten years ago or so, who in Los Angeles had ever considered the possibility that a distinct Ethiopian cuisine might exist? Now all of a sudden we have five or six restaurants serving just that." He goes on to speculate about what folks at M-G-M might have thought in the 1940s if they'd walked out of their front gate to find an Ethiopian restaurant. Ghion was located on Washington Boulevard in Culver City, right across from the M-G-M (now Sony Pictures) studios.

More than a quarter century later, Andrews says he'd never heard of Beyene's restaurant. "My first consciousness of Ethiopian places in LA would have been probably the very late '70s or early '80s," he recalls, with Walia, Red Sea and Addis Ababa the "big names at the time."

As for his question about who would have imagined an Ethiopian cuisine: The answer is — the readers of the Los Angeles Times. In 1974, nine years before his musing, the Times ran a story under the headline "Fuel-Saving Meal Preparation Taught." The piece concerned a program offered at the Van Nuys Community Center by the Department of Water and Power. The May program topic: "Ebony Foods." The first session taught people how to make "*wot* (beef stew), *yemisir selatta* (lentil salad), and *injera* (bread). All are Ethiopian dishes which may be cooked on the surface of an electric range or in a Dutch oven." The month's other programs featured West African cooking and soul food.

The early 1970s also saw the emergence of an Ethiopian community in Tokyo, where the Ethiopian Association of Japan began holding its annual Ethiopian Night for Dance and Cuisine in 1972. The organization celebrated its 35th anniversary event in 2007 with more than 400 people at the gathering.

Charles Perry, a long-time food critic in Los Angeles, began reviewing city restaurants in 1978, and in 1980, he reviewed Almaz, which was located in the Algiers Hotel on South La Brea Avenue. He soon visited Walia, which had "the smallest, most inconspicuous sign of any restaurant ever." He recalls the owner, "a very pretty recent Cal State LA graduate" named Alia Ahmed — a Harari Muslim who served *t'ej*. Addis Ababa opened in 1980, as did Lalibela, with several *mesobs* (unique at the time) and its authentic coffee ceremony, featuring "a long-necked clay pot that rested on a little pillow on the floor, while frankincense was burning."

By 1981, the Los Angeles Times had recognized the mini-explosion, and in a long piece called "A Taste for the Exotic," under the "African" section, John Pashday offered squibs on four of the city's Ethiopian restaurants: Addis Ababa (with the sourest *injera* and tasty *wots*), Almaz (mediocre "coffee-shop quality" food), Red Sea (hard to find but worth the trip), and Walia ("smaller and simpler" than Red Sea but just as good). He also visited Rosalind's West African Cuisine on South La Cienega Boulevard.

A few years later, Rosalind's moved less than two miles away to South Fairfax Avenue, a few blocks from Walia's location on Pico, and changed hands to become Ethiopian. It's still there, and around it, the neighborhood that's now officially called Little Ethiopia has emerged, as have so many others since then, official or not, in big cities around the country.

The Spices of Ethiopian Life

Back in the early '70s, before Ethiopian restaurants or markets began to show up in American cities, Ethiopians here had two choices if they wanted to make authentic cuisine: Get your spices from back home, or become friends with Workinesh Nega.

When Workinesh and her husband, Selashe Kebede, moved to America in 1974, they did so with the intention of pursuing their chosen careers. Workinesh had earned a graduate degree as a nurse anesthetist from the University of Pittsburgh, and that's what she did in Ethiopia when she returned there after college. Selashe, who had a doctorate in agriculture, began work for an Ethiopian company that made spices.

Then came the Derg, and they and their children got out. Selashe joined a spice extraction company in Kalamazoo, Mich., and Workinesh went back to school for some retraining.

This was a time when the small but growing population of Ethiopian-Americans used pancake batter to make ersatz *injera* and cayenne to spice their *wots*. Even people who knew how to cook would rarely bother to search out all the things they needed to do it properly. So Workinesh began to experiment, and soon she started whipping up batches of authentic spices to give as gifts to her Ethiopian-American friends, a circle that included some exiled members of the royal family, many of whom came to America when the Derg deposed their patriarch.

A few years later, Workinesh grew disenchanted with nursing, and she left the field. That's when she created the pioneering company that celebrated 30 years in business in 2008.

Workinesh Spice Blends has always been mom 'n' pop: For many years Workinesh ran it herself, and when Selashe retired in 1996, he joined her in the warehouse-cum-kitchen. For about 10 years after that, their children now grown, the couple began to divide their time between the U.S. and Ethiopia, making sure their clients were well stocked before they left Kalamazoo, and then closing the company for several months of the year.

Workinesh grew up in Gondar, Selashe in Guder, west of Addis Ababa, and after college in America, they lived in Addis before coming to America to stay. For decades in Kalamazoo, they survived in a city and a state with virtually no Ethiopian community. After the fall of the Derg, they got back some of the property they left behind. They finally moved home to Ethiopia for good in 2007, leaving Workinesh Spice Blends in the care of their daughter, Lemlem Kebede, who came to America with them when she was 5 years old, and who has a degree in advertising.

Not that it helps at the company she runs. Workinesh Spice still does business by word of mouth, and it doesn't have a website to sell and promote its spices. For decades now, Ethiopian restaurants, groceries and individuals have simply known that if they want *berbere, mitmita, shiro* and more, they can order one pound or 100 pounds from Workinesh.

The company offers just about any spice on the Ethiopian table, some of them blends, like *mitmita* and *berbere* (in three different heat levels), and some of them pure, like *krinfud* (cloves), *dimbilal* (coriander), *telba* (flax seed), *korerima* (cardamom) or *ird* (turmeric) — more than two dozen in all. It's not that you *can't* get many of these spices at your local grocery store or food co-op. So many Ethiopians have grown accustomed to getting them from Workinesh that they just do. There's also *mekelesha*, a special blend of spices added to make your *wots* extra tasty, and *yekebay manteria kimem* — that is, the spices you add to butter when you boil it to make *kibbee*.

Almost all of the company's hot peppers and other produce come from farms in the South (a few items, such as coffee, come from Ethiopia), and when the goods arrive at the factory, which is now in suburban Minneapolis, Lemlem or her assistant — depending on "who gets stuck doing it each day" — grinds them and mixes them. She uses her mother's and grandmother's recipes, but don't dare ask for preparation tips: "They created them long ago," Lemlem says, "and we continue to use them and keep it secretive."

Workinesh Spice also sells teff, grown on farms in Oklahoma and Kansas, then milled and packaged at their factory. The company buys teff from SS Farms, an Oklahoma enterprise owned by the innovative agrarian Dean Smith, who began to plant teff in 1996 when he learned that the Ethiopian community valued it, and after he found a buyer in Workinesh (see Chapter 6). In 2008, when a Kansas teff project launched, Smith put the growers in touch with Workinesh, and now the company buys the Kansas teff as well. Two bad growing seasons, in 2007 and 2008, left Workinesh without enough teff to satisfy its clients, but things improved in 2009. The company also makes *ambasha* bread, and *injera* sold in packs of five or 10.

The growth of the Ethiopian-American community has been good for Workinesh Spice in the long run, but it's also brought lots of competition. Big NTS Enterprise of Oakland, Calif., which opened in 1984, and once bought spices from Workinesh, now imports directly from suppliers in Ethiopia. Lemlem remembers packing orders for NTS when she was a child. Zelalem Injera ships its bread nationwide from Dallas and D.C., and in the past few years, numerous other smaller companies have launched, most of them with websites.

In the last few years, more American-made Ethiopian products have begun to show up on market shelves. Eleni Woldeyes of Hillsboro, Ore., markets the *berbere*-based simmer sauce *kulet* through her young company, Eleni's Kitchen, and Motherland Oils of Pomona, Calif., bottles *noog* and flax seed oils. Authentic Ethiopian Cuisine of Woodbridge, Va., has created two types of *kibbee,* one for general use, and a special one for *kitfo,* as well as a blend of *sinefitch,* or Ethiopian mustard. These products are sometimes hard to find — for now.

But Workinesh remains, and its clients stretch across the country and around the world to places like Canada, Europe, Japan, Israel and Lebanon.

Name an Ethiopian restaurant or grocery store in the U.S. and Workinesh Spice either supplies it or would like to. Well into the 1980s, the company "had a good majority of the business," Lemlem says. But then NTS began to grow, and in the 1990s, her mother's choice to shut down for a few months each year opened a window and then a door for competition. So now it's a tougher sell for Lemlem, who took over running the company in December 2007.

She does it all in about 5,000 square feet of space, and she dreams of having a bigger factory some day, with more employees to do the work. For now, though, Workinesh Spice Blends is just what it's always been: a family business that serves the greater Ethiopian family around the country and the world.

Communities of Cuisine:
Addis Ababa in America

You almost have to be looking for Skyline Plaza in Falls Church, Va., at the intersection of Seminary Road and South George Mason Drive.

Sure, you might happen upon it during a trip to the bigger nearby Skyline Mall or Northern Virginia Community College. But whether you approach it head on, where Seminary dead ends into South George Mason, or simply pass it while driving to somewhere else, it's unremarkable from the road, just another block-long suburban Virginia strip mall with a few dozen respectable-looking shops.

But look again. For this is one of the largest proximate concentrations of Ethiopian restaurants, grocery stores and businesses in America, a rival to the dizzying U Street corridor in nearby Washington, D.C.

You can't even see all of Skyline Plaza from the road because it's a two-sided complex, with another full row of shops on the back side of the building. Abay Restaurant and Market, Skyline Café and its market, Eyo Restaurant and Sports Bar, Flamingo Restaurant, Birhan Market and Café, Flavor Cake and Pastry, Wube Berha Market, Tenadam International Market, Marhaba Market, Azieb Market, Harambe Travel, Almaz Hair Salon, Sunshine Beauty Salon — these are some of the Ethiopian businesses at the plaza.

Sprinkled among them are shops that cater to neighboring world cultures, like May-May Fashions and Fat Boys restaurant (both Chinese), Carthage and Al Jazeera restaurants (Middle Eastern), Walima Café (Mediterranean cuisine), Fairous Café (Lebanese cuisine), Oasis (an Arabic gift shop), Falika's Fashions (African wear), plus the slightly anomalous Stone Hot Pizza.

And this is just the heart of it all. Around Falls Church, and then into nearby Arlington and Alexandria, are scores of other Ethiopian-owned businesses, all part of the greater Washington area diaspora.

One of the more eminent places at Skyline Plaza is the tiny Abay, which Yonas Alemayehu opened as a market in 2001 and divided six years later into a market and five-table restaurant. The August 2008 issue of Maxim magazine listed his *tere siga* among the nation's best raw meat dishes, and the Travel Channel did a spot on him and his place in 2009.

Yonas has a dramatic history: A native of the southern Sidamo region, known for its coffee, he fought with the Ethiopian People's Revolutionary Party against the repressive Derg regime, and he spent eight years in prison for his part in the rebellion. Here in America, he's still outspoken politically, and he fears for the future of his homeland.

"Things have gone from bad to worse," he says, even thought the Derg is long gone and Ethiopians now participate in quasi-elections. A leader of the revolution, Meles Zenawi, has ruled the country since the fall of the Derg, and freedom remains elusive.

Yonas says that a small bunch of "hooligans" now governs Ethiopia, supported by past U.S. administrations, but if Ethiopia could become a true democracy, the movement would spread through all of Africa, which would be good for the American government. Unfortunately, he says, American diplomats who go to Ethiopia "stay in the hotels and drink whiskey" rather than getting out among the people, so America has sloppy intelligence about Ethiopia and a poor understanding of its problems.

Some people fear that democracy in Ethiopia will lead to a splintering among its many cultures, all of whom are now held in check by a watchful central government. Yonas says that's nonsense. Given true freedom, the Ethiopian people will fight with words, not guns, because at heart, they're all one people, well mixed and intermarried, a blend of the country's many cultures, "like a tiger or a zebra."

"I have some Oromo blood," he says, so if the cultures of Ethiopia begin to divide into separate nations, "I'll have nowhere to go. You cannot separate our people."

Yonas doesn't serve up politics when you order at his restaurant, and he knows he'll only stay in business if his food stands out. "When your place is small," he says, "everything must be tasteful." His national press coverage also doesn't hurt.

One of the newer place at Skyline is Eyo Restaurant and Sports Bar. It opened in April 2008, and by August it was the political place to be: The restaurant hosted a convention party for Ethiopians for Obama, and together the community watched their almost-native son (Obama's father is Kenyan) accept the Democratic nomination. Many such parties took place at restaurants around the D.C. area.

There's really no accounting for why people favor one place over another.

On a warm Saturday afternoon before Memorial Day, Yonas had a steady flow of customers in his market and a few diners in his restaurant. Several storefronts down, Eyo was packed for lunch and abuzz with conversation, as was Flavor, the bakery and coffee shop right next door, where two old friends — one from New York City, one from Atlanta, now both retired and visiting D.C. — sipped coffee and reminisced. All of the restaurants on the strip offer essentially the same dishes, and they're all about the same size. But where its neighboring restaurants all had a little bit of business, Eyo had a lot. Sometimes a place just catches on.

Flavor is the only bakery on the strip, and its young owner, Kidist Assefa, has a degree from Baltimore's International Culinary College. She came to America just after high school, about 15 years ago, and her café offers a variety of pastries and coffees.

But Ethiopia isn't a dessert culture, so Kidist doesn't make any uniquely Ethiopian pastries — at least, not yet. At Dama, an Arlington bakery owned by a well-established Ethiopian pastry chef, you'll find a tall fluffy cake made in part with teff flour. Kidist hasn't mastered that art and hasn't yet created her signature Ethiopian-influenced dessert.

"The consistency of the pastries are different when you make them with teff," she says. "But I have a plan to make something yummy." She would say no more.

Down the strip from Flavor, Andu Bahta and Ali Ashenafi have stopped by to chat with Dag Tegne, the manager of Skyline International Market and its neighboring restaurant. Both are cab drivers — Ali's been here for seven years, Andu for three — and they have a few restaurants that they especially enjoy: Andu likes Dukem in Washington, and Ali savors the *goden tibs* (short ribs) at Meaza, a few miles away in another part of Falls Church.

But even though they have favorites, they don't play favorites. "You taste one, then taste another, and you compare," Andu says. "I taste everything. Everywhere is something special."

The restaurants at Skyline Plaza each have a different character, some homier, some a bit more fancy, but none of them what you would call upscale. What they rarely have is non-Ethiopian customers. Yonas gets some at Abay, but mostly, the businesses at the plaza serve Ethiopians who have made the greater Washington, D.C., area the heartbeat of their country's diaspora. There's nothing from home that the local population can't find at Skyline, from food and groceries to books and videos to *mesobs* and *mitads* and homemade *t'ej* and companies that allow them to make money transfers to Africa.

It's a new Addis Ababa, and one of many Little Ethiopias across America.

THE ETHIOPIAN COMMUNITY of the nation's capital is a cluster and a sprawl.

Along a few blocks of U Street in the northwest District, an area that's become known to some as "Little Ethiopia" (but not without controversy), dozens of Ethiopian-owned businesses thrive, serving people of all communities. Most of them are restaurants, a few are grocery stores, and the rest are mini-marts, nightclubs, liquor stores, bookstores, hair salons and more. It's a city neighborhood like any other, dominated by Ethiopians and their generations.

The U Street cluster began to grow during the 1990s, and as Ethiopian businesses moved in, some of the neighborhood's long-established African-American businesses moved out. This led the African-American community to feel displaced, so much so that residents of the neighborhood have objected to renaming the area. For now, "Little Ethiopia" is an informal sobriquet. The neighborhood's long-standing name is Shaw, and the city promotes the burgeoning nightspot destination as U Street.

All but two or three of the strip's dozens of Ethiopian businesses are on the south side of U Street, and if you turn south onto 9th Street where it intersects U, you'll pass 10 restaurants and several other businesses before reaching the next block. Meanwhile, on the north side of U Street, the businesses that remain serve a largely African-American community. Eventually the street's north side turns into row houses, some occupied and some boarded up.

U Street is a glorious place to be if you crave Ethiopian food, and picking a restaurant from among so many is a challenge. The one thing you don't want to do is look in a window and pass up a place with only a few Ethiopians in conversation around a table. In fact, that's probably just where you want to stop for a meal. Think of it as dropping by your neighbor's kitchen.

Before this Ethiopian cluster emerged in Shaw, people gravitated to 18th Street in the trendy Adams Morgan neighborhood for Ethiopian food. The street still has a lot to offer, like the popular Meskerem, as well as Awash, Dahlak and the tiny Keren (the latter two are Eritrean). Addisu Gebeya is a well-stocked grocery store, and some of the other businesses along this portion of 18th Street — a hardware store, a liquor store, a hair salon, a travel agency — are owned by Ethiopians. These shops join a host of other hip hangouts and culturally diverse restaurants.

But in terms of a destination for Ethiopian food and culture, it's no longer the king of kings. A second market, Merkato, closed a few years ago, as did three other restaurants: Red Sea (one of the city's oldest and best), Addis Ababa (which moved to suburban Maryland), and the big Fasika's (lost to a fire). Some smaller markets have opened and closed in the past few years as well.

Now even the city has recognized the shift: Evening revelers can catch a shuttle bus that runs exclusively between Adams Morgan and U Street. The cost: 25 cents — with all-day runs on Saturday until 3 a.m. Sunday morning. It's a great service, but also a challenge to the dwindling Ethiopian restaurant community in Adams Morgan. And U Street doesn't offer just Ethiopian fare: It has culinary diversity, a few galleries, some jazz clubs, and even Nellie's, a "straight-friendly" sports bar for the gay community.

Adams Morgan might have seen it coming, for the city's Ethiopian restaurant community wasn't born there. In 1978, Desta Bairu, a former cook for Ethiopia's ambassador to the United Nations, lent her name and talent to Mamma Desta, which opened at 4840 Georgia Ave. NW.

The pioneering restaurant — owned by a financier, not by Desta — was quite a novelty when Washington Post writer Robert Asher introduced the place to D.C. readers in his "weekly guide to family dining." He visited Mamma Desta with his wife, their 11-year-old son, and the son's "marvelously willing" same-aged friend.

"When it came to our combined knowledge of Ethiopian cuisine," he wrote, "we could bring to bear two generations of total ignorance." To call the place "unpretentious," Asher said, would be an understatement: "From the outside, it's nothing more than a small yellow sign over a window that you can't see in, on a block that doesn't exactly dazzle." The interior was no more alluring, and the menu offered only three dishes. Their server told them about a fourth option and recommended that they "mix it up" and order three dishes to share between the four of them.

Their next surprise was the lack of silverware, and after that, the taste of the food: They loved it, although it took a moment to adjust to the heat of the spices. The portions were generous, the prices low, and the experience altogether satisfying. They even had leftover *injera*, which the boys "bagged up for keeping either as souvenirs, doorstops or football padding." Asher chatted with the owner, from whom he learned that the cook, Mamma Desta, "decides what's going to be served on a given day. 'She just does what she wants,' he commented with a shrug and a grin."

The Ashers' dinner consisted of spicy lamb, beef with greens and traditional *doro wat*, and the writer concluded: "Even though there's a 'suggestion box' perched above the coat rack, we couldn't begin to tell her how to do any better."

One month later, the Post's long-time restaurant critic, Phyllis Richman, gave it a try. In her column on June 11, 1978, she called it — incorrectly — "the first [Ethiopian restaurant] in this country and maybe the first anywhere outside Africa."

"In Ethiopia," wrote Richman, "the thin, porous pancake called *injera* are gray, fermented from a grain known as tef. In Washington's Ethiopian restaurant, the *injera* are white, like heavy linen pancakes, having been made from wheat fermented six days in plastic buckets. In Ethiopia, the *injera* are cooked on an earthenware griddle over a eucalyptus fire; in Washington, they are cooked in an electric frying pan. But Mamma Desta is inventive and has devised American substitutes to cook Ethiopian food that, according to reliable sources, tastes 80 percent authentic."

Richman notes that "berberi," a red pepper, and "the hottest in Africa," is used to spice Ethiopian dishes. But "Mamma Desta's food does not come close to being even the hottest food on Georgia Avenue."

"What is authentic is the method of eating these pancakes and meats and pounded red pepper pastes," she goes on. "Leave your floppy sleeves and neckties for another day. Roll up your sleeves. You eat with your hands."

To Americans, this must have sounded odd. But to the emerging Ethiopian community, it was a homecoming.

Desta was born in Eritrea, and she arrived in the U.S. in 1959 as a cook for the Ethiopian ambassador to the United Nations. She returned to Ethiopia briefly in the 1970s, then she moved to Washington, D.C., which had a growing Ethiopian community. "When she moved to Washington, she cooked in her apartment until the complaints started," Ghebrai Asmerom, the manager at Mamma Desta, told The Washington Post. "Then we decided it was the right time for a restaurant."

So in February 1978, putting to work her two skills — cooking and diplomacy — she went to work at Mamma Desta, after the rise of the Derg in Ethiopia led to the burgeoning of Washington's Ethiopian population. She remained at the restaurant for a few years and then parted company with its owners, moving to Madison, Wis., where she returned to the kitchen as a caterer, making meals for the community's Ethiopians and *ferenj*. Eventually she moved to Chicago and lent her name once again to a restaurant, the first in that city (see Chapter 12).

A year after Mamma Desta's opened in D.C., Georgia Avenue had four Ethiopian restaurants, including the long-gone Peasant Basket. Owned by an Ethiopian, it served mostly Middle Eastern and Italian dishes. But the menu included a few Ethiopian items, and with some notice, the owner would prepare a full Ethiopian feast for her patrons. By 1984 there were nearly a dozen restaurants around the city, and today there are almost a dozen just on 9th Street in Shaw.

Starting in the 1980s, the Ethiopian population of the District and surrounding Maryland and Virginia grew and grew until it became the epicenter of the culture outside of Ethiopia. But back in those days, the community still wasn't quite large enough to support a company that made *injera* and sold it in markets.

That first *injera* company was owned by Tedla Desta, who began his arc of fame and success in the '60s and '70s in Ethiopia, where he pioneered a system of farming teff. He also designed some innovative tractors for use in Ethiopian farming, but that business suffered under the Derg, which nationalized many industries and began importing tractor parts from Russia.

That's when Tedla came to America, and in the late 1980s, he began making *injera* and delivering it to 7-Eleven stores before the city had Ethiopian markets. His business only lasted a few years, into the early 1990s, because the population wasn't quite large enough yet, and people who wanted *injera* either made it at home or got it at one of the city's restaurants. Now, of course, dozens of companies in the D.C. area — some of them women working out of their homes — make *injera* and sell them in markets and to restaurants.

A few more early entrepreneurs made and sold *injera* around D.C. before Muluken Mehari came on the scene in the early 1990s and added an innovation: He began to sell his product to Indian and Middle Eastern grocery stores, where Ethiopians often shopped for spices and other goods. Muluken mixed his *injera* batter himself, but there weren't enough Ethiopian women to work in his kitchen, so he hired "Spanish girls" to swirl the batter onto *mitads*. After a while he opened a restaurant, Kokeb, at 14th and U streets, the first in the neighborhood. He closed the place after seven or eight years because, he says, "I couldn't handle it, too much work, quite a headache."

Muluken now lives in Virginia, but a few years ago, he began to return to Ethiopia to explore business opportunities. He now owns Maye Trading — the name comes from the initials of his wife and children — importing teff and spices for sale to Ethiopian markets in America. He came here in 1973 to go to college, and he only recently returned home to do business because "even after the Derg, it was not very inviting." There's more opportunity now, he says, although still with too many restraints.

When Muluken arrived in the U.S., there were no Ethiopian restaurants. "We just cooked spaghetti," he recalls. "I never ate rice before I came to this country." He ate a lot of *kitfo*, with bread, and he enjoyed Mamma Desta's back in its day. He even knew Desta casually and would say hello when he visited her restaurant. Then, the restaurant community blossomed, and "it was a new thing and everybody went," Muluken says. "You didn't cook at home at all." *Injera* pieces in those early days were bigger than they are now in America, up to 16 inches, and they contained more teff because that's what people liked.

Georgia Avenue today is no longer the anchor of the District's Ethiopian food community, but it does host one of the city's many mini-clusters: From the point where Georgia Avenue in Silver Spring, Md., turns into Georgia Avenue NW in D.C., more than a dozen Ethiopian restaurants and grocery stores line both sides of the street for the next few miles.

The further down Georgia you go, the closer you get to neighborhoods where Ethiopians tend to live. Ethiopia Restaurant and Market sits far apart from other shops among a small strip of businesses at the corner of Buchanan and 14th, a few blocks west of Georgia. But it's not isolated from the community. Across the street is the Ethio-American Health Center, a free clinic opened in June 2009. Debre Selam Kidest Marian Church, the Ethiopian Orthodox congregation right next door, owns the building and the parking lot between the two places. On the outside wall of the health center, facing the church, a large mural, painted by a Jamaican neighbor as a gift to the community, depicts a cross, a Lalibela rock church, and four faithful ancient Ethiopians.

Travel the length of 14th Street until it reaches P and you come to Lalibela, a places that's popular with both Ethiopians and *ferenj*. It's right across from the city's Studio Theater and half a block from a Whole Foods Market and some shiny new condos. Lalibela is nicely priced and especially big on beef. It has a full bar, but don't try to order a bottle of Mirinda, an orange-flavored Ethiopian soft drink. They haven't been able to get it for a while, and the last bottle, now a keepsake, sits beside a row of Ethiopian beer bottles behind the bar, its name written in English on once side and in Amharic on the other.

Much further north on Georgia, around where the avenue crosses from Maryland into D.C., you'll find nearly a dozen places on the Silver Spring side of Georgia Avenue and its cross streets.

One of the more unusual Maryland places, less than a block from the border, is Tiramisu, an Ethiopian-owned and largely Ethiopian-frequented bakery and coffee shop that serves familiar breakfasts of *chechebsa*, *kinche* and *ful*, all written in Amharic on a chalk board in the window. It's just across the street from the Evangelical Ethiopian Church, above whose side door hovers a large replica of the tablets containing the Ten Commandments, which are written in Hebrew.

The marquee above the bakery presents its name in English and, below that, in Amharic letters that spell out "Tiramisu Kek Bet," or "Tiramisu Cake House." The pastries are international, from chocolate chip cookies to baklava, with lots of mochas and cappuccinos to go with them. The shop also distributes a variety of fliers for Ethiopian-owned businesses and services, like an American real estate company that sells villas, townhouses and condos in Ethiopia to successful Ethio-Americans who want a vacation residence back home.

Tiramisu sits between two Ethiopian grocery stores and around the corner from Nile Restaurant and Market, the first Ethiopian business on Georgia Avenue NW in D.C. From there, as the avenue descends into Washington, past Walter Reed Army Hospital, you can't go more than a few blocks without coming upon another grocery store or restaurant, often with their names in Amharic above the door. Further south, Georgia Avenue moves closer to the parallel 14th Street, where more businesses reside. Drive Georgia for a few miles and you'll eventually arrive at U Street and Little Ethiopia.

Nor would you want to walk from Georgia Avenue to Adams Morgan, which began to steal Georgia Avenue's Ethiopian glory in the 1980s. Mahaba Mohamed manages Meskerem on 18th Street in Adams Morgan with his sister, Nafisa Said, the restaurant's first and only owner. The sibling are Moslems, somewhat rare among Ethiopian restaurant owners in the U.S., and Meskerem, open since 1984, is now the oldest in the city.

Mahaba acknowledges that the rise of the U Street cluster has damaged the critical mass of the Adams Morgan Ethiopian business community. The places that remain seem to do well, and Meskerem is always busy, although Mahaba says he's lost most of his Ethiopian customers, who now spend more time among the U Street restaurants. Adams Morgan remains popular with tourists and young professionals.

The scaling back of 18th Street as the city's Little Ethiopia didn't exactly coincide with the rise of the U Street corridor. With high rents in Adams Morgan, and lower rents in the developing U Street corridor, not all of the 18th Street restaurants and business could thrive. A decade ago, a young Ethiopian woman in Addisu Gebeya market in Adams Morgan told me that "there are too many Ethiopians here," and some need to "move away and start businesses somewhere else." It seems they have.

The adventure of descending U Street to the new heart of it all begins on the 1500 block with Selam, a tiny underground Eritrean restaurant with hearty food and hip music on the weekends. The 1000 block welcomes Almaz, and at the corner of 11th and U street, there's Dukem, the big yuppie hotspot, with a patio for *al fresco* dining that's larger than some of the other restaurants in the neighborhood. It's so touristy that the restaurant bought a large billboard ad in downtown Addis Ababa to promote its D.C. and Baltimore locations. On weekend nights, Dukem is always packed, both indoors and out (when weather permits). But the patrons tend to be far more Anglo-European and Asian than African or African-American. Next on U Street comes Madget, with a witty menu that boats, "Most Ethiopian restaurant owners dine at Madjet ☺."

This part of U Street has nearby restaurants offering the cuisines of other cultures, so it's no surprise that these four places have more non-Ethiopian patrons than their competitors just a few blocks away, at U and 9th streets.

The only exception is Etete, a narrow, tightly packed restaurant and bar right that's the closest one to the corner of 9ᵗʰ and U. It's about as far as most non-Ethiopians seem to venture when coming to Shaw for Ethiopian food.

But keep walking down 9ᵗʰ and you'll encounter a cornucopia of choices: Ethiopian and Eritrean restaurants, grocery stores, music shops, wine shops, and an Ethiopian Community Services and Development Center.

And don't be afraid to stroll even further from the cluster, several more blocks down U Street past 9ᵗʰ, to find Zenebech Injera, Deli & Grocery, where I've never seen a non-Ethiopian, except in the mirror. These friendly folks, like owner/cook Zenebech Dessu, serve fresh meals in their newly remodeled two-table restaurant and make *injera* that they distribute daily to grocery stories in the D.C., Maryland and Virginia.

MOST OF THE RESTAURANTS in this neighborhood — and in fact, all over D.C., Maryland and Virginia — are owned by Ethiopians from the northern part of the country. They tend to be Amhari or Tigrayan, members of the cultures that have ruled Ethiopia for centuries.

But lately, a few Oromo people have opened restaurants. The cuisine is the same, and politics isn't on the menu, which doesn't stop some customers from serving it up anyway.

One such place was Gori Café, located at the corner of 12ᵗʰ and V streets in Shaw, just a block or two from the big 9ᵗʰ Street cluster. Its owner, Yonas Chalka, left his home in Welega in 1994 seeking political asylum, and he drove a cab for many years before opening Gori in late 2008. The name is an Oromo word that means "come in," and he promoted his restaurant and watering hole as "the stop by café."

That was a challenging sell, considering its location. Gori was surrounded for two blocks by newer low-rise condos and nicely maintained older row houses. It's a charming few blocks of residential life in between a more dilapidated few blocks of crumbling businesses, all of it just a short walk from U Street. The place could accommodate about a dozen people, almost always Oromos who were happy to have a place of their own.

"Many Oromos will not go to an Amhari or Tigrayan restaurant," Yonas says. "Even some of my friends who are Amharas do not want to come here. They want me to put up the Ethiopian flag. They see many Oromos sitting here talking their language or listening to Oromo music, and they don't like it." He discusses this without bitterness, just resignation. "That's how it is," he says a few times during the conversation.

Still, he listed the dishes on his menu with their Amharic names rather than their Afaan Oromo ones. "Many of the neighbors, especially the foreigners, know the Amharic names," he says. "They aren't accustomed to the Oromo names." His Oromo customers understood, although he had hoped to re-do the menu some day with the dishes named in both languages. He also points out that it's hard to find an Afaan Oromo equivalent for, say, "zilzil tibs."

Gori served dishes familiar to any Ethiopian restaurant-goer. Rare among the city's restaurants, it offered *chechebsa*, an Oromo contribution to the national cuisine. It's a dish prepared by frying small pieces of wheat dough in spiced butter and then seasoning them with *berbere*. There was *ful* and *kinche* for breakfast along with bagels and oatmeal, a variety of lattes and cappuccinos, homemade telba juice (flax seed, an Ethiopian favorite), as well as chicken and fish sandwiches, and even pasta.

For dinner you could choose beef and lamb but no chicken, and the vegetarian platter was generous in its selections and portions. Other restaurants served chilled Ethiopian-style potato salad, but Gori's preparation was unique: It was made of shredded rather than cubed potatoes, mixed with chopped onions and jalapeños, and flavored with a light lemon dressing.

The restaurant had a full bar with Ethiopian beers and American-made *t'ej*, although on weekends, if you were lucky, you could also find some homemade *t'ej* and even *talla*.

Yonas only sold his *talla* by the bottle, which was no problem for the solo diner: It wasn't too alcoholic, and drinking a full bottle got you about as buzzed as two glasses of wine. It was the color of tea or a dark amber *t'ej*, a little sweet (like cider) and a little grainy (from the barley), with effervescent bubbles. You could taste the malt of the hops, like a microbrew, and the further down the bottle you got, the thicker and chewer it became, so you had to give your bottle a gentle shake to distribute the settled ingredients.

He wouldn't say who made his *talla*, but you could tell that it doesn't come from a winery: It was served in recycled wine bottles, sometimes with the original label, and there was no cork or cap, just a piece of aluminum foil on top to keep it from spilling. It was a unique treat in a city with so many restaurant choices.

But now that choice is gone: In 2010, after less than two years in business, Yonas put his restaurant up for sale, unable to compete with the big U Street restaurants just a few blocks away. He never gave up his day job as a cab driver, so he's still able to sustain himself, albeit in the real world, rather than in the place of his dreams.

You won't find *talla* or any alcohol at the city's biggest Oromo-owned restaurant, and you need to be a member to eat there. The Oromo Center Inc. moved to its location on Upshur Street NW in D.C.'s Petworth neighborhood in 2006 after many years in neighboring Columbia Heights. The community bought the building and operates a restaurant that opens in the late afternoon every day, seating more than three dozen people in its main upstairs dining room, and another three dozen downstairs in a room that doubles as a meeting space (with ping pong, pool and fusball in the room next door).

Back in the kitchen, which is about the size of Gori's entire dining room, Asnaku Biru, a nursing assistant by day, does all of the cooking, except for the *injera*, which they buy from Oromo women in the community. For about $10, with profits benefiting the center, you get a beef *wadi* (*tibs*) and some vegetarian selections. There's no menu, so whatever dishes Asnaku prepares is what patrons can enjoy. The room also hosts Ibssa Corner, where a barista makes cappuccinos and lattes. It's named for Sisai Ibssa, a well-known community member who died in 2006, the year the center opened.

For Edries Jemal, the center is a place of community and pride as well as occasional sustenance. A member of the center's board of directors, he came to the U.S. in 1970, holds two master's degrees, and works for D.C. government. His long time in America has given him a taste for continental cuisine, and he says that he only eats Ethiopian food maybe once a week. He visited Ethiopia in 2004 for the first time since leaving, and hasn't eaten Oromo dishes, like *bunakala* or *marka*, since leaving home 40 years ago.

It's also been a long time since any of Washington's Oromo people have enjoyed or even seen *anchote*, a potato-like plant eaten in Oromia. Asnaku says she would prepare it by boiling the plant and cutting it up into pieces, then seasoning it with garlic, ginger, basil, jalapenos and spiced butter.

The center doesn't try to serve these regional and traditional country dishes because, on the whole, "the food is generally identical," Edrias says. "When you talk about Ethiopia, the Amharas are the people who have a lot of notoriety. But the food is a combination of all cultures." He knows Oromos who go to restaurants owned by Amharas, and he says, "We try to patronize our community, but other than that, there are no hang-ups. Maybe the Amhara have some. When a minority dominates a majority, they have insecurities."

The center is a converted house and looks like it when you pass by, except for a sign above the front window that says "Waltajjii Oromoo" on the bottom and "Oromo Center" above it, with a drawing in the middle of a big green *odaa*, the native tree under which traditional Oromo villages hold meetings and community events. Horizontal bars of black, red and white, the colors of the Oromo national flag, back the words and image. There's room behind the house for American-style cookouts, although the restaurant is just a part of its mission, which includes counseling, language training and translations — anything to help the community become more self-reliant.

Two of suburban Maryland's Oromo-owned restaurants are owned by sisters: In Burtonsville, Genet Gonfo operates Soretti's Ethiopian Cuisine with her husband, Gheleta "Gil" Kitila; and in Hyattsville, older sister Kelem

Lemu and her husband, Adamu Lemu, own Shegga Restaurant and Coffee Shop.

Genet and Gil started their business in January 2008 when they launched Coffee Oromia, which they had planned as a neighborhood coffee shop that offered wraps and sandwiches. But they found that to be a crowded niche, and by mid-2009, they changed their restaurant's name to Soretti and now offer a full menu of Ethiopian dishes. "Soretti" is an Oromo term of affection that means one who brings good luck and life's riches. It's often a nickname given by a woman to her first daughter-in-law, and Genet has liked it since her mother-in-law gave it to her.

Gil visited the U.S. in 1969 as an American Field Service exchange student. He finished high school in Ethiopia, then attended college in the U.S. But he returned home from college to the communist revolution, and he left soon afterwards, making his way to Maryland through India, Germany and Atlanta. Genet arrived in 1984, having worked in restaurants in Ethiopia, and she became an accountant in the U.S. after getting a degree at the University of Maryland. She and Gil owned a General Nutrition Center franchise in D.C. for a decade until a dispute with a landlord forced them to give up the business. That's when they became restaurateurs.

The walls of Soretti's feature matted prints of photos showing Ethiopian life, plus a few pieces of Ethiopian art, and a large poster with a passage from Antony Wild's *The Dark History of Coffee* that discusses coffee rituals in Oromo life.

"We didn't really plan to own an Ethiopian restaurant," Gil says, two years into his new enterprise. "We couldn't make a living with the coffee concept." Fortunately Genet likes to cook, although "I don't know any other way than the way I do it at home," she says.

Gil is very political, and he has an idea about why so few Oromos own restaurants in the U.S. "Oromos have not been business people," he says. "They were colonized and conquered in the 19th Century by Menelik. Of course, Abyssinians consider him their hero, but they remember him for forcing people to be united."

And yet, Soretti's menu names its dishes in Amharic, not Afaan Oromo. They do this to keep from confusing customers. "To me, language is just an instrument of communication," Gil says. "It's not about pride or anything." But he's clearly very proud of his heritage. "The Abyssinians are so controversial," he says, and if his menu were in Afaan Oromo, "they would make a big issue about this."

"We have no problem with other Ethiopians," Genet adds. "They have a problem with us." Their daughter once served an Ethiopian family who asked in Amharic what she spoke, and when she said Oromo, they "gave her a hard time" because she didn't speak much Amharic.

Genet says that her husband opened her eyes to the country's cultural and political conflicts, and she's more quietly passionate than he is. The majority of Amharis she meets are fair and reasonable, but she sometimes still feels like an outsider to the community. "I have a restaurant and they make me feel like I don't have the liberty to call it whatever I want," she says. "I'm not accepted as an Ethiopian if I focus on who I am. I would feel intimidated to speak Oromo among many Ethiopians. It's subtle, but it's there."

If Genet's sister, Kelem Lemu, experiences any of that at Shegga, she doesn't care to talk about it. "It's not my thing," she says of politics. "I believe everybody should work together and have harmony between everyone."

Her restaurant is about a mile from the campus of the University of Maryland, and that makes for a more non-Ethiopian crowd. In fact, on a Thursday afternoon in August, her patrons included a fellow reading The Wall Street Journal, a professor in front of a laptop grading a pile of papers, and a young father with two toddlers who placed his order on the way to a table and ordered extra *injera* for the kids (then later photographed them with his cell phone as they surrounded a tray of half-eaten food).

Shegga, too, began more as a coffeehouse than a restaurant, serving breakfast when it opened. But soon Kelem and Adamu, who runs a van transport serviced, decided to morph it into a restaurant serving only lunch and dinner. Soretti's and Shegga have similar menus and even similar lunch specials for $6.95. But they're 19 miles apart in different towns, so there's no competition. "Shegga" means "beautiful" in Amharic and "good" in Afaan Oromo. Kelem worked in restaurants and drove a cab before launching Shegga, and Adamu still owns his transport service.

The two restaurants are about equal in size. Soretti's has a slick website, and it's a little more trendy, located in a strip mall with other international cuisines nearby. Shegga, with no presence on the web, is more homey but still contemporary, situated next to a Mexican/Salvadoran restaurant and across the street from a Subway. Kelem and Adamu also market Ethiopian Horse Harar, a special blend of coffee created by Caffe Pronto in Annapolis. The brand takes its name from MAO Horse, an Ethiopian coffee export company. Like Soretti's, Shegga names its dishes in Amharic, but for Kelem, it's more a matter of comfort than commerce. "When I grew up," she says, "I just knew it as *injera*."

THE ERITREAN POPULATION in D.C. is considerably smaller than the Ethiopian population, so naturally, there are far fewer restaurants. But the community still has plenty of choices, and lately, a few new restaurants have opened around U Street. These places have all of the familiar dishes, usually presented in Tigrinya rather than Amharic on the menus, and they all serve spaghetti and *cotoletti*.

Two of them are away from the U Street cluster: Over in Adams Morgan, where 18th Street nicks the eastern end of U Street on its way to Dupont Circle, there's Keren, a small place, with an even smaller dinner menu, that specializes in breakfast for its almost exclusively Eritrean clientele; and Dahlak (formerly Harambe), with a much bigger list of entrees. Their separation from even the Adams Morgan mini-cluster a few blocks up 18th Street means they're a destination that you need to know about to discover.

On 9th Street, among the dense row of Ethiopian restaurants and markets, there's Ambassador, a bar and restaurant named for a hotel in Asmara that's a gathering place for young people. Its Italian-influenced breakfast menu includes frittatas, mortadella sandwiches and smoothies. The menu lists its meals in a mix of transliterated Amharic and Tigrinya, and when the owner, Amanual Kiflu, puts the daily specials on a chalkboard in front of his entrance, he writes them in Ethiopic script — using the Amharic rather than the Tigrinya names. It's all part of his design to honor his homeland while bring the two countries together at the table.

A few storefronts away, you'll find Zula, the oldest Eritrean restaurant on the strip, and also the smallest and most unadorned. It has five tables that can seat maybe 15, with room for 10 more at the bar. Two flat-screen TVs play at once, one with American programs (*The Simpsons* around dinnertime), and one with EriTV, both of them silent as Tigrayan music plays on the stereo.

Zula has a small menu with all the basics, including lots of pasta and *cotoletti*, and a full bar with Zibib, the Eritrean-made ouzo. The sparsely decorated yellow walls have only a few pieces of art, including one that depict "Eritrean Coffee," which looks more like chocolate syrup, dripping from the *jebena* into the *sini*.

Such a tiny place can only survive on the loyalty of community members. As I looked at the menu in the window one day, a man out front told me that the food is great and I should try it. The same thing happened a few days earlier at the newer Ambassador, where a man praised its ecumenism: an Eritrean owner, an Ethiopian cook, and servers from both cultures. All of the neighborhood's Eritrean restaurants fly the Eritrean flag, with an American flag as well at Ambassador.

These places are on the south side of 9th Street at its intersection with U. Cross over U and stroll the north side of 9th and the neighborhood changes quickly, from a well-developed restaurant row into a block or two with more dilapidated buildings than developed ones.

On this block you'll find Bella Café and Restaurant, a contemporary-looking, two-level establishment whose name belies its Eritrean cuisine (with Italian dishes on the menu as well). It's in a spot that once housed Asmara Café, another Eritrean restaurant. Nafka, a tiny Eritrean eatery that never really stood much of a chance, opened and closed right next door in less than a year.

And six blocks up U Street from the 9th is the easy-to-miss Selam Restaurant, a homey café that doubles as an eclectic dance club on Friday and Saturday nights. The name on the restaurant's banner suggests Middle Eastern cuisine, until you notice the Eritrean flag beside it. It's small, with room for 20 at tables and 10 more at the bar, and when live music isn't playing, Tigrinya CDs are. You can also watch two wall-mounted flat-screen televisions with the sound turned off, one airing American cable news, and one broadcasting Eri-TV, the all-Eritrean network of news and music.

Selam is quieter on weekdays, but on weekends it hosts a mix of multicultural non-Africans and Eritreans (mostly men) who gather to drink, listen to music, and order a meal. The menu isn't large — five or six veggie selections, and spicy *tibs* of beef, chicken or lamb. But its generous portions are flavorful, spicy and liberal with the jalapeños.

The growth of the city's Eritrean community means more selections for diners. It also means more competition for the largest Eritrean restaurant in town: Far from the U Street cluster, and a few blocks from the district's Convention Center just north of Chinatown, the Eritrean Community and Cultural Center has served meals since its creation in 1990. It opens daily at 9 a.m. for breakfast and closes at 10 p.m., with service until midnight on Friday and Saturday. The restaurant is non-profit, with proceeds benefiting the center, but the wait staff and three cooks — one of whom has worked there for 15 years — are all paid. Meals cost about $10.

The menu, in transliterated Tigrinya, is as big as any commercial restaurant, and in some cases bigger: You can get beef, lamb or chicken *kulwa, hamli, shiro, quanta firfir, gored gored* and more. Breakfast features *ful,* frittatas, or steak and eggs. Henok Tsehaye, a member of the center's board of directors, says the restaurant is especially famous for its *cotoletti* and other sandwiches, including the *imbolito,* a potato sandwich that's another Italian holdover in Eritrean culture.

They get their *injera* from Zenebech in Shaw, even though she's Ethiopian. "We don't have any Eritreans making *injera* in bulk," Henok explains. "It has to do with the population size. Ethiopians have a very large population here."

The restaurant has a full bar with Zibib but no *mes* (that's honey wine in Tigrinya) unless someone makes it for catered special functions. The place is big, with tables and booths that seat around 60 in the main room, plus half a dozen around the bar, and up to 100 in the cafeteria-style back room, which has plenty of space for buffet dinners, a stage for live performances, and a Bingo board, along with a few watercolors of Eritrean life decorating the walls.

Henok concurs that there's not too much difference between Eritrean and Ethiopian cooking. "Ours is probably milder," he says, although he prefers his food spicy, "probably because of how I grew up" in Addis. Eritreans may use more oil and less butter, adds Tedros Asmelash, a patron at the restaurant, so the food sometimes isn't as greasy. Tedros prefers milder cooking, and he says, "Where I come from, my grandmother said that whenever you put too much spice, you lose the taste of what you're cooking."

Henok was born in Eritrea but grew up in Addis Ababa when his family moved there, so he has some perspective on the two cultures. He arrived in D.C. in 1981 and knew of Mamma Desta's restaurant — he's quick to point out that she was Eritrean — but he never got around to eating there before it disappeared. He now works at Reagan National Airport in facilities management, and he spends most of his free time at the center, rarely eating at other Eritrean restaurants around D.C.

But if the occasion arises, he's perfectly happy to eat at an Ethiopian-owned restaurant. He has Ethiopian friends and says he "appreciates the food of certain restaurants. I would say Eritreans here are more lenient toward Ethiopian restaurants versus Ethiopians going to Eritrean restaurants." From the Eritrean point of view, he adds, "that animosity may have been there long ago, but it's something that's fading now."

SO WHERE DO YOU FIND the best Ethiopian food in Washington, and who's the best Ethiopian cook? How about Kebebush Demissie, who prepared three meals a day at 2009 Wyoming Ave. NW.

But don't look for her place on any list of D.C.'s Ethiopian restaurant: It's the address of Ethiopia's ambassador to the United States, and Kebebush, formerly a chef to her country's prime minister, was the personal cook for the ambassador, his wife, and their teen-age daughter from 2005 until late 2009, when Ethiopia recalled Ambassador Samuel Assefa. Prime Minister Meles Zenawi has said that he won't appoint a new ambassador until several months after Ethiopia's May 2010 elections.

Kebebush is so good, her colleagues at the embassy claim, that she once won a cooking competition against Marcus Samuelsson, the Ethiopian-born, Swedish-raised New York City master chef and restaurateur. They say she even chopped onions faster than he did.

There's no kitchen at the embassy, so the building's employees — virtually all of them Ethiopian — have to pack their lunch or go out for their noontime meal (the closest Ethiopian restaurant is about three miles away).

The embassy is located just off of Connecticut Avenue along the horseshoe-shaped International Drive. It's flanked on the left by the embassies of Kuwait, Bahrain and Jordan, and on the right by Bangladesh, Ghana and Israel. Ethiopia has occupied its building since 2000, and the courtyard's northern wall hosts a metal diptych relief — with "Ethiopia" written in fluid Ethiopic script — created by two Ethiopian artists, Skunder Boghossian and Kededech Tekle-Ab. The designs on the two halves of the piece depict images of Ethiopian life, history and culture: a *mesob*, a walia ibex, a nyala, Aksum, Gondar, a *jebena*, a *berele*, Orthodox crosses, and a willowy *odaa* tree.

You can walk right up to the front door of all of the embassies on International Drive except for the gated and guarded one owned by the Israelis, with whom the Ethiopians united in November 2008 for a joint and belated celebration of the new year, according to each culture's calendar (on the American calendar, that's Sept. 12 for the Ethiopians, and some time in September or October for the Israelis). The Ethiopians suggested the event as an outreach to the Jewish community.

When the embassy has a small function — say, for 20 or 30 people — Kebebush prepares the food at the ambassador's residence and they truck it over in serving trays. For gatherings in the hundreds, which happen a few times a year, the embassy reaches out to Ethiopian restaurants in the area. Queen of Sheba in D.C. has catered an affair, and so has Eyo in Falls Church, Va. The food at these big events is almost entirely Ethiopian, with perhaps some appetizers from other cuisines.

At weekday lunch in the embassy's tearoom, where employees gather to eat, the food is usually (although not always) non-Ethiopian. Still, their way of eating sometimes harkens home.

"Ethiopians are incapable of eating alone," says Annette Sheckler, a senior adviser at the embassy, and one of its few non-Ethiopian employees. "They're incapable. If you walk downstairs, somebody will ask you to eat with them." The people who gather in the tearoom will sometimes put the food they packed into the center of the table for all to share. The ambassador even treats the staff now and then by laying out a catered restaurant spread.

Sheckler attended college in Illinois before the state had Ethiopian restaurants, and she first ate the cuisine with some Ethiopian friends, who made their own spices and substituted white bread for *injera*. The first time someone gave her *gursha*, "I thought it was very nice," she says, "but I thought, why are they stuffing my mouth with food."

"I was famous with *gursha* because of my long fingers," adds Solomon Mekonnen, a financial officer at the embassy, holding up his hand to show the half dozen people gathered around a table one afternoon. He once gave *gursha* in the window of a U Street restaurant, and passers-by stopped to watch.

Everyone in the group chuckled, except for Fikerte Kidanemariam, who simply said, "I hate *gursha*. It is too big." She explained that to do it properly, you have to fill your hand with food from fingers to palm, and that's just too much to force into someone else's mouth.

Fikerte was the culinary sage and scholar of the group, the assistant to the ambassador since 1999, the mother of two daughters who came to America before she did, and the grandmother of an 18-year-old grandson born in Dallas. Her sister is married to Daniel Mesfin, the author of *Exotic Ethiopian Cooking*, the most thorough and edifying Ethiopian cookbook you can buy.

What Fikerte doesn't know about Ethiopian food and cooking probably isn't knowable.

Amharic uses the same word, *duba*, to mean pumpkin and squash. So how does a woman indicate the difference if, for example, she sends her daughter to the market to buy one or the other? Before Fikerte could answer, three Ethiopian men at the table said there is no squash in Ethiopia, just pumpkin. Fikerte coolly set them straight, to their great surprise: There certainly is squash, and it's served steamed, but it's never used to make *duba wot*, which requires pumpkin. If Fikerte wants a pumpkin *duba*, as opposed to a squash *duba*, she asks for the "big one." The men then said that they didn't like *duba wot* all that much, but Fikerte again interceded: *Duba wot* cooked well tastes like *doro wot*. The men didn't challenge her.

Fikerte hasn't shopped in an Ethiopian market in the U.S. in her 10-plus years here. Her friends and family bring spices and supplies from home. When she lived in Ethiopia, she even made her own *shiro* and *berbere* powders, but she no longer has the time — nor, one senses, the strong desire — to do it here.

The familiar dish *doro wot* may just look like a chicken leg in a spicy red stew, but preparing it well could change the course of a woman's life. Back in the 1960s, when Fikerte was a bride, if a woman couldn't cook *doro wot*, she wasn't ready to get married. She had to know how to cut the chicken up into 12 parts — no more, no fewer. "They don't bother girls so much now," she says, "but back then, you had to know how to split the chicken properly."

As the conversation went on, two of the diplomats at the table began to recall some foods unique to their cultures. Solomon is Amhari, but Assefa Delil is Gurage, and Fekadu Ayana, the embassy's counselor for community affairs, is a teacher in Ethiopia, and an Oromo.

Here in America, Assefa's wife cooks for him, and he only goes to an Ethiopian restaurant if he wants to show out-of-town guests the community. The Gurage use the word *ajed* to refer to an exceptional cook, and the freshness of an Ethiopian meal matters a lot. If a dish wasn't prepared that day, he says, "I can tell immediately, I can smell it." He can also tell what kind of butter, "a good one or a bad one," the chef used, and he's particularly fond of butter in his coffee, a Gurage and Oromo custom that the others eschew.

The Gurage gave *kitfo* to the wider Ethiopian culture, and they like to mix *gomen* with *ayib* to make a dish they call *zumamojad*. That's something you'll find in Ethiopian restaurants, although not with its Gurage name.

But *oqut*, another Gurage favorite, never quite caught on. It's made from young pumpkin leaves that you boil until the upper part separates from the lower part, and then you mix it with onion, garlic and a lot of butter and *ayib*. This is a dish eaten in the countryside, and Assefa describes it with particular delight and cultural pride. There's also *anebabera*, a slightly thicker type of *injera* made from wheat, and baked in an elaborate process of layering, folding and pressing, then seasoned with butter, *berbere* and coriander.

Fikadu shared memories of *chumbo*, an elaborately prepared bread served only in the western portion of his native Oromia, and also *anchote*, a potato-like plant prepared with jalapeños and garlic. Oromos enjoy *bunakala*, the whole roasted coffee pod, mixed with butter or milk, and *chuko*, roasted barley with lots of butter. These dishes come from very rural cultures, which accounts for the use of so much rich milk and butter to flavor them.

And the group all chuckled when someone mentioned *houza*, a tea made from the mildly hallucinogenic leaf *chat*, which is popular among many Africans — and illegal in some places. Ethiopians also use warmed coffee leaves, or *koti*, as they would tea leaves, adding other spices to create a potable treat.

Ethiopians sometimes call the puny *injera* made in America "forged," and Solomon says that "if you gave American *injera* to an Ethiopian at home, they would think you are stingy." *Injera* is bigger in Ethiopia, sometimes 20 inches in diameter, compared to the usual 12 in the U.S.

One American custom has permeated the households of the diplomats: While they still prefer to eat from a shared plate in the middle of the table, their children have come to shun the practice.

Solomon looked around for a big home serving plate when he moved to the U.S., but "wherever they go," he says of his children, "they see people eating by themselves" from their own plate, so that's what they tend to prefer. Assefa and his wife like to share, but their children prefer their own plates. Fekadu calls this a move "from socialization to individualization."

This doesn't happen at America's Ethiopian restaurants, where people always eat from a plate shared by all. A few places offer silverware to replace fingers and rice to replace *injera*, but that's rare. The first wave of Ethio-

American restaurateurs were traditionalists, and that's how we've come to know Ethiopian dining.

But why don't Ethiopian restaurants serve any of the dishes enjoyed by a wider range of Ethiopian cultures? Why do they only serve what's become known as the national cuisine? Because the first immigrants also were from the north, where the cuisine originated, and because commerce trumps culture, so it's too late to change the American palate. As Assefa puts it: "If restaurants make all the traditional foods, they won't make any profit."

ONE AFTERNOON, as I chatted with a grocery store owner at Skyline Plaza in Falls Church, in walked Zenebech Dessu's son Mente, making the daily delivery of his mother's fresh *injera* from their shop along U Street.

When you talk about "Ethiopians in Washington, D.C.," you need to include cities like Falls Church (with its Skyline Plaza), Arlington and Alexandria in Virginia, or Takoma Park, Silver Spring and Wheaton in Maryland, where Ethiopian restaurants and grocery stores form mini-clusters of a community that has, in fact "moved away" to live and to open businesses.

Sometimes you'll find these suburban businesses in groups of three or four. Others are more scattered, isolated from a cluster, along side streets, and situated in tiny plazas among residential neighborhoods, or just one of dozens of diverse businesses among block after block of commercial property. Skyline Plaza in Falls Church is the largest cluster apart from U Street, but it gets plenty of competition from the other restaurants and grocery stores sprinkled around the suburbs.

Few of them are large, even fewer are fancy, and their customers are largely Ethiopian, except perhaps on weekend nights, when the rest of the neighborhood goes out to dine. Their owners are former cab driver or parking lot attendants or teachers with degrees in biology or chemistry or computer technology, investing in their culture and seeking a place of their own. They tend their businesses from morning to night, some with a few employees, usually young Ethiopian men and women who are new to America. Their places come and go, for as with any business community, they're at the mercy of an economy that offers opportunity to everyone and promises success to no one.

Arlington has a good number of Ethiopian restaurants and businesses, especially along a several-mile stretch of Columbia Pike that turns into Falls Church. The pike's Lalibela II, an offshoot of D.C.'s thriving Lalibela restaurant at 14th and P streets, becomes a hoppin' Ethiopian disco on Friday and Saturday nights, sometimes snarling traffic for several blocks along the highway as people wait to get a parking place.

One special Arlington place is the four-in-one Dama, a restaurant, grocery store bakery and diner on the 1500 block of Columbia Pike. Like so many Ethiopian establishments, it's unspectacular from the road and from its tattered and crowded sloped parking lot. But inside, it's the place to be on Sunday morning, when the neighborhood's Ethiopian Orthodox Christians gather before and after church.

Better yet, its co-owner, Almaz Dama, earned a diploma at the Bethesda, Md., campus of the French *L'Academie de Cuisine*, where her teacher was Roland Mesnier, who served as a White House pastry chef for 25 years. And while most of her baked goods lean toward the continental, she does offer a few Ethiopian-tinged desserts.

Almaz came to America at age 19, earned a degree in nutrition at Howard University, and opened a restaurant called Dama on North Capital Street in Washington in 1983 with her sister. Business wasn't so great, and that enterprise closed four years later. She spent the next decade cooking at other places and learning other chefs' secrets. Then, in 1999, she opened the new Dama with her relatives — two sisters, a brother, and a cousin — and between them they now manage the side-by-side quartet, as well as a Silver Spring, Md., restaurant called Bete that sells Almaz's baked goods in a café alongside a small restaurant.

In her work as a pastry chef, Almaz distinguishes between European-influenced "cake" and Ethiopian "pastry." Ethiopians don't have a cultural tradition of sweet baked goods (see Chapter 1), so her bakery's homeland treats are often fried and not always sweet.

For example, there's *sambussa*, a triangular fried shell of dough stuffed with spicy lentils or beef, served at many restaurants as an appetizer. *Pasti* came to Ethiopia in the last century or so from Italian influence, but Ethiopians have adopted it as their own. It's sweet and dessert-like: moist on the inside, crunchy on the outside (from frying), and somewhat amorphous, shaped like a giant amoeba. Another of Almaz's Italian-influenced treats is a *bombolino*, which she refers to as an "Ethiopian doughnut." It's dark brown and deep-fried, chewy in the middle and peppered with effervescent cumin seeds, denser than an American doughnut, and prepared with much less sugar.

Almaz's original creation is a tall round cake made of teff and other flours. She uses a blend because teff has no gluten, and the cake "needs something to hold it together." It's light brown inside, just like teff, with thin layers of pastry cream throughout, and with chunks of glazed peaches, strawberries and kiwi on top.

It's delicious, and not too sweet. Almaz has altered her recipes over the years to cut down on the sugar because her Ethiopian customers have suggested it. She also uses less cream in her cakes and cookies than an American baker would use, another concession to her clients.

Dama specializes in vegan cakes that Ethiopians can eat during their longest stretch of fasting during the nearly two full months of the Fasika (Easter) season. Fasting forbids the consumption of animal products, so cakes without eggs and milk are a holiday delicacy, and Almaz has become known and appreciated for hers. She even tends to get more non-Ethiopian customers — vegans seeking special treats — during this time of year.

But mostly her customers are Ethiopian and Eritrean, both in the bakery and the restaurant. On Sunday mornings, the café fills up early with people having breakfast, and there's always a line of three or four customers waiting at the bakery counter to pick up cakes and cookies. The restaurant gets busy after 1 p.m. when church lets out. Almaz's sister-in-law, Amsale, works the bakery counter, and Amsale's husband, Hailu, who is Almaz's brother, does the heavy lifting, rolling dollies of supplies back and forth between the restaurant, grocery story and bakery.

The Sunday morning café patrons run a gamut, from tri-generational families to young couples to groups of men who take their time drinking their coffee. Children sometimes run freely about, reigned in when necessary by the parents. People know each other, and Almaz welcomes many of them with a hug, a kiss, or a gentle shoulder bump, a customary Ethiopian greeting.

The café bakery opens into the cramped market, and that opens into the roomier restaurant. The market has spices on one rack, books and videos in a display case surrounding the register, chilled goods in a glass showcase, and a corner rack stacked with *injera* from half a dozen of the area's *injera* bakeries, each with its own label.

Dama doesn't make *injera*, and it doesn't need to: Almaz leaves that specialty to others, serving as distributor for their breads, including several brands of decorative round golden *ambasha*. With so many *injera* labels around the area, most of which deliver, and with so much other cooking going on there day and night, it's just as easy, and certainly just as authentic, to buy *injera* from the places that specialize in it. She does make *dabo kolo*, a doughy European-style bread common in Ethiopia, as well as *kita*, the thin, *berbere*-spiced "Ethiopian pizza" made by heating batter in a stovetop pan.

When catering customers order food, the kitchen packages the variety of dishes in large rectangular buffet-style foil tins, and on weekends, the market's countertops fill up with them as they await pickup or delivery. Dama only has one truck, and on days when they cater three or four weddings, the truck makes multiple runs to venues all around the area, even as far away as Baltimore.

The fourth room of the Dama family enterprise is a diner, located in a separate building just across a side street from the restaurant complex. The diner serves lunch and dinner Monday through Friday, and its menu is entirely non-Ethiopian: You can get a Caesar salad, a turkey club, pasta with marinara, Indian curry chicken, tilapia and a variety of other sandwiches and platters.

There's a U.S. Navy facility not far away, and sometimes the sailors come for lunch. Mostly, though, the customers are Ethiopian. On weekends, Dama rents the place for private events of up to 60 people. When it's not being rented, it's a warehouse for the mountain of *injera* packages necessary to fill each weekend's orders.

To do all of this work, Almaz counts on family. She, sister Lemlem, brother Hailu and his wife, Amsale, own and operate the complex. A bevy of nieces, nephews, cousins and in-laws make up much of the rest of the staff, and she often gives jobs to new people who come over, whether family or not, to help get them started in America.

Dama's nearest restaurant competition is Lalibela II, about a mile up the road. It's a different kind of place, but still a place for Ethiopians to gather, and both seem to thrive. About two miles from Dama on Columbia Pike, there's Meaza, which takes up the 5700 block. It has a big modern wide-open dining room with contemporary furnishings and a stage for performances. Next door, connected to the restaurant, there's a market and café with takeout wine and beer, along with books and videos. There's also a patio for *al fresco* dining.

In nearby Alexandria, Va., there's the only Ethiopian restaurant with two names: To the *ferenj* it's Waterfront Gourmet, but to Ethiopians it's Bahir Dar, the name of a town on the southern shore of Ethiopia's Lake Tana. The stylishly designed, multi-level Bahir Dar is on a waterfront, located inside a snazzy food court that looks out onto the Potomac River in Alexandria's historic Old Town.

Bahir Dar does not — and *will* not — serve its meals on a common platter for all to share. Instead, the patrons get shiny round concave black plates of their own. The dishes they've ordered come in small bowls of different shapes and colors, and the *injera* comes on its own plate as well. Your server gets you started by picking up a piece of *injera* with tongs and unrolling it onto your personal dinner plate. Then, you use a spoon to put your dishes on your *injera*.

The restaurant's owner, Yessi Burouk, does this because of how she was raised by her middle-class family in a changing Ethiopia. Her grandmother served meals in the old-fashioned way, with one central plate from which everyone ate together, and Yessi still values the community of a meal. "I like to eat with people," she says. "But some people, the way they eat" — she stops, then uses her hands and mouth to show how people sometimes sloppily gobble up their food. So she serves her food the way they do in modern Ethiopian homes and restaurants.

Bahir Dar hosts educational tours of high school students, church groups and international tourists. The restaurant's tranquil setting lets patrons look out of its tall windows onto a multi-leveled riverside plaza that dips down toward the Potomac and the sailboats in their docks. There's a cluster of small arts and crafts shops just across the plaza, and kiosks that teach historic lessons about the community and the region.

Yessi promotes her place as "the oldest food in Old Town," a reference to the ancient history of the cuisine. "Ethiopia is the oldest nation on earth," she says, "and we're in synch with Old Town, which is preserving history." She came to the U.S. in the final months of 1974, has a degree in health information management, owned some Greek restaurants in D.C. as far back as the 1980s (her father was educated in Greece), and opened Bahir Dar in 2003. Her Amharic name means "blessed," just like the Hebrew *baruch*, which is akin to "barack."

Ethiopian restaurants don't get much more eclectic than Caboose Café and Bakery, located in Alexandria's Del Ray neighborhood, not far from Bahir Dar. Del Ray bills its Mt. Vernon Avenue stretch of restaurant, antique shops, ice creameries and boutiques as the place "Where Main Street Still Exists," although this 21st Century Main Street hosts Thai, Chinese, Mexican and Ethiopian food, along with cafés, yoga and Pilates.

Caboose serves specialty sandwiches (Cuban, French dip, California croissant), omelets, salads, artisan breads and a good variety of pastries and desserts. There's plenty of coffee, too, including Ethiopian Harar and Yirgacheffe varieties, which you can purchase by the pound in glistening navy blue bags. An awning covers the outdoor patio, and the wine list includes *t'ej*. The tables indoor are all made of wood, and some are tall with stools. The works of local artists hang on the walls, and the whole place is redolent with bakery-fresh delights.

Just one problem: You'd never know this is an Ethiopian restaurant if you didn't already know. Nothing about Caboose says "Ethiopian" until you read the menu. The restaurant offers a dozen beef, chicken and veggie dishes, including traditional combinations, but only after 5 p.m. The takeout menu doesn't mention Ethiopian cuisine, and the decals on the window proclaim "Cake, Pastry, Artisan Bread, Latte, Espresso, Omelets" — a taste of everything except, as the menu says, its "Ethiopian specialties prepared daily on the premises from the finest ingredients."

Owners Rhoda Worku and Meskerem Kifle opened their place in 2004 as a coffee shop and café serving breakfast and lunch, taking its name from a red caboose on the grounds of a school across the street. When they later introduced a dinner menu, some customer began to suggest that they include Ethiopian selections as well.

Rhoda came to the U.S. in 1982 to escape the Derg and lived outside of San Francisco for a few years before settling in the D.C.-Virginia area. She refers to her partner in business as her sister, and they were raised together as part of an extended family of close friends, although they're not actually blood relations.

Their restaurant only serves Ethiopian food for dinner because, Rhoda says, "lunch is usually a quick meal for most people, and Ethiopian food takes more time to eat." A lot of their lunch traffic is also takeout for working people, and that's not so easy to do with Ethiopian food.

Apart from family and friends, Caboose has virtually no Ethiopian customers for dinner, and they don't get a lot of requests for *t'ej*. They don't promote Ethiopian food in the window because when they designed the place, they had no plans to serve it. But because it's a limited Ethiopian menu, and only available for dinner, they've still chosen not to emphasize it.

These are Arlington's and Alexandria's more contemporary places, fancy enough for tourists and the non-Ethiopian neighbors, but with authentic food that satisfies Ethiopians. They're just not Dama, where food, culture and politics all come together for a dynamic experience.

The conversation at Dama ranges from family matters to the week that just ended to politics back in the homeland, and many Ethiopians consider the country's president, Meles Zenawi, to be a dictator who holds office through fraudulent elections.

Hailu welcomes this discourse at his restaurant, and he's happy to take part: Like Yonas in Falls Church, he has strong feelings about the state of things in Ethiopia and what it would take to effect true freedom.

In 1981, under the communist Derg regime, Hailu won a scholarship to study in Cuba. He left Ethiopia with no intention of returning home. He attended school for two years, then moved to Canada and soon to the United States, where members of his family, who came from Ethiopia's Gurage region, slowly joined him. His means of escape was a common one for education-worthy Ethiopians under the Derg.

"It was the cream of the crop that was leaving the country," he recalls, "the top of the top of the students." Back then, the government paid good students $150 a month to go to college. That's what an entire family might earn in a month. The Derg would kill people on the streets and announce it on the radio, Hailu says, but now, with a constitution, the government just doesn't brag when it eliminates the opposition.

"They have certain laws that they break every day," he says. "There are laws that they use when people try to demonstrate without a permit, which you shouldn't need to have, because it's your right to demonstrate. Some of it is unbelievable."

Dama has many Eritrean customers, and while they sometimes discuss politics with their Ethiopian kin, the discourse remains civil. That's what Hailu would like to see among Ethiopia's many cultures, and he says that Meles only foments division by dismissing the country's minority cultures as not being truly "Ethiopian."

When Italy returned an ancient obelisk that it looted during the occupation of the 1930s, Meles said the object had no meaning to the Gurage, the Woylaita and the many other southern cultures that lived so far from the Amhara-Tigray region of Aksum. This offended Hailu, who is proudly Gurage *and* Ethiopian. "It is that history that makes Ethiopian history," he says.

Now he hopes that President Obama will look at Ethiopia's record of human rights and not help the government to continue it. He approves of food aid to Ethiopia, but not aid to a government that engages in abuse. "It's that kind of help," he says, "which is sustaining this."

But he doesn't see change happening any time soon, and he scoffs at Ethiopians who debate whether things were better under the emperor, the Derg or the current government.

"We always argue about when we were better off," he says. "What I say is, we deserve better. When we are allowed to discuss our own problems openly, we will survive as a nation. In Ethiopia, that's what we are missing."

Communities of Cuisine:
Urban Life

Wrigley Field pops up on Chicago's West Addison Street in middle of a city neighborhood like a giant that descended a beanstalk, and on game days, pubs and restaurants in the surrounding blocks teem with fans gorging on burgers, fries, sausage, Guinness and Bud, and spilling out onto the sidewalk at all-American places like Palermo's, Irish Oak, Matsuya, El Burrito and Sluggers Sports Bar & Dueling Pianos.

But on an unusually cool Fourth of July weekend in Chicago, during the summer of 2009, there was another game in town. About a mile west on Addison, at Lane Technical High School's stadium, thousands of fans gathered to watch athletes from around the continent play the world's most popular sport, feasting between matches on *kitfo, siga tibs, sambussa, kolo* and, of course, *injera*.

For the first time in its 26-year history, the Ethiopian Sports Federation in North America chose a Midwestern city to host its annual gathering, where Ethiopians come together for cultural events and soccer matches between teams from the U.S. and Canada. Inside the stadium, two dozen vendors, chosen by lottery, sold homemade-on-the-spot Ethiopian food from their concession booths.

Most of the vendors at the soccer tournament were not restaurateurs: They were just Chicago area Ethiopian-Americans who wanted to take part in the event, and they all had stories to tell about their journeys to America and their love for their native cuisine. They paid $2,500 a piece to set up their short-lived restaurants, and they pretty much all agreed that they wouldn't end up making much profit, if any, for their efforts: Only about 8,000 people came to the gathering, a consequence of the struggling economy, and far short of the 15,000 the organizers had anticipated.

But that didn't seem to matter to the cooks and servers who spent five days — some of them rainy, but mercifully, none too humid — feeding their compatriots.

Each restaurant except for one — there were 24 in all — had a name and created a sign to announce it. They chose names that meant something to them, and often something very personal. Eskinder Tadele, a taxi driver who's lived in Chicago for 14 years, and whose wife is a fine cook, named his restaurant Yoni Café, after his 3-year-old son. Betlehem Yikono, just five years in America, and still speaking tentative English, operated Lili's Restaurant, named for her 3-month-old daughter. Rahel Taye didn't name her Little Ethiopia after Esate, her 5-year-old daughter, but her banner displayed an Ethiopian flag to the left of the restaurant's name and Esate's photo to the right.

Hirut Assefa called her place Tinqsh, after a popular Addis Ababa restaurant owned by the mother of a friend, hoping to capitalize on memories of the original. Altefugn dared you not to stop: The name is an Amharic word that means "just stop by" or "don't pass me by." Chicago Style Restaurant was anything but that with its full menu of Ethiopian dishes, topped by *kitfo* written only in Amharic. Asmaru was named for its owner/chef, Asmaru Ayenew, or "Dr. Injera" as she's been called. Banatu is one of Amsale Fakibelu's favorite restaurants in Addis, so that's what she named her concession.

Only one place had no name, and no wonder: Its menu consisted of hot dogs, cheeseburgers, double cheeseburgers, chicken sandwiches, steak sandwiches and a Good Humor cooler. The closest thing to Ethiopian it cooked was a grilled chicken leg, rescued from becoming *doro wot.*

Some of the names were scrawled in Amharic, English or both on cardboard or construction paper. Some were professionally printed on large vinyl banners, lush with color and hung with brads from the flap of the concession's tent. Altefugn had the most comprehensive banner, featuring the restaurant's name, its numerous dishes, and the prices for everything, all in both Amharic and English. Madura Genet, which means "land of heaven," wrote its name in Amharic with no English translation. (The crowd was almost entirely Ethiopian.) Ye'enat Guada, or "mother's kitchen," offered business cards with its name in big red Amharic letters and a translation in smaller print beneath it. The owner, Hilina Mohammed, who doesn't own a restaurant, created the cards herself for the soccer event.

A prize for originality probably would have gone to the banner for Gojo, which wrote the first two letters of its name using the English letters "G-o," and the last two with the single Amharic letter pronounced "jo." That letter looks a bit like a hut when printed squarely, and that's what a *gojo* is: a thatched-roof dwelling built by people of the Ethiopian countryside. Gojo's sign placed the unique portmanteau spelling on the left, the Amharic words "megeb bet" ("food house," or restaurant) on the right, and in the middle, a drawing of a house, meant to represent a *gojo*, but looking much too boxy, more like something from 1950s suburban America.

Among these many amateurs, half a dozen actual restaurants set up booths to promote themselves. Chicago's big popular uptown Ethiopian Diamond attended, and so did the small downtown La Sera Café, owned by two Ethiopian sisters. Blue Nile of Chicago and Addis Ababa of Evanston served food as well. So did Ledet, a pair of popular Atlanta restaurants, one in the city, one in the suburbs. The owner and her family came to Chicago to set up their kitchen for the week.

The restaurants all offered a vegetarian combination along with lots of beef and some lamb, and very little chicken. But one selection stood out: Every restaurant served *kitfo*, and virtually every one listed it atop its menu. There need be no further proof of the how this Gurage dish has so thoroughly saturated Ethiopian cuisine.

Few Americans eat their *kitfo* raw, in the Ethiopian fashion, and probably even fewer would be tempted to do so at an outdoor concession, even though each booth had a refrigerator, a small stove, and a unit that dispensed non-potable running water. None of this bothered the Ethiopians who enjoyed their mounds of *kitfo* at the picnic tables set up in front of each booth. The event didn't permit alcohol, so the revelers settled for coffee, tea and soft drinks. A sign at the entrance to the field banned outside food, but that didn't stop two young men from sneaking in some McDonald's burgers and fries.

Many of the concessionaires said they came to "feed my people" and just be a part of it all. "I don't think we'll make that much profit," said Rahel Taye of the Little Ethiopia booth, "but it's fun to do this for your own culture."

For some, though, it was an opportunity to promote side businesses and experiment with entrepreneurship.

Amsale Fakibelu works full time as a nanny for a Chicago family, but she also caters, counting on word of mouth. She makes Ethiopian food, and pastries like baklava and tiramisu, and the sign at her Banatu concession named all of the dishes and desserts only in Amharic, except for "hot dog," a treat for the kids.

Amdebirhan Bishu drives a taxi but hopes to open a restaurant in the city some time soon, so his Fasika booth tested the waters. He's a confident young man, a determined entrepreneur, and he says that if he can't open a restaurant, then he'll find another way to go into business for himself. He's one of 10 children in his family, most of the siblings living now in the U.S.

Asmaru Ayenew, a.k.a. "Dr. Injera," doesn't own a restaurant yet, but she may soon: Some friends of hers, who have full-time jobs, also own one of

Chicago's Ethiopian restaurants, and she says they've asked her if she'd like to buy it because it's becoming too much for them to handle. She's pondering the opportunity, but in the meantime, she's content to cater for churches and parties and to make her own brand of *injera*, which she sells in a few convenience stores in the uptown Edgewater neighborhood, where the city's Ethiopian restaurants and residents have clustered.

One of her distributors, an Indian grocer, gave her the moniker that she wears so proudly. "I'm the *injera* doctor," Asmaru says. "That's what they call me: Dr. Asmaru." She makes her *injera* because, she asserts, "not everybody can. They don't know how to. It's hard work. In this country, I have taught a lot of people. Some people become good, and some people just don't catch on."

Asmaru is one of several Ethiopian women in Chicago who package and label their homemade *injera* for sale in small markets. Hirut Assefa, of the Tinqsh booth, made her own *injera* for the tournament but doesn't sell it in stores because there's "not enough profit. We all make our own *injera* at home," she says, "so who's going to buy it?" But Hirut admits that when she doesn't have time to make her own — she works full time for the city of Chicago — she'll pick up a package in a market.

If Asmaru takes over her friends' restaurant, it won't be her first. The intrepid immigrant left Gondar, Ethiopia, on her own in 1982 at age 15 and moved to the Sudan, where she opened Selam, an Ethiopian restaurant, in Gadarif, about 12 hours by car from Khartoum. She was still a teen-ager at the time, and she needed a livelihood. "There was no choice," Asmaru recalls. "In Sudan, you can't do anything. So I had to work." She used Sudanese spices and peppers to create her own *berbere,* an especially impressive feat considering her rather privileged upbringing: She never had to cook at home in Ethiopia because her mother never made her do it. "I was just one," she says, meaning an only child. "I was a spoiled girl." But she had watched her mother in the kitchen, and that was enough to allow her to launch her nascent enterprise.

Hilina Mohammed wants to own a restaurant, too. She's just not sure yet where to own it. She set up her Ye'enat Guada food booth at the 2008 tournament in D.C. and again at the 2009 event in Chicago, searching for the right city to open her place. An Addis Ababa native and a New Yorker now, she came to America in 1999 to attend college and works in internet technology. "It's just a beginning," she says of her summertime culinary sojourns. "As you continue to think about it, you never know what you're going to do."

Chicago's Ethiopian Community Center had the only food booth to offer spaghetti, and at the table in front of the center's concession, four men sat around a single plate, all twirling their forks in noodles covered with a glistening tomato sauce flavored with onions and *berbere*. The meal came with crusty Italian bread, so the forks provided the men with a Western way to eat communally in the absence of *injera*.

At the booth for Atlanta's Ledet, owner Hiwot Kifle worked the kitchen while her son, Yonathan Araya, and her daughter, Ledet Kifle, set up tables and prepared to serve their customers. The siblings have different surnames because Yonathan, in Ethiopian tradition, took his father's first name as his last, and Ledet took her grandfather's (also a custom, less frequently practiced). They were joined by their cousin, Ruth Giday, who studies international business at a Florida university. She's the only Ethiopian in her school, and her aunt sends her Ethiopian food because she can't get any in her college town.

It's an absence she misses, and a while back, after bragging to a friend about her culture's cuisine, they took a road trip to an Ethiopian restaurant. "It had nothing that tasted Ethiopian," says Ruth who, mercifully, wouldn't name the place. "I was actually embarrassed."

The only thing more abundant than food among the concessionaires was cultural pride, and it might as well have been on the menu at Fasilides, where Fanta Agede did the cooking and her daughter, Tezeru Teshome, greeted and served the customers. The women created a tri-fold takeout menu to distribute, even though they don't own a restaurant and have no plans to open one.

At every tournament restaurant, someone was sure to tell you that his wife or mother or sister was the "best cook" in Ethiopia. When Fanta playfully claimed the honor, Tezeru quickly added: "You'll hear that a lot, but this is the truth." Her mother gets all of her ingredients from Ethiopia because "they Americanize their spices here and don't make it authentic." Although Tezeru only eats Ethiopian food at home "at random times, when I crave it, when I'm homesick," it's always available.

And yet, despite this pride in her ancestral cuisine, Tezeru, who's in college studying history, with her eye on law school, doesn't cook. "My mom didn't want to teach me," she says. "I think she wanted to break the cycle of women always cooking. I don't think she would call herself a feminist, but she is."

Tezeru is a modern cultural warrior, proud of her mother and her heritage, but coolly determined to find her own way. She wants to marry an Ethiopian man, then live in Ethiopia to raise their children. "That's where my roots are," she says. "Kids who come from Ethiopia have an aura about them. They're wiser. They're stronger."

A panorama like this could never have happened in Chicago just a decade earlier, when the city had only a few Ethiopian restaurants — most of them located in the Wrigleyville area — and a growing but still largely unnoticeable Ethiopian population. Not any more. Several miles uptown from Wrigley

Field, on North Broadway, a cluster of restaurants and other businesses has formed, creating more choice and competition.

You could say that the story of Ethiopian food in Chicago is the story of two women, each of whom made a very different journey to their American success.

For Zenash Beyene, life began in Balesa, a village near Gondar, the former Ethiopian capital. Zenash is rare among Ethiopians in America: She's Beta Israel — that is, an Ethiopian Jew, a culture that the Orthodox rabbis of Israel have declared to be descendants of one of the 12 Lost Tribes of Israel. Very few Beta Israel remain in Ethiopia, the majority having been airlifted to Israel in Operation Moses and Operation Solomon, two massive and difficult enterprises of the 1980s and 1990s.

Zenash got to America the hardest way. Like tens of thousands of other Jews seeking to leave Ethiopia, she walked to the Sudan in 1974 during the period of the Beta Israel mass exodus from Ethiopia. She was 15, and the mother of an 8-month-old daughter, Marita, whom she left with her mother in Ethiopia. Those two eventually made their way to Israel while Zenash landed in Khartoum, where for a while she ran a small restaurant just to get by. After a short spell in Saudi Arabia, she returned to the Sudan, and eventually, she moved to Chicago.

Sitting at a table in the back of Ras Dashen, her thriving restaurant, Zenash discusses her arduous emigration with a comfortable smile, as if to affirm her triumph. "We walked a lot," she says, without melancholy, of her escape. She arrived in Chicago in 1981 — "November 6, Thursday night," she recalls with a satisfied grin.

In Ethiopia, her father designed knives, tools and furniture and sold them to the Christians, earning good money from his craft. This was a typical profession of Ethiopian Jews, and it made them important merchants in the regions near Gondar where most of them lived. "When I grew up we were very close," she says of the Christian, Jewish and Moslem communities. "We were neighbors."

But Ethiopian Jews also faced hardships and prejudice, and that led to the Israeli migration. Her mother now lives in Israel, and she's visited there a few times. She opened Ras Dashen in 2001 with the help of Kevin Swier, a professor of biology at Chicago State University, and her husband since 1993. The restaurant's business card lists him as owner, but Zenash owns the kitchen. Marita, with whom she's been reunited, manages the place. She doesn't have many Ethiopian Jewish friends in Chicago now — there's her brother, her daughter, and a few visiting Ethio-Israeli students — and she admits, "Sometimes I feel lonely."

Long before Ras Dashen, Zenash cooked for Ethiopians in Chicago. She sold *injera* and catered meals, sometimes for Ethiopian students in the city. There was no teff back then, and when she arrived in Chicago, "for two weeks I cried because I missed *injera* very badly," she recalls. She experimented for a while and came up with a mixture of rice, "dark wheat" and self-rising flours that sufficed until teff became more available.

In the meantime, as Zenash subsisted, along came Tekle Gabriel and the legendary Desta Bairu.

Tekle, a Chicago resident since the 1970s, when he arrived in town to attend college, decided in 1983 that he wanted to open a small business with the capital he had available to him. Some friends persuaded him that his venture should be Chicago's first Ethiopian restaurant.

"I was not enthused about the idea," the wry restaurateur recalls 25 years later. "I had a hard time eating my own cooking."

But he finally agreed, especially after coming upon the idea of recruiting Desta, who was then around 70 years old, to join him.

When Desta left the Washington, D.C., restaurant named for her in the early 1980s, she moved to Madison, Wis., just a few hours by car from Chicago, to live with friends. Erku Yimer, who is now the executive director of Chicago's Ethiopian Cultural Center, was a student back then at the University of Wisconsin at Madison, and he remembers eating at Desta's house and telling others about her. "The lady was very good at public relations," Erku recalls, and if you ordered two or three dishes, she'd sell you on two or three more before your meal ended.

Tekle knew the small Madison community of Ethiopians, and when he began to plan his restaurant, he asked Desta to be his business partner and cook.

She agreed, and Mama Desta's Red Sea opened in January 1984 on Clark Street, not too far from Wrigley Field. Like Zenash, Desta had to make her *injera* with a mix of flours and no teff, just as she did at her Washington restaurant. The partnership lasted only two years before Tekle bought her share, and Desta then lived in numerous other cities. She even returned to Eritrea for a while, where the story goes that President Isaias Afewerki greeted the pioneering cultural entrepreneur at the airport for a red-carpet welcome. But she experienced culture shock there after so many years away, and soon she came back to America.

Finally, well into old age, her memory failing, she returned to Eritrea once more. Erku, who lost touch with her after she left Chicago, believes she died between 1993 and 1998. Tekle believes she was in her 90s.

Chicago's Ethiopian community was small in 1984, so Mama Desta opened in the trendier Wrigleyville area. By the early 1990s, Ethiopian Village and Addis Ababa had joined Mama Desta on Clark Street. But then two things happened to the farther-north Edgewater neighborhood: More Ethiopians began to settle in that part of Chicago, and the neighborhood began to gentrify. It was the perfect combination of elements to invite Ethiopian restaurants.

Ethiopian Diamond opened on North Broadway in Lakeview in 1999, Ras Dashen in 2001, and several others on the surrounding streets in the years after that. Then came some markets, and the home *injera* businesses. Slowly, this shifted the audience for Ethiopian food to the north, leaving Mama Desta as the sole remaining Ethiopian eatery in restaurant-rich Wrigleyville. Ethiopian Village was by then long gone, and Addis Ababa moved north to the town of Evanston a few years ago.

Zenash recalls that some of these restaurants asked her to be their cook. But she says that didn't want to give away her cooking secrets, and she continued to dream of owning her own restaurant. She finally realized that dream in 2001.

So like the spread of human populations from Africa to Europe multi-millennia ago, Chicago's Ethiopian restaurant community has moved north in the past decade. Beginning around the 5800 block of Broadway, 27 blocks north of Mama Desta's, you first encounter the established Ras Dashen, and right next to it the newer, smaller Abyssinia, formerly a grocery store, but now a restaurant that sells a few spices as well.

Walk three blocks more on Broadway and you're at the big Ethiopian Diamond, and across the street from that is Kukulu Market. Between Ras Dashen and Ethiopian Diamond is the Nigerian-owned, pan-African Homeland Market, a grocery store with two shelves of Ethiopian foods, including gesho *inchet* — if they have it in stock. There's also the tiny Peacock Café, an Eritrean restaurant with long hours and a short menu, frequented mostly by the city's small Eritrean population.

Not too far from this cluster, tucked away in a row of businesses on a residential street beneath a railroad trestle, is Blue Nile, where they boast a menu signed by Bob Marley's son Ziggy. They'll give you a takeout menu with a photocopy of the signature if you ask. From there, it's a good walk or a short drive south to the Andersonville neighborhood, where you'll find Demera and Lalibela, two newer restaurants, both elegantly appointed, the former in the midst of a thriving few blocks of restaurants and pubs, the latter a block off the main drag of Clark Street, and run by a plucky husband-and-wife team. Rounding out the community, north of the Broadway cluster, is Ethiopian Diamond II, at a location where African Harambe, an "emporium of cuisines," opened in 2007 with Ethiopian and other African dishes on its menu.

And now a building on West Greenleaf Street at the corner of North

Clark, a few blocks from Ethiopian Diamond II, houses Chicago's new and growing Ethiopian Cultural Center. The place has big constructions plans for 2011, and the remodeled building will include a banquet hall. But they won't cook their own food, which means some good catering business for the city's restaurants.

This isn't quite the concentration of Washington's U Street, but to the Ethiopianist, those several blocks on Broadway offer reassuring sights and a place to get good food or to buy *injera*, *berbere* and gesho.

The newest kids in town have opened their restaurant several miles south of the Broadway cluster on North Wells Street: In the long shadow of the pioneering Zenash and Desta come Askale and Rahel Kebede, two young Ethiopian sisters who bought the Turkish-owned La Sera Café and added some Ethiopian dishes to its already diverse international menu.

La Sera isn't a place you just happen across like you might with the uptown restaurants. Located in a downtown neighborhood that's more residential than commercial, it's surrounded by dozens of high-rise apartments and condos, some 30 stories high, with two veterinary hospitals within a block, and a few other shops and restaurants nearby, none of them as eclectic as La Sera. It's a good client base in a neighborhood with few fine dining options, and when weather permits, *al fresco* diners can look in one direction at the steel arches that proclaim the neighborhood Old Town, and in the other direction at the lofty John Hancock building on the skyline horizon.

Askale, the elder sister, came to America in 1999 and for many years lived in Denver, working at a restaurant. She moved to Chicago in 2007 to join Rahel, who moved there in 2001 when she met her husband, an Ethiopian-American software engineer, during his visit home. Rahel worked at the Sheraton Hotel in Chicago for a while, but then she and Askale decided to go into business. "We wanted to work for ourselves," Rahel says of their decision to buy La Sera. "It's kind of for us."

During the day, a mix of downtown workers, Ethiopian cab drivers and neighborhood people enjoy breakfast and lunch at La Sera. The evening crowd is more from just the neighborhood. For people who don't want Ethiopian food, there's everything from European pancakes and flatbread pizza to hummus, *taouk* (Arabic chicken), salads, panini and a grilled sirloin steak. The Ethiopian menu is still small: *tibs* wrap, *kitfo* wrap (medium rare), a lentil and spinach wrap, and for breakfast, *ful* and *kinche*.

"We wanted people to have different kinds of choices," Rahel says. "That's why we only put three Ethiopian dishes on the menu." They don't promote themselves as an Ethiopian restaurant and don't advertise their Ethiopian dishes. If people take to the cuisine, they plan to offer more, although right now Rahel says it's unlikely they'll become all Ethiopian.

The "wrap" of their Ethiopian dishes is *injera*, although you can ask for the food to be served in the traditional way. Patrons can also ask for pretty much any Ethiopian dish — including *shiro,* which they keep in stock — and the sisters will make it. Their Ethiopian customers naturally want their *kitfo* raw, although the menu says it comes "medium rare," for the benefit of their non-Ethiopian diners. "We cook it a little bit more for them," Rahel says.

La Sera gets all of its *injera* from Kukulu Market, and the owner's son, Bibi, delivers it daily. They get their spices and *shiro* from back home ("When someone goes for a visit," Rahel says, "we ask them to bring a lot.") They do this because it's more economical than buying it retail, and they only make a few Ethiopian dishes, so they're not likely to run out.

The restaurant's décor is contemporary, with hardwood floors, wood tables, and a couch in front of a cocktail table to give the place a café ambience. A small marketplace along one wall sells teas and coffees next to a few traditional clay Ethiopian coffee pots (*jebena*) and cups (*sini*), along with a small decorative carved wooden *jebena* with *sini*.

One of the coffees they sell by the cup or the bag is Royal Ethiopian Coffee, the enterprise of Dawit Bekele, a long-time Ethiopian-American businessman who launched his line in June 2009 and opened the homey uptown café Royal Coffee in Chicago to go with it. Dawit lived in Maryland for many years and raised his family there while traveling a lot for his work exporting Ethiopian foods to Middle Eastern companies.

In 2003, he moved his family to Ethiopia for five years, and that's where his American-born daughter, Leah Bekele, graduated from high school. But in 2008, she entered Columbia College in Chicago as a freshman studying public relations, and a year later, Dawit opened his café on North Sheridan Road, just a few blocks from the heart of Chicago's uptown Loyola University. Leah works in the café during the summer, although after college she dreams of a career in New York.

Royal Coffee is "pure Ethiopian highland coffee," imported raw from Ethiopia by Dawit and roasted here. In the café, you can buy the roasted beans in shiny black bags, or you can buy unroasted beans that you scoop from a burlap sack on the floor in front of the display shelf. The café, about a mile uptown from the North Broadway convergence, sells breakfast items, sandwiches, salads, desserts, crepes and a variety of Ethiopian dishes, along with its brand-name coffee. The walls of the café are all Ethiopian, decorated with poster-sized photographs of plump red coffee beans still on the tree, Ethiopians harvesting and sorting the beans, and a poster that tells "The Story of Coffee," the same tale that appears on the company's coffee bags.

And don't let the name fool you: Royal Coffee is an Ethiopian restaurant. You can order an Ethiopian vegetarian plate with four selections; a *tibs* plate with beef, chicken and lamb; a combination plate of *chechebsa, ful, kinche* and *firfir* with beef, all popular breakfast items; and even *kitfo*. Each dish comes with *injera*.

The growing North Broadway convergence is a big help to Assefa Eshete, who opened Kukulu Market there in 2003. He sells Ethiopian spices, grains, coffee, books and videos, so naturally, his customers are mostly Ethiopians. His shop is small and crowded, and he makes *injera* from time to time on two *mitads* in the back of his shop, selling the bread with the Kukulu label on it.

But in that trade, he competes with Terefech, Yeshu, Mulu, Bethy, Yeshie, "Sara A." and the other Ethiopian women of Chicago who make *injera* in their homes, put small white labels on them, and sell them in markets to the Ethiopian community. Assefa even sells the competitors' *injera* in his shop because he can't make enough of his own. "A lot of ladies make it in their names," he says, "so the competition is high." And he needs help from an employee to make his Kukulu *injera* because, he says, "only the ladies can make it."

For a while he had some competition: Lili Market, about a mile away, was the city's second Ethiopian grocery store for two years, but in 2009, it changed its name and owner and now is a general convenience store. It was a bad location to begin with, too far from the North Broadway cluster, plus Assefa had a good head start. Abyssinia Market, a few blocks from Kukulu, transformed itself in 2008 into Abyssinia Café, an intimate little restaurant right next door to Zenash's bustling Ras Dashen. But just around the corner from Kukulu, Assefa faces even more competition from Happy Grocery, one of a few convenience stores, not owned by an Ethiopian, that stock *injera* made by neighborhood Ethiopian women.

Assefa continues to expand his business, which gets more crowded with supplies every year. He now sells spicy *awaze* sauce and imported "Ethiopian toothbrushes," small pieces of brown wood with grooves carved into them, used by Ethiopians to clean their teeth. Each one costs 99 cents and is good for three or four uses. His son Betre (Bibi) Assefa, who drives a cab, works the counter when he can and delivers *injera* daily to the Kebede sisters at La Sera Café downtown. He also ran Chicago Style Restaurant at the soccer tournament.

Abyssinia Restaurant, owned by Abraha Kidanu, occupies space in a building owned by the same landlord who owns the space that houses the neighboring Ras Dashen, and when Abraha arrived in the U.S. from Sudan in 1982, he ate at Zenash's house when she catered. Now they compete for customers in a growing market. Abraha is from northern Ethiopia, and he'd like to serve *tihlo* — if he can get his wife, who cooks the food at Abyssinia, to sign on to making the time-consuming Tigrayan dish. When he had a market, he sold his own brand of *injera*. He doesn't do that at his restaurant, but he will make pure teff *injera* for some regular customers who must eat gluten-free.

Tekle Gabriel lives up north himself, and during the summer of 2008, he acknowledged the disadvantage of Mama Desta's being the sole Ethiopian restaurant in Wrigleyville. "The cluster puts a focus on the neighborhood," he said of his North Broadway competitors. "I would like to have had a couple of restaurants around here." He was philosophical — and mathematical — about his situation. The Chicago metro area has eight million people, and "if you get a miniscule amount of that eight million," he said, "there's enough business for everybody."

But things didn't add up for Tekle and his pioneering restaurant, which closed in February 2009 when the structural problems of his building became too expensive to repair. He also said he needed a respite from the business after 25 years, although he's pursing investors to reopen somewhere else. So with the loss of Chicago's historic first Ethiopian restaurant, the migration is complete: A new culture of Ethiopian cuisine has settled far north on Broadway, and the post-game Wrigleyville mobs have nothing to choose but burgers and beer, with some Asian and Moroccan thrown in if you know where to look.

San Francisco & the Bay Area

San Francisco's Ethiopian community seems to have left its heart in Oakland.

It's not that the city by the bay doesn't have some good places to get Ethiopian food. There are more than enough, and they offer some intriguing variety. But it's the city *across* the bay where you'll find an ever larger business community, along with a company that pioneered the sale of Ethiopian food and alcohol in America.

Let's begin in San Francisco, which has at least eight restaurants distributed among its trendier communities. Actually, though, they're not all Ethiopian. Three of them are Eritrean, and three of the ones that are Ethiopian have menus that list their dishes in Tigrinya rather than Amharic. These restaurants' owners come from Ethiopia's northern Tigrinya-speaking cities.

Both Ethiopians and Eritreans say their food is indistinguishable, and you have to press hard to get people of either culture to suggest even the slightest difference. Eritrean dishes may be lighter, with less butter or oil, and a bit less spicy. Or they may not be. It seems to depend upon whom you ask and what mood he's in when you ask him. Iyasu Behre, who owns Red Sea in Oakland with his two brothers, notes that in his native Eritrea, people might eat more vegetable dishes than Ethiopians, and "village to village has different kinds of spices for *kibbee* — like house spices." But that only proves that cooking, like politics, is local.

The Ethio-Eritrean restaurant scene of San Francisco pretty much resembles that of any other big city: Some restaurants are fancier and pricier, some are homey, and some are holes in the wall. But if you want some cool jazz with your hot *wot*, then you need to visit a few blocks of San Francisco's Fillmore Street, which the city has developed as a jazz center.

Rasselas, an Ethiopian restaurant owned by Agonafer Shiferaw, opened in the city in 1986 and has had several different locations over the years. It's been on Fillmore since 1999, when Agonafer joined the city's effort to revive jazz in the neighborhood. There's no cover charge for the music, which artists play from a small stage in the dining room, and you can enjoy a variety of traditional Ethiopian dishes with your meal, including *kitfo*, or you can order bar food, like an Ethiopian *sambussa*, ginger chicken or drunken chicken. The restaurant also has a larger back room — with a full stage, a second bar and a balcony — that people can rent for parties or receptions.

Just a block down Fillmore is the more intimate Sheba Lounge, which Agonafer co-owns with Netsanet Alemayehu, who runs the places and serves as hostess. Sheba has a few traditional dinner tables, but most of the seating consists of pneumatic leather couches and armchair situated around cocktail tables. The Ethiopian dishes are a bit more expensive, and there's a drink minimum if you just want to listen to the music. It's the price you pay for a touch of class while you eat your dinner with your hands.

The city's other restaurants are exactly that: no music, just sturdy Ethio-Eritrean food, with more variety and slightly lower prices. Haight Street has two restaurants, including Massawa, which has been on the street's 1500 block, near the corner of Haight and Ashbury, since 1986. It's one of many exotic offering among block after block of multi-cultural restaurants and small shops that throw back to the legendary street's hippie days.

Asmerom Berhe has owned Massawa since 2000. He's the third owner since it opened, and he's in partnership with his two brothers. The three of them also own Red Sea restaurant in Oakland. As Eritreans selling what most people think of as "Ethiopian" food, they need to pay attention to marketing, so they name both cultures on their signage. The dishes are the same, although you'll need to learn that the *tibs* you're accustomed to ordering at an Ethiopian establishment are called *kulwa* in Tigrinya. Asmerom's menu helps by describing each dish.

And how are relations between Ethiopians and Eritreans in the bay area in light of the tensions between the two countries in Africa? That depends upon which brother you ask.

"It's politics, you know," says Asmerom, who notes that Ethiopians and Eritreans live together in many of the city's neighborhoods. "These guys don't even like the government in Ethiopia. If someone passes away, everyone comes to visit."

Across the bay in Oakland, at Red Sea, brother Iyasu Berhe answers more cautiously.

"The Eritreans are always friendly to the Ethiopians," he says, although in the 1990s, when tensions were high between the two countries, and Eritrea was, in Iyasu's view, "occupied" by its neighbor, "Ethiopians had a hard time coming to Eritrean restaurants."

When an Ethiopian restaurant hosts an Amharic singer, Eritreans readily attend because they know the language and the music. But Ethiopians, Iyasu says, don't come to performances by Tigrinya-speaking singers. It's a different language and culture, and they don't seem to be willing to cross over for sake of solidarity.

"It's still tough because of the border issues," Iyasu said, reflecting on things back home. "There's always politics. It's never going to change."

Around San Francisco, diners don't seem to care — or even know — about these tensions. Whether owned by Ethiopians or Eritreans, the city's restaurants do well on prime dining nights.

You can choose from many more restaurants across the bay in Oakland and its little neighbor Berkeley, and that means survival is harder, especially for small places in a competitive industry. Telegraph Avenue in Berkeley has two restaurants about half a mile apart. But once Telegraph Avenue descends into the bigger city of Oakland, around the 6400 block, you'll find more than a dozen restaurants and grocery stores running south to around the 2300 block. Sprinkled among them are myriad other businesses owned by Ethiopians, some of them general convenience stores with a few shelves that sell Ethiopian spices and alcohol.

Ethiopia Restaurant in Berkeley offers 12 different vegetarian dishes, and if you order a combo platter, you can select five of them. Thus the restaurant bills itself as the "home of 792 possible vegetarian combination." A few blocks up the street, Finfiné, with its fancy *accent grave,* sits secluded inside a mini-mall alcove, looking a bit like a Tiki bar.

Then, Telegraph spills into Oakland, and it's place after place after place.

The journey begins with Brundo Market, a tiny, well-stocked shop that sells spices, freshly cut meats, gesho and its brand-name *injera,* which you can watch the employees make behind the counter. Brundo also sells its spices and *injera* online, and its efficient website would probably lead you to picture a much bigger home office. It's affiliated with Café Colucci, a restaurant two storefronts away, with an African gift shop, owned by an Ethiopian, in between. The café is also a caterer, and for around $70, you can get an 18-inch platter of assorted Ethiopian dishes.

From there, you can't walk more than a few blocks without seeing an Ethiopian- or Eritrean-owned restaurant and market: Alcatel, at the corner of Alcatraz and Telegraph avenues, is an Ethiopian-owned convenience store that sells Ethio products, as is U&I Market, which offers Dareye Injera in plastic bags.

That *injera* was the product of a restaurant that began its life as Café Dareye, originally located much further down Telegraph, away from a cluster of restaurants and markets. An enterprise of the Zafu family, the small restaurant opened in 2008, when Taytu "Nunu" Zafu was 21 years old, and an American resident for only six years. The café, named for Nunu's later grandmother, who lived her entire life in Ethiopia, and who owned a restaurant in Addis Ababa, offered good food at low prices, and Nunu ran it with the women of her family.

Nunu's mother, Terufet, cooked all of the food (including their packaged *injera*), and Nunu played host when she wasn't working part-time toward her degree in business at University of San Francisco State. Her father works as a janitor, her sister is at UC Davis, her grown brother drives a cab, and her little brother lives at home. Along with its Ethiopian food, Café Dareye served sandwiches (pastrami, turkey tuna — and ham), as well as favorite Ethiopian drinks, like flax seed juice and sunflower juice.

That was then. Now, it's moved way up Telegraph Avenue, right across the street from the long-established Café Colucci, and it's change its name to Dareye Hide-a-Way. The new place is bigger, fancier and has a diverse and "evolving" menu. The family even hopes to expand into a franchise.

Some time ago, the city of Oakland offered a portion of Telegraph to the Eritrean community to develop as a sort of "Little Eritrea." But the community didn't have the money, recalls Asmerom, so the offer went to a wealthier immigrant community that was "second in line." Now the street is rife with Korean business clusters, including Koreana Plaza, just up the street from where Café Dareye once existed.

All of this Telegraph Avenue action — with a few other restaurants located elsewhere around Oakland — takes place in plain view along a major artery, just what restaurants need to survive.

Not so for NTS Enterprises, a company that pioneered the nationwide sale of Ethiopian food, spices and alcohol in the United States. It's open shop is located in a warehouse down a nondescript residential street many blocks from Telegraph. To find it you have to know where it is, and then some: It's situated behind a house on 19ᵗʰ Street that sports an easy-to-miss wooden sign that declares "NTS Enterprises." The sign hangs at an angle on the front of the house.

This primitive shingle belies a thriving business. Nega Sellassie and Tekle Girmay began their semi-eponymous business — "NTS" stands for "Nega Tekle Shareholders" — across the bay in Daly City in 1984, when Ethiopian restaurants were few and the demand for NTS products was low. They sold their goods nationwide, and before the company grew, Nega and Tekle would ship items to a city — New York, Boston, Washington — fly there, get it off the plane at the other end, rent a car, and deliver the goods themselves. Now they have agents in those cities to unload and deliver their products, and since 1996, they've had a warehouse in Ethiopia from which they ship everything to America.

For a while they sold directly to Ethiopians. They also sold clothing and shoes imported from Italy, as well as Ethiopian clothing, to bring in more money. When NTS began, Nega worked full time as a regional manager for the Church Fried Chicken chain. But when the company wanted to move him to Dallas in 1987, he quit that job to concentrate full time on NTS. He and Tekle moved the company to Oakland the following year.

The hidden 19ᵗʰ Street location is an open shop and occupies about 3,000 square feet. It's a cornucopia of smells, and NTS sells some products that you can't find anywhere else.

Got a tummy ache? Then buy some *fetho*, a small brick red seed that's ground into a powder, dissolved in water, and then soaked up with *injera* to cure stomach ailments. NTS sells *helbet*, a seed grain that's added to pasta sauce and eaten with *injera*; *bula*, the root of the enset plant, used to make soup or porridge; *mokmoko*, a powder that turns water blood red and protects against blood cancer; *kesher*, which you mix with ginger and drink like tea; and *wot mekelesha*, a blend of spices that you add in the last minutes during cooking to enhance the flavor of a spicy *wot*.

NTS has a retailer's license and sells a lot of its products over the counter to people who wander into the warehouse. Throughout the day, Ethiopians and Eritreans trickle in every 15 minutes or so to buy a few items and chat with Nega or Tekle. When neither is at the warehouse, their Spanish-speaking employee tells people what things costs and rings them up. He spends the time between sales at the back of the warehouse, measuring out spices on a scale and putting them in plastic bags that he places on the shelves.

These walk-ins may pay the electric bill, but they don't pay the rent. That's where restaurant and grocery store clients across the country come in. A few blocks away, NTS has a 10,000-square-foot warehouse from which it ships flats of goods every day to restaurants and grocery stores as far away as Washington, D.C., and New York.

In a community divided among Ethiopians and Eritreans, Nega is something of a cultural bridge: His parents were Eritrean, and he was born in the Ethiopian city of Shashemene, which Haile Selassie gave to the Rastafarians as a place of their own in the holy land of Ethiopia. A good-natured fellow with a dry sense of humor, Nega scoffs at the notion of tensions between the cultures, and he unites them in name: Ethiopians and Eritreans together are all "Abyssinians," he says, citing the archaic name for the ancient territory on the Horn of Africa.

The governments of the two countries might have something to say about that, but the people who drop by NTS Enterprises to buy their *berbere* and gesho seem to have no quarrel.

Los Angeles

Can something as small as an atom weigh more than an elephant? Yes, it can, but only if it's so packed with matter that its density trumps its dimensions.

That's how to think of Little Ethiopia, a Los Angeles neighborhood that occupies most of the 1000 block of South Fairfax Avenue. What Little Ethiopia lacks in size it makes up for in concentration: You may spend more time there choosing a restaurant for dinner than you'll spend eating the meal once you settle in.

And better yet, Little Ethiopia is so close to the city's outstanding Los Angeles County Museum of Art, which is open from noon to 8 p.m. most days, that you can easily walk from the museum and conclude your day of culture with an Ethiopian meal — not that most Los Angelenos ever walk *anywhere*, except to their cars.

Los Angeles has one of the nation's largest Ethiopian populations, one that began to form as long ago as the 1950s, when Ethiopians went there to attend college and sometimes stayed. In 1969, on a state visit to United States, Emperor Haile Selassie stopped at UCLA and got a special medal of honor from the chancellor. In the minds of Ethiopians, this further established Los Angeles as a welcoming place to live. A few years earlier, nearby Long Beach had briefly hosted the world's first Ethiopian restaurant, the enterprise of the enigmatic Beyene Guililat (see Chapter 10).

In the 1930s, the 1000 block of South Fairfax hosted a farmers' market, and in the 1950s it became a hub for the city's Jewish merchants. Los Angeles placed blue "Little Ethiopia" street signs at both ends of the block in 2002 to honor the culture that now dominates. It's the strip mall of Ethiopian culture in America's vast multi-cultural west coast capital, the place to be for city residents and tourists who want Ethiopian food, and for Ethiopians who need spices and supplies.

But it's not the only place you'll find Ethiopian restaurants and grocery stores in Los Angeles, and one of the community's pioneering businesses isn't even owned by an Ethiopian.

Tucked away in a back corner of C&K Importing, or Papa Cristo's, as its restaurant is called, you'll find everything you need to make an Ethiopian meal: spices, gesho, barley, teff, *injera,* and even *etan,* an incense sold in the form of small white rocks that are placed on charcoals to burn. It's all there at C&K and has been for decades since the shop's current owner, Chrys S. Chrys, discovered the Ethiopian community in the 1980s and began selling the products they needed among his full line of Greek and Mediterranean goods.

Chrys' father opened C&K Importing in 1948, and the business has since grown into three parts, all side by side on the 2700 block of West Pico Boulevard, and all three opening into each other: On the left is a restaurant, on the right a diner, and in the middle, the grocery store, with freshly baked pastries and, in a back corner, its shelves of Ethiopian supplies, which Chrys has always bought from NTS Enterprises of Oakland.

C&K began selling Ethiopian foods because it was good for business, but the connection between the two cultures goes deeper. Ethiopia's Orthodox Christianity is closer to Greek Orthodoxy than American Christianity, and when Ethiopians began to settle in Los Angeles, they had no Ethiopian Orthodox churches to attend. So some gravitated toward Greek Orthodox churches and even continue to worship there today.

"They're absolutely wonderful people with very similar backgrounds and interests," Chrys says. "I really enjoyed the fact that we could add to our population of nice people."

An established outlet like C&K made things a challenge at first for the affable Amsalework Asfaw, who has owned Selam Market since 1997. But after more than a decade in business on West Pico Boulevard, a few miles from C&K, he's well established among the area's Ethiopian community as another place to go for spices and supplies.

In fact, Selam is a full-service market with more than just Ethiopian goods. The store has a butcher shop that offers fresh cuts of meat, bins of legumes sold in bulk, a long shelf of wines and beers, rows of non-Ethiopian grocery items, and a cooler along the back wall.

Selam is also an *injera* bakery that puts out thousands of piece of *injera* a week from a kitchen in the back of the store, where two employees spend hour after hour pouring cups of fermented batter onto a skillet, swirling it around a few times to distribute the batter, and then placing the skillet on an open flame for about a minute to allow the *injera* to bake.

Amsalework comes from Gondar and was among the first wave of Ethiopian political refugees to seek asylum in America. When he arrived in 1982, the Ethiopian population of Los Angeles was so small that he couldn't find Ethiopian food. So he bought spices at a Korean market to mix his own *berbere*, and he used Pioneer, a brand of French sourdough bread, to scoop up his food. "That was the closest thing we found to *injera*," he says. "It's so sour."

He worked at a bank for about a decade, but when he saw the opportunity to buy a storefront on Pico Boulevard — about 30 long blocks from C&K Importing — he seized it and opened his business.

About 80 percent of his customers now are Ethiopians, and that's just fine with him: Over and over, Amsalework says that his goal is to "feed the family." Beef and lamb are especially popular with his customers, and his meat cooler features homemade *delin*, a sauce of *berbere* and other spices.

"Here you have families who don't even set foot in Little Ethiopia," he says with some pride. His shop doesn't sell cultural artifacts and souvenir items. That's for the Little Ethiopia crowd, a demographic of younger people and tourists.

It certainly is. On a Friday night in Little Ethiopia, the trendier restaurants are packed with mostly non-Ethiopians.

Messob is popular, and the slightly upscale restaurant has its own label of reserve wines, made by a California winery for the restaurant's owners, brothers Berhanu and Getahun Asfaw. The restaurant sells two types of winery *t'ej* and also makes its own. Messob has a banquet room that's even larger than its restaurant. The room is a gathering place for Ethiopians, and Berhanu is president of the Little Ethiopia committee.

The Asfaw brothers are from Mohare, a Gurage town, and their first language is Muhar, one of the dialects of Sabat Bet Gurage, or "seven houses of Gurage." This is rare among Ethiopian restaurant owners in the U.S., and Getahun is especially proud of his restaurant's *kitfo*, the Gurage dish that long ago spread to the wider Ethiopian culture.

Across the street from Messob is Rosalind's, the first Ethiopian restaurant to open on the strip, in 1984. But Rosalind's wasn't Ethiopian when it opened: The owner was Ghanaian, and when she sold it to an Ethiopian businessman, the new owner kept the name and changed the menu, retaining only a few West African appetizers, like *pilli pilli* (a pepper sauce dip), *o jo jo* (balls of ground beef or sweet potatoes) and plantains. The restaurant's Ethiopian entrées include *asa tibs*, described as "Ethiopian-style whole fried rainbow trout fish."

Rosalind's tends to get more Ethiopians for lunch, but its dinner crowd is culturally mixed and largely non-Ethiopian. The restaurant's menu is the most helpful and edifying to Little Ethiopia's first-time diner, although you'll have to choose your favorite spelling of *injera*, which appears as both "enjera" and "ingera" at various places on the menu.

After explaining the basics of using *injera* to pick up your food, the menu cautions diners not to let their fingers touch their mouths, and not to lick their fingers during a meal, all in an effort to be classified "a true Ethiopian gourmet."

But rules are made to be broken, it seems, and customs sometimes change in the U.S. for some Ethiopians.

On one August afternoon at Rosalind's, a family of Ethiopians — two adults, three teen-aged children, and three toddlers — bowed their heads for a blessing before their meal, and then proceeded to use two hands to grab their *injera*. The littlest girl, a very fidgety 3-year-old, let Mommy feed her — when she wasn't running around the table or being corralled by her slightly older sister.

You won't find any of that at Meals by Genet, "the only authentic gourmet Ethiopian restaurant in Los Angeles," and certainly the fanciest restaurant on the strip. Owner Genet Agonafer arrived in the U.S. in 1981 with her 5-year-old son, worked for a while as a waitress and bartender, and opened a catering business about a dozen years ago. She often caters meals for movies in production. There's no Ethiopian food on set, but for wrap parties when production ends, the companies sometimes ask for it.

To protect the privacy of her clients, she doesn't like to talk about the celebrities she's served. But she will say that actors prefer salads, carbs and "chicken, chicken, chicken."

"Sometimes you are on the set for three months," Genet says. "You need to be creative."

At Meals by Genet, the signature restaurant that she opened in 2004, the menu is mostly Ethiopian, but the clientele is about 90 percent American. The servers are not Ethiopian, a rarity in Little Ethiopia, and they dress in white shirts and black vests. The menu literally spells out its prices: A dish may cost "eighteen" or "sixteen," not $18 or $16.

These are the highest prices for Ethiopian food in Little Ethiopia, although you do get to eat amidst low lighting that's too dark for some to read the menu. Jazz music fills the room, linen covers the tables, and Ethiopian art decorates the walls.

Genet says her America customers tend to order Ethiopian dishes — which include the California-friendly tofu *tibs* — and her Ethiopian customers often order from the European side of the menu, where they can enjoy linguini with orange sauce, grilled salmon, chicken curry, ribeye steak or Italian chicken. She cooks the food herself, and she admits that it can "get very tight" on a busy night, with some customers ordering Ethiopian food and some ordering continental.

The rest of Little Ethiopia's restaurants differ in size and clientele, some catering more to Ethiopians. The well-stocked Merkato is the strip's marketplace for spices, alcohol, music and clothing. Merkato has an adjoining restaurant, and the back of the market has a few small tables, where Ethiopian men gather to chat, eat and drink.

At one end of Little Ethiopia, you'll find Jah Lambs & Lions International, a shop, owned by a man from Trinidad, that sells Rastafarian music, clothing and artifacts. At the other end, there's the Herbal Healing Center, which sells medical marijuana — illegal under federal law, but legal in California. The shop promises "highest quality cannabis" and offers "free gram for all first-time patients." The center has business cards in the red, yellow and green colors of the Ethiopian flag (which are also the colors of African solidarity).

And don't overlook Safari Ethiopian Store, a bright clothing store and gift shop. The outfits hang on racks, and the shop is less crowded than Merkato, where all of the clothing items are folded on shelves.

These Ethiopian businesses aren't alone on Fairfax: Sprinkled among them are a bakery that specializes in cakes, a shop called Laundry by "Julia" (the quotation marks are part of the name), and two remnants of the 1950s: the National Council of Jewish Women Thrift Shop, and another thrift shop next to a thrift "gallery" with its storefront sign in English, Hebrew and Arabic.

Then, a few blocks from the strip, on the way to the corner of Fairfax Avenue and West Pico Boulevard, keep an eye open for Amsale Fashion Design and Tailor, a small shop with its sign in both English and Amharic.

A left turn from Fairfax onto Pico, a few blocks from Little Ethiopia, takes you to Selam Market and eventually to C&K Importing, the former close enough to walk. Turn right at that same corner, and you soon come to Mohamed Ibrahim's Awash, which opened in 1991.

Mohamed began in the restaurant business in 1985 when he owned Pico Grill, nearby on Pico Boulevard. That place started with American cuisine, but then Mohamed married a woman who made *injera*, and slowly, he introduced some Ethiopian food at his grill. He now calls his former place "an Ethiopian restaurant, but a little different than your traditional Ethiopian restaurant." Along with his American dishes, he served *tibs* - pan-fried Ethiopian-style beef dishes — but no juicy *siga wot*, and no *doro wot*.

He closed the restaurant in 1991, took six months off, and then discovered the small storefront on West Pico where Awash has been ever since. He's especially proud of his vegetarian food, and during the two-month Lenten holiday, he says, "ours is the busiest restaurant."

Although it's not far from Little Ethiopia, Awash is a destination, and a place frequented mostly by Ethiopians. Mohamed has never regretted opening his restaurant away from the heart of things, and he says with a wry chuckle, "We prefer to stay off Broadway."

If you continue along Fairfax where it intersects Pico barely a block from Awash, the street takes you through a neighborhood of middle-class homes. You'll eventually reach Washington Boulevard and the border of Culver City, one of LA's next towns over. Turn right onto Washington, then follow the winding boulevard through Culver City to Sony Pictures studio, far from Little Ethiopia, and you'll find the location of one of the area's first Ethiopian restaurants.

Around 1982, when the restaurant opened, it was called Ghion, and Mulugeta Lakew, newly arrived from Ethiopia, enjoyed going there for a taste of home. "It was the come-together place," he recalls, "the only place." He got his degree, entered the real estate business, got married and had a family. Ghion closed after a while, and the storefront lay dormant. So in 2003, Mulugeta bought it, remodeled it, reopened it as Fassica, and "hired" his wife as its chef. He got his spices from C&K Enterprises.

His restaurant was a homey place, and Mulugeta even made his own *t'ej*. But the law forbade him to sell homemade alcohol, so he served it gratis to friends and regulars who dined there. His clientele was mixed: some Ethiopians, some students from nearby UCLA dormitories, and even some celebrities from the studio across the street, although "when they come here, they put on big glasses and hats and stuff," Mulugeta said during the summer of 2008, less than a year before his young enterprise closed.

Finally, there are the many little cilia of Ethiopian businesses that reach out across the greater Los Angeles area. Inglewood has a restaurant and a market, and numerous other towns have small Ethiopian markets that serve the community in the many neighborhoods where people live. You can get Ethiopian food with a side of sushi (or vice versa) at Korea Kitchen, a multicultural Lancaster, Calif., restaurant owned by Youngsil Hong and Mulu Alemayehu, who is Ethiopian. And you'll find major clusters of Ethiopians in San Diego, south of LA, which has nearly a dozen small markets, and San Jose, near San Francisco, which has numerous markets and restaurants.

But nowhere else in California will you find a street sign welcoming you to Little Ethiopia, California's one-block, one-stop Ethiopian experience.

New York City

The big city of New York is a small town when it comes to its Ethiopian community.

In a place famous for its Chinatown, Little Italy, Spanish Harlem, Diamond Row and more, there is no cluster of Ethiopians: There are two restaurants in the East and West Village, two near Columbia University, two on the East Side, two in Clinton (née Hell's Kitchen), two between Morningside Heights and Harlem, and two very recently in Brooklyn — in all, 12 restaurants in two boroughs. (Chicago, with half the population, has 10.) If you live in the other three boroughs and you hunger for *tibs* and *t'ej*, then it's a bridge-and-tunnel night out.

The city's Ethiopian population is small compared to the size of the city, and there's no Ethiopian neighborhood. "New York is not always a good place to be," says Yeworkwoha "Workye" Ephrem, one of the deans of Ethiopian food in America. "It's tough. Ethiopians use New York as a stepping stone to other places," such as Atlanta, Dallas, Seattle, D.C. or Denver.

But New York hasn't even had an Ethiopian grocery store since the closing of Abyssinia Market on 116th Street in Harlem a few years ago. Its owner, Mekonnen Tadesse, opened the market in 1995 and converted it to a coffee shop in 1998, continuing to sell a few basic grocery items. He finally closed his place in 2003, done in by rising rents and the rigors of life in New York.

Mekonnen came to the U.S. in 1989 with business in his blood: His family in Ethiopia owned a pastry and coffee shop. "I came here in the spirit of adventure," he says. "I loved this country since I was a little boy." For a while he drove a cab in New York, and when he saw that the city had no Ethiopian market, he opened Abyssinia.

In any other big city, it would have been a great idea. But New York isn't any other big city.

"It was very hard to survive selling spices," Mekonnen says. "We don't have enough of a community. The nature of the people who live in New York City is different than the people who live in D.C. It's hard to stay open in New York because Ethiopians are scattered all over the place."

Even though his shop was more or less in the middle of Manhattan, "for a person to buy *injera* for $10 when he's living somewhere in Queens is very hard." He always got his spices from Workinesh, and he sold everything an Ethiopian kitchen would need: *berbere, shiro,* turmeric, teff, gesho, and even *injera* he made himself.

The city's Ethiopian population is largely professional — new immigrants tend to settle in places with closer, larger communities — and with the changing times, Ethiopians in New York who now want a taste of home can literally get it from there. "Everyone is traveling back home," Mekonnen says. "If you bring back five kilos of *shiro* or *berbere*, you can eat it for a year."

There's also the internet, and of course, the proximity of the huge D.C. community, where Ethiopians in New York all have friends or family. And besides, Mekonnen points out, all an Ethiopian home really needs is *berbere* to spice the red hot dishes, and turmeric and ginger, both easy to find, to spice the milder yellow ones.

Mekonnen, who's lived in Harlem his whole American life, opened a new business, Café Addis, on West 125th Street in 2008, serving a mix of Ethiopian and American food. But within a year, the struggling economy led him to turn his place into a neighborhood bar that just serves sandwiches. When he craves Ethiopian food made by someone else, he gets it at Queen of Sheba because "their cooking is very close to home."

In the absence of a market or bakery in the city, restaurants make their own *injera*, and everyday folks who don't have time to cook can buy it from a handful of women whose uptown Manhattan kitchens double as bakery and storefront. As Mekonnen says of life in busy New York: "You get used to it, and you just eat what's here."

But some key players in New York's community think it might be time for another market to step up. Many Ethiopians work downtown, so a market around 40th Street, rather than on 116th Street, might have a chance. And now that Americans in big cities have embraced the cuisine, "people know enough about Ethiopian food that they might attempt it at home," says Hibist Legesse, who co-owns Bati restaurant in Brooklyn.

Ethiopian food débuted in Manhattan in July 1979 when Sheba opened at 151 Hudson St. in Soho, near the entrance to the Holland Tunnel. The owners were a group of "relatives" that included Araya Selassie Yibrehu, a young Ethiopian businessman, and Workye, who was then a U.N. employee. Workye's sister, Encou, did some of the cooking, and a few other relatives and friends joined the sisters and Araya in the enterprise.

The endeavor to open Sheba began around 1977, when the investors bought a shabby 1,000-square-foot building in an underdeveloped part of Soho and turned it into a 56-seat restaurant. The food was authentic, although the furniture was not: Sheba had no *mesobs*, just American-style dinner tables. And because this cuisine was so new to New York, the menu also offered burgers and omelets.

On Dec. 7, 1979, The New York Times took notice, commending the restaurant's Ethiopian fare, cautioning people about the "incendiary Ethiopian spice paste, bereberé," and observing that the "satisfying, savory [dishes] would probably be considered entertaining by venturesome eaters in search of the exotic. The food and sauces seemed overcooked and just a bit greasy," the critic wrote, "but most of the dishes we tried were satisfying and savory." The writer especially liked *kitfo*, "ground raw beef much like steak tartar, with its bright red freshness of color and its convincing belt of hot spices." Clearly, a sophisticated palate.

When Araya calls the partners in this enterprise "relatives," he's using the term in the Ethiopian sense. Families raised together in a city or village think of one another and their children as relatives, so "if I make some mischief," Araya says, "and the next door neighbor knows my father, he can discipline me. They're friends, but they're more like family, even though there's no blood relationship. Sometimes they don't even get married to one another."

Teff was unavailable in America back then, so Sheba used self-rising flour to make its *injera*. The batter was slightly fermented, but not nearly as much as *injera* that uses teff. *Injera* demands altitude to ferment well, Workye says, and even now, at her restaurant in Brooklyn, she uses some self-rising flour when she makes *injera*. Sheba couldn't get *berbere* either, so the cooks made their own from the available spices.

The restaurant's customers were mostly non-Ethiopians, although when Ethiopians came, Workye recalls, they often brought their American friends to teach them about their culture's cuisine. Decades later, when Workye opened Ghenet in Soho, customers would recall their first Ethiopian meal at Sheba, and "when I told them it was me, it was like a family reunion."

A year or so after Sheba opened, Araya bought out his partners. This began his pioneering effort to spread Ethiopian food around New York. He and a new business partner, Michael Winn, later opened Abyssinia, with *mesobs* and no tables. Then they opened Blue Nile, a larger restaurant, at 77th and Columbus. This place, too, had only *mesobs*, and people loved it.

So began the spread of Ethiopian food in New York. On Nov. 9, 1983, The New York Times published a lengthy article about the cuisine, told through the experience of Queens resident Sarah Wolde Selassie, a well-educated Ethiopian-American woman — the wife of a former Ethiopian Airlines employee — who said that families in Ethiopia usually eat at home and "only go out to dinner for European food."

In one way or another, Araya has been in the Ethiopian food business ever since he opened Sheba: His restaurants have closed, but in the late 1990s, he created Sheba Tej. His mother and sister came from Ethiopia to perfect the recipe, and with a business partner, Araya took his endeavor to Brotherhood Winery, the oldest in the United States. A while after selling his interest in Sheba Tej, he remerged with his own company, Heritage Winery, which now makes four varieties of *t'ej*, all flavored and fermented with gesho, and two of them — Axum Tej and Saba Tej — adding a touch of hard-to-get Ethiopian honey.

Workye had come to America a year before Sheba opened with her husband, a lawyer, and their two children, seeking more freedom than Ethiopia's increasingly heavy-handed Communist dictators allowed. She worked at the U.N. for 18 years in administration and human resources, even spending two years with a peacekeeping mission on the Israel-Lebanon border, and after she sold her partnership in Sheba, she took a long break from the restaurant business.

She returned in 1998, her three children now grown, to open Ghenet in Soho, which she operated until 2009, when her rent nearly doubled, forcing her to close. That's when she opened a new Ghenet in Brooklyn's trendy Park Slope neighborhood.

Ghenet has a few rare touches among Ethiopian restaurants. Each table has a small glass silver-topped shaker with *mitmita,* the incendiary red pepper powder. Before a meal, patrons get a packaged towel to wash their hands. It's no skimpy moist towelette, but rather a sturdy towel about the size of a washcloth. You also get a dish of *dirkosh,* or dried pieces of *injera,* to munch, and some hummus in which to dip it. It's Ghenet's Ethiopian equivalent of chips and salsa, or fried noodles and duck sauce.

Workye says she makes her *injera* with 80 percent teff for better fermentation, mixing it with 10 percent barley and 10 percent self-rising flour. It's a little darker than most other New York *injera.*

She sees her new restaurant as "more of a teaching place. I want to introduce the culture and the different kinds of food Ethiopia has. What we have here is the tip of the iceberg. There are a lot of different foods that have not been discovered."

To that end, she's now working on a cookbook that will include dishes not commonly found in Ethiopian restaurants. She has a ghost writer helping her, and she hopes to travel to Ethiopia with a photographer to research and illustrate the book.

And Workye — whose full name, Yeworkwoha, means "water of gold" — has another dream enterprise in mind: She wants to start a line of frozen Ethiopian foods. She doesn't have a backer yet, so right now, you can only taste her cooking in two ways: by visiting Ghenet, or by being one of her children, to whom she sometimes overnights a home-cooked meal — even to her daughter in Washington, D.C., with its abundance of Ethiopian restaurants. "They like mummy's cooking, I guess," she says with a contented grin.

As Ghenet continues to thrive in uptown Brooklyn, a new kid in the neighborhood has found its own niche. Bati opened in early 2009 in Fort Greene, an eclectic Brooklyn neighborhood about a mile closer to Manhattan than Park Slope. The restaurant is just blocks from the Brooklyn Academy of

Music (BAM), and its young co-owner, Hibist Legesse, hopes the arty crowd will help her restaurant grow and thrive.

The daughter of an Ethiopian banker, Hibist came to American in 1992 to attend a private high school near Buffalo and has lived here ever since. She had her first Ethiopian restaurant meal in the 1990s at Araya's Abyssinia in Manhattan. She didn't much care for frigid upstate New York, and in her loneliness back then, she would sometimes ask friends to drive her to Buffalo, where she looked for Ethiopian names in the phone book. Her own means "manna" in Amharic, and it derives from *hbst*, the ancient Ge'ez word for "bread."

In 2008, while remodeling the storefront that became Bati, Hibist returned to Ethiopia for the first time since leaving there, and she brought back some work by contemporary Ethiopian painters to adorn the walls of Bati. The restaurant is intimate and crowded when it's busy, but in a warm way. From table to table, and even at each table, her customers are diverse and, she says, "savvy as hell" — educated and curious. Some neighborhood folks even stopped in during construction to ask about the place, and after she opened, bloggers spread the word. She hopes her proximity to BAM will even bring Manhattanites to her table.

Hibist's arrival in Brooklyn's nascent Ethiopian restaurant community, even before the opening of Ghenet, feels like the passing of a torch from the veteran Workye to a new generation, although the two restaurants are now in competition with one another. Fortunately, they're in a borough and a city that's big enough to allow both to thrive, and just far enough apart to draw from different neighborhoods.

On a Sunday evening in March, just a month after Bati opened, the place was packed and stayed that way, clearly something the neighborhood needs and wants. A couple with a baby in a stroller required a high chair, and when they learned that Bati didn't have one, they decided not to stay. But they came back 10 minutes later, parked the stroller next to their table, and improvised.

They were first-timers with Ethiopian cuisine, and when their food arrived, they glanced casually around the room to see exactly how to do it before they began to eat. Their baby was too young for the food, but across the room, a 3-year-old Japanese-American girl with her parents mastered *injera* quickly and began to grab chunks of mildly spiced lamb.

Hibist wants Bati to specialize in healthy food and fast friendly service. Once a "horrible waitress" herself, she knows what *not* to do. She makes her *injera* with 60 percent teff because it doesn't work out right otherwise. "The hardest thing about this restaurant is *injera* making," she says, and she admits it wasn't too tasty when she opened. She's never made it for herself at home and would never attempt to do so.

This new Brooklyn contingent of Ethiopian food is encouraging, although it's hard to imagine the cuisine spreading to all five boroughs. Manhattan is still the quickest fix for New Yorkers and tourists. With the loss of Ghenet in Soho, Village people now only have the modest Awash and the diner-like Meskerem. Both are fine choices, the latter located in a storefront below ground level along a bustling little street filled with everything from a hummus restaurant to an Irish pub.

Near Times Square, there's Queen of Sheba, which has become popular with the city's Ethiopian community, and another Meskerem (once owned by the same people as the downtown restaurant, but now no longer). These two competitors are around the corner from one another in a gentrified Hell's Kitchen, and both are a good safe walk from the heart of Broadway. And now there's Lalibela in suburban Mt. Kisco, one of only three Ethiopian restaurants in New York state that's not in New York City (the other two are both in Rochester).

You'll find no Ethiopian food further uptown in Manhattan than Zoma, located on Frederick Douglas Boulevard (Eighth Avenue) and 113th Street in Morningside Heights. It's the city's trendiest Ethiopian restaurant, with a glassy bar illuminated in a rainbow of colors, and decorations that mix modern art and Ethiopian tribal headrests.

The owner, Henock Kejela, is tall, trim and fit, with short silvering hair that makes him look slightly older than his early 40-some years. He comes to work in blue jeans and a long-sleeve collarless white knit top. A resident of the neighborhood, he worked in finance for many years before opening Zoma, and after hearing a community development group bemoan its lack of culinary diversity, he became "an accidental restaurateur."

Henock came to America in 1984 at age 16 to live with his sister in Dallas. A few moves and a college degree later, he landed in New York. His wife, Jote Kassa, is a corporate attorney and a great-granddaughter of Haile Selassie. His full birth name is Henock Kejela Tesfaye, but when he got to Ellis Island, an immigration officer thought two names were more than enough. He still uses "Tesfaye" in his e-mail address, and he took T. as his middle initial.

For now, Zoma doesn't serve lunch on weekdays, a victim of poor foot traffic in a gentrifying West Side neighborhood. Henock looks forward to more development and growth in the coming years. The enterprise is new to him, but it's partly in his blood: Back home, his mother owned a restaurant for several years along Addis Ababa's bustling Bole Road.

When Henock came to America, he says, "as a newcomer, I wanted to experiment with new kinds of foods," so he really didn't miss Ethiopian food very much. Before opening Zoma, he would eat it a few times a week. But now it's back in his life full time, and even his 7-year-old twins, a boy and girl, are starting to eat it. His own return to the cuisine doesn't really surprise him.

"Everyone has their stories," he says. "I circled back. When you get older, and you get hungry, that's what you want."

Communities of Cuisine:
Village Life

Forget about your Ethiopian feast around a *mesob*, sipping *t'ej* as you eat, and listening to a *begena* or *masinko* playing over a tinny stereo, all in the venue of a cozy urban restaurant with four sturdy wall.

For a brief while, if you wanted Ethiopian food in Alaska, you had to visit the neighborhood yurt.

And it was a big neighborhood. In all of Alaska, there has been only one Ethiopian restaurant: Tekul, formerly located on College Road, just a few minutes from the campus of the University of Fairbanks, and now closed, its owner says, after a "successful and disastrous" brief life.

Alex Antohin, a great-great-grandson of Ethiopia's last emperor, opened Tekul in June 2007, a few months after graduating with a degree in sociology from the University of Fairbanks. He did it to honor his Ethiopian heritage and the food he grew up loving, but also as an experiment to bring some culinary diversity to a place with almost none.

Born in Virginia, Antohin grew up mostly in Fairbanks, where his Russian-born father is a professor of theater at the university, and his Ethiopian-born mother, a great-granddaughter of Emperor Haile Selassie, is a teacher and anthropologist. He named his restaurant for a kind of traditional Ethiopian wood hut, his maternal culture's version of a yurt — that is, an Alaskan native home made of a cloth tent, draped in the shape of a dome over a framework constructed from tree branches.

"There isn't a lot of choice, food-wise, in my town," Antohin says of Fairbanks, where you can get Thai, Chinese, pizza, and little more that isn't simply America. How, he wondered, could a nascent entrepreneur remedy that absence in an economical way, using the money his relatives gave him for graduation. He didn't want to (and couldn't afford to) take out a lease on a building. So he approached a businessman who owned a large office building and an empty parking lot, and he leased a corner of the lot month to month.

With the help of a business partner, and a hand here and there from friends and curious passers-by, Antohin built his yurt from latticed boughs of Alaskan birch in about six weeks, opening Tekul in mid-June 2007. The yurt had a 30-foot diameter and reached up 14 feet to the crisp blue Alaskan sky. His edge of the parking lot touched a grassy field with a cluster of trees. The restaurant had a sign on the front with its name written in English and Amharic on a small replica of the Ethiopian flag.

Although Antohin's yurt had room for seating, Tekul was takeout only, with a window on one side to order, and a window on the other side to pick up your food. He made each dish from scratch on stovetop burners fueled by an oil-fired generator. His customers often liked to stand outside the pickup window and look into the kitchen as he cooked their meals. They even watched him chop the onions and cut the meats and vegetables — something he watched his mother do while he was growing up.

The menu was modest: *shiro, azifa, kategna, ayib, sambussa*, lentil salad, *fitfit*, and *wots* made of beef, chicken or vegetables. Antohin got his *berbere, shiro* and other supplies shipped from Ethiopia, and although he served *injera*, it wasn't fermented. He tried at first making his *injera* with teff shipped from an Ethiopian market in Denver, where his brother lives, but Alaska was just too cold to provoke fermentation. So he used whole wheat flour and baking powder to make *injera* that had authentic-looking "eyes" but a paler hue and no bitter taste. Tekul even presented a coffee ceremony on Sundays, and Antohin encouraged patrons to take some *injera* home and try cooking Ethiopian food themselves.

During the construction of Tekul, curious townspeople would stop by to ask why someone would built a yurt on an asphalt parking lot. These folks became his first customers. His kitchen had a few single metal burners, like a stovetop, and two flat pans for making the *injera*. Except for the occasional patron who had eaten Ethiopian food in Washington, nobody noticed the missing element of his *injera*.

His customers at Tekul were mostly Alaskan transplants or people born and raised there, but almost never people of indigenous Alaskan cultures. He only remembers serving one Ethiopian, a vacationing professor on sabbatical who was delighted to find home cooking so close to the Arctic Circle.

A few early customers at Tekul were "a little scared and insulting at first," making comments about starving Ethiopians. But once people began to try the food, he had repeat customers. His only common complaint came from people who had to wait while he made big orders for them.

Antohin did all the cooking, something he learned to do from his mother, and he spent one of his college years in San Jose, where he made Ethiopian food for friends. Before Tekul opened, he got a quick refresher course from his mother, who was "one of our best customers because she was so happy to have Ethiopian food."

Growing up in Fairbanks, Antohin could request that his mother make an Ethiopian meal whenever he wanted it, and he'd have it about once a week. He especially liked his mother's *doro wot,* and he admits that his doesn't taste anything like mom's did. His father didn't care for the spicy cuisine all that much. Antohin had no Ethiopian community growing up, just his mother and some visits with family members. And although the family lived in Russian for two years when Antohin was a child, he says he still feels closer to his Ethiopian heritage.

"I don't know why I lean more toward my Ethiopian background than my Russian," he says. "I have a stronger sense of wanting to help out Ethiopia. It's in a very demoralized and tough state. Most Ethiopians' lives have been very hard. I feel I have a duty to help out because it's half of my heritage."

Of course, he is Ethiopian royalty, so that might have something to do with it. His mother, Esther, was born in Ethiopia in 1960, one of numerous great-granddaughters of the emperor.

This is all very far removed from Antohin's all-American life, although being a prince is literally in his blood. "When I'm in Ethiopia, I definitely feel it a little more," he admits. "I'm very happy and proud of it, but I don't let it work on my thinking in any way."

After two good months in business, Antohin knew he had to close Tekul for the harsh Alaskan winter that begins in late August. He intended to return to his enterprise in May, and he went to Ethiopia for a three months in the interim to teach in a primary school. But before the winter ended, Tekul's roof caved in from the weight of the unrelenting snow, and that was that. Antohin dismantled his yurt and, eventually, moved to San Diego, where he took a job as a teacher's aide.

He dreams of reopening Tekul or something like it in Alaska if his life ever leads him back there. His next move will probably be to Denver, where his brother is raising four adopted Ethiopian children, all from the same family. He feels a longing to get closer to his African roots, and he trains in tapoeira, a form of Afro-Brazilian martial arts.

"A lot of people were sad to see us go," he says, reflecting on his short-lived adventure as a restaurateur, "and that's why I want to open it again. It was a sociological experiment, and I think they were really happy to have the choice."

Mirror Images

Since Eritrea won its independence from Ethiopia in 1994, the two countries have continued to engage in border wars, usually small but sometimes heavily armed. Meanwhile, within Ethiopia, the majority Oromo culture has long felt oppressed by the ruling Amhari-Tigrayan government, and some activists want Oromia to become an independent country.

In Columbus, you'll find an emerging community whose neo-American entrepreneurs reflect these conflicts, still widespread in the homelands they left behind.

The Ohio city's "Ethiopian" community has significant elements of all three cultures, or nationalities, as Eritreans and especially Oromos prefer to say: Its numerous restaurants and businesses are owned by Amharis, Eritreans and Oromos. They co-exist because they must in a pluralistic country, but in some ways their intermingled communities resemble the United States in the early 20th Century, when a generation of immigrant cultures kept to themselves as much as they could and quietly condemned their new American brothers and sisters.

Ask an Oromo in Columbus if he's Ethiopian, and after a very loaded pause, he'll give you one of two answers: "I'm Oromo," or, "*No*, I'm Oromo." The former answer is the polite response, the latter more emotional and aggrieved.

This tends to divide the business community, although the biggest division is the one between the Oromos and everyone else. At Lalibela, owned by Amharis, and at Selam Olympic, owned by Eritreans, all of the dishes on each restaurant's menu appear in three languages: English, transliterated Amharic, and transliterated Tigrinya. This invites three cultures to order in their own languages. It leaves Oromos nowhere to dine but at home.

It's not that Oromos don't know two or even all three of those languages. It's just that some would rather not patronize restaurants owned by people from cultures against whom they have such a painful and long-standing grievance.

Morkataa Dhinaa, an affable young Oromo businessman, greets every customer who enters his Odaa International convenience store, and if you're a few coins short of his price for the item you're buying, he'll let it slide. But he remembers what happened to him at a cultural fair a few years ago: After he set up his booth, complete with the Oromo national flag, an Ethiopian man — that is, an Amhari — told him he shouldn't have that flag and should just join the Ethiopian booth. Morkataa declined, believing he wouldn't really be welcomed.

Odaa sells *injera* and *berbere*, but it's not an Oromo or Ethiopian market.

Its wares are what you'd find in any well-stocked convenience store across America. Morkataa's *injera* comes only from the city's Awash Enjera Bakery, owned by Yadessa Berhanu and his wife, Ashla Tigro, both of whom are Oromo. He says that 95 percent of his customers are Americans, but of the remaining five percent, 90 percent of those are Oromo, a few are Eritrean, and very few are Amhari.

Politics aside, Columbus does have a booming community, the largest in Ohio. Half a dozen companies bake and label their own *injera,* just like in Chicago and D.C. There's a 68-page Ethiopian Yellow Pages published in the city. And on the 3900 block of East Main Street, in a neighborhood where you'll find many of the businesses, a branch of Central Ohio Healthcare Systems displays a large sign with the Ethiopian flag (but not the Eritrean or Oromo flags).

It's a relatively new community that grew quickly, dwarfing nearby metropolitan areas like Cleveland to the north and Pittsburgh to the east.

In 1994, the city got its first restaurant thanks to Tekle Beyene, who bought a building that had housed a French restaurant and turned it into Ethiopian-Eritrean Cuisine. The place did well, his customers liked the food, and he got a good review in the newspaper. But the restaurant shared space with his other business, a small convenience store, and in 1996, he decided to close the restaurant and just operate his A&B Market. He now owns the small strip mall on East Livingston Avenue where A&B still sits, and he leases the other storefronts to places like a beauty salon and an Italian pizza and sub shop.

Over the next decade, the Ethiopian, Eritrean and Oromo communities in Columbus grew and grew. The city and its adjacent suburb Whitehall now have four or five restaurants — business being tough, they tend to come and go — half a dozen markets with large supplies of Ethiopian foods, and numerous other markets, like Odaa, trading largely in non-Ethiopian goods, with a few basic food items for their countrymen who need it in a pinch.

These businesses come in all sizes, with proprietors of all cultures. But two restaurants, just a few blocks from each other along an unguarded border on South Hamilton Road, nicely illustrate the interplay of politics and business.

Lalibela, owned by an Amhari, and Selam, owned by an Eritrean, each has a menu with its dishes named in English, Amharic and Tigrinya. But Selam calls itself an "Ethiopian and Eritrean restaurant," while Lalibela is just "Ethiopian." No Ethiopian restaurant would ever call itself Ethiopian *and* Eritrean, partly for political reasons, but also because "Ethiopian" is the brand name. For Selam, it's a matter of both awareness and politics: Americans might not know the cuisines are the same, and Eritreans would surely be offended if the restaurant didn't mention their culture.

At Lalibela, you can order such dishes as greens/*hamli/gomen*, beef/*kelwa sega/yesega tibs*, chicken/*dohro kelwa/yedoro tibs* or hot chicken/*zebhi dohro/ doro watt*. The Eritrean word for the familiar Ethiopian *tibs* is *kelwa*, and the word for *wot* is *zebhi* or *tsebhi*. Selam's menu offers the same array of dishes, again named in triplicate. Lalibela is the larger of the two, with a circular bar in the center and a pool room at the front. Selam also has a bar, much smaller than Lalibela's, and each place has a stage for live performances — Amharic singers at Lalibela, Tigrinya singers at Selam.

Just down the strip mall from Selam, Mihret Brhane's One Stop Market has the number "1" in Amharic on its marquee and business card, but only the card says "Meskerem," the first month of the Ethiopian calendar, in Amharic. The vivacious young businesswoman has two shelves of Ethiopian foods and household items along with other standard convenience store items. She's Eritrean, and unconcerned with politics, focusing instead on business and good cheer when customers enter her store.

Ashe Bekele's Addisu Bakery & Carry Out sells its own brand-name *injera* exclusively at its shop. "We make it and we sell it here," brags the company's business card. Ashe, who's from Addis Ababa, opened the shop in 2008. Not too far away, Walt's Carry Out and Beauty Shop sells Ethiopian wines, spices and several brands of *injera*. In Amharic on its window are the transliterated American words "Walt's Grocery."

Redda Mehari opened Warka Market after decades as the administrator of a non-profit center for refugees and immigrants in Las Vegas. He first came to America in the early 1970s to get a degree at the University of the District of Columbia. He then returned to Ethiopia, but in 1983, he left again and arrived in the U.S. as a refugee himself. Now retired from his long-time profession, he recently moved to Columbus to be closer to his sister in Dayton, and he opened Warka, a convenience store, internet café and small restaurant.

Redda grew up in Addis Ababa, the son of Eritrean parents. Back when he first came to America, he says, he got plenty of Ethiopian food, although "we never, ever bought any of those things. It became a tradition to bring a lot with you from home and to share with everyone." He also had his wife to cook for him, just as she does now at Warka. The place began as a coffee shop, but that didn't bring in much income, so they added a small selection of Ethiopian dishes. "It's keeping us alive," he says of his expanded menu, although it's still a struggle.

When Redda lived in D.C. in early 1970s, the city had no sense of Ethiopian community. So his group of young immigrants, attending college on student visas, established one around 18th and Columbia, in Adams Morgan, where a cluster of trendy Ethiopian restaurants later emerged in the 1980s. His café continues an enterprise that he began some 35 years ago: *Warka* is the Amharic word for an oak tree with big encompassing branches and leaves, and in traditional Ethiopian cultures, people come together under a *warka* to sell goods on market days and to conduct community affairs. (The tree is called an *odaa* in Afaan Oromo.)

At Sunny Café, you can only get one Ethiopian dish: *misir wot* on *injera*. That's because the café trades in American-style deli sandwiches, pastries and coffee. It has four small tables with chairs, and three cushy couches that surround a cocktail table.

The café opened in 2003 when the two young adult children of current owners Mulushewa Belayneh and her husband, Gebre Berhe, launched the fledgling family business. Their daughter, the older of the two, named if after herself. Both kids have now gone off to college to enter the field of nursing — Mulushewa was a nurse technician in her earlier career — leaving mom and pop to run the business.

But Sunny Café's sandwiches have a difference: Mulushewa sprinkles them with a touch of *mitmita* to give them some Ethiopian flare. She also makes an Ethiopian bread, or *dabo,* lightly seasoned with cumin. And if you ask, she'll serve your sandwich as an *injera* wrap.

Like so many of these small Columbus businesses, Sunny Café struggles, and Mulushewa has a theory to explain it. "[Ethiopians] who live in Columbus cook in their homes," she says. "They don't go out. We come from Addis, so we know the enjoyment. Many of them come from the countryside and don't spend that much money." This makes it hard for community restaurants, despite the presence of an Ethio-Eritrean population.

But she's happy to say that the new young generation of Ethiopians in Columbus embrace American-style food, so her sandwiches are popular takeout items in her neighborhood. She'd even like to begin importing some natural food items from Ethiopia to sell at Sunny's.

Abyssinia restaurant serves delicious food, but you have to find the place first. It's way back off the road in a strip mall, and you can't see it from the four-lane highway that passes the cluster of shops. Owner Admassu Worku, a salesman back in Ethiopia, and his wife, Tiruwork ("good gold") Hailelegiorgis, who does the cooking, came to the U.S. a decade ago seeking opportunities for themselves and their three young children. They opened Abyssinia in November 2005.

The mini-complex has three rooms: a register and small gift shop in the center, a crowded poolhall with two tables on the left, and their roomy restaurant on the right, where Tiruwork serves generous portions. The *injera* comes naked on a tray, with your dishes in small bowls and tins. It's your job to pour each dish onto your *injera*, all at once or little by little.

These businesses are on the city's east side, slowly spreading west over two or three miles. About 10 miles away, practically on the campus of Ohio State University, you'll find Columbus' sole west side Ethiopian restaurant, Blue Nile, now the oldest in the city, opened in the mid-1990s. It's smaller than it should be, considering its proximity to the university. The clientele is heavily non-Ethiopian, and the politics are more of the blue-state-red-state variety.

You don't hear a lot of political talk from the city's Amhari business owners. From their point of view, there's very little politics in everyday life. But of course, it's a different story when you talk with Eritrean and Oromo people.

Tekle Beyene, the city's pioneering restaurateur, and an Eritrean, has a lot to say, and he's not easy on his homeland's government. He's also more hopeful about the prospect for reconciliation among the communities in America. He dreams of a democratic Eritrea with closer ties to Ethiopia and other neighboring African countries, and he'd like to see the government develop its economy and help the masses the way he sees the Ethiopian government doing.

"There is always politics, but the people are very close to each other," he says. "We are tied to the same culture and history. We are intermingled with blood and relations." It's not the split from Ethiopia that hurt his homeland, he says, but rather an oppressive government doing nothing to develop the country economically for the benefit of all.

"Eritreans are hard-working people," Tekle says. "That wouldn't be a problem if they had the opportunity. But all the government wants is war. You don't benefit from two countries fighting."

Morkataa wants the same thing for Oromia, located within Ethiopia, but he doesn't think it will happen any time soon. He'd like to stock more Oromo foods at his market — things like *anchote, enset* and *bunakala*, whole coffee pods that Oromo people cook with spiced butter. But he says the government over there makes it hard to get such things because they're part of Oromo culture.

On a breezy Saturday in June at Odaa, the conversation turned to politics thanks to a passionate older Oromo fellow who would only say his name was "Y. Tucho." A long-time educator, and an American now for 20 years or so, he's writing a book about relations between the Ethiopians and the Oromos.

As we talked, he asked me several times — only half playfully — if I worked for the Ethiopian government. He seemed to believe me when I said that I didn't. And as Morkataa tended his shop, nodding in agreement now and then, Tucho let loose the passion of his people.

"They have bugs in their heads about us," he says of the ruling Amhari. "They take us to be stupid. They're extremely hostile and unfriendly. They want to maintain there hegemony, and they don't understand that it's out of their hands. Every human being is equal. I just can't put up with the myth they have about themselves. They can't manage our cultural lives. The Gurages are there. The Woylaita are there. The Oromos are there. You are not going to hide them or put them in a box."

Steel City Ethiopians

In Pittsburgh, a city with more than 70 neighborhoods — each with a name, and many with an ethnic or cultural identity — observant Moslems can buy halal meats at Salem's. If you're Jewish and you keep kosher, no problem: Six days a week, Murray Avenue Prime Kosher will set your table. You'll find Indian, Asian, Greek and Italian grocery stores, and you can make an authentic meal at home in all of these cultures, buying your supplies from Old Country grocers or their second- and third-generation progeny.

But if you're Ethiopian, you can't buy *berbere, kibbee* or other kitchen staples in your adopted hometown.

Pittsburgh doesn't have an Ethiopian grocery store, and Ethiopians who want *berbere* either bring it back from visits home or buy it in cities that have it. This is typical of many — even *most* — American cities (including New York) where you find Ethiopian cuisine. But now Pittsburgh has two Ethiopian restaurants, and it's an excellent laboratory for observing how Ethiopians live and eat when they settle in a city without a community large enough to support restaurants and grocery stores.

Although some of Pittsburgh's Ethiopians have lived here for 25, the city only got its first Ethiopian restaurant, Abay, in May 2004, and that restaurant has its *injera* shipped from bakeries in Washington, D.C. The restaurant's owner, James Wallace, is African-American and was a corporate attorney who stopped working as a lawyer to pursue his dream of owning an Ethiopian restaurant. He had two partners — a young Ethiopian-American woman pursing a master's degree in Pittsburgh, and a middle-aged Ethiopian-American woman from Washington, D.C. But they just helped him get started, and now he runs the place himself.

Tana, the city's second Ethiopian restaurant, opened in January 2008, and since then it's become a gathering place for the city's youngest Ethiopian population. Once a month or so, families from Western Pennsylvania and West Virginia gather there with their adopted Ethiopian children. It's a chance to socialize, but also to make sure their new family members grow up with a taste for their native cuisine. Some of the parents have even learned to make Ethiopian food at home, although they say it's nothing like the real thing they get at a restaurant run by Ethiopians.

Tana makes its own *injera*, and the presence of two restaurants means that Ethiopians in Pittsburgh can now buy *injera* locally if they want it. But what did they do in the past? The extended Birru family tells a typical story. Most of the Birrus have lived elsewhere over the years, but now a dozen or so family members have lived in Pittsburgh for two decades or more. With no place to get Ethiopian food until recently, they adapted their tables and their palates.

Elizabeth Birru was born in Ethiopia, the first child of an Ethiopian father and an African-American mother who met in college in the U.S., then married and moved to Ethiopia for his work. Liz spoke Amharic those first four years, but she lost it soon after the family returned to America, where sisters Mehret and Rahel were born. It didn't help Liz's Amharic that her mother never learned to speak it, so it wasn't spoken at home in America.

She remembers almost nothing about her Ethiopian childhood, and certainly nothing about food. Growing up American in the 1980s, in Florida and Pittsburgh, the family couldn't get teff, so when they had *injera*, it was made with white flour. The family lived in Chicago for a while and got fermented teff *injera* at restaurants. After they settled in Pittsburgh, where the sisters mostly grew up, an uncle would bring teff *injera* from D.C. when he visited. Relatives would also bring *ambasha* — the big, doughy Ethiopian bread — and they would freeze it.

Their Ethiopian grandmother lived with them from time to time, and when she did, she cooked. The wives of her father's brothers would also prepare Ethiopian family meals. Mehret didn't like spicy Ethiopian dishes as a child and remembers sitting on her grandmother's lap, picking away at the mild *alichas* on grandma's *injera*-covered plate. Liz "liked it spicy from day one," Mehret recalls, especially when their grandmother cooked, and now she's largely vegetarian (with a little chicken on occasion).

As for *injera*, Mehret preferred the white flour variety as a child and tended to shun true fermented teff *injera*. Even now, she says the spongier white *injera* soaks up the juices better, although she favors the real thing to grab the food. She eats all kinds of dishes these days, and both sisters fondly recall growing up with *chechebsa* made by their Eritrean aunt, the wife of one of their father's brothers. When grandma was around, sometimes even breakfast would be Ethiopian: some *ambasha* toast, sweetened with honey.

But when their Ethiopian relatives weren't there to cook, they enjoyed their mother's American cuisine. She would occasionally make *alichas*, and from time to time she even tried *injera*, never with great success. Their father fasts for Christian holidays, and the family eats more vegetables then. Today, as adults and young professionals (Liz is in business, Mehret in medical school), they eat like Americans and get their Ethiopian food at restaurants and family gatherings.

The Birru sisters have enjoyed many of their Ethiopian meals in the Pittsburgh home of their uncle and aunt, Tsegaye and Selam Beru (same family, same name, different spelling), who have two children, a teen-age son and a pre-teen daughter.

For Selam's nephew, Seifu Haileyesus, life in America was different when he arrived here more than 20 years ago. He came to attend college, and at school — inexperienced in American cuisine — he ate a lot of salad and bread at first. "Everyone was wondering about me," he recalls. "When they had spaghetti, I got happy." His family would send him *berbere, kibbee* and *dirkosh* (dried pieces of *injera*), and with that, he could make a spicy Ethiopian *wot*. But Seifu is a meat eater, so he took a liking to places like Ground Round.

Growing up in Addis Ababa, he ate only Ethiopian food at home, along with pasta from time to time, prepared by the family's housekeeper/cook under the supervision of the lady of the house. His mother also owned a *t'ej bet* for a time, but Seifu doesn't drink *t'ej* because he has a bad reaction to honey. As a child, adults always ate first. That's an Ethiopian custom still practiced by some families. As he got older, they all ate together, and sometimes they would have their own plates rather than eating communally. With pasta, though, everyone always had an individual plate because it made eating much easier. Beginning in high school, he'd go with friends to a *shai bet* ("tea house") for tea, pastries and music. If he went to a restaurant, it was an Italian one.

Today he owns Tana, where his sister is one of the cooks, and he gets all the Ethiopian food he wants. But before that, at home, he made salads, steaks, soup, chicken breasts, and from time to time some Ethiopian beef dishes, like *siga wot* and *kitfo*. His pattern is typical for Ethiopians living in cities with no community and no place to buy staples. Fortunately, Selam and her family eventually settled in Pittsburgh as well, so he'd get Ethiopian food with them. But now he's virtually all American at home, starting with breakfast, which is oatmeal or cold cereal with milk.

Martha Agedew Vasser, who works and hosts at Seifu's restaurant, has a slightly different story. Her parents attended college in America, and her father, an educator, has traveled extensively. She was raised in Ethiopia eating mostly Ethiopian food, but sometimes her mother would make dishes of chicken and rice, something she learned to do in America. She also made salads, roasts, and a stuffed cabbage that Martha still misses after more than

20 years away from Ethiopia. They would sometimes end dinner with a European-style salad of romaine lettuce, tomato, onions and peppers.

But even with this culinary diversity, Martha recalls that 90 percent of the food at home growing up was Ethiopian. They never went to restaurants for the evening meal. Rather, they would sometimes meet friends at cafés, bakeries or "hamburger joints" to socialize and order a little something to eat.

Now that Tana has opened, Martha says, Ethiopians feel they have a place to gather, and she's met some Ethiopians she didn't even know lived in Pittsburgh. "Social life is an integral part of their existence," she says, and over the years, she saw many leave Pittsburgh for cities with more community. Tana now offers a lavish buffet each September to mark Meskerem, the Ethiopian new year.

Martha came to America for college, and for a while, she couldn't get Ethiopian food. "I missed it to death," she admits, but thanks to family in New Jersey, and her own effort at cooking, she got an occasional fix. She's "tried for years to make *injera*, but I did not succeed." Eventually she married an African-American Pittsburgher and raised two children.

Her son, in college, is a difficult eater in any cuisine. But her daughter, still in high school, likes Ethiopian food and makes it at home (along with soul food). She especially likes *doro wot* with *ayib*. Martha used to cook Ethiopian food maybe once a week for her family. Now that they're grown and spending time with friends, she doesn't do it nearly as often.

These adaptations are typical of Ethiopians who live in places with virtually no community, and most say they don't expect their children to live by *injera* alone — if at all. It will certainly take some effort on their part, as well as a commitment to their ancestral culture.

"A couple of my cousins are more into the pizza and American foods than *injera* and *wots*," Liz Birru says of this American-raised generation. "But I can promise you that I'll take Ethiopian over those items any day."

Mesob Across America

MICHIGAN'S PIONEERING Ethiopian restaurant, The Blue Nile in Ann Arbor, does a hearty business thanks to the presence of the University of Michigan. It's one of the more all-American Ethiopian restaurants: Rather than getting its spices from Ethiopia through a distributor in the U.S., Habte Dadi and his wife, Almaz Lessanewerk, buy *berbere* and *shiro* from another pioneer of Ethiopian food, Workinesh Spice Blends of Minnesota.

Blue Nile also doesn't use any teff in its *injera* and doesn't ferment the batter, so there's no sourdough taste. Their bread is snow white, but its texture and bubbly top perfectly mimic the slightly darker *injera* made with teff. This choice is a throwback to the restaurant's early days. When the original Blue Nile opened in Detroit in 1984, Habte says, people knew so little about Ethiopian food that the restaurant didn't want to make the experience any more foreign than it needed to be. It also was very hard to get teff back then. They make their *injera* on square skillets rather than a big round *mitad*, and one person does it for six hours a day to keep the busy restaurant stocked. They once tried shipping fermented *injera* from a D.C. company, but they found it didn't stay fresh long enough.

Blue Nile is a popular place in Ann Arbor, always packed on weekends and often on weekdays, and a few years ago, Habte and Almaz bought a neighboring storefront to expand. They now have two intimate rooms in which they host banquets, conferences and parties, and they're open for lunch, serving Ethiopian food and a few non-Ethiopian fusion dishes.

The method of cooking at Blue Nile is a little more "mechanized" (Habte's word) than at other Ethiopian restaurants. Rather than cooking in open pots, Blue Nile prepares its food in large pressure cookers. Habte says this avoids direct contact with heat and cooks the food more slowly to preserve its flavor. It also allows the restaurant to make large quantities and save time. In their home, Habte and Almaz cook food in the traditional way, in an open pot. But they don't ferment their personal *injera*. "We do miss it," Habte says, "but after so many years, you get used to it."

The couple came to America in the early 1980s, and Almaz got lucky right away: She had an Ethiopian meal the day she arrived because she stayed with relatives. Habte had to learn to cook for himself (the couple met in America), and now he sees those days as a time of experiencing new things. "In order to miss something, you have to get other things," he says. "It was kind of fun." And he adds, with a smile: "When I came here, I didn't expect to find *injera*."

Habte and Almaz aren't the original owners of Blue Nile, which was launched in Detroit by Almaz's brother, Seifu Lessanewerk, in 1984. Five years later, he opened the Ann Arbor location. The couple joined him in the business in 1993. Seifu was a pioneering Ethiopian-American restaurateur, and Blue Nile sells a honey wine called Seifu's Tej. It's made by a New York winery and was created at Seifu's behest for the restaurant. You can now buy it in wine shops in Michigan and find it at restaurants in a few other states, and Seifu Haileyesus sells it at Tana in Pittsburgh. The restaurant also sells packets and tins of its own Ethiopian tea, a blend of orange peels, lemon peels, cloves, chamomile, rose hips, wood betony and cinnamon.

Just a few miles away from Ann Arbor, in nearby working-class Ypsilanti, the mom-'n'-pop Red Sea restaurant struggles, too far from a population center that may only be large enough to support one restaurant.

Red Sea's original owner, who was Eritrean, gave up in 2007, selling the business to Dereje Retta, an engineer at a local company, and his wife, Roza Tesfaye. They retained the restaurant's name and menu, and they make fermented teff *injera*, unlike Blue Nile.

But the Ann Arbor area has few Ethiopians, so both Blue Nile and Red Sea count on non-Ethiopians to survive. As for community, the restaurateurs have none: Dereje only moved to Michigan because of his work as an engineer.

A night at Red Sea is almost like spending a night at home with Dereje and Roza. The couple has two pre-teen daughter, Phevan and Lydia, who often spend time at the restaurant in the evenings and on breaks from school.

The girls were born in America, but they love their parents' native cuisine. Phevan is especially fond of *kitfo*, "but not raw," because she's not old enough yet to eat it that way. She also likes *shiro*, especially the authentic Ethiopian kind that her uncle brings when he visits. "They make it way better there," she says. Perhaps Uncle's home delivery enhances the flavor: Her mother also serves the same type of Ethiopian *shiro* at the restaurant.

Roza prepares Ethiopian food almost exclusively at home, with the occasional macaroni and cheese as a treat for the kids, or maybe some ribs or a steak now and then. Phevan is quick to interject that she likes *kategna*, a dish of toasted *injera* soaked in *berbere* and *kibbee*. Pointing to Lydia, she adds, "She likes it *real* hot!"

Dereje came to America in 1990, a year before the demise of the Derg. He was an Ethiopian Airline pilot, and one day he flew to Yemen and never went back. He got an engineering degree at the University of Dayton, and he met Roza in America, where she was a college student. Dereje had access to Ethiopian food in the 1990s because nearby Columbus had a grocery store, and he sometimes made his own *tibs* and *shiro*.

When Roza arrive here, she brought *berbere* and *shiro* from home, and it lasted many months. But she didn't bring teff, and she could only get white flour for *injera*, so she came to prefer regular bread with her *wot*. She sometimes went as long as a year without real *injera*. Teff is much easier to get now, and Roza uses it in her *injera* at Red Sea, although it's still a challenge: Even her visiting mother, an experienced cook, had trouble at first making it in America. Like many Ethiopians in America, they say *injera* doesn't work as well with American water. Her mother finally stoked the fermentation process by using club soda and letting the batter sit outside for a few days.

The only thing missing now for Dereje and Roza is an Ethiopian community in little Ypsilanti. Their restaurant, and their spirited *shiro*-phile daughters, are almost all they have of home. There are Ethiopians in the Ann

Arbor area — just not too many, and not enough to keep a restaurant afloat. Red Sea doesn't sell alcohol, but sometimes Roza will make *t'ej* and serve it to Ethiopian friends from her church when they gather at the restaurant for a party. Roza prefers hers sweeter. Dereje likes the strong stuff.

Somewhat surprisingly, nearby Detroit has a relatively small Ethiopian community and only a few Ethiopian restaurants. Meskerem (Meskie) Assefa, who owns two of them, says the Ethiopians she knows eat a mix of foods at home, with Ethiopian cuisine more likely around the holidays. By the time she and her engineer-husband moved to Detroit in 2004 — from Toronto, where she also owned a restaurant — she had no trouble getting teff. But when she arrived in Canada in 1981, she counted on her father to bring teff from Ethiopia when he visited, and even then, *injera* was hard.

"The way we do it in Ethiopia, it didn't come out really well here," she recalls. So she tinkered with the preparation, and "after trial and error, it worked." Her kids, all North American-born, love Ethiopian food, even *kitfo*. "Any Ethiopian kids, if you introduce them at a young age, definitely, they love it," she says. "They just love the sourness of the bread." Her daughter, who's 27 and lives in California, even makes some Ethiopian food now at home.

Meskie has settled into her life in Detroit since moving there because of her husband's job. Her restaurant customers are mostly non-Ethiopian, with the occasional Ethiopian passing through to buy some takeout *injera*. She misses the big Ethiopian community she left behind in Toronto, where she was very involved with the local association. A trip to Ethiopia in 2009 for her sister's funeral further reminded her of the solace of home and community.

Once you leave the urban density of eastern Michigan, you'll find only three other Ethiopian restaurants in the state: Altu's, in East Lansing, named for its affable owner/chef, Altaye Tadesse; GoJo, in Grand Rapids, opened in 2007 when its owners, Sam and Sharon Terfa, brought Sam's native cuisine back to their Midwestern town; and the vegan Little Africa, also in Grand Rapids, owned by Loul Negesh, who also has a company called Teshlou Imports.

East Lansing is the home of Michigan State University, a solid and adventuresome young and educated client base for an Ethiopian restaurant in a smaller town. Altu serves all the familiar dishes in the traditional way, but the menu makes it especially easy to order: There are no Amharic names, just descriptive names like spicy chicken stew, spicy lentils, spicy ground peas or collard greens, with brief descriptions of each dish. Diners can eat at contemporary tables or at one of the restaurant's numerous *mesobs* surrounded by wicker-and-metal chair. Beverages — including Ethiopian spiced tea — are self-serve, and so are forks, if you dare. Some diners use a mix of forks and hands, picking at some dishes with metal, then switching to *injera* for others. The décor is mostly modern, with grass skirts hanging from the ceiling around the perimeter of the dining room to complement the *mesobs*.

Altu describes her dishes in English, without naming them in Amharic, because people in central Michigan aren't usually too familiar with Ethiopian food. And although she's Oromo, she never considered naming the dishes in Afaan Oromo for a crowd that might not even recognize the more familiar Amharic names.

Altu's also caters private parties, either at the restaurant on Sundays and Mondays, when it's closed for regular business, or at the place of your choice.

East Lansing was an unusual small-town Ethiopian hub for many years thanks to the presence of the late Harold Marcus, a renowned scholar of Ethiopian history and culture, who taught at Michigan State University for decades. Marcus used his love of the culture to bring together a community of Ethiopian and Eritrean students and their families for social and cultural events.

At one such event, an African festival in 1980, James McCann recalls cooking *doro wot* for 300 guests using a university kitchen. McCann, who has lived in Ethiopia, is now a leading scholar of Ethiopian culture and the author of *People of the Plow*, a history of Ethiopian agriculture, and *Stirring the Pot*, a book about African cuisine with two Ethiopia chapters, drawn from his research and travels there. He learned to cook *doro wot* from his maid when he lived in the northwestern Ethiopian city of Gojjam.

At the festival three decades ago, McCann and his Ethiopian cooking partner, Astair, had real *berbere* to make their *wot* but only buckwheat for the bread. "It was an abomination," he recalls of the *injera*. "That part was done by an Ethiopian woman who did the best she could using the technology of that time." Back in those days, Ethiopians who wanted more authentic teff *injera* would, if they could get it, use reconstituted *dirkosh*. McCann would sometimes bring huge sacks of *dirkosh* with him from Ethiopia to give to friends in America, and later that year, he visited Astair's mother in Addis Ababa's famous Merkato market when he returned to Ethiopia for field work.

"The techniques were evolving and the audience was sympathetic," McCann says of the 1980 *gebr* (feast). But despite his love for Ethiopian food and culture — or perhaps because of it — he rarely eats in Ethio-American restaurants because "they almost always disappoint me." When he returned to East Lansing for a semester in 2004, he knew about Altu's but didn't try it, although he did get some good *injera* made by the wife of an Eritrean graduate student. "It was a definite improvement from the earlier stuff," he says, "but still heavy. *Shiro* powder is the number one seller among those folks, and that is what most people ask me to carry when I come back. It is a delicate blend."

The menu at GoJo is thoroughly Ethiopian, but if you ask for it, they'll give you silverware. They also offer four "non-traditional dishes," each one a familiar Ethiopian meat dish that comes with rice rather than *injera*. Not too many people request these items, and most of GoJo's customers seem to know what they want and what they're getting when they visit.

"To our pleasant surprise," Sam says, "many people do their homework before coming to eat and don't even ask for any silverware." The drop-ins, caught off guard, sometimes request it. He doesn't serve *kitfo* out of concern for health department regulations. But he doesn't get many Ethiopian customers anyway, and Americans rarely eat raw beef at Ethiopian restaurants.

Sam has lived in Michigan for decades, and back in the 1980s, he sometimes sought Ethiopian food at Mama Desta's in Chicago or at Blue Nile in Detroit. He even got it in Grand Rapids now and then: The city has had other Ethiopian restaurants over the years, but none of them succeeded.

Sam hopes his enterprise adds up to a better result, and he's expanding GoJo's profile by taking part in Taste of Grand Rapids, an annual fair where people can sample many cuisines, and where his young restaurant won first place in the best booth competition in 2008. Venues like that aren't conducive to a big round *gebeta* covered with many dishes, so Sam serves his meals there in an *injera* wrap.

GoJo is in the city's artsy-cum-bohemian Eastown neighborhood, which hosts a hookah lounge, some antique shops and a used book store. Sam's culinary competition is Chinese, Indian, Middle Eastern and Greek.

It's hard to make a small restaurant in a mini-strip mall look like a *gojo*, which is a traditional Ethiopian thatch hut (like a *tekul*), but Sam has done his best. Tall bamboo barriers separate a few of the tables by the window, and grass skirts hang from the interior of the windows and from the ceiling against the opposite wall. He has no *mesobs*, but a few of his tables are round pieces of black painted wood atop yellow metal barrels. A floral print couch greets people at the entrance, and the restaurant's far wall is decorated with four large chalkboard, scrawled with the names and thoughts of patrons written in English, and with the Amharic names of some of the Ethiopian children adopted by Grand Rapids residents. The restaurant's window features a painting of a golden Ethiopian countryside speckled with *gojos*. Two local college students created the scene after Sam gave them a sketch of what he wanted.

Sam arrived in the U.S. in 1974 from Ethiopia's Oromo region, studied mathematics in Holland, Mich., and cooked food for the family hosting him.

He's never gone back to his homeland — never had a very strong desire, he says — and he doesn't like to talk about Ethiopian and Oromo politics. He comes from a big scattered family: one sister in England, one in Australia, one in D.C. and two back home. The ones back home send him spices for GoJo, and they get them not from wholesalers but from individuals, which Sam says insures better quality control and a personal touch.

He worked for many years as a math teacher and tutor after college, and he's always cooked for friends and family. He had no teff back in the '70s and '80s — "like the rest," he recalls, "I also missed *injera* very much" — so he just used regular bread. Like most Ethiopian restaurants, GoJo's *injera* blends teff with other flours, and if diners give him three days notice, he'll prepare a gluten-free variety.

Best of all, his menu includes a delectable iced Ethiopian tea that he sells on his website as GoJo Ethiopian Loose Leaf Spiced Tea. It's a blend of — well, a host of spices that Sam won't reveal. The mixture if proprietary, and Sam intends to keep it that way. It's worth a trip to Grand Rapids or the internet, whichever is closer.

IF YOU WANT ETHIOPIAN FOOD IN CINCINNATI, do not pass Emanu, and do not look for any other restaurant: This East African eatery has a monopoly on the cuisine, but not for lack of other people trying. In the past several years, three Ethiopian restaurants — Queen of Sheba, Little Ethiopia and Addis Zemen — have come and gone. So has Emanu: It was called East African Restaurant a while back before it moved a block up the street and reinvented itself with a new name.

It's not like Cincy is a hamlet: Its metro area has 2.2 million people, just about the same as Cleveland's, and it has both Ethiopian and Eritrean Orthodox churches. This speaks to a measurable population. But Cleveland also only has one restaurant, down from two a few years ago, and neither city has an Ethiopian grocery store. Meanwhile, about two interstate hours away from each city, there's Columbus, with its blossoming population.

The family that owns Emanu is Eritrean, and its menu of familiar dishes is written in transliterated Tigrinya rather than Amharic. Yhedgo Beyene worked for Ethiopian Airlines for many years, and he came to the U.S. with his wife, Emanu Mogos, in 1991, five years after their son Samuel Yhedgo, a co-owner of the restaurant, moved to Wisconsin and then to Cincinnati for college. Both were born in Eritrea, but because of Yhedgo's work, they lived for many years in Addis Ababa, and they consider themselves to be just as Ethiopian as they are Eritrean.

Emanu's menu offers the Amharic names of the dishes in parentheses after their Tigrinya names, which fosters both commerce and harmony, especially with Emanu being the only restaurant in town. You can order "*kilwa derho (doro tibs),*" "*ades (misir wot),*" or the always popular "*hiwswas (beyaynetu)*" combination platter. There are desserts like baklava, papaya pound cake and honey cheesecake because, as the menu says, "dessert it not a native course in Ethiopia." Emanu recommends coffee with dessert for $1.50 a cup, or $5 for a coffee ceremony.

Yhedgo graduated in 1957 from the Eritrean Vocational Technical School, which opened in 1954 and is now called Asmara Technical School. He carries in his wallet a laminated alumni card issued to mark the school's golden anniversary. He worked first for the Ethiopian highway commission, and then for 23 years as a welder for Ethiopian Airlines. When he retired in 1991, he and Emanu joined their sons in America.

They launched East African Restaurant in 2001, with Emanu as cook, and closed it six years later. Soon they re-opened as Emanu, moving from the first floor of a two-story house on Montgomery Avenue, in the Pleasant Ridge neighborhood, to a more contemporary setting, a few Montgomery storefronts closer to the business district. The competing Little Ethiopia restaurant took over their old address for a while, but it didn't last very long. An American-style café now occupies the spot.

Emanu and her extended family have become Cincinnati's brand name for Ethio-Eritrean food. They've cornered the market, both figuratively and literally: Their restaurant sits at the meeting of Woodford and Montgomery streets at Dallman's Corners, a suburban enclave of businesses that include an antique shop, a tattoo parlor, a comics shop, a music store (with used vinyl), and an assortment of restaurants, bars and cafés, none of them ethnic, unless you count Maggie Malone's, an Irish pub that welcomes dogs on its outdoor patio. It's a good location at a busy intersection, with a bus stop on the corner, although its sign, Emanu East African Restaurant, proclaims the restaurant modestly.

There are no Ethiopian markets in Cincinnati, but you can get a larger takeout order of *injera* if you give Emanu one day's notice, and her son Melake Yhedgo owns Queen City Market, a convenience store, where he soon hopes to sell Ethiopian spices.

Haile Besera — Melake's cousin and Emanu's nephew — owns Fairmont Carryout, a general convenience store located about 12 miles from the restaurant. He sells *berbere, mitmita, shiro* and other basics when he can get them, and he sells *injera* baked by several local women when they can get teff and are able to make it. Unfortunately for his community, that's not all the time, so he doesn't always have the items in stock. Haile says it's a dearth that sends people to Columbus, about 110 miles away, to get what they need.

He would gladly sell his Aunt Emanu's *injera*, but she's too busy with the restaurant to bake enough of it.

Even Emanu seems to have a hard time finding her spices: She now gets them from people back home, or from Columbus, or even in Canada once when she went there for a wedding. There's really plenty of *berbere* and *shiro* out there, but it seems as if Emanu and Yhedgo are so busy with daily business that they don't have time to shop and network. Asked why all of the other Ethiopian restaurants in the city have failed, Emanu speculates: "It is not easy. It's a hard job. I come in at 8 o'clock and I am here all day. The kitchen is very hard."

Emanu is pretty much a two-person operation, with Yhedgo seating customers and taking their orders, which Emanu prepares herself. On a surprisingly busy Tuesday evening in July, she served a table of six with a few squirmy children, another table of six women ranging in ages from 20s to about 50, a younger couple, and a middle-aged couple who took food from a shared plate but asked for separate plates onto which they placed their morsels and *injera*. It's BYOB, although Emanu will sometimes make *t'ej* at home for people who request it.

Yhedgo says their customers are almost exclusively Anglo-European, with a few African-Americans from time to time, and rarely Ethiopians or Eritreans, whom Yhedgo says usually just eat at home. Emanu estimates the city's Ethio-Eritrean population in the hundreds rather than the thousands, which could also account for their infrequency at the restaurant. Nearby Columbus is a much better place to be if you want more community.

Despite her kitchen responsibilities, Emanu still finds time to emerge throughout the evening — in her apron and hairnet — to say hello to all of her guest. She's spry, round and very friendly, whereas Yhedgo, just as convivial and eager to please, moves more slowly, although he never stops moving. And she has no time for politics. "It's crazy," she says of the tensions between her two native countries and cultures. "It's not necessary in America. Some are more conservative, but I'm not. We're together here now."

TALL INDIANA has three Ethiopian restaurants in two different cities, all toward the center of the state. In Bloomington, there's Ashenda's, easy to miss if you're not looking for it (and maybe even if you are), located in a quaint and lovely old yellow house. It's half of the Italian restaurant Puccini's La Dolce Vita, and when you enter, they'll ask you which cuisine you've come for and seat you on the appropriate side. The décor is authentic, with African pottery, masks and instruments on shelves and walls. So is the cuisine — and the eponymous owner, Ashenda Hagos, who's also affiliated with the Italian side of the place.

The epicenter of Indiana's Ethiopian cuisine is Indianapolis, with its whopping two restaurants, and for a short while recently, an Ethiopian grocery store, which didn't last very long.

The city's two restaurants, Abyssinia and Major, have a lot in common. Both owners get their spices from back home, sell *injera* in 10-packs, perform coffee ceremonies and offer homemade *t'ej*, and both have similar décor: glass-top tables with linen tablecloths, each one decorated with the symbols and colors of Ethiopian culture.

But Abyssinia is located in a brightly lit strip mall in a busy commercial neighborhood, and it's surrounded by international cuisine: Mexican, Peruvian, Japanese, Middle Eastern, an Oriental market, a tae kwan do studio, and a Best Buy that anchors the development. Major is a few miles away in a slightly frayed working-class ethnic neighborhood, in an uninviting complex of half a dozen businesses, some of them closed, that requires a very sharp driver-unfriendly turn off of busy Washington Road.

That's too bad, because the food and the hosts at both places are equally fine and friendly. The new kid in town is Eden Major, whose eponymous restaurant opened in 2008, replacing a Mexican restaurant whose name still tops the marquee that people see when they find Plaza Del Sol, the mini-strip that hosts Major. Eden's storefront itself is more welcoming, with her restaurant's name in English and Amharic.

Her neighbors on the strip are largely Hispanic-owned businesses, but a block away, there's Somali House of Coffee, and a few blocks after that, Safari Restaurant, a steamy Somali eatery that serves chicken, beef, goat, *ful* and *angera*, the Somali version of the Ethiopian bread. Between them is Pawn Mart, and nearby, the airport, with planes flying so close over the neighborhood that you can practically see inside the windows.

Eden runs the place almost by herself. Her husband, Tesfu Maru, drives a taxi and helps her in the evenings, and on busy weekends, she recruits two cousins. The family has two children, Aaron and Cannan, whose pictures, blown up to poster size, adorn one of the walls among images of Ethiopian cultural life. Friends and family look after the kids during the day when their parents are working. The restaurant is open every day for lunch and dinner, although Eden opens at 1 p.m. on Sunday so she can go to church in the morning.

Eden was raised in Eritrea — she calls her restaurant "East African," not "Ethiopian" — and moved with her family to Yemen when she was 11. They lived there for 14 years, and she grew up watching her father operate a restaurant in Saan'a, the Yemeni capital. He died in 2006, but her mother still lives there and runs a market for the city's Ethio-Eritrean community, which worships together at a combined Orthodox church.

Eden met her husband, who's from Dessie, Ethiopia, in Yemen, and the Catholic Church sponsored their move to America in 2002, just as it has for numerous other Ethiopians and Eritreans in the Indianapolis area, creating a cluster large enough to support one Ethiopian and two Eritrean Orthodox churches. Eden says that Ethiopians and Eritreans from Yemen "are like brothers and sisters," and they don't engage in the politics of back home.

Major serves most of its customers on tables, but on one side of the restaurant, on a slightly raised platform, Eden has set up four *mesobs* with wicker chairs and a mural of Ethiopian life behind them. It's almost like a patio, and she says her customers often ask to be seated there because they find it to be relaxing.

Eden gets her spices and gesho from friends back home every few months, and she serves homemade *t'ej* along with a selection of Ethiopian beers and *t'ej* made by American wineries. Her customers are American, Somali and Sudanese — but mostly American, and rarely Ethiopian or Eritrean. "Everybody has family," Eden speculates about her dearth of native customers. "You're married, you have kids, you cook for your house. It's expensive to take a family out to a restaurant."

That's certainly true. But a few miles away, at the more established Abyssinia, Ethiopians find their way to supper. Owner Abraha Belachew also says that most of his customers are non-Ethiopians because "Ethiopians usually cook at home." Still, on a Wednesday evening in July, his culturally mixed clients included an Ethiopian family, Indian and Asian men, lots of Anglo-Americans, and three 20-something first-timers who asked for his help in ordering.

Abraha came to the U.S. in 1988 from Gondar as a refugee and lived in San Diego for a while. He visited a friend in Indianapolis, which he calls a "quiet city," in 1996, and he liked it enough to move there. He drove a cab for a while and went into business in 2003. On a trip home to Gondar in 1998, he met Tiruye, who became his wife. Their families knew each other when the children were growing up.

Abyssinia is an unusually patriarchal Ethiopian restaurant. Although Tiruye makes the *injera*, Abraha cooks the food, and young Ethiopian-American men make up his wait staff, a rarity at Ethiopian restaurants. "I cook like back home, not like in America," he boasts, although he'll adjust the spice levels for Midwestern palates. He's decorated the walls of Abyssinia with Ethiopian musical instruments, artifacts, mini-*mesobs*, and paintings and posters with scenes of Ethiopian life.

At Major, you can buy a 10-pack of Eden's *injera* for $6. Abyssinia sells

Teruye's *injera* in packs of 10 for $7, but Abraha has upped the ante: He also hosts a small market on a set of shelves by his cash register, selling *berbere, shiro*, lentils, yellow peas and Ethiopian coffee. His *berbere* sells for $8 to $10 a pound, depending upon what he has to pay to get it from back home, and in a glass case beneath his cash register, he sells Ethiopian CDs and gift items.

For a while, Indianapolis had Addis Market, but it didn't last very long. The community just wasn't big enough. So Abraha's spice rack now provides a small service to a population that's probably more Eritrean than Ethiopian. This invites politics, but with such a small community, it's really not an issue. "About religion we don't have a problem," Abraha says with confidence. "And we know the politics, but we don't talk about it."

UNTIL RECENTLY a city with no Ethiopian restaurants — and still one with very few Ethiopians — Milwaukee suddenly has two of them. Ethiopian Cottage is owned by Yigletu Debebe, an Ethiopian who worked for many years as an educator in the public school system, and Alem Ethiopian Village is owned by Zerihun Bekele, whose downtown business district location presents him with a few challenges.

Zerihun came to U.S. in 1985 to attend college in Chicago and moved to Milwaukee in 2002. He owns the restaurant with his four brothers, who named the place after their mother, Alemnesh, who lived in the U.S. for more than 20 years before her death a few years ago. He estimates that Milwaukee has about 500 Ethiopians, so that means he counts on non-Ethiopians to stay in business. And it's a challenge.

"For most of them it's an adventure," Zerihun says of his Midwestern patrons. "It's a new experience for a lot of people. The dishes that are red in color, people shy away from. They think it's hot and spicy and will make them sweat." The yellow and green foods go over better.

His customers are also sometimes reluctant to eat with their hands, so Zerihun decided to institute a new policy: "They're going to have to ask three, four, five times to get a fork. If you use a fork, you're going to disconnect yourself from the food." He sells Ethiopians beers, and he used to serve Nigest Honey Wine, made in Ethiopia, but his customers found the taste to be too sharp. Now he serves an American-made *t'ej* that people seem to enjoy.

"Compared to Chicago," Zerihun says, " this is a very small town."

The sole Ethiopian restaurant in Madison, Wis., is Buraka, and it's owned by Markos Regassa, an Ethiopian who graduated from the University of Wisconsin. He got there the long way, leaving Ethiopia in 1986 for Madrid, where he met his wife, a Madisonian. They returned to her home town, and Markos got a degree in business at the university.

A year later, in 1992, he opened an outdoor Ethiopian food cart on the university's Library Mall, joining other vendors with his unique cuisine. He had a small carryout restaurant for a while in a bad location, and in 2000, he opened Buraka along State Street, a busy strip of places to eat and shop that runs from the Capitol building in Madison to one edge of the University of Wisconsin campus, right in front of the library, where it all began for him and his cart. His sole competitor, a restaurant called Yirgalem, closed a few years ago. He named his restaurant after his great-grandfather, but it's also the Afaan Oromo word for "great joy or contentment." That, he says, is what food brings us.

Markos is Oromo, but he uses the Amharic names of the dishes on his menu because, he says, "I don't really want to mix business with politics." Nor does he want to see an independent Oromo nation separate from the whole of Ethiopia.

"Emotionally, people can say that," he says. "But it is a very costly process. It's all about power. The Oromos are a huge number, and I don't think [the current leaders] want to open a door for them. We need a good government first, and in Ethiopia, they have a very good constitution. Most of the problems we have in Africa are about economic resources."

If you visit Buraka, be sure to ask that your food be served in the traditional Ethiopian manner: with a piece of *injera* laid flat on a serving plate and the food on top. Otherwise, it comes as a sort of *injera* sandwich, with the *injera* rolled over the food, and with a knife and fork to eat it.

Markos says he began this accommodation in part to please American patrons not accustomed to Ethiopian food, but also to conform to Wisconsin law, which requires that vendors who sell food from carts do so in a way that people can eat it with cutlery. His cart customers became accustomed to his *injera* wraps, so he continues the practice at his restaurant. You can ask for your meal family style, and a few customers do. But most are happy with wraps, and even those folks who want to share usually ask for a small empty plate of their own as well.

Markos gets his essential spices from Ethiopia a few times a year, although he sometimes blends them with basic spices that he buys at specialty and Indian stores in America. He prefers the stuff from home and says the taste of *berbere* made here just isn't the same. His menu has all the familiar dishes, with one exception: no *kitfo*. "Too risky," he says, which a chuckle, of the raw beef dish so popular back home.

FOR ETHIOPIAN FOOD IN IOWA, there's only one place to go: David's Place, opened in 2006 by Dawit Kidane. Born in Eritrea, he lived in Ethiopia for several years as well before an American woman, who had lived in Ethiopia and knew his family, adopted him at age 15 in 1975. He moved to Iowa with his new American family and finished high school, and except for six years in Florida, he's been there ever since.

Now fully American, he remembers his shock upon arriving more than 30 years ago and encountering some American customs — for example, the phenomenon of the couch potato. "We didn't have TVs in Ethiopia, and you always played outside," he says. "But here, I thought it was strange that everyone after school goes home, and that's that." He had his first hot dog with friends in a school cafeteria, and when he saw someone smothering one with mustard, he did the same. He ended up spitting out his first bite.

And then there was the paltry American school lunch. "Back home," he says, "we go eat lunch at home and eat *injera*. We don't have five dishes of food on the plate, but everyone eats together. But here, I can't believe you eat a bologna sandwich, an apple and a carton of milk. I was really amazed at how you only get small portions."

For the longest time, Dawit had no Ethiopian community with which to connect in Iowa. His American mother "tried her best" to make *injera* and Ethiopian food, and Dawit enjoyed it. "But my American brothers complained, 'Why do we have to eat this hot spicy food.'" Soon he adapted to American family cuisine. In time, he brought his parents and four siblings to America, and he has cousins in Washington. On his first trip to D.C. as a young man, he was so overjoyed to see so many Ethiopians that he said hello to every Ethiopian stranger he passed on the street. "I was very excited," he recalls, "but nobody was saying 'hi' to me."

Now he's a restaurateur, and he always tries to be at David's Place — Dawit is the Ethiopian version of David — to help first-timers. Some customers ask for forks despite his lessons, and "some people just have no coordination. I tell them you can hold *injera* as tight as you want, and it doesn't break. Some of them try to make it like a taco. But when I show them how, most of them can do it. I make sure my waiters know that if somebody asks them about anything, they come get me."

When he opened his restaurant, he struggled with making good *injera*. For a while he bought it in Chicago, about four hours away, and then he got an idea: He asked his mother, now living in Florida, to make the *injera* and overnight it to him three times a week. That worked until he mastered the art, no thanks to the unpredictable Iowa weather, which he says makes it hard to get the "eyes" on the *injera* right. He's a pro at it now, and he's trained his kitchen employees, many of them Mexican men and women, to make perfect *injera* and all of the restaurant's dishes.

Dawit doesn't cook his dishes with *kibbee* because, he says, "that's too much butter in your body, and it's not really good for you." He only uses *kibbee* for his *kitfo*, a dish he didn't serve at first, until people — especially his few Ethiopian customers — began asking him for it. *Kitfo* just isn't *kitfo* without *kibbee*, and he makes his own with the fresh unsalted butter he buys from the nearby Amish community.

IN THE NORTHERN TIP OF IDAHO, Ethiopians have to get their cooking supplies by mail and their Ethiopian meals at home: The closest restaurants are 300 or 400 miles way in Seattle and Portland, two cities with large communities.

Wudneh Admassu is a professor of chemical engineering at the University of Idaho and the inventor of the Zelalem Injera Machine (see Chapter 6), which makes *injera* by automation. He's fortunate to have an Ethiopian wife who cooks the family meals, and because he's so busy — and so in love with his native cuisine — he usually skips lunch when he's on campus all day.

But when he arrived in America in 1974, just out of high school in Addis Ababa, he lost a lot of weight in those first few months.

Wudneh was raised in the much more traditional Sidama region, and he was born in Yirgacheffe, a town that lends its name to a prized Ethiopian coffee. He had a religious upbringing, which meant no meat on Wednesdays and Fridays. He didn't care for American food when he arrived, and it took him almost a year to learn to eat it.

"Everyone now thinks I'm a big city boy," he says, "but I was raised in a church kind of thing." He lived in Seattle back then with a cousin, and while the city now has plenty of Ethiopian cuisine, it didn't in 1974. The first time friends took him to a burger place, he was so unaccustomed to the way they prepared the meat that he threw it away and just ate the bread.

So he decided to fend for himself: "I went to the Goodwill store, bought a small pan — I still have it — and I used it to make *wot* almost every day." He had no *injera*, so he used poor substitutes, sometimes even Wonder Bread, and in the absence of *berbere*, he used chili powder to spice it up, or he would get supplies from home, or his Ethiopian friends would share what they had. When a small Ethiopian restaurant finally opened in Seattle in the early 1980s, "that was a very big thing for us." There still was no teff, so the restaurant used self-rising flour, and "you could tell it was not *injera*," he recalls.

But after a while, Wudneh decided that "God doesn't want me to die," so he expanded his personal menu to include American fare when necessary.

Now it's Ethiopian most of the time, thanks to his wife, Elizabeth. His 13-year-old son wants *injera* and *wot* every day and won't eat school food, but his 11-year-old son is more Americanized and eats everything. The older boy only enjoys pizza and burgers with his friend. Elizabeth makes *injera*, too, which is just a bit of an irony: The man who invented a machine that makes thousands of pieces of *injera* every day still has his prepared the old-fashioned way, one piece at a time.

WHAT ARE THE CHANCES of finding an Ethiopian restaurant in Sioux Falls, S.D.? How about three or four of them, along with a few markets and a growing Ethiopian community?

The city's proximity to Minneapolis, just a few hours away, has helped its Ethiopian population to grow and feel at home. So has the John Morrell food plant, which employs more than 3,000 people, and which has attracted Ethiopians at least since the early '90s with the offer of good jobs.

One of the more unusual Ethiopian grocery stores in Sioux Falls is Tidy House Laundry, where you can buy fresh *berbere* while you wash the stains from last night's *wot* out of your good white tablecloth. The shop's owner, Ayalew Abebe, came to America in 1992, lived in San Diego for a few years, then went to Sioux Falls to visit a friend. He ended up staying.

Ayalew says he opened a laundry, rather than a market, because he didn't want to specialize in an ethnic business. But three years later, to bring in more income, he added Ethiopian foods, including gesho. Local women make his brand name Golden Injera, and he gets his grocery items from NTS Enterprises in Oakland. He has competition from a few other markets in town, including Mercato, just two miles away. It's owned by his brother, Benay Abebe, who joined Ayalew in the U.S. about six years ago. The family comes from Gojjam, a northwest Ethiopian town tucked into a bend in the Abay River.

Mulugeta Endayehu opened Lalibela restaurant and bar in 2003, pursuing his vocation and his dream. His wife, Marta, was raised in Ethiopia and came to America as a refugee. She settled in Sioux Falls, and on a visit home, she met Mulugeta. They married in 1999, moved to America, and opened their restaurant four years later.

For Mulugeta, it was a return to the profession he left behind: He owned a restaurant in Kombolcha, a town in north central Ethiopia, and came to America with the dream of opening another one. He named his restaurant after his parents' historic hometown. His place does well, and it keeps him busy, for it's largely a two-person operation: Marta cooks, and most of the time Mulugeta takes care of everything other than the kitchen. His restaurant is a popular gathering place for the city's Ethiopian community, and sometimes Mulugeta hosts over-21 dances for the Sioux Falls community.

Amanual Liben works as a loan document specialist by day and co-owner of Shalom Ethiopian Coffee House and Restaurant when he has the time. He bought the place from its previous owners in late 2008, in partnership with his brother-in-law, and reopened it July 2009, expanded its menu and making it more of a gathering place for the city's African community.

For his customers who can't handle spicy Ethiopian food, he added burgers, fries and fried chicken to the menu. For the many Sudanese people in Sioux Falls — the internationally known "Lost Boys," who suffered in Sudan's civil war — he's added a game room on the lower floor. If workers at the local John Morrell plant, many of them African, don't want American food for lunch, they only have to call Shalom, and they can have a home-cooked lunch delivered. He offers free coffee to customers on Sundays with a full Ethiopian coffee ceremony, and once a month, he brings in touring Ethiopian musicians to perform.

Amanual came to America in 1989 at age 14 with his oldest brother, and he's been in Sioux Falls since 1994. Back home, his father is a Lutheran pastor, so Amanual was raised in that faith, and not the Ethiopian Orthodox Church. He's also Oromo, but unlike so many other Oromos in Ethiopia and America, he doesn't see Oromia as an occupied country that deserves to be independent. He says that his restaurant serves "the national dishes of Ethiopia," and his menu uses the Amharic names for the dishes, not the less familiar Afaan Oromo names.

"Ethiopia is not even as big as Texas," he says, "and [Oromos] having their own country is impossible. The fact that we are so diverse in Ethiopia, that's what makes it so hard for the leaders to give what each and every tribe needs." But he believes they're trying, and to Oromos who feel oppressed, he points out that there are cultures in every country who feel that way. In America, he says, some Ethiopian immigrants feel like they're not treated equally. He'd rather see all Ethiopians come together than continue to pull apart. "I love everyone from Ethiopia, any tribe," he says. "God made us that way, and it's our unity. We should combine our differences to make a stronger Ethiopia."

Ojulu Oballa visited a friend in Sioux Falls in 1995 and moved there a year later. It's a choice he's never regretted, and now he's a big promoter of his new hometown. "The place is easy to live," he says. "It's not very complicated like a lot of big cities, but it's growing up. It's a very friendly city."

In 1997, he brought Ethiopian food to Sioux Falls when he opened Blue Nile, a restaurant and nightclub. The business was a challenge, and he closed it in 1999. Four years later, he opened Ethiopian Food & Carry Out, a homey little restaurant, painted white with bright red trim around the windows and doors. It's been his livelihood ever since, and his wife, Almaz Tsege, cooks the food.

Ojulu's restaurant is small — just four tables — so that's why he has carry out: Most of the people who eat there don't actually eat there. His also sells Ethiopian spices, which he gets from suppliers in Minneapolis, and he gets his teff directly from Teff Co. in Idaho. A few other markets around town sell Ethiopian goods as well, and before the city's emerging Ethiopian population had local markets, they got their supplies on trips to Minneapolis.

Back when he opened Blue Nile, the locals took to his unusual cuisine with a pioneer spirit. "Americans are good at trying everything," Ojulu says, "so we were okay. If they don't like something, they tell you. If they liked it, they come back." He guesses that the city had about 1,000 Ethiopians a decade ago and how has maybe 3,000. The entire Sioux Falls area counts only about 160,000 people, making its significant Ethiopian food community one of the most concentrated in the country. Many bigger, more urban areas have far fewer Ethiopians and only a restaurant or two.

The city also has two Ethiopian Orthodox churches, but Ojulu is rare among Ethiopian Christians: He's Presbyterian, a result of his having been educated in missionary schools back home. He comes from Ethiopia's southwestern Gambela region, which borders the Sudan, and he's involved with the Luo United Communities Organization. Luo is a family of Nilotic languages spoken in Ethiopia, Sudan, Uganda and Kenya, and Ojulu speaks the Luo language Anuak, as well as Amharic, Arabic, and five others. The group is more concerned with preserving its cultural heritage than with airing grievances against the ruling cultures in the countries where they live.

"We're trying to organize ourselves as the people who speak the same language," Ojulu says. "We've lost our identify, and we just want to identify ourselves for who we are. We need everyone to respect us as human beings." Sioux Falls has a small population of Luo speakers, but many more live among Minneapolis' big Ethiopian community. And Sioux Falls has people of many other African cultures, all of whom get along better here than they do back in Africa. "Everybody is sharing," Ojulu says. "We share everything. We go to Somali grocery stores, too."

IN SALT LAKE CITY — and in all of Utah — the small Ethiopian community has only one place to go for a meal from home, and it's all thanks to Rundassa Eshete, a local businessman, teacher and writer who owns African Restaurant & Mini Mart. The market part of his business sells items that appeal to a few African communities, and his restaurant serves food familiar to anyone who's eaten at Ethiopian restaurants in other cities.

Just be careful not to ask for *injera*. His restaurant serves it, and his sister Bullalle Eshete does the cooking. But if you want to get on Rundassa's good side, you should use the bread's Afaan Oromo name, *budeena*.

Rundassa is a real estate developer with a master's degree in business from Brigham Young University. He's taught at Salt Lake Community College, and he's the chairman of the Oromian National Academy, a group that "hopes to resurrect the Oromo language, culture and norms that have been destroyed by the Ethiopian ruling class." He's passionate about the cause of his culture, and he operates a website to exchange ideas about it.

He opened African Restaurant & Mini Mart in 2004 as a service to Salt Lake City's small African community, selling items to his Ethiopian, Sudanese and West African customers. He guesses that the city has fewer than a dozen Oromo people and fewer than 100 Ethiopians — or as he calls them, "Abyssinians." Utah is also home to a small community of Italians whose families lived for generations in Ethiopia, and who left when the communist Derg took over. They come to his restaurant in groups, some even speaking broken Amharic, and they're among his most convivial customers. "Italians are the friendliest people," Rundassa says. "They get along with everyone."

Unfortunately, not everyone in Salt Lake City gets along with his cuisine. His market-cum-restaurant struggles to survive, partly because of its location on the city's industrial west side, far from the more adventuresome college crowd, and partly because "Utahans are not outgoing about eating African food." He also has some trouble finding people who can cook the food properly, so many of his employees are family members who have come to America recently as refugees. He sees the business as a way to help them get started. And he has some competition: There are a few other pan-African markets in the city, at least one owned by an Ethiopian, although only Rundassa has a restaurant to accompany his grocery store.

Rundassa was born in Ambo, the city that gives its name to the bottled Ambo Mineral Water, popular back home and among Ethiopians in America. In fact, he says, his family owned much of the mountain land that produces the water — until the imperial government took it from them and jailed his father. When the emperor fell, his father was freed, then jailed again for most of the Derg years. He finally got out of prison in 1991, when the Derg fell, and died in 1998.

During the turmoil, Rundassa left Ethiopia in 1989 to study in the Ukraine, where he was treated as a cultural oddity: Russians would sometimes ask to touch his hair to see if it was made of wire. He came to the U.S. to study at Brigham Young, where he met his wife, Jan. His brother-in-law is now one of his best customers, always craving Ethiopian food.

But Rundassa doesn't like that term, and not surprisingly, the menu at his restaurant names its dishes in Afaan Oromo, not Amharic. When he gets Amhari customers, he talks to them in English, even though he speaks

Amharic. "They tell me we're all the same," he says, "and I say no, we're not the same."

So rather than asking for *misir wot, gomen* or *doro wot,* you can order *kochee misira, raafuu* or *kochee handaanqoo.* The variety plate called *beyaynetu* in Amharic is *wal-maka* (Afaan Oromo for "combination") on Rundassa's menu. The dishes all come with *budeena,* and many are made with *qimamii,* known in Amharic as *kibbee.* He also serves *marqa,* the Oromo corn or barley porridge, although it's not on the menu, so not many people ask for it. West Africans call this *fufu,* and in Swahili it's called *ugalii.* It's a simple dish, he says, but customers have to wait 45 minutes because it takes a while to prepare.

Although Rundassa sells the products of several African cultures, his restaurant dishes are all familiar to anyone who knows Ethiopian cuisine. He calls his place African Restaurant because he would *never* label it an Ethiopian restaurant. He doesn't even eat "Ethiopian" food, and he was raised Waqeffanna, a traditional Oromo religion that believes everything is interconnected. His wife was raised Mormon.

In his many years of living in Salt Lake City, Rundassa has met "a lot of Utahans who you would never imagine had worked in Ethiopia." These encounters are sometimes difficult for him because people usually don't know much about the tensions between the Oromos and the Amharis. Back home in Ethiopia, he says he was forced to go by the first name Alemayehu because he would have been teased if he had used his given Oromo name.

"It's really hard for me to talk passionately about Ethiopia," Rundassa admits. "I have my limitations about it. I miss nothing out of Ethiopia, not even the food. My wife cooks whatever Americans eat here, and it works for my stomach, a lot better than Ethiopian food. I can't handle spicy, especially after you've lived in Russia, where it's such a mellow food. I like the smell of Ethiopian food, but I get ulcers in my stomach if I eat it."

YOU'LL ONLY FIND a smattering of Ethiopian restaurants in the South between the D.C. suburbs in Virginia and the more metropolitan cities like Atlanta, Dallas and Houston, which all have Ethiopian communities, restaurants and markets. Tennessee and Kentucky each have a few restaurants, and Florida has some restaurants and markets sprinkled across several of its cities. But if you live in Alabama, Mississippi, Louisiana, West Virginia, Arkansas, or anywhere in Georgia other than Atlanta, you'll have to get accustomed to ribs, collard greens and grits instead of *tibs, gomen* and *kinche.*

One recent exception is South Carolina, where Redi-Et Ethiopian

Restaurant opened in upscale touristy Myrtle Beach in May 2008, with owner Sara Seyoum supervising the kitchen. The business was successful enough to outgrow its original location, moving to a new place in 2010. Sara came to the U.S. with her husband in 1998, and in Ethiopia, she owned a restaurant, so she knows the business and the cuisine. She chose to open her place in South Carolina because she saw a business opportunity in a state that had no Ethiopian food, although she does offer a kids' menu with chicken fingers, hot dogs, hamburgers, onion rings, French fries and chips, plus a selection of cheesecakes for dessert. Sara also caters parties, performs the coffee ceremony for customers at the restaurant, and on Valentine's Day, rewards people with free Ethiopian coffee.

Three of North Carolina's college towns — Charlotte, Raleigh, and Chapel Hill — have four restaurants between them. One of them is Meskerem, a branch of the New York City restaurant, and owned by a family member who moved to Charlotte. It joined Red Sea, which opened in Charlotte more than a decade ago. Durham, N.C., once had an Ethiopian restaurant, but it doesn't any more.

You can also get Ethiopian food if you live in the upscale mountain town of Asheville, N.C., although not all the time (at least for now), and only if you stay alert or get on the mailing list. Judah Selassie and Getenesh Ketema opened Abaye Cuisine Catering in Asheville in 2008 to see if folks would embrace Ethiopian food, and also to lay the groundwork for a restaurant they hope to open if the cuisine catches on.

So far, so good: The company hosts dinners every month or two at local halls and community centers, and they've done so well — about 150 people at each gathering — that they now have two servings a night.

Abaye's monthly events lean toward vegetarian dishes because Judah is a vegetarian, and because he's found that Asheville has many vegetarians as well. For $13, guests get a plate with four dishes, a salad and a drink. Sometimes, though, there's a meat option, which comes with two veggie sides. That's $16. He doesn't serve the food on a big central *gebeta* for all to share: Each person gets a plate with the three or four dishes atop the *injera*. There's silverware available for people to take it they want it, but Judah says they rarely do.

Getenesh and an Ethiopian friend cook the food in the commercial kitchen of a nearby community college and then take it to a dinner's venue. Ethiopian music plays during the meal, and Judah decorates the hall with cultural artifacts. He sets up a small table to sell clothing and crosses from Ethiopia, and he offers *injera* for takeout. For a while he presented slide shows about Ethiopian culture, but that stopped when he noticed that "people weren't as interested as they were in the food." Between dinner events, he'll take orders for people who want *injera*, and Getenesh has conducted a few cooking classes.

Their gatherings get some first-timers who heard about them through word of mouth, but mostly, Judah says, "everyone knows what they're coming to. I keep getting more and more surprised at how many people know about it. The interest has been very high."

This is due partly to the fact that many people in affluent Asheville have adopted Ethiopian babies. "There's a huge community for that," Judah says, "and they've been following us." The phenomenon conflicts him: He's happy to see the children have a chance at a better life, but he would also like to see Americans support Ethiopian families, both adults and children. He does some of that himself.

In time, Judah and Getenesh hope to open a restaurant in Asheville, if they think the town can support it, and if the economy makes it possible. Ethiopians who open restaurants often have a lot of friends and family to help, but that wouldn't be the case for theirs. "I cook," he says, "but my hand is not in the pot when it comes to that." So Judah worries about Getenesh taking on too much.

Judah was born in New Jersey to America-born parents of Ethiopian ancestry, and he studied environmental science at Rutgers. He's lived in Ethiopia for stretches of time and now holds citizenship in both countries. Getenesh was born in Ethiopia, where she learned to cook by watching older women do it. The two met there in 1998 and married three years later. They've lived in Asheville since 2004, moving there from New York, where Judah was a partner in a downtown American café and Getenesh worked at Queen of Sheba restaurant. When they decided to have children, they thought it would be better to raise them in a more hospitable place.

Their son was born in 2004, and his diet is all Ethiopian. "He's been eating spicy foods since he was 1," Judah says. "*Injera* was really his first food, just because it was the healthiest thing we could give him." They mashed up the *injera* with vegetables and *shiro*, and now he even likes *mitmita*, the hottest Ethiopian spice. His name is Amanuel Judah, which is somewhat rare among Ethiopian-American children: Parents here tend to give children their father's last name, rather than using the Ethiopian naming custom, where the father's first name becomes the child's last name. But Judah is very close to his ancestral culture, so he went with tradition. "I do what I can do," he says.

IN ALL OF NEW ENGLAND, you'll only find Ethiopian restaurants in four cities, and most of those are in Boston and its neighboring towns and suburbs. There are no markets in the region, although one Ethiopian family provides the growing Boston community with the goods that people need for home cooking.

Connecticut has two restaurants. Lalibela, open since 1999, has a great location on Temple Street in New Haven, just around the corner from Yale University's small but impressive art gallery, in a neighborhood with several blocks of shops, cafés and competing international cuisines. About 45 miles north, in Hartford's West End, there's Abyssinian Ethiopian and Eritrean Cuisine, one of half a dozen shops on a block-long city strip. It's flanked by a Mexican restaurant and a pizza shop, with Japanese/Korean food and a Burger King just across the street. Both Connecticut place have small bars, both have framed posters and photos on the wall, and both have glass tabletops over tablecloths. Abyssinian is Eritrean-owned, or else the name of the restaurant would never mention Eritrea.

Don't be fooled by the sign above the window at 15 Oak St. in Portland, Maine. It says "Asmara — An Eritrean Restaurant," but in all of New England north of Boston, there are no others, and no Ethiopian restaurants at all. It's a risky business strategy — not labeling the place "Ethiopian," even though the food is the same — but so far, it's been a success for its hard-working owner/chef.

Asmarat Teklu opened the restaurant, located on a quiet side street, just a few blocks from city hall, after working for several years at Barber Foods, a major employer in the area. Her husband still works there and helps her with the restaurant on busy weekends. He came to the U.S. through Sudan as a refugee in 1991, during the waning days of the Derg, and she followed seven years later taking the same rugged route. They now have two young all-American children and a successful restaurant.

Asmara is open six days a week for lunch and dinner, and Asmarat rents the space on Sundays for private functions. The restaurant seats about two dozen people, including two at a small *mesob* tucked in a corner behind a booth by the window. She pretty much works the kitchen and dining room alone, making *injera*, one piece at a time, between the lunch and dinner shifts, swirling her batter on a *mogogo* from Seattle's Niat Products, the enterprise of a fellow Eritrean (see Chapter 6). It didn't take long for word to spread about the restaurant, the first of its kind in the state. "When they saw the sign or something in the newspaper," Asmarat says, "they were excited to try our food." She has silverware, but few people ask for it. Asmarat tells her patrons, "You have to use nature's fork."

Along with her Eritrean menu, Asmarat offers a Sudanese-inspired dessert called *ligamat* — fried dough balls, spiced with cayenne and sweetened with honey — and baklava. "We don't use a lot of sweets in our culture," Asmarat says, "but here in America, they like to eat sweets after a meal." She also serves homemade *mes* (the Tigrinya word for *t'ej*) and performs the coffee ceremony for patrons who order it. Her *injera* is almost pure teff, with a bit of yellow corn flour added to the mix.

Asmarat says the Portland area has maybe 40 or 50 Ethiopian and Eritrean families, and they tend to eat their meals at home rather than at restaurants. "There is no politics here," she says, "everyone is friendly," and they even worship together at the city's Greek Orthodox church. During touristy summers, Asmara hosts patrons from Boston, New York and other big cities.

Not that Bostonians *need* to travel to Portland for Ethiopian food: The area has six restaurants that offer a range of atmospheres.

The restaurants in Boston and Cambridge (very near Harvard) provide the fanciest décor — and the highest prices. Addis Red Sea has two locations — one in Boston's South End, and one north of the Harvard campus on Massachusetts Avenue. Asmara, south of Harvard on Mass Ave., bills itself as "Eritrean and Ethiopian," which of course means its owner is Eritrean.

Much further down the avenue, across the Charles River in Boston, there's the trendy new Lucy Ethiopian Café, where the menu is on a chalkboard that lists offerings in English and Amharic letters, along with lessons on Amharic numbers, days of the week and helpful phrases. The Addis Combo is a veggie platter, and they also serve *chechebsa* and a *besso* milkshake. Entrées include *kitfo* and *tibs*, along with lots of coffees, teas, cappuccinos, hummus, and non-Ethiopian wraps and sandwiches. The Ethiopian dishes come in small bowls, with *injera* on the side for grabbing it.

In multi-ethnic neighboring Somerville, Fasika serves the local Ethiopian community, as well as upscale *ferenj* willing to make the trek (an easy train ride on the Orange line from Boston, followed by a short walk). There's a bar on one side and a restaurant on the other, with separate street entrances for each. A wall of wood and glass separates them, and you go from one side to the other through a door. The bartender is a hefty silver-haired fellow with a Boston accent.

The restaurant side is a gathering place for Ethiopian friends and families, and on a weeknight in August, a table with three or four young men kept growing and growing as more friends entered. They all greeted each other with ebullient handshakes, hugs and shoulder bumps, and before long, the circle was so wide that some of the revelers were practically sitting at the neighboring table. Meanwhile, across the room, an American couple asked their server to explain each dish on their platter, and before their meal ended, they took a picture of themselves leaning into their leftovers. The restaurant also serves homemade *t'ej* in *berele*, a rarity among Ethiopian restaurants in the U.S.

Go a little further on the Orange line and you'll end up in Malden, where just a few blocks from the train station you can have a hearty meal at Habesha, another gathering place in a town with a sizeable Ethiopian population. It's the best-priced Ethiopian food in the Boston area, with many Ethiopian beer and *t'ej* choices.

Those are the place where you can go if you want an Ethiopian night out in Boston. But what if you just want some *injera* and *berbere* to prepare the family meal? There are no Ethiopian markets in the area, but thanks to an enterprising Ethiopian family, there's fresh *injera* daily, and all the supplies you need to cook a meal and make *t'ej*.

South End Food Emporium looks a lot like any neighborhood mini-mart, with several aisles of standard fare. The dozen or so types of coffee — two of them Ethiopian — distinguish it a bit, as does the deli counter, where you can get made-to-order sandwiches.

But look to the left of the cash register and you'll see a pile of *injera*, along with an explanation. "Hi, my name is *injera* and I am from Ethiopia," says a note on the box. "I am a soft, spongy and very delicious bread. They make me from a cereal grain known as teff. Researchers tell me that I was born about 3,000 years ago. I nourish my lovers with high levels of iron, calcium, potassium and other nutrients. Try me!! You will fall in love with me!" Next to the *injera* are several full *ambasha* breads, and a few single triangles of *ambasha* in plastic bags.

Then, on some shelves just a few feet away, you can find bags of teff, gesho (three kinds), and all of the spices and ingredients you need to stock the pantry of an Ethiopian kitchen — even incense rocks and sticks from Ethiopia.

The market is the enterprise of Wandossan Alemu Desta, and the *injera* comes from Family Injera, a business run by his sister, Rahel Desta, and located several miles away in the adjacent community of Arlington, where the family lives just a few blocks from the bakery.

Rahel begins work at 3 or 4 a.m. to make the day's *injera*, which she packages in bags of seven pieces for sale at South End Food Emporium and a dozen or so other convenience stores around the area. The storefront is small, with nine *mitads* on two long metal tables, and four more tables for packaging. The batter ferments in large gray rubber garbage cans (typical of *injera*-making places). The family rents the space from a Greek-owned construction company whose office is next door.

Boston's community grew for the same reason that other Ethiopian communities grew in America: After a few people begin to settle there, family members — which includes "friends who grew up together," Wandossan says — joined them when they won the right to emigrate. The metro area now has as many as 15,000 Ethiopians, and South End Food Emporium is the only place within hundreds of miles where they can buy spices from home.

The family business began about 20 years ago when Wandossan left Ethiopia to escape the political turmoil. He opened South End Food Emporium on Columbus Avenue and he's been there ever since. Other siblings and family members followed, and Family Injera opened about 14 years ago. Every day at South End, Wandossan sells 30 or 40 packages of *injera*, and lots more sell at other distribution points around the area.

But don't imagine Ethiopians buying all of that *injera*: About 30 or 35 percent of it sells to non-Ethiopians, and among that subset, maybe a third of the buyers are Indians. "They have culturally the same kind of bread," Wandossan's Indian customers tell him, and a friend who owns an Ethiopian restaurant told him that a plurality of his diners are Indian.

This is really no surprise, for in the past few decades, Boston's South End has become upscale and educated, which means its residents are adventuresome at the table. Wandossan says non-Ethiopians also buy his spices, and they ask for instructions on how to make Ethiopian food. They eat their *injera* with hummus or pâté, or they use it to make a *berbere*-spiced wrap, or as a steak sauce when they mix *berbere* with a little water to form *awaze*. It's a phenomenon that's sure to increase as Ethiopian food becomes more familiar across the country. "Ninety-five percent of the people who come into our store are Americans," Wandossan says, "and when they see the *injera*, they like to try it."

PHILADELPHIA'S ETHIOPIAN COMMUNITY exists somewhere between big-city Chicago and small-town Sioux Falls. With its proximity to New York, and to D.C. just a few hours away, it's not the first place you think of when you think about big Ethiopian communities. Yet the city has about half a dozen restaurants, plus a number of markets, in a cluster spread out over a mile or so on the city's west side, most of them along or near Baltimore Avenue in a multi-cultural neighborhood called University City, not too far from the University of Pennsylvania and Drexel.

A few blocks north of the Baltimore Avenue restaurants, Chestnut Street hosts the Ethiopian Community Association of Greater Philadelphia, which formed in 1984, and which makes the neighborhood feel like a little "Little Ethiopia." Not far away, a few blocks south of the Baltimore restaurants, there's an Oromo Community Association of Greater Philadelphia, and elsewhere in the city, an Oromo Evangelical Church, and a chapter of the Oromo Liberation Front. A few miles further to the west, there's an Eritrean community center, and across the Schuylkill River, the city's east side has three more restaurants.

So it's a good-sized community, and in some ways it tops New York, which has no markets and no convergence of businesses, although the Philly restaurants survive on the city's non-Ethiopian community, for very few of their owners say they have very many Ethiopian customers, and some admit they have virtually none at all.

If one thing stands out about this mid-sized community, it's style: No two restaurants are exactly alike, and each has the unique touch of its owner.

The Baltimore Avenue cluster hosts three restaurants sprinkled among a several-block run of shops and restaurants of other cultures. There's a noticeable African influence, and if Ethiopian isn't your thing, you can shop or eat at The Nigerian African Food Market, La Calebasse West African Restaurant, African Food Market, Desi Village Indian restaurant (which replaced Blue Nile Ethiopian Restaurant in 2009), Baltimore African Market, and Sunshine Market African and Asian Foods, whose owners are Asian.

The Ethiopian adventure begins with Queen of Sheba, where Genet Abebe cooks and her husband, Wobeshet "Manny" Gebreamanuel, oversees their business. They have a bar on one side, a restaurant on the other, and a single *mesob*, surrounded by cushioned seats, at the back of the dining room.

The wall of the restaurant side of the place features what Manny calls his "Historic Museum," a row of posters and photos of Ethiopian life, history and culture, from the Queen of Sheba through Haile Selassie and, at the end of the gallery, a framed poster of President Barack Obama. A nearby wall shows Martin Luther King Jr. delivering his "I Have a Dream" speech, with those resonant words atop the poster.

And then there's the restaurant's back wall, above the *mesob*. Thursday is karaoke night, popular with students, and when you sing, you get your name on a star cut out of colored construction paper. These stars saturate the wall, often overlapping one another.

A quarter of a century ago, Manny helped to create the city's Ethiopian Community Center, owned by its members, and in the 1980s, the community was tight. But in the 1990s, he says, things got more political as younger people came from post-Derg Ethiopia. "All of this division didn't help our community come together," says Manny, who speaks Amharic and Afaan Oromo (his mother's culture and language), and who just "listens" in Tigrinya.

Across the street from Queen of Sheba, on the same block, sits Gojjo, the growing enterprise of owner Habtamu Shitaye. When he bought the building, in 1996, it was the Cherry Tree Inn, a neighborhood tavern. Habtamu kept the rustic wooden barroom, into which you enter, much like it was when he took over, and above the cash register is an illuminated stained glass sign with its former name.

Walk through the bar and you find a dimly lit dining room with half a dozen tables. Up the stairs, there's another bar, a bocce table, a small dining room, a sunroom with tables, and then, out the back door, a two-tiered wooden deck for *al fresco* dining. The upstairs indoor dining room has a wall covered with a mural, painted by an artist from Mozambique, that depicts a row of Ethiopians enjoying many *berele* of *t'ej* back home. The building's third floor is the home of Habtamu, his wife, and their two children.

A native of Ethiopia's southwest Omo region — he won't be more specific, he says, because he shuns identity politics — Habtamu came to the U.S. in 1987, got an associate's degree, and soon, he says with a smile, "became a hustler for money," working as a taxi driver and at other jobs until he opened his restaurant and moved in above it. He's proud of how Gojjo has grown, and he says, "The good thing that we learned is that customers appreciate how we upgrade and maintain the business. The American dream sometimes makes you crazy. So I have a conflict in myself. You think you can have everything. I believe you should enjoy it, not be controlled by things you buy."

His customers are international, but as usual at Ethiopian restaurants, he sees few African-Americans. "I encourage them to try it," Habtamu says. "It's better than the other food you see on television. If you're curious, you'll find we have a lot in common."

He seems to hold television partly responsible for corrupting the American palate in general, and if only Ethiopian food had the profile of McDonald's, it would be even more popular. "It's just lack of exposure," he says. "If you blind yourself not to try, if you think it's poison that's going to make you sick…" His voice trails off with a playful smile.

Gojjo's menu is typical and diverse, and it includes *ugali na nyam*, a chicken dish that his wife learned to cook when she lived for a while in Kenya. Also on the menu: Ethiopian Cheese Steak, made with Ethiopian spices and a secret sauce. "We're famous for that here," says Habtamu's 17-year-old son, Allen. They also offer a regular Philly Cheese Steak for the less daring.

Allen now attends a multicultural magnet high school, but in his youth, friends would be a little amazed to learn that he came from a culture of people who eat everything with their hands. "They're not accustomed to sharing," he says, "and it's a new experience for them." So he brings friends to Gojjo to introduce them to the cuisine. Habtamu says he missed his native cuisine when he arrived in the U.S. in 1987, but he soon adapted. "There was a craving, of course," he recalls. "But when you go to Rome, you have to act like Romans."

The last University City restaurant, a few blocks west on Baltimore, is Dahlak, the only Eritrean-owned restaurant in the neighborhood. It's a curious mixture of upscale and back home: on one side, you can dine at tables with glass over traditional cloth designs, and in another room, it's all *mesobs*, surrounded by a pastiche of cushioned stools, and with one *mesob* in the back of the room on a rustic hardwood floor, with a mural of village life behind it. The restaurant's owner, Neghesti Gabrehiwet, has been successful enough to open a second location of Dahlak across the river in the city's Germantown neighborhood.

Walking north from Baltimore Avenue, along 45th Street, it's a short hike to Abyssinia, now the city's oldest restaurant (although the place was called Red Sea in the 1980s when it opened), located on a corner in a residential neighborhood between the business districts of Baltimore and Walnut streets.

It doesn't look like much when you enter: a bar with stools, and three small tables. But there's a back room and an upstairs, an Ethiopian jukebox, Italian billiards, a gallery, and a performance space with live Ethiopian music on some weekends. It's beloved in the neighborhood, whose population has grown younger over the years, and the restaurant is a hangout for college students (who take their parents there), young bohemians and new college grads, as well as nearby Ethiopians.

The menu includes some Ethiopian-style sandwiches filled with *kitfo*, beef, lamb, chicken or vegetables. And these *are* Ethiopian sandwiches: The description for "Chicken Sandwich" says, "For ingredient information, see menu item #14," which is the familiar *doro tibs*. The place isn't open for breakfast, but from 10 a.m. to 2 p.m. it serves brunch items like Ethiopian omelets, *ful*, *sheya* (beef with *ful* or eggs), and the spicy *sils fitfit* (*injera* mixed with onions, olive oil, *berbere* and tomato sauce).

Finally, if you walk a few more blocks north to Chestnut Street, you'll find Kaffa Crossing, a café and restaurant with a big menu, even for breakfast. Close to a few city universities, which makes it a good place to study, the café attracts students with its free wireless, and it hosts parties, college readings, author book signings, and teachers who bring their classes there to meet.

Two shelves in the back display Ethiopian artifacts — coffee pots, instruments, baskets, two miniature *gojos*, wood crosses — and from another shelf, you can buy Ethiopian scarves, shawls, t-shirts, baby clothing and a few books in Amharic. The café's lunch and dinner menu includes such rarely found dishes as okra *wot*, eggplant *wot*, and the rather un-Ethiopian tofu *wot*, a concession to its trendy young clientele. They also offer tuna salad, a hummus platter and an *injera* wrap with *yemisir wot*, *kik alicha* or tofu *wot* inside.

This all dwarfs the tiny Ethio Café & Carry Out, which rents its space from the Ethiopian Community Center, just across the street from Kaffa. Genet Bersoma and Solomon Gebreab own it, and their daughter, Melat Solomon, joins her mother in cooking the food and running the place on alternate days. They opened in September 2008, and because they're part of the community center, most of their customers are Ethiopian, although they get some students now and then. The restaurant seats about 20, and in an adjoining room, the women chop vegetables in full view of their customers, with a kitchen in back that's smaller than the one the family had in its Addis Ababa home. They make their own *injera* and sell it in packs of 10 for $6.25.

It's a homey, intimate place, and Melat says that "everyone knows each other here, that's one thing I've noticed." But she doesn't hear a lot of political chatter because "with the kind of place this is, it's too small. There's no bar, so people just come to eat. It's kind of neutral." The heavily vegetarian menu, with its choices written in transliterated Amharic, briefly describes each dish, except for *dulet*, the one dish that probably most needs to be described (it's liver and tripe). Ethiopians, of course, will know what it is, so if you have to ask, you probably shouldn't order it.

The city has two more Ethiopian restaurants, but you'll need some wheels to get to them from the University City area.

On the east side of the Schuylkill River, in Philly's Center City, there's Almaz Café, with its Ethiopian and American menu and industrial-boho décor. The sides that aren't painted various shades of green or blue are made of large metal sheets bolted to the ceiling and the walls, and a stairway leads to an upstairs balcony with a few tables and a low roof. There's also a small counter at the window with bar stools so patrons can look out at the bustling city. The stereo system plays Amharic jazz and American soft pop.

The fare includes wraps (turkey, barbecue chicken, veggie), sandwiches, soups, salads, and a full Ethiopian menu. They sell more Ethiopian food at dinner, more sandwiches for lunch, and coffee and pastry all day long. The dinner menu includes the breakfast favorite *ful*, and for a while they served *kinche*, but people didn't take to it. They preferred omelets, French toast and other American breakfast standards.

Co-owner Almaz Haile opened the place with a partner, Solomon Getnet, three years ago. She guesses that her customers are 97 percent American, although Ethiopians who work in Center City stop by, usually for an American-style lunch or for coffee. She serves a lot of students, doctors, businessmen and even TV news people from a nearby station. The café is the only Ethiopian restaurant in Center City, and it's not far from the University of Pennsylvania. Almaz makes her own *injera*, and she gets her spices in "pillow-case-sized bags" from back home, even though she could get them locally from any of the three markets that sell Ethiopian spices.

Finally, there's Era, perhaps the quirkiest of the city's venues. A neighborhood restaurant in every sense, it's a typical hole in the wall, open daily from 4 to 10 p.m., with more seats (about 20) around a circular bar in the front room than in the restaurant (about 16) out back, and with a pool table in the barroom area that takes up about as much room as the restaurant.

But Era has a full menu of Ethiopian dishes, along with a bar menu of standard finger foods, and owner Akliku Senbeth admits that he sells more alcohol than food. "I don't have Ethiopian customers," he says. "A lot of people around the neighborhood just like the food."

Era doesn't hide its Ethiopian flavor. Its sign, which juts out from the building, proclaims its name against the colors of the Ethiopian flag, and it welcomes passers-by with the promise of "Fine Ethiopian Dining." It's an odd thing to encounter on a corner in a tightly packed residential neighborhood with as many nicely maintained row houses and sidewalks as tattered ones. But he's been in business since 2002, and his venture seems to be working.

Akliku is Oromo, from the countryside near the southern city of Welega, and before opening a restaurant, he drove a cab, worked at a hospital parking lot, and did refugee outreach for the city. He arrived in the U.S. in 1982 and just happened to land in Philly, which has always been his home. He raised two sons there, and they both now attend Villanova on scholarship, one studying civil engineering and the other computer engineering. His daughter is still in high school. Aklilu named his restaurant Era in part because he hopes to stick around. But the letters are also an acronym for Ellal, Robbera and Aklilu — that is, his two sons and him.

The menu at Era is in transliterated Amharic, not Afaan Oromo, because that's how people know Ethiopian food. But Akliku is a very proud Oromo and a founder of the city's Oromo Community Center, which promotes the culture and serves as a gathering place. He's very ecumenical about Ethiopia's many cultures, and he wants Era to be a respite, not a battlefield. He sometimes even takes his customers to other Ethiopian restaurants in the city.

"All of my customers are my friends," he says, "and sometimes they want to see what others do. When I opened my business, I didn't want to get involved in politics. If I do politics, I do *only* politics."

There's one noticeable common element among the city's restaurants: They don't try very hard to get Ethiopian beer or *t'ej*, and many of the owners don't even seem to know that they can. This is partly due to Pennsylvania's difficult state-owned liquor control system, where restaurants can't serve any brand of alcohol unless the state approves it. But if a restaurant wants a particular import, or a type of ethnic beer or alcohol, all an owner has to do is tell the state's Liquor Control Board where to get it, and they'll oblige. The out-of-state supplier will then need to buy a license to sell in Pennsylvania. Tana Ethiopian Cuisine in Pittsburgh sells several brands of Ethiopian beer and three types of *t'ej*, and the restaurant's supplier, Global Air and Transport in Maryland, already has a Pennsylvania license. The company would certainly be glad to get its money's worth out of the license by selling to more restaurants in the state.

Philly also has a few grocery stores that sell spices and *injera*, all in the University City area, and none that sell Ethiopian goods exclusively.

The small Addis Market, right next door to Abyssinia, offers a few spices, Zelalem Injera shipped from D.C., and a few other convenience store items. It's pretty bare bones, without much room to grow, and it's located in a residential neighborhood, where parking is a challenge.

A few blocks away, there's the full-scale convenience store Super 7 Market, owned by an Ethiopian husband and wife, that promotes its Ethiopian spices and *injera* in its window in Amharic writing. "American, Ethiopian and Middle Eastern Foods" proclaims the marquee, in English, above the door, which faces the store's convenient parking lot at the corner of 46th and Walnut. They've even branded their *injera*, spices and legumes, which they sell under their own Blue Nile Falls label.

Super 7's big competitor, just east on Walnut Street, is International Foods & Spices, an Indian-Pakistani market that began selling Ethiopian spices a few years ago. The shop gets its *injera* from Ethiopian women in the community, and on Tuesdays, when it's closed, Super 7 sees a spike in its *injera* sales.

Mohnednur Salih and his wife, Zemzem Salih, bought Super 7 in 2007 and for a while considered changing its name to Blue Nile Market. He scrapped that idea because Philly already had a Blue Nile restaurant (now closed), and he didn't want to confuse people. Then he considered Ethio Market. But he has a lot of North African, Middle Eastern and American customers, and when he informally surveyed them and the people in the neighborhood, he found that they preferred he keep the name Super 7. So now, as a compromise, he's added a mention of "Ethiopian" to his marquee and put some Amharic promotion in the front window.

Zemzem made the store's *injera* at home for a while. Business grew, and now she's busy tending the store (with help from her brother-in-law), so they get their *injera* from two community women, who make it for them on alternate days.

Mohnednur and Zemzem are Moslems whose families knew each other back home in Ethiopia when their children were growing up. Zemzem's family later moved to Saudi Arabia, where the couple married. To make it easier for her to return with him to America, she took his last name, rare among Ethiopian wives. Their daughter is 19 and a student at Temple University studying to become a pharmacist, and their pre-teen son helps out around the store during the summer and joins his parents' conversations with visitors.

Their enterprise is still rather new, so Mohnednur hasn't given up his full-time job working in parking and transportation at the University of Pennsylvania. The tuition benefit for his daughter is another incentive, and the two jobs keep him very busy.

As for his unique position — a Moslem Ethiopian businessman in a largely Christian community — Mohnednur finds Philly to be a welcoming place, without the friction of the D.C. community, which is big enough for people to divide.

"We grew up together," he says of his multi-cultural Ethiopian compatriots. "Your interests are the same, the way you eat your food is the same. There's no conflict here in terms of politics. When you have a business, you don't have to focus on politics, you have to accommodate everyone. I'm not there. I'm here."

Preparing an Ethiopian Feast

First, the good news: You can prepare an Ethiopian meal for four in little more than three hours over the course of a few days. You can serve your guests juicy, spicy *doro tibs wot*, effervescent *kitfo* with a side of *ayib,* fresh lemony *butecha*, hearty *atakilt alicha*, and to cool things down a bit, *azifa*, a flavorful chilled lentil dish.

There is no bad news, although unless your town has an Ethiopian restaurant or market, you'll need to go online to buy *berbere, mitmita, injera* and gesho. And once you begin cooking, you'll work steadily for about two hours before you serve the meal: Ethiopian cooking is rather labor-intensive. You can pop a turkey or a brisket or a pork loin into the oven and forget it for a few hours. Ethiopian dishes demand your attention.

Fortunately, almost every dish is a stew — that is, something you make in one pot. But for most of the dishes, it'll be a watched pot, and you'll need to keep the ingredients moving.

In fact, the feast I propose requires some preparation a few *weeks* in advance, and then two blocks of time on the day of the feast. You'll need to make the *azifa* in the morning to let it chill for dinner. *Butecha,* too, must be prepared in advance to allow it to thicken as it chills.

My feast also includes a tandem of two easy-to-make and especially delicious dishes for carnivores: *kitfo*, a beef dish eaten raw in Ethiopia (I'll teach you to make it *yebesele*, or fully cooked); and *ayib*, or Ethiopian cheese, the traditional accompaniment for *kitfo*. You'll need to make the *kitfo* last, just before you're ready to serve your guests. *Ayib* also makes an excellent appetizer at an Ethiopian meal, especially when mixed with a touch of *mitmita* to spice it up, or stuffed inside a gutted *karya* (jalapeño pepper) to create a treat called *sinig*.

Most Ethiopian vegetable dishes reheat well, so advance preparation is a good way to break up your work and have more time to spend with your guests while you cook the dishes best prepared just before eating them. You can make the vegetable dishes a little bit in advance, and then let them sit in the pot while the chicken stews. Or vice verse: If the chicken is ready first, let it relax while the vegetables cook. Everything will be fine.

At Ethiopian restaurants, vegetable dishes are rarely made to order: The cook prepares most recipes in large quantities and then dishes out portions as needed, sometimes at room temperature. A lid on the pot keeps them warm, and you can always pump a little more heat through them just before serving. Ethiopian food is malleable in ways that make your dinner party easier to manage.

What follows is a thoroughly annotated, day-by-day, step-by-step guide to making your meal, beginning with a shopping list, followed by the preparations, and ending with some notes on the *injera*. Appendix A tells you where to buy the specialty items that you can't get at your local market, and Appendix C presents all eight of the recipes — the six dishes for the feast, plus *t'ej* and *niter kibbee* — as they would appear in a recipe book.

Now let's get cooking.

The Harvest

My proposed menu provides a balanced selection of popular Ethiopian dishes: *doro tibs wot,* a spicy dish made with chunks of chicken breast; *kitfo,* for the beef eaters, and its accompanying cheese, *ayib; atakilt alicha*, a stew of potatoes, carrots and green beans; *butecha*, prepared from chick pea powder, and accented with chopped onions and jalapeños; and *azifa*, a lentil salad with a blend of flavors and ingredients. All of these dishes include "king onion," along with a variety of other spices and ingredients, and the ensemble gives the herbivores plenty to eat while still sating the omnivores (Ethiopians often choose beef over chicken or vegetables if given a choice).

If you're cooking for four, here are the ingredients you'll need, plus perhaps a little extra (better not to get caught with a hungry guest):

- Two large or three small boneless chicken breasts, about one and one-half pounds in all
- One pound of lean ground beef
- A 32-ounce container of plain yogurt or buttermilk
- Two large red onions, about two heaping cups finely chopped
- Six tablespoons of chick pea powder (sometimes called gram powder)
- Two large carrots
- Two medium potatoes
- One-third pound of green beans

- One and a half cups of green lentils
- Six or seven jalapeño peppers
- Lemon juice, about three or four tablespoons
- Lime juice, about three or four tablespoons
- Turmeric powder
- Ginger powder
- Crushed garlic
- A quarter cup of red wine or *t'ej*
- Olive oil, used in preparing the vegetable dishes and possibly the meat dishes.

Next come some of your optional ingredients if you want to prepare your own *t'ej*, and if you want to use Ethiopian spiced butter (*niter kibbee*) instead of Indian ghee or olive oil in the meat dishes. If you choose not to prepare these elements yourself, other sections of this book will tell you where to buy them or find substitutes. Olive oil can easily substitute for *kibbee* in the chicken dish but not in the beef dish. (Oh, okay: You can use olive oil for the *kitfo*, but it's better with *kibbee* or ghee.)

- 32 solid ounces of honey for making *t'ej*. This will be about 21 or 22 liquid ounces.
- One-third of a pound of gesho stick for making the *t'ej*.
- One pound of unsalted butter for making *niter kibbee*, unless you decide to use store-bought ghee or *kibbee* as a substitute.
- A small portion (less than a teaspoon) of the following powdered spices for the *niter kibbee*: ginger, basil, cumin, cardamom, turmeric, fenugreek. You also need some fresh crushed garlic and some chopped onions.
- Ten pieces of *injera*. Appendix A tells you where to order it online. Two alternatives: Use Middle Eastern *pita* bread or Indian *nan* as a surrogate; or try making some yourself by visiting Heather Moore's blog (see the note at the end of this chapter). I recommend the online option: By the time you get done experimenting, weeks in advance, to see if you can successfully make edible *injera*, you'll have spent much more time and money than if you simply have *injera* shipped to you.
- *Berbere* and *mitmita*, the Ethiopian red pepper spices you'll need to flavor your chicken and beef dish authentically. Once again, consult Appendix A for places to buy them online.

Now your kitchen is stocked, and it's time to cook. With apologies to Virginia Woolf and Mrs. Dalloway, here are the hours and days of your adventure.

Six or Seven Weeks Before the Feast

This is a good time to decide whether you want to make your own *t'ej* or buy some from a winery. If you make your own, you'll need gesho. You'll also need *berbere* to make your *doro tibs wot* and *mitmita* for your *kitfo*. If you live in a city with Ethiopian grocery stores or restaurants, you may be able to buy these items locally. But if not, you'll need to do some shopping online. Just make sure your stuff gets to you on time.

Appendix A will lead you to numerous options for ordering *injera* and spices online, and most of the companies have convenient websites that allow you to order your goods. Consult this chapter, spend a little time online, and order your spices well in advance. They'll stay fresh for a long time. You should order the *injera* a few days before the meal, or you can order it early and freeze it.

To freeze the *injera*, fold each round piece in half, then in half again, and then in half again. This gives you a thick triangle of *injera*. Wrap each piece separately and tightly in aluminum foil, then put them all in the freezer.

So take stock of how intrepid you want to be, and make sure you order your specialty items early enough for them to arrive when you need them.

Five Weeks Before the Feast

This is when you need to begin fermenting your *t'ej* if you choose to go all out and make it yourself. If you choose instead to buy a bottle made by a winery, Chapter 8 tells you where to order it. Or you can simply serve your favorite white or red wine, or a traditional mead of another culture.

To make your own *t'ej*, mix one part honey to three parts water in whatever quantity you think will be enough for your party, using a glass jug large enough to hold the liquid without being filled to the top. To generously serve four, use 22 ounces of liquid honey (just buy a two-pound container) and 66 ounces of water. Your final volume of *t'ej* will be about 20 percent less than the volume of liquid when you mix it.

Stir the liquid thoroughly until it achieves a uniform color. Add a third of a pound of gesho stick, then mix it into the liquid, making sure all of the gesho is moistened. Place the lid lightly on the jar and set it aside. Don't seal the lid: Give it just a little room to breathe.

Chapter 8 of this book has a detailed annotated *t'ej* preparation, so consult that as well. This concise version will get you through the process.

Four Weeks Before the Feast

Open the jug of *t'ej*, stir it for about 20 seconds, then place the lid lightly on the jar again and set it aside. You should see fuzzy microbes forming on the gesho. This is part of the fermentation process. Stir the fuzz into the liquid.

Three Weeks Before the Feast

Open the jar of *t'ej*, stir it again, and then remove the gesho. Do this with tongs, or anything that allows you to pluck out the floating sticks. You needn't get every last piece out, but do your best to remove as much as you can. A few remaining floaters won't hurt anything. When the gesho is out, stir the liquid again, then place the lid lightly on the jar and set it aside.

Two Weeks Before the Feast

Open the jug of *t'ej*, stir the liquid for about 10 seconds, then place the lid lightly on the jar again and set it aside.

One Week Before the Feast

Open the jug of *t'ej*, stir the liquid for about 10 seconds, then place the lid lightly on the jar again and set it aside.

And while you're at it, why not make your own *niter kibbee*.

In a non-stick pot, over low heat, slowly melt one pound of unsalted butter. When it liquefies, add all of the other ingredients: ¼ teaspoon each of powdered ginger, basil, cumin, cardamom, turmeric, fenugreek; one tablespoon of chopped onions; and ½ teaspoon of minced garlic. Stir them into the butter.

Bring the mixture to a low boil, and let it boil for at least one half hour. After a while, you'll see thick milky solids in the bottom of the pot and a translucent yellow liquid above it.

When the liquid and solids seem to be fully separated, the *kibbee* is ready. Remove it from the heat, then pour the liquid through cheesecloth into the container in which you intend to store it. The cheesecloth will catch the milk solids and spices.

Now, refrigerate the container — uncovered at first, to allow heat to escape. When the butter begins to solidify, cover the container. Your *kibbee* is now ready to use on the day of the feast.

Three to Five Days Before the Feast

If you've decided to order *injera* online, place your order today or tomorrow. You can freeze the *injera* when it arrives. If you've given your *injera* company of choice a trial run, and you know it delivers on time, then you might wait another day to order and have it arrive on the day of your feast to avoid the hassle of having to wrap and freeze it. If you've bravely decided to make your own *injera,* consult Heather Moore's blog for instructions. But once again, I recommend ordering authentic *injera* online. Appendix A tells you how you can do it.

The Day Before the Feast

It's time to strain, bottle and chill your *t'ej.* Take a piece of cheesecloth and place it in a wire mesh strainer. Set the strainer over the top of a large pitcher or pot. Slowly pour the *t'ej* through the cheesecloth and mesh strainer to fill the container

After you've strained all of the *t'ej* through the apparatus, pour it into bottles, seal the bottle, and put it in the refrigerator to chill.

The Day of the Feast

It's Saturday morning, and your guests arrive at 7 p.m. So let's get to work.

9 a.m. — *Azifa* and *Butecha*

Before you start on the morning vegetable dishes, you need to tend to the chicken breasts.

If they're fresh, you have nothing to do right now. If they're frozen, take them out of the freezer and let them begin to defrost in the refrigerator. In fact, you can put them in the refrigerator the night before, and by morning, they'll be defrosted enough to cut into bite-sized pieces for the *doro tibs wot.* But if you take them out in the morning, you'll need to return to them by mid-afternoon. It's easier to cut a chicken breast into pieces when its still semi-frozen than when it's slippery and thawed.

Now we'll start with the *azifa.* Measure one and a half cups of green lentils, put them into a large pot filled with water boiling water, and let them cook until they're tender. This should take about 45 minutes.

While the lentils are cooking, begin work on the *butecha.* Measure two cups of water into a bowl. Add to this six tablespoons of chick pea flour — that's three for each cup of liquid — and stir it with a wire whip until the flour dissolves in the water. Then add two tablespoons of olive oil, two tablespoons of lemon juice, one quarter of a teaspoon of turmeric powder, and one-half teaspoon of ginger powder. You can forego the turmeric if you find the taste of this tart spice to be too strong or overwhelming.

When the mixture is smooth, put it into a large pot. Turn on the heat to low-medium, and bring it to a lightly bubbling boil. When the mixture begins to bubble, adjust the heat so that it doesn't spit and splatter. You may want to put some aluminum foil loosely over the top. Don't put a lid on it! The *butecha* needs to thicken, and that happens when the water slowly boils away. The volume will reduce as it cooks.

Once the *butecha* begins to boil, you have to stir it regularly — every three or four minutes. Scrape any residue off the spoon and the sides and bottom of the pot. A non-stick pot is your best choice.

Now you have two dishes cooking, and you're keeping a close eye on one of them, stirring the *butecha* regularly and the softening lentils every now and then. It's time to begin chopping.

For this portion of the dinner, you'll need about one-third to one-half of a cup of finely chopped red onions and two jalapeños.

For the *azifa*: Prepare about one fourth of a cup of onions and one jalapeño chopped into very small pieces. For the *butecha*: prepare one fourth of a cup of finely chopped red onions and one finely chopped jalapeños. Do *not* put this mixture into a food processor.

After about 30 to 45 minutes, your lentils will be soft and your *butecha* will be thickened. Leave the *butecha* in the pot while you tend to the lentils. This allows the *butecha* to thicken even more after you turn off the heat.

Thoroughly strain the water from the lentils, rinse them in cold water while still in the strainer, and keep running cold water over the lentils until the water comes out clear through the bottom of the strainer. Put the lentils in a deep bowl, and mash them gently with a spatula.

When the lentils are mashed, stir in the chopped onions and jalapeños. Then, add one teaspoon of ginger powder, one-quarter teaspoon of turmeric powder, three tablespoons of lime juice and four tablespoons of olive oil. Mix them all well. Taste the *azifa*, and add a touch more of any ingredient if the flavor of that ingredient doesn't peek through. Add a bit more onion and jalapeño if you can't taste them, and then a bit more until you get the flavors balanced well.

Finally, you have an option: You can continue to mash the *azifa* well, or you can put it all in a food processor and blend it on low. I've had it both ways in restaurants and I've prepared it both ways. When you're done mashing or blending, your *azifa* is ready to refrigerate. Stir it now and then to make sure it gets colder and colder as the day goes on.

Finally, it's back to the *butecha*. Scoop it from the pot into a large bowl, and stir in the chopped onions and chopped jalapeño. Do this gradually, until you see onions and jalapeños sprinkled through the dish but not overwhelmed by them. When it's all mixed, put it into the refrigerator. A few hours later, take it out and stir it. You'll find that the mixture has firmed up considerably. When you stir it, it'll begin to look like scrambled eggs. That's just how you want it to look. Stir it a few more times later in the day.

Your morning preparation is done. You've been working for about an hour. Enjoy the rest of your day. You'll be back in the kitchen about 90 minutes before your guests arrive.

4 p.m. — Tending to Your *Injera*

Now is the time to take your *injera* out of the freezer. Unwrap each piece, put them all on a plate to begin defrosting at room temperature, and cover the plate lightly with foil or wax paper. Check it now and then. When it begins to soften, gently open each piece to hasten the process of defrosting.

You can begin this step a little later if it's warm in your home and the *injera* is likely to defrost more quickly. You can even take the *injera* out at 5 p.m., when you begin making the last two dishes, and use your microwave to hasten the process. Microwave the frozen *injera* on the defrost setting until it's no longer frozen. Then, just before you're ready to serve the meal, heat it at a higher setting to make it warm and moist, just like it would be when it comes off of the *mitad*.

Count on using at least two piece of *injera* as the plate under the dishes, and figure that each guest will have his or her own piece of *injera* to grab the food. Then, have a few extras ready, just in case your guests have big appetites and want more. That's eight or nine pieces of *injera* for a dinner party with four people. And remember, you have to eat the plate! The *injera* under the food is delicious when it's soaked with sauces.

5 p.m. — The *Atakilt Alicha, Doro Tibs Wot, Ayib* and *Kitfo*

Time to get back to cooking your main courses. Begin this heat by stirring the *azifa* and *butecha* once again.

Next, it's time to make your *ayib*. Into a deep saucepan, pour a 32-ounce container of plain yogurt or buttermilk that has no flavorings and no added sodium. Low-fat yogurt is okay, but avoid the non-fat variety. Heat the yogurt or buttermilk over a very low flame for about 20 minutes at a very low gentle boil. Do *not* stir once it begins to boil. Within five minutes, you'll see the liquid (whey) separating from the white solids (curds).

When it's done cooking, remove it from the heat and gingerly pour off the liquid that's formed. Don't use a strainer: The soft solid white *ayib*, which you want to keep, could come through the strainer. Take your thoroughly drained cheese and put it into the covered container in which you'll refrigerate it. Stir it a little to enhance its appearance and consistency.

Now chop the onions. You want them to be very fine, almost liquefied, although I wouldn't recommend using a food processor. I use a hand chopper. You'll want one cup of finely chopped onions for each of the dishes that requires onion.

Next, for the *atakilt alicha*, prepare the vegetables: two medium potatoes, peeled and cut into bite-sized pieces; two large carrots, scraped and cut into angular or oval bite-sized pieces; one third of a pound of green beans, cut into thirds; and two jalapeños, seeded and julienned. While you're doing this, you should also julienne two more jalapeños for the *doro tibs wot*.

To cook your *atakilt*, put a third of a cup of olive oil in a non-stick pot and let it begin to heat. Then, add a cup of chopped onions and let them cook in the oil, stirring frequently. When the onion begins to liquefy and turn translucent, add the spices: half a teaspoon of chopped garlic, and two teaspoons of ginger powder. Blend the spices into the mixture and let them cook for a minute or two, stirring constantly.

Now add the vegetables to the pot and stir it all around, coating all of the vegetables with the onion and spices. Do this for a minute or two: The ingredients will sizzle, but don't let them burn. Finally, add about a cup of water — just enough to cover the vegetables — and stir it all again. Bring it to a very low, gentle boil, and stir every five minutes or so. You may want to add more water from time to time to keep it moist without soaking it.

With your *atakilt* cooking, you can turn to the chicken.

Place a cup of onions in a non-stick pan and let them begin to cook and caramelize. Stir them constantly, tossing and turning them in the pan as they sizzle. *Do not let them burn!* You can add a tablespoon of water if you like to keep them from burning. When they become translucent and a little brown, add four tablespoons of *niter kibbee* or its substitute (ghee or olive oil). If you want your dish to be especially rich, use five or six tablespoons, or even more, to taste. But four is the minimum here.

As the *kibbee* melts, stir it around in the cooked onions to get everything moist. As soon as the *kibbee* is melted (or the oil is hot and sizzling), add three-fourths to one tablespoon of *berbere* and blend it well into the *kibbee*-soaked onions. Let this cook for a minute or two, then pour in a quarter of a cup of red wine or *t'ej*. The sweet fermented liquid will sizzle when it hits the pan.

Now, toss in your pieces of chicken, and let them "fry" for a few minutes, until each piece is no longer pink on the outside. Then, add one-third to one-half cup of water, stir it again, and add the jalapeños. Stir it all well and let it simmer at a very low boil.

The *doro tibs* will need to cook for about 15 to 20 minutes. Swirl the ingredients around every few minutes, and thoroughly stir the *atakilt*, moving the ingredients from top to bottom and coating them with the liquid that remains as it cooks down.

The *atakilt* is ready when the water has reduced and the vegetables are tender, although you can turn of the heat while there's still some liquid in the pot. This will be a thick sauce flavored with onions and ginger.

The *doro tibs* are ready when most of the liquid has reduced, leaving the meat coated with a thick red sauce.

When the other dishes are almost ready, it's time to make your *kitfo*.

In a skillet, cook one pound of ground beef for about a minute. Carve out a hole in the middle of the skillet and add at least four tablespoons of *niter kibbee*. As the *kibbee* melts, stir it thoroughly into the beef, making sure to moisten all of the beef with the *kibbee*.

When the beef is cooked to your taste — well done, medium well, rare — sprinkle it with one teaspoon of *mitmita* and one teaspoon of cardamom, then mix the ingredients well. You can use a little more of each, to taste, but be careful: *mitmita* is hotter than *berbere*! You can substitute *ghee* for *kibbee*, but you really shouldn't use oil. You need some form of clarified butter. *Berbere* as a substitute for *mitmita* also won't do.

By the way, Ethiopians enjoy *kitfo* raw, or *tere,* and you can as well. For that preparation, begin by heating the *kibbee* in a skillet until it melts, then remove the skillet from the heat. Mix in the beef, stirring the ingredients thoroughly, then add the spices and mix well again. If you return it to the heat and cook it very slightly, you'll be preparing it *lebleb*. Ethiopian cooks will often stir the mixture by hand.

Kitfo cooks up quickly, even when you make it *yebesele* (well done)*,* and more than any other dish at your feast, you want to serve it hot. So when it's done, it's time to eat.

There's just one more thing to do, and you can do it while the *kitfo* comes to fruition: Reheat the *butecha* in the microwave. You can serve it cold as well, but I've found it to be a better complement to the meal when it's hot, especially when you serve cold *azifa* as one of your dishes. As an alternative to heating it, let the *butecha* sit out for a while to reach room temperature.

Okay: It's time to eat. This is the easy part. Place two or three piece of *injera* on a large round serving plate, at least 12 inches in diameter. The pieces will overlap. (If you're using some other kind of unleavened bread, cover the plate with it, just as you would cover it with *injera*.) Scoop out portions of each dish, and arrange them artfully on the *injera*. Put the *doro tibs* in the middle, with the other dishes organized around it. Serve the *ayib* in dollops around the *kitfo* on the platter. If you bought or made some *t'ej*, pop the cork and pour it.

Now call your guests to the table, and dig in.

A Few Words on Your Injera

So what *do* you do about the *injera*, the hardest ingredient of your Ethiopian dinner party to make?

Your meal won't be "authentic" if you don't serve the food on *injera*. But if you can't get any from a restaurant or grocery story in your community, and you aren't up to the enormous challenge of making it yourself, and you don't want to bother ordering it online, then you'll need to improvise.

A nice moist store-bought Middle Eastern *pita* or Indian *nan* makes a suitable surrogate dinner plate and silverware set. In the worst-case scenario, you may simply have to serve your meal on a plate and eat it with a fork. Think of it this way: When in Rome, you can't always eat like an Ethiopian.

If you order *injera* online or get it from a local vendor, it will freeze well, although it does take up a good bit of space in your freezer.

If you don't have an Ethiopian market within driving distance, your next option is to buy some *injera* from internet companies that ship it nationwide. So why not splurge and have some fresh *injera* sent to you? When you figure in the relatively low cost of the ingredients used to make your entrées, your feast will ultimately cost no more than dinner for four (including tip) at a good Ethiopian restaurant.

Appendix A will direct you to companies that sell *injera* by mail. Most make the *injera* fresh each day and get it to you within 48 hours. You can time the delivery for the day of the feast, but I'd recommend having it arrive a few days before and then freezing it. You wouldn't want to be caught without *injera* because it didn't get to you on time.

Finally, for the biggest adventure, you can try making it yourself. I'd recommend doing it a few times for practice before the day of your feast. You'll need teff, but you should be able to get that at a good specialty market or natural foods store in your community. You can also order teff flour by mail — once again, consult Appendix A — or you can make your *injera* with whole wheat flour.

Several things have to go well for your *injera* to turn out right.

First, you have to get the right proportion of water to flour. It should be a little runny, like a thin pancake batter. About one cup of water for every one cup of flour is a good proportion.

Then, you need to allow it to ferment. This is the easiest part, and after three or four days in a bowl, you should have a batter that will taste properly sour when you bake it.

Finally, there's the challenge of turning batter into bread. This requires a large round surface with a high even temperature. But even with that, it's not as easy as pouring the batter onto the skillet and lifting off a piece of bread a minute or two later. The bread will stick, or it will burn, or it won't form bubbles on the top and look like *injera* — or all of the above. *Injera* is a very temperamental bread.

Heather Moore, an American woman who's visited Ethiopia, has a very helpful blog with instructions on making *injera* at http://burakaeyae.blogspot. com/2007/02/ step-by-step-injera-instructions-real.html. She learned how to make *injera* from an Ethiopian friend. The site includes excellent step-by-step video so you can see her technique. There are also myriad *injera* preparations available online. Just search the term "making *injera*" and you'll find them.

So there it is. Serving an Ethiopian feast isn't as simple as stuffing a chicken, whipping up some mashed potatoes, and steaming some broccoli. But if you've come this far in your journey, then admit it: You're intrigued. Just take it slow, do some online shopping, embrace your inner Ethiopian, and enjoy your culinary odyssey.

Some Ethiopian Cookbooks

If you'd like a little more help in becoming an Ethiopian chef at home, here are a few cookbooks that offer a wide variety of dishes. Most are in print, and you can usually find the ones that aren't on websites that sell used books.

Just one caveat: Ethiopian cooks all say they don't use measurements in their cooking — they go by instinct and tradition — and that makes it hard to get a recipe anything close to a "standard" in Ethiopian cookbooks. Recipes for the same dish can vary greatly from book to book in almost mind-boggling ways.

For example, take *yemisir wot*, the popular red lentil stew spiced with *berbere*. One book tells you to add four tablespoons of *berbere* to a cup of cooked lentils. Another calls for five to seven tablespoons. And one calls for a half cup of *berbere*! That much pepper will add more *moq'ta* ("heat") than even an Ethiopian couldn't survive.

Or *kik wot*, a spicy dish made with split yellow peas: In one recipe, you need a quarter cup of olive oil, in another a half cup, and in another a full cup, all for the same quantity of peas. Two of the books call for a cup of chopped onions in your *kik wot*, and another calls for a whopping *three* cups. The *berbere* for these disparate recipes range from four tablespoons to half a cup. Or *azifa*, your chilled lentil dish with many ingredients: Is it one, two or three whole chopped onions, the juice of two limes or the juice of three? Picking a book means picking your proportions, and the proportions aren't always what they should be — the result of turning an oral tradition into a written one.

I've adapted the recipes in this chapter from these books, working out proportions that seem right. So if you follow a cookbook, be careful. I recommend that you prepare any recipe for yourself and tailor it to your taste before you serve it to guests.

♦ *Exotic Ethiopian Cooking* by Daniel J. Mesfin. This is the most thorough cookbook available. It includes nearly 200 recipes, nutritional charts, color photographs, a glossary, and more than 40 pages of introductory material on Ethiopian food and culture.

♦ *Taste of Ethiopia,* by Webayehu Tsegaye and Tamiru Degefa. Filled with color photographs of Ethiopian dishes, this book offers several dozen popular recipes, with glossaries describing commonly used grains, flours, legumes and spices, as well as the names for many dishes and ingredients in Amharic and English.

♦ *Taste of Eritrea* by Olivia Warren. This nicely done little book has an introduction about cultural influences on Eritrea and its cuisine, followed by dozens of recipes, many of them familiar to fans of Ethiopian food, along with numerous Italian-influenced dishes popular in Eritrea. The recipe for making beer — *talla* in Amharic, *suwa* in Tigrinya — is easy to do in your kitchen.

♦ *The Recipe of Love: An Ethiopian Cookbook* by Aster Ketsela Belayneh. The author of this big bright book owns Addis Ababa, an Ethiopian restaurant in Toronto, which she opened in 1992 at the age of 26. The photography is vivid, the recipes are diverse, and the author's life-affirming philosophy winnows through the book.

♦ *A tavola con le Regina di Saba/Dining with the Queen of Sheba* by Teshome Berhe. The author lives in Italy, where he owns an Ethiopian restaurant, and his book features each recipe in English and Italian on facing pages. The 20-page introduction to Ethiopian cuisine is also in both languages.

♦ *Foods of Ethiopia* by Barbara Sheen. This book was written to teach young readers about Ethiopian food and culture, but it includes nine recipes, some of them very authentic, and some adapted for easier preparation (the *kategna* uses tortillas rather than *injera*). It's liberally illustrated with color photos, and it's a fine primer for young readers and chefs.

♦ *Ethiopian Delights Cookbook* by Karen Jean Matsko Hood. Due for publication in 2010, this latest offering by the prolific cookbook author promises 250 recipes, along with information on Ethiopian history, culture and folklore.

♦ *Cook Book* by AACASA. Published by the Australian African Children's Aid Support Association, this little book illustrates some of its recipes with step-by-step photos. Many other photos of dishes and ingredients, both in color and in black and white, accompany the recipes.

♦ ***Ethiopian American Cookbook.*** This remarkable little book — which is nearly impossible to find, and very interesting as a cultural artifact — was printed in Asmara in the 1970s (it has no copyright date), by the National Literacy Campaign Organization, to foster understanding between its two cultures. Half of the book is Ethiopian recipes for Americans to try, and the other half is American recipes for Ethiopians. Each page appears in each language, with the English and Amharic pages facing each other.

The Introduction to the book says it's "the result of the combined interest and contribution of a group of American and Ethiopian women in Addis Ababa," and the acknowledgement page thanks the Ethiopian-American Women's Committee for helping to compile the recipes.

Clubs for Ethiopian women and girls were common in Addis Ababa at the time, says Wilhelmine Stordiau, who was raised in Ethiopia, and who now bottles Begena Tedj in Frankfurt. These clubs united Ethiopian women with women from other countries, and their meetings took place at the homes of the members and at the foreign embassies of the non-Ethiopian women.

"The hostess had to prepare tea, coffee and cake snacks," recalls Stordiau, whose great-grandmother was Ethiopian. "The preparation used to take one day at our place, and the house employees, especially the cook, hated these days as it was a lot of work. After having had their tea, the women sat down to do some charity work: preparation of fundraising parties, making bandages for hospitals, stitching — and writing cookbooks!"

This particular book may intimidate the modern American chef because, it seems, the Ethiopians who contributed recipes didn't understand the American supermarket. Pages 47 to 49 offer detailed instructions on how to prepare a freshly killed chicken for cooking. "Take off its head and the big feathers," the book instructs. "Dip the chicken into a pot of boiling water holding it by its feet. Take off quickly the small feathers." And so on, through 20 numbered instructions.

The book's recipes are authentic and easy to follow, but don't miss page 17. It offers measurement equivalents, so you can translate a recipe's instruction for "two ladles butter" and "½ ladle red pepper" into more familiar proportions: "1 ladle = 10 tbsp. or ¾ cup," the instructions say. A page on the Ethiopian side offers the Amharic names for spices with their English counterparts, although two of them, "kebebe sine" (a pepper-like plant that tastes like allspice) and "hidar filfile," have no translation. The American portion explains protein, calcium, iron, fats, carbohydrates and five types of vitamins, telling readers the foods in which they're found, and recommending a daily allowance for each type of nutrition.

The American recipes, by the way, include egg salad sandwiches, tomato soup, hamburgers, brownies, Sunday chocolate cake, lemonade, crabmeat rounds — and a martini. *Letenachin*!

An Epilogue: Ferenj Tales

Stanford University is thousands of miles and a few thousand dollars in airfare from southwest Ethiopia. But the metaphoric distance between the two is immeasurable.

One is an enclave of education and the privilege that comes with it. The other is a place where people spend their hours and days doing things outdoors by hand that Westerners do indoors in minutes with a machine (or better yet, they hire someone to do it for them).

But twice in the past few years, teams of engineers in a program at Stanford have developed affordable products that make the lives of Ethiopians — and especially the women who cook the family meal — much easier.

It happened at Stanford's Institute of Design (the "d-school") in a course called Design for Extreme Affordability. In 2008, a team of graduate students discovered that a piece of metal could lengthen the longevity and durability of the most important item in an Ethiopian woman's cooking repertoire. And a year later, another team took some of the tears out of making Ethiopian spices.

The course lasts for six months and assigns its graduate students to teams that must come up with solutions to help one of the five countries chosen by the instructors. They don't have to produce a finished product, just a prototype, although some of the teams form companies when the term ends and pursue ways to market their inventions. They can create whatever they want, as long as it's affordable and helpful to the cultures to which they've been assigned.

When Dave Evans and his team — Emilie Fetscher, Jeannie Rosenthal and Abby Schlatter — began work on a project for Ethiopia in March 2008, they had two ideas in mind: finding a way to strip kernels more efficiently from dried corncobs, and working on an industrial-capacity stove to make low-cost *injera*. The stove idea was too big, so Evans and Fetscher spent a week traveling around Ethiopia, collecting information and taking photos, looking for a problem to solve.

Their visit occurred during the dry season, and Evans recalls that "everyone was waiting for the rain and had nothing to do, so we drew pretty big crowds." They interviewed women one on one, and sometimes dozens and dozens of villagers would gather around to listen. "We were all over the map trying to find something that would stick and that people would care about," Evans says. They left Ethiopia without a solid idea.

When they got home, they began to process it all. "One of the things we saw as we looked at cooking was that it's terrible from a Western perspective," Evans recalls more than a year later. "It's women's work in a patriarchal society, and the kitchens are sort of run down." Among the material they brought back with them, they found eight photos of cracked or broken clay *mitads*, but they hadn't asked anything about them, and it never came up in conversation. "It was the status quo that these pieces of clay were very fragile," Evans says.

The *mitad* is essential to every Ethiopian kitchen, and the traditional country *mitad* is a simple piece of equipment: a circle of clay, up to 24 inches in diameter, that a woman heats over hot coals. She pours the fermented *injera* batter onto it, covers it for a minute or two, and soon she has *injera* to place under the evening meal.

But *mitads* don't last very long: They break every few months, often at the slightest jostle or unavoidable provocation (like the family's cow or goat stepping on it). For families who live on a dollar a day, replacing an essential item that costs about $4 isn't easy. Some families have to replace their *mitad* four times a year, and if they can't afford it, they'll borrow a neighbor's until they can.

So Evans and his team saw an opportunity when they stumbled across their *mitad* photos. If they could find a way to make a *mitad* more durable, they could allow Ethiopian families to save money and frustration.

They first studied the clay-making process, and then tried to create a *mitad* reinforced with steel. Neither option got them too far. Soon they wondered what might happen if they compressed the clay by clamping a steel band around it, a feat of engineering, when used in a more complex way, that creates bridges. They tested their theories using hose clamps around clay discs three inches in diameter, and it worked.

But would it work on a huge clay *mitad*, which they couldn't get in California? "It was one thing to test something in the vacuum of the university," Evans says, "but it was another thing to take it out into the culture."

This meant another trip to Ethiopia, which Evans took solo for a month in the fall of 2008. "The tests went better than we could have hoped for," says

Evans. "And the people loved it. We had people coming by the office for weeks asking where they could buy it." His remarkable film of the trip to Ethiopia shows him slamming a steel-rimmed *mitad* on the ground without harming it. A *mitad* without the steel band shatters at the tap of a hammer.

In Ethiopia, Evans lived in the southwestern city of Awassa and worked with Fekadu Haile, a native of the area and a self-made businessman whose company, Dama Enterprises, manufactures furniture, and who was looking for a project that would allow him to "give back profitably" to the poorer people of his community.

Fekadu and his wife hosted Evans for the month he spent in Awassa, and by late 2009, Dama had sold more than 2,000 steel bands and had turned a profit on the team's invention, which Fetscher dubbed The Mighty Mitad — or simply The Mighty, as its satisfied customers in Ethiopia now call it.

The Mighty Mitad costs the equivalent of about $3 to $4, less then the cost of a new *mitad*. If every household in the country owed one, the inventors estimate, Ethiopians would save $200 million and a billion pounds of clay annually. The money they save might also allow them to afford stoves that burn wood more efficiently. Ethiopia is deforesting itself to fuel its traditional country stoves, and "people burn everything they have for fuel. Around 6 p.m.," Evans says, "the whole country becomes smoky."

It's a serious problem that the Mighty Mitad can't solve. Fortunately, at the Aprovecho Research Center in Oregon, inventors are working to make cleaner-burning stoves for the world's poorest people, and one team has developed an *injera* stove that researchers hope will help preserve what's left of Ethiopia's forests, 90 percent of which have disappeared since the early 1960s. The challenge is one of engineering, but also one of convincing Ethiopians to accept a new way of doing things, even though some people travel hundreds of miles to get wood for their inefficient old stoves.

For the past decade or so, several projects have brought solar cooking to Ethiopia (and other poor countries) with greater success. Solar cookers can allow up to 20 families to cook without the use of firewood, saving time, money and deforestation, and mitigating the dangerous smoke of wood stoves. The Arba Minch Solar Initiative has seen some success, and other projects dating back more than a decade have also helped.

If the Mighty Mitad, efficient stoves and solar cookers are feats of technology and engineering that can save Ethiopian forests, then you could say the Pepper Eater is an invention that saves the trees.

The 2009 Ethiopia team at Stanford first wanted to create something having to do with water technology. But when they traveled to Ethiopia in March 2009, they walked through a market and found a group of women grinding chili peppers, an ingredient used liberally in Ethiopian cuisine (and not just as the key spice in *berbere*). After working for a while, the women would sometimes crouch down in pain because of the pepper oil they got in their eyes.

The students talked with vegetable sellers, all of them coughing and sneezing from contact with the peppers. Even women back in their homes registered the effect of the peppers from having worked with them all day.

"It kind of hit us in the face," says Sam Hamner, who's getting his doctorate in mechanical engineering. "These peppers are really potent, and the women are doing it by hand."

Hamner and his colleagues — Scott Sadlon, Megan Kerins and Siobhan Nolan — continued to talk with farmers, and they came home with a lot of information on irrigation and "a little bit of information on peppers," Sadlon says. They talked it all over, and finally decided to pursue a way to make it easier for women to grind peppers.

The traditional method of grinding peppers begins by laying them out on tarp to dry in the sun. The people who grind the peppers can do it in two ways: by hand, crumbling them into flakes, and preserving the valuable seeds for other purposes (like making the ultra-fiery *mitmita*); or with a giant pestle, in a mortar large enough to bathe a child. The former process brings their hands into contact with so much pepper oil that it hurts; the latter process is very physically demanding.

"The women who do this are resilient," Hamner says. "They just deal with it. From a western mentality, you would think that people would complain. But it's really hard to get people in Ethiopia to complain about anything."

So the team set out to create a device that would save time and pain. Each prototype they made — one with a small blade, one with stones in a jar — addressed an aspect of the task and helped them answer a design question. Finally, they came up with a successful prototype: a silver metal cube with rotating steel blades and a handle to crank them. Using it requires minimal hand contact with the peppers — you can drop whole peppers into the device — and with a combination of pressure and sheer, their Pepper Eater makes nice flakes and has a receptacle to catch the seeds.

In September 2009, they returned to Ethiopia with enough material to assemble 10 machines. The spent a week in the poor rural southwest, traveling to Zway, Alaba and Awassa, dropping off machines along the way, and teaching people how to use them. They returned to each town a few days later to learn what people thought.

The women who prepared their peppers by hand agreed that the Pepper Eater made the job faster for them, and the team sold all of their prototypes to a cooperative of women who were delighted with the device. But the women who worked with a mortal and pestle found that the machine didn't save any time, and so they didn't like it, even thought it meant fewer calluses and no pepper oil on their hands. It just wasn't more efficient, and they preferred to stay with the more physically demanding traditional way. "They were willing to deal with the discomfort of the manual process," Hamner says. "We need to give them something better for them to want to buy it."

Since the course ended, team members have spent their time promoting the Pepper Eater in Ethiopia (to the mayor of Bahir Dir, a city on Lake Tana) and in America (to the owners of the Oakland, Calif., restaurant Café Colucci). If they can begin to manufacture their machine, each one will cost about $25. That's a lot for an Ethiopian who earns less than a dollar a day. But with an efficient machine, women who earn $285 a year grinding peppers can earn $463 a year, the company says, so the Pepper Eater would double their output and pay for itself many times over in just one year.

The team has identified three categories of people who might use their machine: large-scale producers, women's cooperatives, and individuals in their homes. The challenge now is to create a larger Pepper Eater to serve the mass-production needs of the first two groups. In April, they presented a business plan as semi-finalists in the Stanford Social-E Challenge, a contest that awards a $25,000 development grant to the winner. Winning the grant will help them implement their $50,000 design and production plan.

Hamner and Sadlon encountered Ethiopian cuisine at different times in their lives. For Hamner, a native of Jacksonville, Fla., it happened during his undergraduate years at the University of Florida at a restaurant where, a few years later — after his trip to Ethiopia — he returned with an aunt who wanted to try the cuisine. Sadlon's initiation came when he was 10, when his Massachusetts family vacationed in Washington, D.C., and his parents wanted to expose him to different cultures.

In Ethiopia, they tended to eat in restaurants, although they sometimes bought food and prepared it themselves. They ate *kitfo*, both cooked and raw, and they were surprised to find popcorn — with lots of sugar on it. The tea was unusually sweet as well. In Zway, a town near a lake, they had a delicious fish stew that reminded them of goulash.

Ethiopians fast on Wednesdays and Fridays, so they couldn't get meat on those days, which suited Hamner, who's a "pescetarian" — that is, a vegetarian who also eats fish. "But if we asked for vegetarian food on any other days," Hamner says, "the people would wonder why we were ordering this." This attests once again to the Ethiopian predilection for meat when its permitted and available.

Their September trip occurred during Meskerem, the Ethiopian new year, a family-oriented affair that left them with time to themselves. On New Year's Day, their favorite breakfast restaurant was closed, and they could only find a *kitfo* house. An Ethiopian man more conversant in English than their server helped them to get their *kitfo* cooked rather than having it served raw.

This was quite a concession for Hamner, although he necessarily compromised his pescetarianism while traveling around Ethiopia. During their March trip, they stayed with a family of five in Zway, pitching a tent outside of their home and sharing the evening meal with the father while the mother and children ate in the other room. The meal consisted of an appetizer of roasted lentils or beans (they're not sure which), some fried bread (*dabo*), and a main meal of beets, onions, kale, and carrots that they harvested themselves from the family's garden.

The meal was wonderful, but unfortunately, the visitors didn't know about Ethiopian hospitality. When you're a guest at someone's home, your host always wants to make sure you get enough to eat, so as soon as you finish your food, you'll be offered more. The only way to stop the flow is to leave a little bit of food in front of you.

"I would eat, eat, eat," Hamner recalls of the evening meal. "Then the wife would bring out more food, and the father would tell me to eat more food. I ate until I was about to explode."

Dave Evans grew up in Silicon Valley, not far from the Ethiopian restaurant Zeni in San Jose. And yet, he'd never tasted the cuisine until just before leaving for Ethiopia, when he finally had a meal at Zeni. During his trips to Ethiopia, he only had a few meals in restaurants: some terrible pizza in Awassa, a "fabulous" fish fry in the lake town of Arba Minch, and a decent meal at an Addis Ababa restaurant pitched to him as being "traditional," but which was, in fact, "considerably kind of dumbed down in flavor for tourists."

Evans loves to cook, so on his long second trip to Ethiopia, he decided to learn from the best, which was much easier said than done: "As a man," he says, "especially as a white man, I was shoved out of the kitchen."

But he persisted, setting himself the goal of learning to make *doro wot*, a favorite dish, and *injera*, the *sine qua non* of the Ethiopian meal.

The *injera*, he soon learned, was the easiest thing to fail at making. "It was a pain," he says, "even beyond making the batter." You have to get it to cook properly, pouring it onto the *mitad* in a spiral — not too quickly, not too slowly, and from not too high above the cooking surface. Lifting it off the hot *mitad* was also a challenge. "I probably tried 10 times," he says, "and I maybe got one piece that they actually let me serve to the family."

As for the *doro wot*, it's not that there's anything too difficult about the preparation. It's just that it can take several days.

His lesson began with instructions on how to properly clean the freshly killed chicken, which you must wash "until it stops smelling bad," his hostess taught him. This means filling buckets with water and then adding lots of salt and lime, then shaking the chicken in the mixture vigorously for five minutes, then doing it again and again, sometimes for six or seven hours. Then, you cook the sauce, which simmers for three or four hours, and then you add the chicken to the sauce — for another few hours,

"It became pretty clear that I wasn't going to do it in the home kitchen," he recalls. "The difference between Ethiopian food in the U.S. and Ethiopian food over there is the culture that surrounds it. You can take the time to lovingly prepare it. And of course, it's fabulous, because you've been working on it for two days."

He did bring one culinary lesson home with him. Coffee is as much a staple in Ethiopian cuisine as *injera*, and it's made from scratch as well: The woman roasts the raw beans, grinds them, performs the coffee ceremony, and then serves three cups of very strong *buna* to her guests. This taught Evans a lesson he could live with.

"We think the only people who can make good coffee are the specialized roasters who have big equipment," he says. So now he does it at home, buying green beans and roasting them himself.

The beans, of course, are always Ethiopian.

WHEN YOU LIVE in a foreign country for more than just a summer vacation, you naturally have to get accustomed to eating the local cuisine. Carl and Pat Templin enjoyed some delicious Nile perch during their stay in Ethiopia. They ate bananas, papayas, mangos, corn and the occasional crocodile, and Pat would sometimes even cook crocodile tail.

But during their decade of living and working in an Anuak village in southwest Ethiopia, the Templins drew the line at rat.

It wasn't a common food — in fact, not even a delicacy. It was just something the children of the village did for fun in the morning. The kids would sometimes place a piece of corn as bait under a heavy dried circle of mud attached to a string, and when the rat reached for the corn, down would come the crushing weight. Or sometimes they'd build a device like a Chinese finger trap: The rat would enter to get some corn and then couldn't get out. The kids roasted their catch until the fur singed off and the meat was tender enough to eat.

This wasn't typical Anuak cuisine. But neither was the national cuisine that the Templins ate on their rare trips to Addis Ababa, or even to Gambella, the nearest place they could call a city, about 25 miles away.

Carl Templin visited Ethiopia for the first time in 1958. A "new Christian, trying to find out what God wanted me to do with my life," the 21-year-old from Pittsburgh spent a year helping to plant a church in the Anuak village of Akado. The missionaries called the village Pokwo, a word that means "village of life" in Anuak, the eponymous Nilotic language spoken by the culture, whose people were divided in the 19th Century by the modern border between western Ethiopia and eastern Sudan.

Carl returned home after his year abroad, met and married Pat, who has a degree in home economics from Ohio Wesleyan University, and by the mid-1980s, had earned his doctorate in international and development education at the University of Pittsburgh. But in 1963, the parents of a 6-month-old son, they decided to return to Ethiopia, where they spent the next 11 years. Their two daughters were born there, and their kids grew up in their village alongside the Anuak children.

They left Ethiopia in 1974, and they've remained close to the culture, the people, and the friends they made when they lived there. They've visited over the years as well, and they enjoy Ethiopian food in America whenever they can — sometimes in their home, where Pat cooks it now and then. But their most revealing memories of "Ethiopian" cuisine throw back to the '60s and '70s, when the Anuak people were even far more isolated than they are now from the central Amhari-Tigrayan culture.

The Anuak had no *injera*. Instead, their staple starch was *kwon*, a thick cornmeal that the women of the village made with the help of nature's oven. The preparation began with the strenuous job of pounding and crushing corn using a heavy mahogany log and a deep wooden bowl — the Anuak version of a mortal and pestle. Next, over a wide area of bare earth in front of their thatched-roof huts, they spread a thin layer of a clay-like substance, taken from the bank of the local river, and with their hands, they smeared the mashed corn atop the clay. This was their oven, where the cornmeal would dry and bake in the searing African sun.

When the corn was ready to eat, the cook mixed it with water to form a porridge that grew thicker as it sat and cooled. This was *kwon*, which people ate for the evening meal, sometimes sprinkled with sesame seeds. If the Templins gave an Anuak family some potatoes or rice, they would gladly eat it. But afterwards, they would say, "I want real food." They meant *kwon*.

"They were way out," Pat recalls of the places she and Carl lived among the Anuak community. "They didn't have commerce. This was a marginal society with no surplus and no food supply. Their diet was very poor and plain." The Anuak had one meal a day: always *kwon*, and sometimes a stew, in water, of meat, fish or even grass, seasoned with salt if they had it, but nothing more (certainly no *berbere*). They used clam shells as spoons, scooping up some *kwon* and dipping it in the stew.

During their long stretch in Ethiopia — from 1963 to 1974, with one year in the middle back in the states — Carl worked at the mission developing curriculum for the people who taught reading, writing and arithmetic to the local children, who also learned Amharic. Pat worked with the women of the village, teaching them to read and sew. After their return to America, Carl created a ministry in Pittsburgh for international students and visiting scholars. He retired from there in 2002. Pat spent the better part of those decades putting their kids through school by selling real estate.

But their 10 years in Ethiopia exposed them to a lifetime of memories about the culture and cuisine of the Anuak people.

The Anuak practice an animist religion and call their deity Jwok, which means "creator." In the culture's creation story, Jwok created humans, who caroused and drank, so he called a meeting of the animals and gave them deadly weapons, like sharp teeth, claws and poison, and he told them to kill the humans. But the dogs liked the humans and warned them, so the humans were prepared and fought off the other animals, who have enmity toward humans and dogs to this day. Anuak villages have dogs living among them, although not as pets, and villagers will sometimes throw them scraps of food. These feral dogs are lean and look like greyhounds.

Pat found it to be hard to teach the Anuaks entrepreneurship because they live in such an egalitarian society. They're now helping an Anuak woman get a college degree in Nairobi, and Pat wants to help form some women's groups to make baskets and sell them, "if not as fair trade items, then as fairly trade items." To win their goods the "fair trade" certification on the international market, the sellers would have to pay an annual fee, and they can't afford that.

In addition to the staple food *kwon*, and the treat of a freshly caught Nile perch from the local Opeeno River, the Anuak would dry their corn, then roast it over a flame in a broken pot, gourd or piece of metal (if they could get it) until the corn popped. Another *injera* substitute was *kisera*, a dish made of corn or sorghum flour that they spread into a thin crepe, then cooked over a grass fire.

For meat, there were cows now and then. They would butcher them by peeling off the skin and spreading it out on the ground, then cutting the meat on the skin to keep it from touching the dirt. Crocodile meat provided some protein, and the mission helped them raise pigs to eat. Sometimes village hunters would even snare a wild boar.

Carl never tasted groundhog, an occasional meal for the Anuak, but on a visit to a nearby village one day, he saw one cooking. "It was a beautifully roasted animal," he recalls, "and I'll tell you, it smelled delicious." They once had an Anuak student visiting them in Pittsburgh, and when he saw a groundhog on the yard of their suburban home, he wanted to trap it and cook it. The Templins stopped him, but considering the damage that the rodent did to their garden, they briefly contemplated allowing their visitor to go through with his plan.

The men of the Templins' Anuak village would hunt various kinds of game deer, and when someone made a kill, Pat and Carl would sometimes buy some of the meat and store it in their refrigerator, which ran on a kerosene generator (there was no electricity in their village). Pat had to butcher and refrigerate the kill within two hours or else it would spoil, and she turned some of the meat into hamburger. The Templins would occasionally buy some other grocery items in the village, and the people would use the money they earned to buy locally made alcohol, or they would walk more than 20 miles to Gambella to spend it.

The Anuak ate bananas when they could pick them and sold some in nearby larger towns. The mission tried to teach them to grow mangos, but it takes seven years for a mango tree to sprout fruit, and the average life span of an Anuak was a mere 27 years. "They said that if you planted a mango tree," Carl recalls, "you wouldn't live to see the fruit. They thought we were trying to kill them." The missionaries also tried to introduce okra and eggplant, but the villagers didn't have oil to fry the vegetables. Cucumbers didn't catch on with the Anuak either.

When the waters of the local river receded, the Anuak would enjoy the abundance of Nile perch, which became much easier to catch. The men stood in a line along the shore, spearing the fish during this dry season. They also ate a smaller river fish, about the size of a sardine, scooping them up with wicker baskets, then cooking them immediately or drying them in the sun.

The Anuak had some chickens, which they mostly used for eggs, although the eggs were small. Fires during the dry season could send sparks into the air that would burn and destroy homes and entire villages, and the Templins have pictures of a woman sitting on the ground among a charred village, eating some roasted chicken that had just been cooked by a forest fire, and that would have gone to waste had she not eaten it on the spot.

At the evening meal, the Anuak sat on the bare ground or on animal skins. Life was very dull, and they spent much of the meal talking about the same things day after day. But in recent years, smaller towns in the region have gained electricity, and even the most isolated villages have battery-powered radios. People are also better nourished in the region now with the spread of national education, and many educated young people have moved to towns and cities like Gambella. But many people still continue to live the traditional village life, eating as they always did, and ignorant of the national cuisine.

During their time in Ethiopia, the Templins rarely ate national cuisine, but they didn't live on Anuak cuisine either. Pat usually cooked Western-style foods and would have supplies sent to them once a year: powdered milk, cheese in tins from the U.K., and flour, which they had to sift often to keep the weevils out. But they did try to eat as much local food as they could, and they would make yogurt with starter that they got from other Westerners.

At home in America, Pat cooks *wots* of *doro*, *gomen* and *misir*. She's tried *injera* with "every *ferenj* recipe, from buckwheat to flour to beer," but none of it was ever good enough to serve, and she hasn't tried it in a long while. When she makes Ethiopian food at home, which she only does now and then, she sometimes uses a flat thin bread called *mar'u*, which she gets at a nearby Middle Eastern grocery.

Although the Templins left Ethiopia 35 years ago, they've maintained ties to the country and the culture. They've visited numerous times since then, and with the advent of new technologies in many parts of the country, they're able to keep in touch with friends in the region where they lived by using e-mail (Gambella, much more developed now than in the 1970s, has internet cafés).

Their last trip to Ethiopia was in 2008, and it wasn't a satisfying one. Back in the 1970s, Carl says, "it was refreshing to go to Addis. It wasn't cluttered, just some people from the countryside walking in the streets, not realizing they could get run over." But now, instead of the occasional animal to avoid, Addis has four lanes of traffic in some places, and Carl found it disconcerting. He suspects he'll never return.

So they cherish their wonderful memories, among them a thick scrapbook of digitalized photos made from their myriad slides. The pictures remind them of the many friendships they made during their stay and over the years.

Pat doesn't cook Ethiopian food at home too often because it's time consuming to make a variety of dishes (who wants to eat just one dish?). She gets her *berbere* once a year from friends who visit or come from Ethiopia, and she often uses it to spice American dishes, like stews, chili or spaghetti sauce. She gets *injera* from Tana, the Pittsburgh restaurant owned by an Ethiopian, and *kibbee* and a special family blend of spices from Martha Agedew, who works at Tana, and whom they've known for many years.

To keep close to the culture that's been so important in their lives, the Templins enjoy meeting Ethiopians who move to the area or who just live there temporarily. They assembled a gathering of Ethiopian friends at their home in May 2009: Each woman brought a *wot* to share, and Pat made a few herself.

And 10 years ago, they hosted a dinner for some Ethiopian women attending a Pittsburgh college. The visiting women cooked in the truest tradition of their national cuisine, with *lots* of onions in their *wots*. Like the food itself, it's a memory that lingers, and a decade later, Carl recalls: "The onion smell in the house for weeks was wonderful."

Appendix A:
Finding Ethiopian Restaurants & Markets

If you're looking for an Ethiopian or Eritrean meal on your trip across America, I've created an accompanying website that I believe is the most thorough listing of Ethiopian and Eritrean restaurants available on the internet. This website also has a link that tells you all about Ethiopian *gebeya* (markets) in the U.S., along with information on where and how to buy spices, *injera* and gesho to make Ethiopian food or *t'ej*.

The restaurant business is a perilous one: 25% of new restaurants fail in the first year, and by their third year, the attrition rate is 61%. So call ahead to make sure your chosen *megeb bet* still exists. All of the restaurants on my list were still open at the beginning of 2010. Many of the restaurants have websites, and some of the websites have menus. I link to these on my website. But sometimes a website long outlives a restaurant — another reason to call first.

Markets, too, can come and go, especially small neighborhood markets. A quick phone call is recommended before you plan a shopping trip.

But even if you do have Ethiopian markets in your area, it may help to shop around.

Prices vary wildly from place to place. *Berbere* can cost $10 a pound at one market and $14 a pound at a market around the corner or across town. Many places sell imported *niter kibbee*: Made from the milk of Ethiopian cows, it's lighter in color and richer in flavor than *kibbee* made by Ethiopians in America. You'll pay around $22 a pound in most markets - unless you happen upon the one D.C. market that sells it for just $12 a pound.

Gesho once ranged from $13 at one Maryland market to $16.50 an another market right across the street. As the product becomes more precious and popular, prices have risen. But at these two competitors — one small and homey, one bigger and fancier — there's still a $3.50 difference in price between a pound of gesho stick. A few miles away, in D.C., another market sells it for an appealing $7.95 a pound.

And there's no consistency to these disparities. A market that sells *kibbee* for $22 a pound sells *bula*, or powdered enset, for $7.50. A few miles away, at another market, you can get *kibbee* for $12 a pound, but you'll pay $10.50 a pound for *bula*.

Ask the owners about this and they'll say a particular product is "hard to get." But that can't account for why one market brims with gesho and *bula* when the owner of another nearby market says he's out of both because of "the government," meaning that the Ethiopian bureaucracy makes it hard for them to be assured of a reliable supply of exported goods. Chances are the gesho-less fellow just isn't as good a businessman as his competitor, and that the grocers who charge more count on a loyal neighborhood customer base.

Some of these shops get their supplies directly from back home, which cuts out the wholesaler. Some order from supply companies in the U.S. owned by Ethiopian-American businessmen, like NTS Enterprises in Oakland, Calif., which leads to higher retail prices. And some just sell things for lower prices, surviving less on volume than on a more subsistence storefront (and possibly homefront).

If you have an Ethiopian restaurant in your town, you can probably buy some *injera* from the restaurant to use at your homemade Ethiopian feast. Most restaurants will sell take-out pieces for around $1.50 to $2 each. This is actually *more* than you'll pay for each piece of *injera* if you buy a 10-pack and have it shipped to you. But it may be more convenient to shop locally if you can.

If you're not lucky enough to live in a city with even one Ethiopian *gebeya* or restaurant, then you'll have to turn to the internet for authentic Ethiopian spices and *injera*. You'll have plenty of options.

Very few small Ethiopian markets will ship their food, although it's worth a try if you know of a market in your state or region. You can buy your *berbere, shiro,* gesho for making *t'ej,* and even some Ethiopian coffee from a market, although you might be able to find the coffee at a supermarket or specialty store in your town. Several American spice companies sell *berbere,* but most Ethiopian markets import theirs from back home.

A few new companies also make "authentic" Ethiopian food accompaniments in America: jars of *kibbee,* for example, and *kulet,* a *berbere*-spiced sauce for making *wots.* You can buy from these companies online as well, or you can find their products in Ethiopian grocery stores.

A neighborhood Ethiopian market probably won't ship *injera,* which takes special packaging. But several internet companies that sell *injera* also sell *berbere, shiro* and other spices and supplies, so you might be able to get everything from one place.

ALMOST 32 MILLION AMERICANS will have to cross state lines, international borders or the Pacific Ocean to get Ethiopian food. The nation's 22 most populous states have Ethiopian or Eritrean restaurants, and many of those have markets. But 17 states have neither: Alabama, Arkansas, Delaware, Hawaii, Idaho, Kansas, Louisiana, Mississippi, Montana, New Hampshire, New Mexico, North Dakota, Rhode Island, Vermont, West Virginia, Wyoming — and of course, Alaska, which actually had one for a few months in 2007 (see Chapter 11).

Some states, like South Carolina and Iowa, have just one restaurant, usually in tourist or college towns (Myrtle Beach and Iowa City, respectively). And surprisingly, despite its many casino buffets, Las Vegas has a dozen of them. So I guess you could say, "*Wot* happens in Vegas."

I've collected my data from websites, phone books and internet sites that allow people to rate and discuss restaurants. If I couldn't confirm online that a restaurant was still in business, I called to be sure.

Sometimes it's impossible to know from a phone book that a restaurant is Ethiopian: Who would think that T's Place in Minneapolis or Snelling Café in St. Paul are Ethiopian? But T's Place serves Ethiopian and Asian cuisine (one owner is from Ethiopia, one is from Singapore), and Snelling Café is simply named after the street on which it's located.

Because of tricks and traps like these, I'm certain that I've overlooked some restaurants and that I've listed places that no longer exist. I welcome additions and corrections to the online list.

You can find all of the restaurant and market information at this site, which previews *Mesob Across America* and has links to the restaurant list, which itself has links to videos on the web that allow you to "visit" some of the restaurants:

http://www.pitt.edu/~kloman/mesobacrossamerica.html

Or if you want to go directly to the full restaurant guide, which includes a link to the market guide, then here it is:

http://www.pitt.edu/~kloman/ethiopianrestaurantguide.html

I hope this book and its accompanying website will inspire some pioneering Ethiopians in America to set out for unexplored culinary territory and bring their food to those 17 unfortunate states. I welcome additions to or deletions from this list, which I'll keep updated online.

Appendix B:
Restaurant Names

If an Ethiopian restaurant isn't named after its owner — or its owner's parent, child or home town in Ethiopia, or after a famous Ethiopian emperor or empress — it may have one of these popular names drawn from Ethiopian history, culture and geography:

Abay. The Amharic name for the **Blue Nile.**

Abol. In the Ethiopian coffee ceremony, the "abol" is the first of three cups consumed by the celebrants.

Abyssinia. The ancient name for the country now known as Ethiopia.

Addis Ababa. The capital city of Ethiopia since 1889. The name means "new flower" in Amharic. Some restaurants will just take the name **Addis.**

Adulis. The name of an ancient port on the Red Sea, now a part of Eritrea.

Arada. A neighborhood in Addis Ababa with a large marketplace built in the 1980s.

Asmara. The capital of Eritrea. A restaurant with this name is almost certainly owned by Eritreans.

Awash. A major river in eastern Ethiopia.

Aksum or Axum. The capital of the ancient Axumite empire, the first great civilization in Ethiopia.

Blue Nile. The famous river that begins in the Ethiopian highlands and wends its way through the country, meeting the White Nile at Khartoum to form the Nile, which journeys on to Egypt. The Blue Nile, called the Abay in Amharic, contributes about 75 percent of the water to the Nile.

Dahlak. An archipelago of islands off the coast of Eritrea.

Demera. This Amharic word means "bonfire." A *demera* often refers to a bonfire of twigs set in celebration or joy.

Dukem. The name of a small city south of Addis Ababa.

Enat. The Amharic word for "mother."

Empress Taytu. The wife of Menelik, the emperor (1889-1913) who brought Ethiopia into the modern era.

Fasika. The Amharic name for Easter. The word has numerous different spellings in English.

Finfiné. In Afaan Oromo, the most widely spoken first language in Ethiopia, this means "natural hot spring." It's also the Afaan Oromo name for Addis Ababa.

Ghenet/Ghion. The river mentioned in the Bible that flows out of Eden. "Ghenet" is the river's name in Amharic. Today, the Biblical reference is believed by some to be to the **Abay,** or **Blue Nile.**

Gojo. The Amharic word for a traditional Ethiopian hut.

Habesha. An ancient name, preceding Abyssinian and Ethiopian, for the people who occupied the northern portion of what is now Ethiopia. The word Abyssinia comes from Habesha.

Harar. A major eastern city of Ethiopia where excellent coffee is grown. The city is largely Moslem in population and character.

Ibex. A type of antelope native to Ethiopia.

Kokeb. The Amharic word for "star."

Lalibela. A legendary emperor of Ethiopia (1189-1229) who ordered the construction of stunning churches hewn from the rocks of the rugged northern Ethiopian terrain. Many of these churches still stand today and are a popular tourist attraction. The city named Lalibela was, before the emperor's reign, called **Roha**, and some Ethiopian restaurants take this name.

Langano. One of Ethiopia's largest lakes, located in the great Rift Valley.

Massawa. A Red Sea port on the coast of Eritrea. A restaurant with this name is probably Eritrean-owned.

Meskerem. The first month of the Ethiopian calendar, and the Amharic word for "spring."

Merkato. The name of a large, well-known, open-air market in Addis Ababa.

Mesob. The large round colorful wicker basket on which the plate of food is placed for all to share.

Meskel. An Ethiopian Christian holiday that celebrates the discovery of the true crucifixion cross in the fourth century. A *demera* is lit at the celebration (see above).

Nyala. A type of antelope native to Ethiopia.

Queen Makeda. Makeda is the name of the monarch known to history and the Bible as the Queen of Sheba or Saba.

Queen of Sheba. According to legend, Makeda was the queen of the land of Saba (known to us as Sheba) in what is now Ethiopia. She bore a child with King Solomon, and that child began the Solomonic dynasty of Ethiopian rulers. There is no historic evidence for this, but the story remains a cornerstone of Ethiopian cultural identity.

Ras. An Amharic word that means "governor" or "regional ruler." Most restaurants with "Ras" as their first word pay tribute to a figure from history, with the exception of **Ras Dashen.**

Rasselas. The name given by Samuel Johnson to his fictional Ethiopian ruler in his 1759 novella, *The History of Rasselas, Prince of Abyssinia.*

Ras Dashen. The highest mountain peak in Ethiopia.

Red Sea. The famous body of water that separates the horn of Africa from Arabia. Ethiopian territory once included the province of Eritrea, which is now an independent country. With Eritrea's independence, Ethiopia became landlocked. A restaurant with this name is probably owned by Eritreans.

Roha. The ancient name for the city now known as Lalibela.

Sawa. A city in Eritrea.

Shashemene. A town given by Emperor Haile Selassie to a group of Rastafarians.

Sidamo. A region in western Ethiopia famous for its coffee.

Sodere. The name of a resort town east of Addis Ababa, known for its hot mineral springs.

Shebele. A river in Ethiopia.

Tana. The Ethiopian highland lake that's the source of the **Abay**, or **Blue Nile.**

Appendix C:
The Recipes for the Feast

Azifa

1½ cups green lentils
1 large jalapeño pepper, seeded and finely chopped
¼ to 1/3 cup finely chopped onions
1 teaspoon ginger powder, or to taste
¼ teaspoons of turmeric powder, or to taste
3 tablespoons lime juice, or to taste
4 tablespoons olive oil

Boil the lentils in water until they're soft, about 30 minutes. Then, drain them well using a strainer, rinse them with cold water, and put them into a mixing bowl.

Using a large spatula, stir the lentils until they begin to become somewhat mashed. Chop the onions and jalapeños into very small pieces but do not liquefy them.

Mix the onions, jalapeño, ginger, turmeric, lime juice and olive oil into the lentils. Stir them together well. When it's all mixed, taste the *azifa*. If the flavor or any one ingredient doesn't peek through, add a bit more of that ingredient. You should be able to taste the flavors of the various elements, all blended harmoniously. You might also add a little bit of each ingredient, then more of it until you have a nice balance of distinct flavors. Put it in the refrigerator to chill for dinner.

OPTIONAL STEP: Some cooks put their *azifa* into a food processor and serve it as a purée.

Butecha

6 tablespoons chick pea flour
2 tablespoons lemon juice
¼ teaspoon turmeric powder (optional)
½ teaspoon ginger powder
1 large jalapeño, seeded and finely chopped
¼ cup finely chopped onions
2 cups water
2 tablespoons olive oil

Measure two cups of water into a bowl, and dissolve about 6 tablespoons of chick pea flour in the water (three tablespoons for every cup of water, plus just a touch more). Add the olive oil and the lemon juice, mix the ingredients, then add the turmeric and ginger. You can forego the turmeric if you find the taste of this tart spice to be too strong or overwhelming.

When the mixture is smooth, put it into a large pot. Turn on the heat to low-medium, and bring it to a lightly bubbling boil. When the mixture begins to bubble, adjust the heat so that it doesn't spit and splatter. You may want to put some aluminum foil loosely over the top. Don't put a lid on it! The *butecha* needs to thicken, and that happens when the water slowly boils away. The volume will reduce as it cooks.

When it's thickened, which will take at least half an hour, remove it from the heat and pour the *butecha* into the bowl in which you will refrigerate it.

Add the finely chopped onions and jalapeño. Stir it all together thoroughly. You can add a little extra onion and jalapeño if you like, but don't overwhelm it with these ingredients. Refrigerate the *butecha*, and stir it thoroughly a few hours later. It should look like scrambled eggs after you stir it.

Serve hot or cold, reheating in a microwave before serving if you prefer it hot. Mix the ingredients one more time before reheating.

Atakilt Alicha

2 small to medium potatoes
2 large carrots
1/3 pound green beans
2 jalapeños, seeded and cut into slices
½ teaspoon minced garlic
1-2 teaspoons ginger powder
1 cup very finely chopped onions
1/3 cup olive oil
1 cup or so of water (see below)

Peel the potatoes, then cut the potatoes and carrots into bite-sized pieces. Cut each green bean into three pieces, and cut the jalapeños into thin slices.

In a large pot, sauté the onions in the olive oil until they're translucent and almost liquefied but not browned. Stir them frequently as they cook.

Add the garlic, ginger and turmeric to taste to the well-cooked onions and stir the spices into the onions well. Let them cook for a minute.

Now add the vegetables to the pot, and stir them around in the onions and spices until they're coated with the mixture. Add water slowly, just enough to cover the vegetables. Cook on low heat for about 30 minutes, until most of the water has evaporated. Stir the *alicha* every few minutes while it's cooking, and taste the carrots and green beans to see if they're tender. If too much of the water evaporates before the vegetables are tender, add a little more water. Just don't let it get too dry.

Doro Tibs Wot

2 large or 3 small chicken breast fillets
1 cup very finely chopped onions
¼ cup red wine or *t'ej*
¾ to 1 tablespoon *berbere*, to taste
2 jalapeños, seeded and cut into slices
4 tablespoons *niter kibbee* or olive oil
Water (see below)

Cut the chicken into bite-sized pieces.

In a hot frying pan over medium heat, cook the onions, turning and stirring them often, until they begin to lightly brown and caramelize. Don't let them burn.

When they seem like they might soon begin to burn if you cook them any longer, add the *kibbee* or oil, and stir the mixture. If you use *kibbee*, wait until it's all melted until you add the next ingredients.

Add the *berbere*, and stir it into the moist sizzling onions. Let it cook for a minute, stirring it constantly. Then add the wine, and mix the ingredients together well. The wine will begin to cook off almost immediately.

Add the chicken and stir the mixture, then let it cook for a few minutes until the chicken begins to turn white on the outside. Slowly add ½ to ¾ cups of water, bring it just to a boil, and reduce the heat. Finally, add the sliced jalapeños.

Let it all simmer until the liquid is almost cooked off and the *doro tibs* remain in a thick red sauce, about 15 to 20 minutes.

Kitfo

1 pound ground beef, preferably low in fat
4 tablespoons *niter kibbee* (Indian *ghee* will suffice; olive oil will not)
1 teaspoon *mitmita* powder, or more to taste (*berbere* will not suffice)
1 teaspoon cardamom powder, or more to taste

In a skillet, cook the beef for about a minute. Carve out a hole in the middle of the skillet and add the *niter kibbee*. As it melts, stir it thoroughly into the beef.

When the beef is cooked to your taste — well done, medium well, rare — sprinkle it all with the *mitmita* and cardamom and mix the ingredients well.

Serve the *kitfo* with dollops of *ayib* surrounding it, or mix some *ayib* right into the *kitfo*.

NOTE: Ethiopians enjoy *kitfo* raw, and you can as well. For that preparation, heat the *kibbee* in a skillet until it melts, then remove the skillet from the heat. Mix in the beef, stir it thoroughly, then add the spices and mix well again. Serve with *ayib*.

Ayib

32 ounces yogurt, low-fat yogurt, or buttermilk

In a deep saucepan, heat the yogurt or buttermilk over a very low flame for about 20 minutes. Bring it to a very low gentle boil, and do not stir once it comes to a boil.

Remove it from the heat and gingerly pour off the liquid that's formed. Don't use a strainer: The soft solid white *ayib*, which you want to keep, could come through the strainer. Put your soft white cheese into a covered container and refrigerate it for an hour or so to let it cool. Stir it a little to enhance its appearance and consistency.

NOTE: *Ayib* is also a delicious appetizer with an Ethiopian meal. You can stir in a bit of garlic, or better yet, some red hot *mitmita*. Eat it with *injera,* or with any kind of bread. You may need cutlery if you're not grabbing it with a piece of *injera*. You can also use *ayib* as an appetizer by making *sinig,* a stuffed jalapeño pepper. Cut off the top and bottom of the pepper, score it down the middle on one side but do *not* cut it into halves, and remove everything inside, including the seeds. Then, fill the center with *ayib*. One per guest should be plenty!

Niter Kibbee

1 pound unsalted butter
¼ teaspoon each powdered ginger, basil, cumin, cardamom, turmeric, fenugreek
1 tablespoon chopped onions
½ teaspoon minced garlic
Cheesecloth

In a pot, slowly melt the butter over a medium heat. When it liquefies, add all of the other ingredients and stir well.

Continue to heat the mixture at a very low boil. In 15 or 20 minutes, you will see the liquid and solid separate, with a transparent yellow liquid on top and white solid spirals on the bottom. Continue to cook this for a total of 30 or 40 minutes to allow the flavor of the spices to permeate the liquid.

Strain the mixture through cheesecloth. Put the strained yellow liquid into a container with a tight lid, and refrigerate it. Several hours later, it will be hardened. This is *niter kibbee*. Use it as the recipes require.

NOTE: You can substitute vegetable oil or Indian ghee for *kibbee* in all recipes except the *kitfo*.

T'ej

2 pounds honey (this will equal about 21-22 liquid ounces)
60-66 ounces water
1/3 pound gesho stick

In a one-gallon jar with a lid, mix the honey and the water by volume, one part liquid honey to three parts water, and *stir* rigorously to blend the ingredients. When the liquid is mixed well, add the gesho stick and stir it into the liquid, making sure all of the gesho is moistened. Put the lid on the jar, but don't seal it tightly. Give it just a little room to breathe.

After a few days, the liquid will begin to produce small bubbles, and microbes (mold and fuzz) will form on the top.

Stir the mixture after one week, then put the lid on it again. Stir it again at the end of the second week, and then remove the gesho stick using tongs. Put the lid back on the jar.

Stir it at the end of the third week, then replace the lid. Stir it at the end of the fourth week, then replace the lid.

At the end of the fifth week, stir the liquid. Strain it through cheesecloth twice, and then bottle it. Serve chilled.

If you let it go an extra week or two, stir at the end of each week. The longer it ferments, the stronger it gets. A five-week batch, mixed in these proportions, will be about 8 or 9 percent alcohol and will have about 250 calories in an eight-ounce glass.

NOTES

♦ You can make *t'ej* in any quantity. This recipe will produce about three 750ml bottles of *t'ej*. If you make it in smaller quantities, reduce the amount of gesho a bit, although using "too much" gesho will only make the flavor stronger. It's best to keep *t'ej* as warm as possible during the fermentation process. In Ethiopia, if the weather turns colder, women will wrap their fermenting *t'ej* in blankets.

♦ If you like, you can rinse the gesho stick for a few minutes in cold water before putting it into the well-stirred mixture of honey and water. Some Ethiopian *t'ej* makers recommend this. Others don't bother doing it.

♦ You can flavor your *t'ej* with fresh slices of ginger, orange peel, banana, jalapeño peppers, even coffee. Add a small amount of your desired flavoring for the last three days of the fermentation process, then remove the flavoring before you bottle and chill the *t'ej*.

♦ If you want your *t'ej* to be clearer, then before you bottle it, put it in a pitcher and let it chill for 48 hours. You'll see the yeast come out of solution and settle in the bottom of the pitcher. Now, slowly pour or ladle the *t'ej* from the pitcher into a bottle, leaving the settled yeast behind. If you don't do this step, the yeast will settle in the bottle, making the *t'ej* above it clearer.

Sources Cited

Mesob Acrsoss America draws its information from the many books and essays written by scholars during a period of more than 800 years, as well as from my own conversations with Ethiopians and my own foray into Ethiopian cooking. The works cited here provide opportunities for further reading.

Books and Articles

Almeida, Manoel de. *Some Records of Ethiopia, 1593-1646.* Hakluyt Society edition. 1954.

Alvares, Francisco. *The Prester John of the Indies.* 1540. Hakluyt Society edition. 1961.

Arkell, A.J. *Four Occupation Sites in Agordat.* 1954.

Bahiru, Bekele. "Chemical and Nutritional Properties of Tej." *The Journal of Food Technology in Africa.* Vol. 6, No. 3, July-Sept. 2001.

Bahiru, Bekele. "Yeast and Lactic Acid Flora in Tej." *Food Microbiology* 23. 2006.

Barker, James. *Narrative of a Journey to Shoa.* 1868.

Barnett, Anna. "Northern Ethiopia: What's on the Menu?" *Nutrition and Food Science.* Vol. 31, No. 1. 2001.

Barnett, Tertia. *The Emergency of Food Production in Ethiopia.* 1999.

Behre, Teshome. *A tavola con la Regina di Saba/Cooking with the Queen of Sheba*. 2005.

Belayneh, Aster Ketsela. *The Recipe of Love*. 2006.

Bilger, Burkhard. "Hearth Surgery." The New Yorker, Dec. 21 & 28, 2009.

Board on Science and Technology for International Development, Office of International Affairs, National Research Council. *Lost Crops of Africa: Volume 1 — Grains*. 1996.

Boardman, Sheila. "The Agricultural Foundation of the Aksumite Empire, Ethiopia." In Van Der Veen, Marijke, ed., *The Exploitation of Plant Resources in Ancient Africa*. 1999.

Brady, Thomas F. "Tickling Africans' Palate." The New York Times. Nov. 19, 1966.

Bulatovich, Alexander. *Ethiopia Through Russian Eyes*. 2000. Translated by Richard Seltzer. Original edition 1897.

Bulletin of the Museum of Fine Arts. Boston: 1945.

Burstein, Stanley, ed. *Kush and Aksum*. 1998.

Chacko, Elizabeth. "Ethiopian Ethos and the Making of Ethnic Places in the Washington Metropolitan Area." *Journal of Cultural Geography*. Spring/Summer 2003.

Chemical Society of Ethiopia. *Proceedings of the Workshop of Modern and Traditional Brewing in Ethiopia*. 2000.

Claiborne, Craig. "Ethiopian Food: Love It or Leave It." The New York Times. Dec. 15, 1970.

Cosson, Emilius. *The Cradle of the Blue Nile*. 1877.

Costanza, S.H., *et al.* "Literature Review and Numerical Taxonomy of Eragrostis Tef (T'ef)." In *Economic Botany*, Vol. 3, No. 4. 1979.

Crane, Eva. *The World History of Beekeeping and Honey Hunting*. 1999.

Crawford, O.G.S., ed. *Ethiopian Itineraries, circa 1400-1524*. Hakluyt Society. 1958.

Cycon, Dean. *Javatrekker: Dispatches from the World of Fair Trade Coffee.* 2007.

D'Andrea, Catherine, *et al.* "Ethnoarchaeological Approaches to the Study of Prehistoric Agriculture in the Ethiopian Highlands." In Van der Veen, Marijke, ed., *The Exploitation of Plant Resources in Ancient Africa.* 1999.

D'Andrea, Catherine. Personal correspondence. 2008.

De Wolfe, Evelyn. "Princess' Hands Guide Ethiopian Welfare Work." The Los Angeles Times. Oct. 30, 1964.

De Wolfe, Evelyn. "Ethiopia for Gods, Guys, Gals." The Los Angeles Times. Oct. 30, 1964.

Doresse, Jean. *Ethiopia.* 1959

Dufton, Henry. *Narrative of a Journey Through Ethiopia.* 1867.

Dwan, Lois. "All's Fare." The Los Angeles Times, Aug. 14, 1979.

Eadie, J.I. *The Amharic Reader.* 1924.

Edwards, Sue. Personal correspondence. 2008.

Egziabher, Tewolde Berhan Gebre. "Some Important New World Plants in Ethiopia." Published in *Proceedings of the Seventh International Conference of Ethiopian Studies 1982.* 1984.

Ehret, Christopher. "On the Antiquity of Agriculture in Ethiopia." *The Journal of African History*, Vol. 20, No. 2. 1979.

Ehret, Christopher. Personal correspondence. 2008.

Eng, Monica. "Mastering Ethiopia's Injera." The Chicago Tribune, March 16, 2006.

Eshetu, Alem. *Amharic for Foreign Beginners,* fourth edition. 2004.

Fattovich, Rodolfo. "The development of urbanism in the northern Horn of Africa in ancient and medieval times." Published in the proceedings of Urban Origins in Eastern Africa conference, Mombasa, Kenya, 1993.

Fattovich, Rodolfo. *Remarks on the Pre-Aksumite Period in Northern Ethiopia.* 1990.

Finneran, Niall. *The Archaeology of Ethiopia*. 2007.

Gebrehiwet-Buckner, Hagossa. *Ethiopian Recipes Revised Edition*. 2007.

Getahun, Solomon Addis. *The History of Ethiopian Immigration and Refugees in America, 1900-2000*. 2007.

Gleichen, Edward. *With the Mission to Menelik*. 1898.

Haile, Mesfin *et al*. "Market Access Versus Productivity: The Case of Teff." 2004.

Harris, W. Cornwallis. *Highlands of Ethiopia* (three volumes). 1844.

Hultin, Paul *et al*. *Luigi Balugani's Drawings of African Plants*. 1991.

Ingram A.L., *et al*. "The origin and evolution of *Eragrostis tef* (Poaceae) and related polyploids: Evidence from nuclear waxy and plastid rps16." *American Journal of Botany* 90 (1). 2003.

Kassa, Daniel Worku. *English-Amharic Dictionary*. 1997.

Ketema, Seyfu. *Tef*. Prepared for the Biodiversity Institute, Addis Ababa, Ethiopia. 1997.

Kifleyesus, Abbebe. "Muslims and Meals: The Social and Symbolic Function of Foods in Changing Socio-Economic Environments." *Africa: Journal of the International African Institute*. Vol. 72, No. 2. 2002.

Kifleyesus, Abbebe. "The Construction of Ethiopian National Cuisine." Published online at http://www.ethnorema.it. 2004.

Kitchen, K.A. "The Land of Punt." *The Archaeology of Africa*. Shaw, Thurstan, *et al*, eds. 1993.

Krasnow, Iris. "Ethiopian Eateries Off to a Mixed Start." United Press International article in the Los Angeles Times, April 21, 1985.

Kropp, Manfred. *The Serata Gebr: A Mirror View of the Daily Life at the Ethiopian Royal Court in the Middle Ages*. 1988.

Kropp, Manfred. Personal correspondence. 2008-10.

Leslau, Wolf. *Concise Amharic Dictionary*. 2004.

Leslau, Wolf. *Etymological Dictionary of Gurage (Ethiopic)*. 1979.

Levine, Donald. *Wax & Gold: Tradition and Innovation in Ethiopian Culture.* 1965.

Lobo, Jerome. *A Voyage to Abyssinia.* 1789.

Ludolphus, Job. *A New History of Ethiopia.* 1682.

Lyons, Diana. "Integrating Africans Cuisines: Rural cuisine and identity in Tigray, highland Ethiopia." *Journal of Social Archaeology.* 2007.

McCann, James. *People of the Plow. An Agricultural History of Ethiopia, 1800-1990.* 1995.

McCann, James. *Stirring the Pot: A History of African Cuisine.* 2009.

McGrail, Jean. "Ethiopia Straddles History." Los Angeles Times. Sept. 29, 1968.

McSpadden, Lucia Ann. "Ethiopian Refugee Resettlement in the Western United States: Social Context and Psychological Well Being." *International Migration Review.* Autumn 1987.

Mesfin, Daniel J. *Exotic Ethiopian Cooking.* 1990.

Ministry of Information. *Ethiopia: The Official Handbook.* University Press of Africa. 1969.

Munro-Hay, Stuart. *Aksum: A Civilization of Late Antiquity.* 1991.

Munro-Hay, Stuart. *Excavations at Aksum.* 1989.

Nishikazi, Nobuko. *Resisting Imposed Wildlife Conservation: Arssi Oromo and the Senkelle Swayne's Hartebeest Sanctuary, Ethiopia.* 2004.

Pais, A. "A Gust of Ethiopian Restaurants." American Visions. February/March 1992.

Pankhurst, Richard. *An Introduction to the Economic History of Ethiopia.* 1961.

Pankhurst, Richard. "Ethiopia Across the Red Sea and Indian Ocean." Addis Tribune, 1999.

Pankhurst, Richard. *The Ethiopian Borderlands.* 1997.

Pankhurst, Richard. *The Ethiopian Royal Chronicles.* 1967.

Pankhurst, Richard. *Travellers in Ethiopia.* 1965.

Permagent, Danielle. "Where the Dinner Table Is an Altar of Thanks." The New York Times, March 18, 2007.

Phillips, Jacke. "Punt and Aksum: Egypt and the Horn of Africa." *The Journal of African History*, Vol. 38. No. 3. 1997

Phillipson, David W. *Ancient Ethiopia.* 1998.

Phillipson, David W. *Archaeology at Aksum, 1993-7.* 2000.

Phillipson, David W. "Excavations at Aksum, Ethiopia, 1993-4." *The Antiquaries Journal.* 1995.

Phillipson, David W. "The Antiquity of Cultivation and Herding in Ethiopia." *The Archaeology of Africa.*" Shaw, Thurstan, *et al*, eds. 1993.

Plowden, Walter. *Travels in Abyssinia and the Galla Country.* 1848.

Powell-Cotton, P.H.G. *A Sporting Trip Through Abyssinia.* 1902.

Power, Lawrence. "Living 'Off' the Fat of the Land." Los Angeles Times, May 6, 1979.

Reich, Ken. "Ethiopia — Beneath the Glitter, Africa's Ancient Ways Persist." The Los Angeles Times. March 9, 1969.

Rogers, J.A. *The Real Facts about Ethiopia.* 1936.

Sagawa, Toru. "Wives' Domestic and Political Activities at Home: The Space of Coffee Drinking Among the Daasanetch of Southwestern Ethiopia." 2006.

Salt, Henry. *A Voyage to Abyssinia and Travels to the Interior of That Country.* 1814.

Samuelsson, Marcus. *The Soul of a New Cuisine.* 2008.

Schuyler, George S. *Ethiopian Stories.* 1994.

Sellassié, Guèbrè (Selasse, Gabra). *Chroniques du Règne de Ménélik II.* 1930.

Shack, William. *Hunger, Anxiety and Ritual: Deprivation and Spirit Possession Among the Gurage of Ethiopia.* 1971.

Silvester, Hans. *Ethiopia: Peoples of the Omo Valley*. 2006.

Southard, Addison. *Abyssinia: Present Commercial Status of the Country with Special Reference to the Possibilities of American Trade*. 1918.

Stewart, Robert B. and Asnake Getachew. "Investigations of the Nature of Injera." *Economic Botany*. 1962.

Telles, Baltazar. *The Travels of the Jesuits in Ethiopia*. 1710.

Trotter, Alessandro. *Zuccagni e Tef Etiopico*. 1938.

Ullendorff, Edward. *The Ethiopians*. 1960.

UNICEF. *Education Statistics: Ethiopia*. 2008.

Wild, Antony. *Coffee: A Dark History*. 2004.

Wondimu, Habtamu. "Ethiopia." *African Higher Education: An International Reference Handbook,* Damtew Teferra and Philip G. Altbach, eds. 2003.

Wood, Rebecca Theurer. "Teff: Ethiopia's Wonder Grain." *East/West*. August 1988.

Woredework, Ephrem Assefa. *English-Afaan Oromoo-Amharic Dictionary*. 1995.

Woredework, Ephrem Assefa. *English-Amharic Dictionary*. 1998.

Yefru, Wosene. "The Pre-Axumite Period: Historiographical Inquiry of Classical Ethiopia in Antiquity." *Henok*. Vol. 2, August 1991.

Zuccagni, Attilio. *Dissertazione Concernante Tef.* 1775.

Websites

Hay and Forest Grower. http://hayandforage.com/hay/farming_tons_teff/?cid=most-popular

Heavens, Andrew. Meskel Square blog. http://www.meskelsquare.com/

Patterson, James. M. *Acreage and Small Farm Insights*. University of Nebraska at Lincoln. http://acreage.unl.edu/News/News/Teff.htm.

Horse Talk. http://www.horse-talk.com/hay.html

Breinigsville, PA USA
18 October 2010
247581BV00001B/15/P